THE ROAD TO
VALLEY FORGE

THE ROAD TO
VALLEY FORGE

*How Washington Built the Army
that Won the Revolution*

JOHN BUCHANAN

**BARNES
&NOBLE**

NEW YORK

For Susi

George Washington by Charles Willson Peale

Contents

Illustrations and Maps

Preface

The impact of war upon society, both during and after wars, is undeniable. Our own times bear witness to this truth. We will, therefore, from time to time comment on the effect the War of the American Revolution had on civilian society—but only in passing, for that is not the focus of this book. Although politicians make revolutions and civilians suffer through them, it is soldiers who win them. After the Adamses and Jeffersons and Clintons and Draytons and others provided the agitation and propaganda and literature of revolution, then the Washingtons, the Greenes, the Morgans, the Glovers, and the mute thousands they led suffered the dirt and blood and horror and, in Winston Churchill's memorable words written about his great ancestor Marlborough, "all the chances and baffling accidents of war" to make the dreams of politicians come true.[1]

This, then, is a book about men at war and the general who led them during the most critical period of the War of the American Revolution: August 1776 through the winter of 1777–1778. It was during this period that Great Britain had its best chances to destroy the Continental Army and crush the rebellion. But it also was during this period that George Washington evolved from a mistake-prone backwoods soldier to a wiser commander in chief of a regular army that in turn developed from rabble into the makings of a professional force.

We will also take more than a passing look at Washington's main opponents during these early years of the war, General Sir William Howe and the British and German regulars he commanded, as well as Sir William's elder brother, Admiral Richard, Lord Howe. But the main focus will be on George Washington the soldier and the Continental Army.

The reader also will note in the following pages a phenomenon that was then probably peculiar to British North America and remains a character trait of modern Americans—a concept of personal liberty that often bedeviled Washington's attempts to fashion a professional fighting force out of raw, untrained men and boys. Although this trait may have been more pronounced among the Yankees of New England, it was widespread in British North America south of Canada. It had been growing for more than a century and a half, and by the time of the Revolution it was deeply embedded in the character of the people. A lack of deference, a questioning of authority, a deep-rooted love of personal liberty. The British statesman Edmund Burke thought that "a fierce spirit of liberty" was "stronger in the English colonies, probably, than in any other people of the earth."[2]

These people were not yet full-blown Americans—that would not come until after the Revolution, during the birthing years of the early republic. They were still in large part New Englanders and Southerners, Rhode Islanders and South Carolinians, Pennsylvanians and New Yorkers, and this was another of Washington's problems as he tried to build a national army. But there was a slow, gravitational pull toward the center that grew stronger over the long colonial decades, marked by a cultural icon common to all: Liberty! The Revolution, first in the minds and hearts of the people, to use John Adams's words, radicalized during the turmoil in the decade preceding armed revolt, cemented by eight years of struggle that beneath the veneer of eighteenth-century civility was vicious and deadly serious, was more than a war of independence. It was truly a revolution that aimed at the overthrow in British North America of a monarchy and the establishment of a then scorned form of government called a republic. That it neither envisioned nor resulted in the overthrow of a social class, such as occurred in the French, Russian, and Chinese Revolutions, is irrelevant, for we are not discussing nineteenth- and twentieth-century events, with their own peculiar historical circumstances of entrenched and obsolete royalty, aristocracy, and mandarinate. Our concern is an eighteenth-century event with its own historical baggage. In eighteenth-century terms the world was truly turned upside down when a king and the concept of monarchy were sent packing by the most successful political revolution of modern times.

Technical Notes

What we now call the Hudson River in the eighteenth century was more often called the North River, and I have retained that usage in quotations where it appears; but when writing in my own words I use the modern name: Hudson River. With one exception, I have followed that rule throughout when the modern name is so familiar that it would be confusing to inflict the eighteenth-century term on the reader. The exception is the Battle of Long Island. It is now fashionable to call it the Battle of Brooklyn, and it is true that the maneuvers and action took place within the modern borough of Brooklyn. But Brooklyn in the eighteenth century was just a tiny village where the battle ended. Contemporaries referred to the battle as being fought on Long Island, and in the nineteenth century it was called the Battle of Long Island, and I have chosen to follow tradition.

William Howe did not become Sir William until the fall of 1776, when he received his knighthood in the Order of Bath, but generally I have chosen to use Sir William throughout.

As in my previous books, readers who regard endnotes as a nuisance, interrupting the flow of the narrative, may safely ignore them, as they are merely citations to the evidence presented and are included because some readers demand supporting apparatus. There are two exceptions: chapter 7, note 22, on the eighteenth-century meaning of the word *plantation;* and chapter 8, note 20, on Horatio Gates.

Acknowledgments

I will find it difficult to repay my friend and fellow student of the Revolution, Arthur Lefkowitz, for sharing with me his deep knowledge of the war and guiding me through muddy woods on a lovely March day to Washington's Rock, from which the Great Virginian himself gazed across the Raritan River far below to the Jersey coastal plain and watched the skirmishing between American and British troops.

The gifted historical editor Dennis Conrad took time out from his own busy schedule to track down an important citation I had misplaced, and I am deeply beholden to him.

I am also grateful to Alex Kidson, Curator of British Art, The Walker, Liverpool, for guiding me to the owners of two portraits, and to Laura Valentine, Picture Library manager at the Royal Academy of Arts, for similar assistance.

The librarians of the New York Public Library and the New York Society Library have once more been generous and efficient in their assistance. Carol Briggs, librarian of the Hillsdale Library in Hillsdale, New York, again cheerfully obtained interlibrary loan requests of works not normally requested by that institution. At The Metropolitan Museum of Art I owe grateful thanks to Connie McPhee and Steve Bentkowski of the Print Study Room, and to the cheerful generosity of Claire Conway of American Paintings and Sculpture. At the Frick Art Reference Library Mariko Iida kindly and patiently revealed the riches of another of the nation's treasures.

I thank John Elsberg, editor in chief, Center of Military History, U.S. Army; Robert S. Cox of the American Philosophical Society; Patrice M. Kane, Fordham University Library; Louise Reeves, Museum of Fine Arts, St. Petersburg, Florida; Irene Falnov, Det Nationalhistoriske

Museum på Frederiksborg, Denmark; Katharine Mair, the National Trust, London.

I also must thank Janet Bloom of the William L. Clements Library; Fred Bauman of the Library of Congress; Juan Izquierdo of the Massachusetts State Archives; James Lewis of the New Jersey Historical Society; Anna Lee Pauls of the Princeton University Library; Michael Paul and other members of the staff of Special Collections, University of Virginia Library. And I must not forget Scott Howting of Valley Forge National Historic Park for doing some extra digging for me.

As always, special thanks must go to our dear friends Charles and Sandy Ellis, whose generosity and help are always in mind.

I have written elsewhere that my editor, Hana Lane, possesses what I consider the most valued editorial gift, that of restraint, and she has once more practiced her art with excellence. I am also delighted once more to experience the professionalism of John Simko, production editor.

Susi, to whom this book is dedicated, is not only first reader but also inspires me more than she knows.

1

Invasion! 1776

"One of the best young officers in the army"

At 6:00 A.M. Saturday, 29 June 1776, following ten days of "very calm weather . . . with light breezes from the east," a British fleet out of Halifax, Nova Scotia, arrived off Sandy Hook, which marks the roadstead of New York Harbor, and by 3:00 P.M. had safely anchored behind the hook. More ships arrived the next day, until the armada numbered 130 ships of war and troop transports carrying 9,300 troops. On 1 July, at 4:40 P.M., Admiral Molyneaux Shuldham signaled his command to get under way. An hour later the ships were "under sail for the Narrows with a fair wind," navigating the tricky passage over the great East Bank sandbar, and at about eight o'clock that evening dropped anchors some two miles off Gravesend. They weighed anchors the next morning at ten o'clock and headed once again for the Narrows, a channel about a mile wide, and safe anchorage in New York City's Upper Bay. But then a law of nature and capricious winds, or lack of them, revealed how in the age of sail the stately passage of tall ships could quickly become a shambles. A captain of Royal Engineers, Archibald Robertson, was there and left a description for us:

> The tide turn'd and becoming allmost Calm and the wind ahead the transports fell into great Confusion all dropping upon one another without steerage way which obliged us to come to Anchor. Some of the ships with in 7 or 800 yards of Long Island. . . . About 12 of the ships

nearest us were ordered to drop down with the Tide, lucky for us the Rebels had no Cannon here or we must have suffered a good deal.[1]

Thus the awkward arrival of the advance elements of a British expeditionary force that would eventually number about 32,000 troops, the largest army the British government had ever sent overseas. Its commander, General Sir William Howe (1729–1814), was aboard HMS *Greyhound*. Six feet, of swarthy complexion, by nature taciturn, he was described by a Quaker lad, Joseph Townsend, who saw him up close the following year. "The General was a large, portly man, of coarse features. He appeared to have lost his teeth, as his mouth had fallen in. As I stood alongside I had a full opportunity of viewing him as he sat on horseback, and had to observe his large legs and boots, with flourishing spurs thereon."[2]

Howe's appearance in America sent a Tory poet, Joseph Stansbury, into a paroxysm of joy:

He comes, he comes, the Hero comes:
Sound, sound your trumpets, beat your drums.
From port to port let cannon roar
Howe's welcome to this western shore.[3]

Howe was of that small, privileged class that then ruled England. He was the younger son of the 2nd Viscount Howe and Mary Sophia, eldest daughter of Baron Kielmansegge. His maternal grandfather was rumored to have been the first Hanoverian king of England, George I. Educated by private tutors and at Eton, he had been a soldier for thirty years. Howe was a man of wide military experience and an expert on the training and deployment of light infantry, a type of unit especially suited to North American conditions. As a young officer during the War of the Austrian Succession, he had served in Flanders with his regiment, the prestigious Duke of Cumberland's Light Dragoons. In 1747, at the Battle of Lauffeld, he took part in the famous charge of his regiment, along with Scots Greys and Inniskillings, all under that old warhorse General Sir John Ligonier. After the war, when a Captain in 20th Foot, he became friends with an officer who eventually entered the British pantheon, James Wolfe. Howe first came to America as a lieutenant colonel in 1758, when he brought his regiment, 58th Foot, from Ireland and led it at the siege and capture of Louisburg during the French and

Major Archibald Robertson of Lawers, 1782,
by George Romney

Indian War. Of his performance, his friend Wolfe wrote, "Our old comrade, Howe, is at the head of the best trained battalion in all America,
and his conduct in the last campaign corresponded entirely with the
opinion we had formed of him."[4]

Howe commanded a light infantry battalion during the Quebec campaign of 1759. Wolfe's confidence in him was displayed at Quebec when
Howe was chosen to lead the forlorn hope of two dozen soldiers who
preceded Wolfe's entire force on that predawn climb by the narrow path
that led up precipitous cliffs from the St. Lawrence River to the Plains
of Abraham, the daring maneuver that led to the famous British victory
that was a giant step toward France's expulsion from North America.

He continued to excel at his trade, at Quebec City that winter, at
Montreal, praised as a brigade commander at the siege of Belle Isle on

the coast of France in the spring of 1761, appointed adjutant general for the British conquest of Havana the following year. Little wonder, then, that at this point in his career a historian described him as "one of the best young officers in the army."

His postwar career continued onward and upward. He obtained the colonelcy of 46th Foot in Ireland in 1764, and four years later was appointed lieutenant governor of the Isle of Wight. In 1772 he was made major general and chosen to train light infantry companies, units of picked men of intelligence, courage, marksmanship, agility, speed afoot, and other attributes that made them roughly equivalent to today's special forces.

Contemplating this distinguished record, and borrowing a phrase from our own time, it would be natural for one to assume that Major General William Howe was among the best and the brightest England had to offer.

While his military career advanced without a hitch, Howe was at the same time a member of the Whig opposition to the Tory government. He entered politics and was elected to Parliament representing Nottinghamshire. He was opposed to the government's American policy, and the voters of his borough recalled that he had told them he would never accept a command in America. Yet in the year 1775 he sailed for Boston, and there on 17 June led the bloody frontal assault on Bunker Hill, where once again he exhibited the personal courage expected of a British officer. He was promoted to lieutenant general that year. On 10 October he succeeded General Thomas Gage as commander in chief, North America. Given Howe's opposition to his government's American policy, that bears looking into. But it can await the arrival on the American scene of Sir William's brother Lord Howe, with whom he would act in tandem.

Sir William Howe would later face accusations of being slow moving and failing to take advantage of opportunities, but on this occasion he intended to strike fast and decisively. According to Major Sir Charles Stuart, a battalion commander in 43rd Foot, "Preparations were made immediately for landing on Long Island and taking possession of a Hill which the enemy had strongly fortified . . . as it commanded Brooklyn's Ferry and the town of New York." But at the last minute Major General James Robertson talked Howe out of this plan, arguing, "if you beat the rebels before the reinforcements arrive, you disgrace the ministry for sending them; if you are defeated, they will be of no use when they come. Land, therefore, on Staten Island."⁵

On the night of 2 July, in a heavy rain, wrote Captain Archibald Robertson, the "1st division of Transports got under way with the first of the flood Tide, and about 9 we got up to the Watering Place on Staaten Island where the 3 men of war had hauled close inshore" and troops under Major Generals Robertson and Leslie "landed immediately without opposition" and "lay near the landing Place all night."

Meanwhile, at about midnight on the previous day, Captain Ephraim Manning of 20th Continental Regiment had received orders from New York City to help remove livestock from Staten Island. On the 2nd, the day the first British troops landed, on the advice of other officers he began at about 3:00 P.M. to evacuate the island and cross to New Jersey, because, he reported, "the Inhabitants being unfriendly & the Enemy so near & my Party so small, had I staid longer we must have fallen into their Hands, as they were surrounding the Island with their shipping, & not long after we crossed the Ferry there came up two Armd Vessels."⁶

The following day, at about 6:00 A.M., Sir William went ashore. Staten Island had been chosen as an invasion base because it had a dependable water supply, was protected on all sides by water—in effect, a giant moat—and was large enough to hold an army. The 2,300 troops who had landed the previous night began spreading out. The next day the rest of the troops disembarked, the first shots were exchanged with the Rebels, and five sailors were killed or wounded. The British attempt to reconquer the rebellious thirteen states had begun. It was the 4th of July 1776.⁷

"The want of experience to move upon a large Scale"

Across the Upper Harbor, on that long, narrow island called Manhattan, another commander in chief had been informed of the British arrival and had given Captain Manning his orders. Did any man ever look better in the role of commander in chief? Contrasting him to George III, Abigail Adams described his "grace dignity & ease, that leaves Royal George far behind him," and Benjamin Rush wrote at the beginning of the war, "There is not a king in Europe that would not look like a valet de chambre by his side." He had in addition a well-developed sense of theater, and was aware of the effect he had on his contemporaries. He was a big, strong, enduring man: six-feet-two in his stocking feet, wide-shouldered, narrow-waisted, broad-hipped, with long, muscular arms and legs. His head was somewhat small for his big body, but "gracefully poised on a superb neck," wrote his close friend and old comrade in arms George Mercer. His eyes, observed Mercer, were "blue-grey" and "penetrating" and "widely separated" over "high round cheek bones." Adding to his imposing—to some, overwhelming—presence, in an age of ubiquitous horsemen he was a magnificent rider. Thomas Jefferson called him "the best horseman of his age, and the most graceful figure that could be seen on horseback."[8]

It has been commonly said of him that he was fearless in battle, but can that really be said of any man? It seems more likely that he possessed in heroic measure what we call grace under pressure. Certainly all of the evidence presented by his contemporaries convinces us that in battle the big man, conspicuously tall in the saddle, time after time exposed himself to enemy fire and never flinched or gave any sign of fear.

He also had two attributes essential to a commanding officer: a strong physical constitution and a temperament that enabled him to meet and surmount the vicissitudes of war. For if either the body or the mind break down, all else mean nothing.

This forty-four-year-old Virginia planter has come down to us as a distant man, reserved and aloof. It was an age of deference, formal manners, and dignified bearing, but this man's remoteness from even his closest friends carried the notions of his time and class to extraordinary lengths and was often remarked upon by his contemporaries. He would never be, as we might say today, one of the boys. The very idea would have left him speechless, and he would have regarded with icy disdain any suggestion that he behave in such a manner.

A story that highlights this character trait took place after the war, during the Constitutional Convention in Philadelphia in 1787. Gouverneur Morris of New York, a patrician snob of the first order, told a group of the commander's old friends and comrades that he could be as free and easy with the great Virginian as with any of his friends. Alexander Hamilton immediately bet Morris a dinner and wine for twelve if Morris would approach their old commander, pat his shoulder, and say, "My dear General, how happy I am to see you looking so well." At the next reception given by the great man, Morris walked up to him, bowed and shook hands, then placed his hand on the Virginian's shoulder and said, "My dear General, I am very happy to see you look so well."

Whereupon George Washington removed Gouverneur Morris's hand from his shoulder and stepped back. He remained silent, fixing Morris with an icy glare. Morris retreated in confusion to the comfort of his friends. There is no evidence that such an incident ever occurred again.[9]

But there was another side to him, tales of laughter, wrote a contemporary, "till the tears ran down his eyes," letters revealing wit, sometimes biting, and subtle humor. One of the best examples of his sense of humor is when, without using the same language, he anticipated Mark Twain's famous quip by 142 years. He wrote to his brother after the Battle of Monongahela (1755), "As I heard . . . a circumstantial account of my death and dying Speech, I take this early opportunity of contradicting the first, and of assuring you that I have not, as yet composed the latter." The man who wrote that was not devoid of humor. But he was young then. By the time he became president, Abigail Adams, who saw him often then, would write, "He has a dignity which forbids Familiarity." The tremendous responsibilities he took on, first as commander in chief of a revolutionary army that challenged the world's greatest military power, later as first president of the new nation, setting precedents with almost every act, and his knowledge that he was forever on stage, subject to constant observation and critique by his fellow Americans and the world beyond, all of that certainly led to the public mask that rarely revealed the very human side of the man on the performing side of the footlights.[10]

Yet even during the war there are glimpses of a relaxed, even playful, Washington, who enjoyed informal social occasions and the company of women. Along with other wives of officers, including Martha Washington, twenty-five-year-old Martha Daingerfield Bland visited her husband, the Virginia cavalryman Colonel Theodoric Bland, at the army's 1777 winter encampment in Morristown, New Jersey. She wrote to her sister-in-law that she and her husband visited the Washingtons socially by invitation two or three times a week and "Every day frequently from inclination. He is generally busy in the forenoon, but from dinner till night he is free for all company. His worthy lady seems to be in perfect felicity, while she is by the side of her 'Old Man,' as she calls him. We often make parties on horseback, the general, his lady, Miss Livingston, his aides-de-camp . . . at which time General Washington throws off the hero and takes on the chatty agreeable companion. He can be downright impudent sometimes, such impudence, Fanny, as you and I like."[11]

Of one thing we can be sure. In 1776, George Washington's military experience came nowhere near his opponents'. He was aware of that, and of the mighty task he had undertaken. Four days after Congress had "Unanimously made its choice of him to be General & Commander in Chief of the American forces," he wrote to his brother-in-law, "I am now Imbarked on a tempestuous Ocean from whence, perhaps, no friendly harbour is to be found."[12]

He was right, of course, but we must note that he did not decline the appointment, and there is evidence that this intensely ambitious man very much wanted to be commander in chief. He silently lobbied for the appointment while a delegate to the Continental Congress by appearing at its sessions resplendent in his Virginia regimentals.

When Washington took command of the Rebel army outside Boston on 2 July 1775, his experience had been limited to wilderness travel and soldiering. In 1753, at age twenty-one, he was sent by Governor Robert Dinwiddie of Virginia, with six companions, on a 900-mile winter journey from Williamsburg, Virginia, to go to the French Fort LeBoeuf (now Waterford, Pennsylvania) and return. He carried a letter to the French commandant in the Ohio Country demanding that the French evacuate the area. He was also instructed to gain the support of the Indians. In neither was he successful. His performance on that 2½-month expedition, in which he suffered deep snows, numbing cold, and drenching in the icy waters of the Allegheny River, revealed his physical toughness and determination, but it also highlighted his inexperience.[13]

His next assignment ended in disaster when he returned to the Ohio Country in May 1754, with orders to evict the French, and was obliged to surrender hastily built Fort Necessity to the enemy. He and his command of Virginia militia were allowed to march out with the honors of war and return home unmolested by either the French or their Indian allies, but the generous terms could not bely that inexperience, imprudence, and a numerically superior enemy had led to total failure. The great Pennsylvania Indian agent Conrad Weiser wrote that the Seneca chief Half King "complained very much of the Behaviour of Coll. Washington to him (though in a very Moderate way Saying the Coll. was a good-natured man but had no Experience) saying that he took upon him to Command the Indians as his Slaves . . . that he would by no Means take advise from the Indians . . . that he (the Half King) had carryed off his Wife and Children, so did the other Indians, before the Battle begun, because Coll. Washington would never listen to them, but always driving them on to fight by his directions." This apt characterization also helps to reveal a part of Washington that we must always keep in mind when studying him. He had the instincts of a fighter. From the raw lad in over his head in the Pennsylvania woods to the mature commander in chief of a revolutionary army, George Washington was a fighting soldier. He grew wiser, he learned prudence, but he remained a fighter, and that instinct sometimes led him astray. It got him into big trouble in the Ohio Country. It would get him into bigger trouble in New York.[14]

He got out of it whole in 1754, and in that regard fortune continued to smile on him during the ensuing French and Indian War (1754–1763). He was the ranking provincial officer with Major General Edward Braddock's expedition that ended with a British catastrophe on 9 July 1755 along the Monongahela River in the deep forests of southwestern Pennsylvania. The fault was not his, and he behaved with great coolness during the rout of the British regulars by a mixed force of French, Canadians, and Indians. It was on that bloody field that his personal luck in battle first occurred, for "I luckily escapd witht a wound, tho' I had four Bullets through my Coat, and two Horses shot under me."[15]

Washington commanded militia, but he did not consider himself a militia officer. His model, despite Braddock's debacle, was the regular British army, and during those years of colonial twilight he yearned and lobbied for a commission as an officer in that army. But such commissions were few and far between, and the provincial colonel from Virginia was not among the chosen. Nor was the regiment he commanded on the Virginia frontier taken into the British service as a regular unit, as he fervently wished. But between 1755 and 1758, by dint of his own knowledge gained through experience, wide reading in military treatises, and devotion to high standards of discipline and honor, Washington raised the Virginia Regiment to a level of professionalism that he regarded as equal to that of regulars. He learned much during the Braddock campaign, and even more serving under that fine field commander and military administrator Brigadier General John Forbes. Forbes had a low opinion of provincial officers, labeling them a "bad Collection of broken Innkeepers, Horse Jockeys, & Indian traders," but he had a high regard for Washington. He may in fact have used in part Washington's plan, drawn up at the request of Forbes's regimental commanders, for an army of 4,000 men to march and fight in a country of deep forests. Although the British advance through the rugged western Pennsylvania wilderness against the outnumbered French at Fort Duquesne (modern Pittsburgh) offered no fighting, all the myriad of administrative details necessary to maintain an army in the field were not lost on the young Virginian. By the end of the war he was in many respects a professional officer.[16]

Nevertheless, on the eve of the British invasion of New York in 1776, Washington remained on the basis of experience a frontier commander, and, despite all the nonsense written about American riflemen winning the war by hiding behind trees and picking off blundering Redcoats, overall the tactics of frontier warfare would not decide the test of arms between the thirteen states and the mother country. He had, to be sure, conducted a successful siege of Boston, which ended with a humiliating British evacuation. But the cards had been all his: a countryside swarming with Rebels, a commanding position on Dorchester Heights overlooking the city, and the captured guns of Ticonderoga to bombard the enemy. And for an inexperienced commander and his equally inexperienced army, static siege warfare could not be compared with the deployment and maneuvering of large bodies of troops in open country, or with the test of formal battles, regiments against regiments, armies against armies, when in the eighteenth-century manner men advanced in formation and delivered volleys upon command before charging with fixed bayonets. Those were the moments of truth separating trained, disciplined regulars from rabble.

To his credit, Washington was quite aware of his shortcomings and admitted them. In a letter assessing the abilities of General John Sullivan of New Hampshire, Washington approached the matter with candor. "His wants are common to us all; the want of experience to move upon a large Scale." He admitted to a "limited, and contracted knowledge . . . in military matters." But he defended Sullivan, and in effect himself and other subordinates, by maintaining that the limitations were "greatly overbalanced by sound judgement of Men and Books; especially when accompanied by an enterprizing genius, which I must do gen'l Sullivan the justice to say, I think he possesses."[17]

But were these abilities, which he and others did possess (although not Sullivan), enough to carry out the most difficult mission attempted by Washington and his army during the War of the Revolution: the defense of New York City? Which brings us immediately to another question. Why New York? Why did Washington send the highly regarded but exceedingly eccentric Major General Charles Lee to New York in January 1776 with orders to occupy the city and plan and build a system of defensive works? Why did Washington leave Boston on 4 April 1776 with two aides, William Palfrey and Stephen Moylan, and his adjutant general, the self-deluded Horatio Gates, and arrive in New York City on 13 April? Why did General Sir William Howe sail from Halifax, Nova Scotia, on 10 June, destination, New York? Why were all the proud regiments on their way from the British Isles and Germany to join him?[18]

"No Effort to secure it ought to be omitted"

A look at a map of eastern North America helps provide the answer to our question. Lying along the Atlantic seacoast, only some 200 miles north of the divide between the northern and southern states, the city provided one of the world's great natural harbors, one that was generally ice-free. From here a British fleet lying in protected waters had access northward via the East River and Long Island Sound to New England and the Maritime Provinces of Canada. To the south, once clearing Sandy Hook, it was a straight run down the coast to Delaware Bay and the water route to Philadelphia, or on to Chesapeake Bay and Virginia, a hotbed of rebellion. Farther south, once the rightly feared waters off Cape Hatteras were cleared, the way was open to the Carolinas, where Charleston, South Carolina, then the richest city in America, would lure the British in this second year of the war and later tempt them even more. But that is another story.[19]

Another look at our map reveals more proof of New York's strategic position in those days, when overland travel was more often than not an extreme form of physical punishment, especially when travelers, or an army, entered the American Back Country, which then was not far from the coast. Thus travel by water was prized, and of all the cities in North America only Quebec, Montreal, and New Orleans could rival New York's water route into the interior. On the map follow the Hudson River—or North River, as it was called in early times—from where it empties into Upper New York Bay northward about 150 miles to Albany. From there follow the Mohawk River west. It was navigable to within about 20 miles of Fort Oswego, New York, on the shores of Lake

Eastern North America, 1776

Ontario. The short portage opened up great possibilities to eighteenth-century traders, explorers, and soldiers. Northward via Lake Ontario and the St. Lawrence River lay Canada. Westward by way of Ontario and the other Great Lakes lay an immense interior and a network of rivers connecting with the mightiest of them all, the Mississippi. Contemporaries saw it clearly. In his orders to General Charles Lee, Washington wrote, "it is a matter of the utmost Importance to prevent the Enemy from taking possession of the City of New York & the North

River as they will thereby Command the country, & the Communication with Canada, it is of too much consequence . . . to hazard such a Post at so alarming a crisis." To another of his generals he drove the point home: "my feelings upon this Subject are so Strong that I woud not wish to give the enemy a Chance of Succeeding." One of the key revolutionary politicians, John Adams, was as one with Washington on the "vast importance of that City, Province, and the North River which is in it, in the Progress of this War, as it is the Nexus of the Northern and Southern Colonies, as a Kind of Key to the whole Continent, as it is a Passage to Canada and to the Great Lakes and to all the Indian Nations. No Effort to secure it ought to be omitted."[20]

We can agree with Washington and Adams on the strategic location of New York City and the Hudson Highlands flanking the Hudson River to the north, but can we agree that securing the city, and holding it, against a British attack was in the best strategic interests of the Rebels? More to the immediate point, could New York City be successfully defended? These are questions we shall be returning to in our narrative.

Meanwhile, for our story we should return to Albany and look directly north. Stretching before us is the classic invasion route between the United States and Canada. With relatively easy portages, the way is clear via the Richelieu River in Quebec, Lake Champlain, Lake George, and a portage to the Hudson at Albany. Contesting forces had been using that route since early in the seventeenth century, and both American and British leaders had their eyes on it in 1776. And New York City and its hinterland were the keys. The British thought that if they controlled them, they could cut off New England, which they considered the seat of rebellion, from the rest of the country. That this was a dubious proposition is irrelevant, for both the British and the Americans believed it.

For the Americans, securing New York City was easy. In the absence of British ground forces, they simply marched in and took control. Its defense, however, presented a serious problem. In January 1776, prior to being ordered by Washington to New York to take over the city and prepare its defenses, General Charles Lee claimed to be losing sleep over the thought of the British taking New York. "The consequence of the Enemy's possessing themselves of New York have appeared to me so terrible that I have scarcely been able to sleep from apprehensions on the subject—these apprehensions daily increase." Given the ambitious Lee's subsequent history, we can be excused our suspicion that his hyperbole masked an itch to put distance between himself and Washington, whom he considered his inferior as a general, and operate without his chief in the immediate vicinity. Whatever Lee thought, once he arrived in the city and reconnoitered its land and waters, he saw the problem clearly and changed his tune:

> What to do with the city, I own puzzles me, it is so encircle'd with deep, navigable water, that whoever commands the Sea must command the Town.

In the same letter he also strongly implied that New York City could not be held:

> I shall begin to dismantle that part of the Fort next the Town to prevent it's being converted into a Citadel. I shall barrier the principal Streets, and at least if I cannot make it a Continental Garrison, it shall be a disputable field of battle.[21]

How that battle turned out Lee would learn at long distance, for on 1 March he was ordered by Congress to take command of the Southern Department, encompassing Virginia, the Carolinas, and Georgia, where his turbulent nature and brutal candor would vex the proud Rice Kings of the South Carolina Low Country. He will return to our story, however, to also vex his long-suffering commander in chief.[22]

Lee left New York on 7 March for Philadelphia and the South. He was succeeded by the hard-drinking, high-living, bogus Scottish nobleman Brigadier General William Alexander (1726–1783), traditionally known as Lord Stirling, who was a brave and active officer and dedicated to the cause. Stirling took up what Lee had ably planned but hardly begun during his short tenure, and he faced the same problem described by Lee: what to do with the city.

The map bears Lee out. New York City and its environs are laced with waterways that are key to both defending and attacking the city. To completely control the Hudson River one had to control Manhattan Island, the opposite New Jersey shore, and the Hudson Highlands north of Tappan Zee. But to hold Manhattan one had to control the western shores of Long Island, which comprised Kings County (modern Brooklyn) and Queens County (modern Queens). Jutting out from Kings County, on the southern side of Wallabout Bay, is Brooklyn Heights, where the well heeled now live and play. Brooklyn Heights overlooks the lower tip of Manhattan, which was the city in 1776, with a population of some 25,000. Artillery mounted on Brooklyn Heights could destroy the city and its docks, as well as ships in the East River anchorage, for the seaport in 1776 was on the east side. On the west side, cliffs then rose from the waters of the Hudson, making access to the streets difficult.

Other important reasons why New York's seaport was on the east side are the prevailing winds and the nature of the waters surrounding Manhattan. The winds, westerly and northwesterly, made it much easier in the age of sail to go up the East River instead of beating to windward up the Hudson. The Hudson River is a stratified estuary, with fresh water on top and salt water below. Thus the Hudson can and sometimes does freeze over, and the climate then was much colder than now, being at the tail end of the Little Ice Age that prevailed in the Northern Hemisphere from about 1300 to 1850. The East River, on the other hand, is not a river but a tidal estuary of salt water that normally does not freeze over. In addition, Lower New York Bay south of the Narrows was clogged by sand, through which a narrow channel flowed toward Sandy Hook, so it was faster getting out of port by sailing about sixteen miles up the East River and out through Hell Gate to Long Island Sound. It also was thirty-one miles closer to England; and the sound, between the southern New England coast and Long Island, was a protected body of water.[23]

But all of this was for naught unless it could be held, and to hold Manhattan the Americans had to hold Brooklyn Heights. Washington assigned that mission to a man he liked and respected, a portly, thirty-four-year-old ironmonger and merchant from Rhode Island even more inexperienced than Washington, "to move upon a large Scale." It remains a mystery why on 8 May 1775 the Rhode Island legislature promoted Nathanael Greene from private to brigadier general, probably the biggest leap in rank in American military history. The records are silent. Greene's sole military experience had been the militia parade ground. When Washington placed him in command of the troops on Long Island, Greene had never led men in battle. In fact, he had never seen a battle. But he was highly intelligent and an avid student of the art of war, widely read in the subject. Upon receiving his new command Nathanael Greene immediately did what any commander in such a situation should do: ride the ground, study the lay of the land, try to anticipate by firsthand reconnaissance from which direction the enemy might come.

"I think we shall fight to-day. Black Dick has been smiling."

On 12 July 1776, HMS *Eagle* (64 guns), Captain Henry Duncan commanding, bearing the flag of the admiral of the British fleet on the North American station, passed Sandy Hook, navigated the Narrows, and dropped anchor off the eastern side of Staten Island. In the armada were 150 ships of war and troop transports. Ambrose Serle, a civilian secretary aboard *Eagle*, confided to his journal, "We were saluted by all the Ships of War in the Harbour, by the cheers of the Sailors all along the Ships, and by those of the Soldiers on the Shore." Also aboard *Eagle* was Serle's employer, a man whom officers and men of the navy fondly referred to as Black Dick. He was Sir William Howe's elder brother, Vice Admiral Richard, 4th Viscount Howe (1726–1799).[24]

The appointments of the Howe brothers to sea and ground command in America has intrigued historians for more than two hundred years. They were Whigs, opposed to the Tories who controlled the government. They were sympathetic to the Americans. The memory of their older brother, George Augustus, 3rd Viscount Howe, who was killed in action near Fort Ticonderoga in 1758, was revered by colonists. He had been so popular among Massachusetts troops that the province erected a monument to George Augustus in Westminster Abbey. Despite all this, and despite Lord Howe's well-known conviction that conciliation, not force, was the answer to American rebellion, the admiral was chosen not only to command in North American waters but also authorized to extend a limited olive branch to the Rebels. This, I think the reader will agree, bears examination. First, however, let us take a brief look at Sir William's elder brother.

As was the custom then, he went to sea early, in his case at age fourteen, and steadily climbed in rank through many situations and climes. He first saw combat at sixteen, was wounded at twenty, and made flag captain at twenty-two. Like his brother, he saw extensive action in the Seven Years' War. Lord Howe was a solid professional: a careful naval tactician, a close student of soundings, currents, tides, and signals. If anything, he was more taciturn than his brother. Horace Walpole related an incident that occurred in 1758 at Cancale Bay, during an amphibious action on the French coast, when Howe formed a poor opinion of the generalship of Lord George Sackville—later Lord George Germain, to whom Howe would report as peace commissioner to the colonies. Sack-

Richard, Earl Howe by Thomas Gainsborough

ville put several questions to Howe, who silently ignored him, where-upon an exasperated Sackville asked, "Mr. Howe, don't you hear me?" Howe replied, "I don't love questions."[25]

In a 1758 amphibious operation against Cherbourg, Howe played an important role in the destruction of the port, and in the failed attack on St. Malo he saved many of the landing force through his own gallant efforts. In 1759 he was in the thick of the action at the great English naval victory at Quiberon Bay, Brittany. He became a rear admiral and commander in chief, Mediterranean, in 1770. In 1775 he was appointed vice admiral, and in December of that year made commander in chief of

naval forces, North America, where he would join Sir William as war-
rior and diplomat.

Richard, 4th Viscount Howe, was a man of high character and
courage, but temperamentally disinclined to talk, as Germain had discovered at Cancale Bay. Walpole wrote that he was as "undaunted as a
rock, and as silent." At first thought, one might wonder about the
choice of such a man as a peace envoy, for whom speech is the chief
tool of the trade; but only if one also assumes that the king and his ministers were truly interested in that aspect of Lord Howe's dual appointment. His contemporaries disagreed sharply on his personality. He was
either "liberal, kind, and gentle," or "haughty, morose, hard-hearted,
and inflexible." But of his popularity in the navy there can be no doubt,
for in such matters we should always trust the opinion of the other
ranks. Despite strong, harsh features, the grim and forbidding figure he
cut, Lord Howe was a good commander, solicitous of his men's well-
being, and they repaid him and took to his peculiar nature and expression. One sailor said before an action, "I think we shall fight to-day.
Black Dick has been smiling."

Now that we have been introduced to our chief protagonists and
the general lay of the land and waters they would initially contest, it is
time to examine the choice of Black Dick and his brother to command
in America and the curious nature of their assignment.

"We must either master them or totally leave them to themselves"

The American Revolution was very much about power and who would
wield it in America. In 1774 Lord Dartmouth, at the time secretary of
state for the American colonies, wrote to the then commander in chief
in America, General Thomas Gage:

> the Sovereignty of the King in His Parliament, over the Colonies
> requires a full and absolute submission.[26]

The colonists, on the other hand, had made quite clear their con-
tention that in all domestic matters colonial legislatures, not the British
Parliament, should prevail. Consider this statement from the First Continental Congress, meeting in Philadelphia in the fall of 1774:

That the foundation of English liberty, and of all free government is a right in the people to participate in their legislative council: and as the English colonists are not represented, and from their local and other circumstances, cannot properly be represented in the British parliament, they are entitled to a free and exclusive power of legislation in their several provincial legislatures, where their right of representation can alone be preserved, in all cases of taxation and internal polity, subject only to the negative of their sovereign, in such manner as has been heretofore used and accustomed.[27]

Could the delegates have been clearer? Parliament in London rules on external affairs, but on domestic matters, including taxation, their own legislatures govern. For the colonists, Parliament was the problem, not their sovereign, the king. But neither the king nor his ministers bought that argument, and the king did not separate his authority from that of Parliament's. The idea of colonial self-government was almost a century ahead of its time. Not until 1867 would Britain, under the British North America Act, grant home rule to Canada. George III, his ministers and Parliament, believed to the very cores of their beings that in all legislative matters, whether at home or in the overseas colonies, Parliament was supreme. The king wrote, "I do not want to drive them to despair but to Submission, which nothing but feeling the inconvenience of their situation can bring their pride to submit to." The operative word, of course, was "Submission." This theme appears again and again in his correspondence; for example, "we must either master them or totally leave them to themselves and treat them as Aliens." The rigid, unbending nature of George III would be an important factor in the coming struggle, and he was equally clear in that regard, too. As events moved inexorably toward the point of no return, he wrote to his chief minister, "I entirely place my security in the protection of the Divine Disposer of All Things, and shall never look to the right or left but steadily pursue the Track which my Conscience dictates to be the right one." He was supported by his ministers and Parliament, who were insulted by the challenge to parliamentary authority, and the colonial belief that their liberties were at stake was to them a notion to be scoffed at. The king, his ministers, and Parliament would have agreed with an English traveler who found himself trapped in revolutionary America that the "sweet enjoyment of real and happy liberty was already theirs."[28]

That much was clear to London. What was not at all clear was how to deal with the rebellious Americans. What would it be: coercion or compromise? It is not our purpose to delve into the intricacies of this argument, which consumed official and unofficial Britain. Nobody, even the most hawkish, wanted a war, but once London decided on coercion, a shooting war awaited only the tinder to set the blaze. That came at Lexington and Concord on 19 April 1775, and for the men in London wrestling with the problem, the bloody encounter between the New England militia and British regulars at Bunker Hill on 17 June sealed the issue.[29]

But who would command? General Thomas Gage, in command in America, had fallen out of favor, largely because of his preference for conciliation. This is ironic, because the Howe brothers, especially the admiral, also favored conciliation. Yet Sir William was chosen to succeed Gage, while Lord Howe, in addition to his combat command, was commissioned within a very narrow scope to bring the Rebels back into the fold. Let us briefly consider how this came about.[30]

Sir William's appointment to serve under Gage and, as he hoped and expected, to eventually succeed him, was relatively simple, in contrast to the protracted negotiations that led to his brother's dual appointment as commander in chief of the North American station and peace commissioner. Sir William was firmly opposed to American independence, but he believed that negotiation was the correct road to ironing out differences between the colonies and London. He also realized, however, that the threat of force was a necessary backdrop to conciliation, and he was an ambitious soldier, thirsting for fame and glory in his chosen profession. Thus he dissembled, never revealing to the ministers responsible for his appointment his true aim in America, although his ties to the colonies, especially Massachusetts, through his dead brother, George Augustus, and his zeal for conciliation were not unknown to both official and unofficial London and were commented upon at the time. Yet on two occasions, in writing, he stated unequivocally to Lord Germain that the Rebel army had to be destroyed: first, in late April 1776, "A decisive Action, that which nothing is more to be desired or sought for by us as the most effective Means to terminate this expensive War"; and in early July, shortly after he had landed on Staten Island, he was "still of the opinion that peace will not be restored in America until the Rebel Army is defeated."[31]

His brother Richard, Lord Howe, also attempted to conceal his intentions, but both the king and his ministers were not unaware of Lord Howe's feelings, which is highlighted by an amusing story that also reveals that the king, rigid as he might be, was not the one-dimensional character who has come down in popular opinion. The incident occurred when General Sir Charles Hotham Thompson was traveling from Bath to London in the company of Lord Howe and another gentleman not named. They stopped on the way to dine, and their conversation centered on the troubles in America. According to Sir Charles, Howe "became very warm upon the subject." He said that Lord North deserved to be impeached, convicted, and hanged. But even worse, said Howe, was the "persevering and invincible obstinacy of the King." Now it so happened that Sir Charles was also groom of the bedchamber to George III, and the next time he was at court waiting upon His Majesty, the king asked him point-blank whether on his recent journey from Bath a certain conversation had taken place. Sir Charles, horrified and embarrassed, admitted it had and waited for the ax to fall. But the king laughed loudly and said, "Well, well, every man has a right to his own opinion in public affairs; but I have too high an esteem for Lord Howe not to advise him, through you, at any future time, before he brings his Minister to the scaffold, and inveighs against my '*persevering and invincible obstinancy*,' to take the precaution of sending the common waiters of an inn out of the room first."[32]

So the king, it appeared, would not be an impediment to the admiral's appointment. But because Lord Howe was actually being appointed peace commissioner, and because the moderate Lord Dartmouth was replaced as colonial secretary by the belligerent Lord George Germain, negotiations between Lord Howe and the ministry with regard to his instructions as commissioner dragged on for months and at times seemed to break down. But Lord Howe campaigned assiduously and cleverly for the assignment. It is too long and tangled a tale for us to follow its many paths and byways, but we must consider its highlights to understand what followed in America.

Lord Germain was suspicious of Lord Howe from the beginning, but overcame his doubts. And he had convinced himself in the case of Sir William that the soldier would not allow his preference for conciliation to deter him from applying necessary force. How much force was necessary, of course, was another question, and one that apparently did not figure much in the discussions leading to Sir William's appointment. In similar fashion, Germain decided that the admiral also would do his duty.

But Germain also tried to stack the deck by adding to the commission somebody who opposed conciliation, and especially concessions. Lord Howe balked, declaring that the first minister, Lord North, had promised that he would be the only commissioner. By that time, however, Lord Howe's younger brother Sir William had replaced General Gage as commander in chief in America, and Lord Howe agreed to serve with another commissioner, provided it was his brother. Germain reluctantly conceded, believing that Sir William would act as a brake on the admiral. Did he not realize, however, that Lord Howe was the more serious-minded of the brothers, and the stronger in character of the two? Lord Howe was also head of the family, to whom Sir William had written upon the elder's accession to the title, "live and be a Comfort to us all. Remember how much our dependence is on you. If we lose your only support left to us we shall fall never to rise again. Excuse me and think of a Family whose only hope now is your safety."[33]

Lord Howe's campaign for the appointment, which began early in 1775, did not end until 27 April 1776, when he and his brother were appointed peace commissioners. His written instructions were detailed and stringent, as Germain attempted to hamstring him. The key word to describe Howe's instructions was *Submission*. Lord Howe could offer pardons to Rebels who took an oath of allegiance to the king. The Rebels must submit and dissolve illegal representative bodies and royal government must be restored and parliamentary supremacy acknowledged before any discussions of a modified relationship between the colonies and the mother country could take place. And everything Lord Howe did in his role as peace commissioner was subject to ratification by London.

Germain and most of the ministry assumed that Lord Howe would follow his instructions to the letter, that he would not enter into any talks with the Rebels until they had submitted, until force had crushed the rebellion. The sword was to take precedence over diplomacy.

The question was: Could Lord Howe, a strong-minded man who shrank from the thought of civil war, who firmly believed that conciliation was the realistic answer to the rebellion—could he be trusted not to deviate from his instructions?

2

"I scarcely know which way to turn"

"At their cups or whoring"

At 2:30 P.M. on 12 July, four hours before Lord Howe's flagship dropped anchor off Staten Island, the first serious action began between the rival forces contesting New York Harbor and the Hudson River. Against the judgment of Vice Admiral Molyneaux Shuldham and his captains, who thought the "consequences you seem to expect from such a measure . . . not equal to the risk of two of his Majesty's ships," Sir William Howe insisted that a small naval detachment be sent up the Hudson to cut waterborne communications between northern New York and the American army at the mouth of the Hudson, and, wrote Sir William, "particularly in distressing the army upon the island of New York by obstructing their supplies through that channel."[1]

Sir William overrode Admiral Shuldham's objections, and at 2:30 on the afternoon of the 12th, HMS *Phoenix* (44 guns), Captain Hyde Parker Jr. (1739–1807) commanding, weighed anchor and on the flood tide stood for Manhattan and the Hudson. Captain Parker was a tough, experienced sailor who had first gone to sea at age twelve. *Phoenix* was joined half an hour later by HMS *Rose* (20 guns), Captain James Wallace commanding. The two frigates were accompanied by the schooner *Trial* and the tenders *Charlotta* and *Shuldham*. Commanding one of the tenders was Lieutenant Lancelot Brown Jr., son of the famous English landscape gardener Lancelot Brown, more familiarly known as "Capability" Brown. Parker, who commanded the flotilla, was well acquainted with the waters around New York. Such capable sailors were needed for this expedition, because the Rebels had been working hard for months to prevent just such an undertaking from succeeding.[2]

From Red Hook in Brooklyn to Governor's Island in the Upper Bay to Fort George on the tip of Manhattan, on to the rocky cliffs of western Manhattan and across the waters to Paulus Hook (modern Jersey City), grim defensive works bristling with artillery had risen. Digging and hauling dirt and moving cannons to create these and other defensive works had been going on since General Charles Lee had arrived in New York in January, when he wrote to Washington that the people on "The whole shew a wonderfull alacrity—and in removing the Cannon Men and Boys of all ages work'd with the greatest zeal and pleasure." At the end of March Benjamin Franklin wrote:

> I have been riding round the Skirts of this Town to view the Works; they are but lately begun, but prodigously forward; all Ranks of People working at them as Volunteers without Pay, to have them ready for the Reception of Gen. Howe, who having finish'd his Visit to Boston is daily expected here.
>
> What will you do with this Spirit? You can have no Conception of Merchants & Gentlemen working with Spades & Wheelbarrows among Porters & Negroes. I suppose you will scarce believe it.[3]

Farther up Manhattan's shoreline, in the rugged hills making up the northwestern part of the island, the British ships would face another obstacle. There the Rebels had built Fort Washington on the highest point on the island, where the Hudson flanking Manhattan is at its narrowest; and across the river in New Jersey, Fort Constitution (later Fort Lee) had been built to complement Fort Washington, although it did not yet contain artillery.

The little squadron, wrote George Washington, "availing themselves of a brisk & favourable breeze with a flowing Tide," sailed across the Upper Bay toward the mouth of the river. At 3:15 P.M. the big Rebel guns opened up in a mounting crescendo described by a British onlooker as a "most terrible fire." But the British captains on their quarterdecks were undeterred. As cannonballs whistled through the rigging above them, they sailed on, holding their fire. Washington reported that a

Captain Sir Hyde Parker by George Romney

"heavy and Incessant Cannonade was kept up from our several Batteries here as well as from that at paulus Hook." On Staten Island and aboard the fleet anxious British eyes watched as the little squadron sailed into a storm of fire. An engineering officer counted the Rebel shots: Red Hook, 27; Governor's Island, 16; Paulus Hook, 27; Manhattan, 126. Through a gauntlet of 196 firings *Phoenix*, *Rose,* and the smaller vessels silently stayed their course, until about 4:10 P.M., between the western shore of Manhattan and Paulus Hook, opposite Trinity Church, British broadsides thundered in both directions, with most of the return fire directed against New York City.[4]

Pandemonium gripped the populace. A Moravian minister witnessed it:

> The balls and bullets went through several houses between here and Greenwich, [and] The smoke of the firing drew over our street [modern Fulton Street] like a cloud; and the air was filled with the smell of powder. This affair caused a great fright in the city. Women, and children, and some with their bundles came from the lower parts, and walked to the Bowery, which was lined with people.[5]

George Washington was even more vivid in his description of the impact of the bombardment on civilians. "When the Men of War passed up the River the Shrieks & Cries of these poor creatures running every way with their Children was truly distressing & I fear will have an unhappy effect on the Ears & Minds of our Young & Inexperienced Soldiery."

As for that "Soldiery," he was exasperated by the reaction of many:

> The General was sorry to observe Yesterday that many of the officers and a number of men instead of attending to their duty at the Beat of the Drum, continued along the banks of the North river, gazing at the Ships; such unsoldierly conduct must grieve every good officer, and give the enemy a *mean* opinion of the Army, as nothing shews the brave and good soldier more than in case of Alarms, cooly and calmly repairing to his post and there waiting his orders; whereas a weak curiosity at such a time makes a man look mean and contemptible.[6]

One of their comrades was pithier, and accused the more than half who did not even man their guns but chased upriver in their desire to follow the progress of the ships, of being "at their cups or whoring." At the main battery on Manhattan, others who may have been drunk neglected to swab the barrel of a cannon thoroughly after firing, whereupon a cartridge caught fire when it was rammed down the barrel and the gun blew up, killing five and wounding three. Meanwhile, the British squadron was soon out of reach. It safely passed the cannon and rifle fire directed at them from Fort Washington, and thirty miles upriver weighed anchor in the Tappan Zee. Captains Parker and Wallace had, in the words of a Briton, "forced their Passage up the River in Defiance of all their vaunted Batteries," with relatively little damage and only four men wounded. It was a blow to American morale, and the presence of British ships on the Hudson a constant worry to Washington.[7]

He would have had even more to worry about had Sir William acted on the suggestion of his deputy, Major General Sir Henry Clinton (1730–1795). Clinton wrote that he was so

> encouraged by our having got some ships of war up the North River, and nearly 10,000 troops in high health and spirits, to propose to the Commander in Chief the landing of a sufficient corps at Spuyten Duyvill in order to lay hold of the strong eminence adjoining, for the purpose of commanding the important pass of King's Bridge and thereby embarrassing the Rebel Operations.

But according to Clinton, Sir William, never a daring commander, told him that "he had no intention of acting offensively before the arrival of the Hessians, nor did he think it advisable to stir a day's march from his cantonements before the troops had their camp equipage."[8]

Meanwhile, the militia in the counties bordering the Hudson beyond New York City would have to deal with any action undertaken by Parker and Wallace. But most militiamen were farmers, and it was the harvest season, of which Washington was well aware. Two days after the British forced the Hudson, he wrote to the Orange County Committee of Safety that at this "extreem busy season I cannot recommend your keeping the Regiment embodied," but "it would be well to notify them all to be ready at a moments warning to Assemble at any place they may be call'd too." Throughout the war, the harvest was a continual concern of militia. At Tappan Zee 400 men of the Haverstraw regiment of the Orange County militia immediately turned out and prevented a British landing, but its colonel, Ann Hawkes Hayes, wrote on 14 July that after being on "Duty night and day" since the evening of the 12th the men "are greatly fatigued with the service," and "express great uneasiness under Apprehension that they Shall loose their Harvest as the grain is now fit to gather and no Person to take it in if they are obliged to gaurd the Shore." Yet Brigadier General George Clinton, commanding the militias of Orange and Ulster Counties, reported that "The men turn out of their Harvest Fields to defend their Country with surprizing alacrity," although he admitted that "The absence of so many of them . . . at this Time when their Harvests are perishing for want of the Sickle will greatly distress the country." His solution mirrored Washington's suggestion to the Orange County Committee of Safety. "Many of the militia may be calld in in 8 hours some in a much less Time should there be occasion for them."[9]

Washington was deeply concerned about raiding parties from the ships and Tories along the Hudson. "Every precaution ought to be taken to prevent the Men of War from getting any supplies of fresh Provisions or keeping up any intercourse or Correspondence with the disaffected inhabitants; shall be much obliged for timely Information of every Manoever of the ships & tenders up the River, & hope that every necessary Step will be taken to prevent any of our Vessels falling into their hands." When he learned that the British ships were moving farther upriver, to the Hudson Highlands in the vicinity of Haverstraw Bay, he took immediate steps to counter the possibility that there might be troops aboard the ships, their aim occupation of the strategic passes through the Highlands, thus cutting off communications with Albany.[10]

This was not the case, but Washington could not know that, and he wrote Egbert Benson, chairman of the Committee of Safety of Dutchess County, and General Clinton of his fears of a British landing in his rear and a Tory insurrection. There were no troops on board the ships, of course, and British landing parties managed to destroy only a few unguarded farms and steal some pigs. For the militia, not only in the counties on both banks of the river but also from nearby Connecticut and Massachusetts, had turned out in the hundreds. To be sure, many were ineffective, firing muskets from the banks at British ships more than a mile away, thus provoking shelling. At Haverstraw General Clinton[11]

> went down there myself. I found the shores guarded or rather lined by an undisciplined Rable under no kind of Subordination to Col. Hay & Capt. Keene who were active in doing all they could but had little in their Power. I caused the Cattle, Sheep, etc., contiguous to the Shores, to be removed to Places of safety & ordered out 100 of their Militia and placed them under the Command of My Officer for the protection of that Neighborhood & to prevent (them) from get supplies of Fresh Provisions & Water.

The upshot of all of this militia activity and the efforts of men such as Clinton, Benson, and Hayes was that the British ship commanders were deeply frustrated, and as the days and weeks dragged on, from July into August, the Rebel militia mounted dangerous efforts to destroy the little squadron, first by attacking the ships with row galleys, then with dreaded fireships. Both efforts failed, but in the case of the fireships it was a very close thing. *Phoenix* was saved from a fireship by the wind and the gallant efforts of its crew. The tender *Charlotta* burned and had to be abandoned. This occurred on the night of 16 August. Unable to get fresh water and provisions and low on ammunition, with the possibility of more attacks by the feared fireships, Parker decided that his command should return to the fleet. Once again the citizens of New York were treated to a booming exchange of artillery fire as the British squadron ran the gauntlet on 18 August, again safely, and dropped anchors off Staten Island. For his exploit in breaching the Rebels' water defenses and returning safely, Captain Parker was knighted in 1779.[12]

The much-maligned militia had done its job in actions to which it was suited: swarming in the face of a British offensive, denying them the fruits of the land, and almost pulling off a coup in the fireship attack. Admiral Shuldham reported to the Admiralty his opinion that it had been a "fruitless expedition" in which the ships had lain "useless for six weeks" up the Hudson and had been lucky to escape and rejoin the fleet. His opinion notwithstanding, if we look on the British expedition as a trial run to test American artillery, it had been a spectacular success and augured future British naval expeditions. The fight for the Hudson was by no means over.[13]

"George Washington, Esq."

Two days after the gallant little British squadron made a mockery of the Rebels' "vaunted batteries" in its first run up the Hudson, the newly arrived Lord Howe began his mission of conciliation. What transpired seems a ridiculous matter of protocol, yet in part it gives insight into the long-festering relationship between two governing classes who were now antagonists. It began with the dispatch of Lieutenant Philip Brown of HMS *Eagle* under a flag of truce to deliver a letter from Lord Howe to Mr. Washington. He was stopped between Governor's Island and Staten Island by three Rebel boats. Upon learning his business, one boat went to shore and returned with three American officers led by the army's adjutant general, Colonel Joseph Reed (1741–1785). Not, however, before Reed had received instructions from General Washington, who later informed the president of the Continental Congress that upon learning of Lieutenant Brown's business and the address on the letter, "I immediately convened such of the Genl officers who were not upon other duty who agreed in opinion that I ought not to receive any Letter directed to me as a private Gentleman. . . ." One of the American officers accompanying Colonel Reed was Colonel Henry Knox, who two days later described to his wife what transpired.

> When we came to them, the officer . . . rose up and bowed, keeping his hat off.
>
> "I have a letter, sir, from Lord Howe to Mr. Washington."
>
> "Sir," says Colonel Reed, "we have no person in our army with that address."
>
> "Sir," says the officer, "will you look at the address?" He took out of his pocket a letter which was thus addressed: 'George Washington, Esq., New York.' . . .
>
> "No, sir," says Colonel Reed, "I cannot receive that letter."
>
> "I am very sorry," says the officer, "and so will be Lord Howe, that any error in the superscription should prevent the letter being received by *General Washington*."
>
> "Why, sir," says Colonel Reed, "I must obey my orders."
>
> "Oh, yes, sir, you must obey orders, to be sure."
>
> Then . . . we stood off, having saluted and bowed to each other. After we had got a little way, the officer put about his barge and stood for us and asked by what particular title he chose to be addressed.
>
> Colonel Reed said, "You are sensible, sir, of the rank of General Washington in our army?"
>
> "Yes, sir, we are. I am sure my Lord Howe will lament exceedingly this affair, as the letter is quite of a civil nature and not a military one. He laments exceedingly that he was not here a little sooner"; which we suppose to allude to the Declaration of Independence; upon which we bowed and parted in the most genteel terms imaginable.[14]

On that same day Washington reported to John Hancock that the British officer conveying the letter had told Colonel Reed "That he (Ld Howe) had great Powers," by which he obviously meant powers of negotiation, which we know was not true. Washington further wrote, "I would not upon any occasion sacrifice Essentials to Punctilio, but in this Instance . . . I deemed It a duty to my Country and my appointment to insist upon that respect which in any other than a public view I would willingly have waived." On 17 July Congress "highly" approved Washington's action and directed that this policy be followed not only by the commander in chief but also by other American commanders.[15]

Actually, the meat of Lord Howe's short letter gave nothing away and did not claim "great Powers":

The Situation in which you are placed and the acknowledged liberality of your Sentiments, induce me very much to wish for an opportunity to converse with you on the Subject of the Commission with which I have the honor to be charged; As I trust that a dispassionate consideration of the Kings benevolent intentions, may be the means of preventing the further Effusion of Blood, and become productive of Peace and lasting Union between Great Britain and America.[16]

Lord Howe also sought other ways to inform Americans of his purpose. On 13 July, the day before he approached Washington, he sent Lieutenant Samuel Reeves of *Eagle* under a flag of truce to the American post of Perth Amboy, New Jersey, to deliver dispatches to the Rebel commander, Brigadier General Hugh Mercer. The dispatches were ostensibly meant for the royal governors of the thirteen colonies, all of whom had by then been overthrown, and included notice of his arrival, his commission, and a declaration for them to publish. But Lord Howe deliberately left them unsealed as a means of spreading his message through gossip as the dispatches made their eventual way to Congress. Howe's secretary, Ambrose Serle, wrote, "This was a prudent and decent Way of acquainting the People of America, that the Door was yet open for Reconciliation; for it was expected they would have the curiousity to read the Inclosures . . . being their Interest & Concern more than that of the Governors."[17]

General Mercer immediately sent the dispatches to Washington, who promptly forwarded them to Congress, and their appearance and rumors as to what they might contain did have the effect of reopening the debate between radicals and conservatives among the American revolutionaries. As it turned out, Howe had little to offer, and the radicals, who controlled Congress, were so contemptuous of the declaration and dispatches they had them published.[18]

Lord Howe, ever hopeful for accommodation, continued his efforts to contact Washington, who on 15 July had written to Sir William Howe and General John Burgoyne, enclosing congressional resolutions about the alleged mistreatment of American prisoners in Canada. Sir William replied the following day, but the letter was refused for the same reason that his brother's letter had been rejected on the 14th. The Howe brothers then took another tack. On 19 July a barge appeared with a white flag. It was again met by Colonel Reed accompanied by one of Washington's aides, Lieutenant Colonel Samuel Blachley Webb

(1753–1807). Webb reported that the bearer, an aide-de-camp to General Howe, "said, as there appeared an insurmountable obstacle between the two generals, by way of Corresponding, General Howe desired his Adjutant General might be admitted to an Interview with his Excellency General Washington. On which Colo. Reed, in the name of General Washington, consented." At noon on the 20th Webb met Lieutenant Colonel James Paterson of 63rd Foot and took him to Colonel Henry Knox's quarters, where, Webb wrote, "Washington attended with his suit and Life Guards . . . and had an Interview of about an hour with him."[19]

Henry Knox described the setting with appropriate hyperbole. "General Washington was very handsomely dressed and made a most elegant appearance. Colonel Paterson appeared awe-struck, as if he was before something supernatural. Indeed I don't wonder at it. He was before a very great man indeed."[20]

It was all very, very polite, and I will not try the reader's patience with a full rendition of the accounts of the meeting by either Washington or Paterson. With great civility they agreed to disagree with regard to the proper forms of address and discussed the treatment of prisoners by each army. Then, about to take his leave, Paterson went beyond his brief, in his account admitting to Washington that he

> could not resist the temptation . . . of pointing out the King's most gracious disposition towards the Americans so strongly manifested in the Powers he had granted and the Choice he had made of Persons unconnected with Ministerial Arrangements, to whom His Majesty had thought proper to delegate the full & free Execution of those great Powers.[21]

Joseph Reed's memorandum of the meeting recorded the following exchange: Washington replied, "he was not vested with any Powers on this Subject by those from whom he derived his Authority and Power. But from what had appeared or transpired on this Head Ld Howe and Gen. Howe were only to grant Pardons—that those who committed no Fault wanted no Pardon: that we were only defending what we deemed our indisputable Rights." Whereupon Colonel Paterson "said that that would open a very wide Field for Argument."[22]

That brief exchange summed up matters perfectly. The Howe brothers had no power to negotiate, much less "great Powers," and the rebels knew it. Too much had happened since Lexington and Concord, the division ran deep, the issue was fairly joined. But at least everybody was exquisitely polite. "Col. Paterson," the American report stated, "behaved with the greatest Politeness and Attention during the whole Business," and when they were finished, Colonel Paterson wrote, "the General . . . with a great deal of Attention and Civility permitted me to take my leave." On the way to his barge, wrote Samuel Blachley Webb, Colonel Paterson was "Sociable and Chatty all the way."[23]

One positive, if minor, note came out of the meeting. On 6 August Sir William Howe wrote to Lord Germain that the interview, although more polite than interesting, had induced him when writing Washington to substitute "General" for "Esq."[24]

But prior to his brother's acceptance of reality, on 30 July Lord Howe had received aboard his flagship *Eagle*, under a flag of truce, the American paymaster general, William Palfrey, who reported that His Lordship "spoke with the highest respect of General Washington, and lamented the nice distinctions which . . . prevented his addressing General Washington," and wished to write him "in any mode of address that might prevent his being blamed by the King, his master. In all discourse, called him *General* Washington, and frequently said, the States of America." Howe urged Palfrey to take the letter back but without the title. Palfrey respectfully declined, "especially as it was against the express direction of Congress."

Contemplating this affair, on the surface comic opera, one wonders how much Howe's reluctance to address Washington by his proper title was fear of riling the king and how much was upper-class British snobbery toward colonials, which was very real. While messengers were coming and going, Ambrose Serle described Washington in his journal as "a little paltry Colonel of Militia at the head of a Banditti or Rebels." Later Major John André, in his own journal kept in 1777–1778, repeatedly referred to Washington as Major Washington, demoting him even from his colonial rank of colonel.[25]

"Sickness, Disorder, and Discord reign triumphant"

Throughout July to mid-August 1776, British reinforcements streamed into New York Harbor and disembarked on Staten Island. Yet no move was made against the Rebels. Washington was puzzled by British inaction and behavior. "Very unexpectedly to me, another revolving Monday is arrived before an Attack upon this City, or a movment of the Enemy—the reason for this is incomprehensible to me." He found "exceedingly misterious . . . the conduct of the enemy. Lord Howe takes the pains to throw out, upon every occasion, that he is the Messenger of Peace—that he wants to accomodate matters—nay, has Insinuated, that he thinks himself authorized to do it upon the terms mentioned in the last Petiition to the King of G Britain."[26]

Washington was referring to the Olive Branch Petition of 5 July 1775, sent a year before by the Continental Congress to the king, asking for a cease-fire and the repeal of all laws objected to by the colonies. But even before the petition could be delivered, the king and other hawks in London had prevailed over moderates and issued on 23 August 1775 the Proclamation for Suppressing Rebellion and Sedition. The Olive Branch Petition was therefore a dead letter. Yet if Washington was right in his assessment of Lord Howe's actions, the admiral was exceeding the strict instructions given to him prior to his departure for America.[27]

In the meantime, American reinforcements also were arriving, and by mid-August Washington estimated his army "in this City and the Posts round about, to about 23,000 men." They were not, of course, of the same caliber as Sir William Howe's forces. Militia made up the bulk of the Rebel army, and the Continental regulars were green and not highly trained. For who was to train them in the arts of battlefield maneuvering necessary for eighteenth-century Western armies, given the state of weaponry at that time? The single-shot musket, which was the standard infantry weapon, was accurate up to about eighty yards; thus the necessity of training and disciplining men to maneuver and fight in close formation to bring to bear massive firepower at short range before closing with the favorite British weapon, the bayonet. The overwhelming majority of American officers had no experience in this type of set-piece, open-field fighting, and were temperamentally disinclined to render such training even had they possessed the necessary knowledge and experience. They may have been colonials, but they were also overwhelmingly British in descent and tradition, and in the British army training was a job for sergeants, not officers and gentlemen. But the sergeants also lacked experience. The forced participation of American officers in training troops awaited the arrival of a particular European professional soldier, but the contribution of the hard-bitten drillmaster of the American army awaits its place in the narrative.[28]

At the same time, Washington, as commander in chief, was beleaguered by the timeless burden of varied administrative details that are
sheer drudgery and often frustrating but are neglected at one's peril.
Later in the war, during the Carolina campaign, Lord Cornwallis would
neglect this essential component of generalship. Not Washington. "For
attention to business perhaps he has no equal," wrote Timothy Pickering (1745–1829) of Massachusetts, who would later become adjutant
general of the army. Unfortunately for Washington the modern staff system was in embryonic stage, and then only in Prussia, where it was
developed, so it all fell on him. He had aides-de-camp, of course, who
prepared drafts of letters and general orders and took dictation, but it was
Washington who had to ponder all matters ranging from petty to major
and try to come up with solutions to problems often unsolvable. A major
problem, the inexperience of officers from juniors to seniors, was widespread. Read the forlorn plea from Elizabethtown, New Jersey, of Brigadier General William Livingston (1723–1790), commanding New Jersey
militia, to Washington on, appropriately, the Fourth of July 1776:

> Your Excellency must be sensible that as the department I now act in
> is to me entirely new, I must be desirous of every aid that can possibly
> be obtained. If you Sir could spare a few experienced Officers to assist
> me in this important Business, it might be of essential Service. Our
> men are raw and inexperienced. Our officers mostly absent. Want of
> discipline is inevitable, while we are greatly exposed for the distance
> of 12 or 14 Miles.

Washington's reply described precisely his own unenviable situation:

> You also request some experienced officers to be sent over. Which I
> would gladly comply with if in my Power but I have few of that Char-
> acter, and those are so necessarily engaged here, that for the present
> I must refer you to General [Hugh] Mercer whose Judgement & Expe-
> rience may be depended upon. I have wrote him that I should endeav-
> our to send over an Engineer as soon as possible.[29]

The only answer to this problem was time in service and learning on
the job. Meanwhile, officers, who were mostly merchants, had to fly by
the seats of their pants and hope they were making the right decisions.
    Much of Washington's time was taken with correspondence to and
from successive presidents of the Continental Congress, to whom he

reported his activities in great detail. Washington was never a military adventurer. He was very much aware that Congress was his boss, and throughout the war he laid the groundwork for one of his greatest gifts to the nation: the primacy of civil authority. But he also repeatedly called upon Congress for the necessary articles that writers like to call the sinews of war. The flintlock musket, for example, would not fire without a flint, thus the absolute necessity of obtaining them, not only for his own forces in New York, but also as commander in chief for other commands, such as General Philip Schuyler's troops on New York's northern frontier, to whom he wrote in June, "I have ordered a Ton of Powder, half a Ton of Lead, five Thousand Flints, some Cannon, Intrenching Tools & a Dozen Whip Saws & files to be immediately sent to You, which You will receive in two or three Days, with a List of them & Every other Article sent from hence at this Time." He also encouraged Schuyler to take advantage of local sources for his own needs and the American army then campaigning in that American will-o'-the-wisp, Canada. For "It will be less troublesome & expensive than sending Articles from hence." Washington made that absolutely clear to Schuyler, and also revealed the pressure he was under:

> I wish you to get Every Thing You want & that Can be had Either in Albany or Its Vicinity rather than to send here for them, I am really so immersed in Buisiness & have such a Variety of Things to attend to, That I scarcely know which way to turn myself."[30]

Such as reminding John Hancock (1737–1793), president of the Continental Congress, "I must entreat your attention to an Application I made some time ago for Flints, we are extremely deficient in this necessary Article, and shall be greatly distressed if we cannot obtain a supply." Lead, however, was not a problem, for "we have a sufficient quantity for the whole Campaign taken off the Houses here."[31]

An experienced military administrator such as a former British career officer, Major General Horatio Gates, could have relieved Washington of much of his burden had he been willing, but Gates labored under delusions of grandeur, fancying himself a great captain, as did certain members of Congress, which had ordered Washington to appoint Gates to the Canadian command.[32]

So the burden was Washington's, and one must read his correspondence, letter after letter, often several on a single day, to realize the crushing nature of his command. He dealt with everything, from nuts-and-bolts supply problems to grand strategy. But one of the most nagging matters was the unprofessional nature of his army, both officers and men. Discipline and the lack of it reared almost constantly, and to dwell on it overlong would make dreary reading. Consider, however, one example of many, reported to Washington by General Schuyler, commanding the Northern Department:

> The most descriptive pen cannot describe the Condition of our Army. Sickness, Disorder, and Discord reign triumphant: the latter occasioned by an illiberal and destructive Jealousy, which unhappily subsists between the Troops raised in different Colonies.[33]

Schuyler had raised a subject that also commanded Washington's attention in New York. As soon as Pennsylvania and southern troops had joined New England soldiers outside Boston in 1775, sectional intolerance had arisen, and it continued to roil the army after it moved to New York. It would never die out, for the seeds had already been planted that would lead eighty-six years later to civil war between North and South. But on this matter Washington the Virginia planter and slaveholder also was Washington the nationalist, and he displayed in striking fashion his talent for coalition command, a gift that would stand him in equal stead when the French joined the war as American allies. In General Orders of 1 August 1776, he sent an impassioned appeal to the army:

> It is with great concern, the General understands, that Jealousies, etc., are arisen among the troops from the different Provinces, of reflections frequently thrown out, which can only tend to irritate each other, and injure the noble cause in which we are engaged, and which we ought to support with one hand and one heart . . . the officers, and soldiers . . . can no way assist our cruel enemies more effectually, than making division among ourselves; That the Honor and Success of the army, and the safety of our bleeding Country, depends upon harmony and good agreement with each other; That the Provinces are all United to oppose the common enemy, and all distinctions sunk in the name of an American . . . ought to be our only emulation, and he will be the best Soldier, and the best Patriot, who contributes most to this glorious work, whatever his station, or from whatever part of the Continent he may come. Let all distinctions of Nations, Countries, and Provinces, therefore be lost in the Generous contest.

In the final sentence, Washington the nationalist made absolutely clear his seriousness of purpose:

> If there are any officers, or soldiers, so lost to virtue and a love of their Country, as to continue in such practices after this order; the General assures them, and is directed by Congress to declare, to the whole Army, that such persons shall be severely punished and dismissed the service with disgrace.[34]

The tender feelings of officers who had endured slights, alleged slights, being passed over for promotion, and other indignities real or spurious were, of course, brought to Washington for adjudication. On 14 August, with an offensive by General Howe expected daily, Colonel James Mitchell Varnum of Rhode Island "has been with me this Morning to resign his Commission, conceiving himself to be greatly Injured in not having been Noticed in the Late Arrangements, & promotions, of General Officers. I remonstrated against the Impropriety of the measure at this time and he has consented to stay till Affairs wear a different Aspect than what they do at present." But Washington had not heard the last from Varnum on the subject of promotion. British senior officers in this war have often been criticized for their fumings and feudings, but their American counterparts ran them at least a close second in this regard.[35]

The army on Manhattan was dependent on farmers coming into the city to sell meat and produce, but many soldiers behaved toward them like thugs and common thieves. On 2 July Washington ordered that "No Sentries are to stop or molest the Country people coming to Market or going from it." A little more than a month later he issued with obvious exasperation another order:

> Nowithstanding the orders issued, and the interest the troops have in it; Complaints are made of the bad behaviour of the troops to people at market; taking and destroying their things. The General declares for the last time, that he will punish such offenders most severely; and in order that they may be detected, an officer from each of the guards, nearest to those Markets where the Country People is, to attend from sunrise till twelve O'Clock, and he is strictly enjoined to prevent any abuses of this kind; to seize any offender and send him immediately to the Guard house, reporting him also at Headquarters. The officers of guards in future will be answerable if there are any more Complaints

unless they apprehend the offender. A copy of this order will be put up in every Guard House in the City.[36]

In an age when sickness and disease felled more soldiers than battle, mundane housekeeping activities also could not be neglected by the commander in chief, due to the inexperience of his officers:

> As the weather is very warm, there will be the greatest danger of the Troops growing unhealthy, unless both officers and men are attentive to cleanliness, in their persons and quarters. The officers are required to visit the men frequently in their quarters to impress on them the necessity of frequently changing their linen, cleaning their persons, and where it can be avoided not to cook their victuals in the same room where they sleep. If any of the officers apprehend themselves crowded in their quarters they are to represent it to the Barrack Master who is ordered to accommodate them in such a manner as to be most conducive to health and convenience. The good of the service, the comfort of the men, and the merit of the officers will be so much advanced, by keeping the troops as neat and clean as possible, that the General hopes that there will be an emulation upon this head.[37]

He also made it clear that his order would not be governed by the honor system, advising that "as a scrutiny will soon be made, those who shall be found negligent will be punished, and the deserving rewarded."

Then there was the matter of the Connecticut Light Horse, 400 to 500 strong, "most of them, If not all, Men of reputation & of property." Like cavalrymen everywhere, at all times, they were mightily attached to their horses, and considering themselves gentlemen disdained the common fatigue duties required of every soldier. Washington told them early on that he appreciated their "zeal and laudable attachment to the cause of their Country," but he wrote to Colonel Gold Silliman, "what to do with the horses of this reinforcemt I am at a loss to determine. It will be impossible to support 'em, & if it could be done, the Expence would be enormous. I cannot think myself at liberty to consent to the Horses coming." As for the men, however, "The Exigency of our Affairs calls aloud for their Assistance." According to Washington's aide-de-camp, Samuel Blachley Webb, "It was only requested they should mount guard, which they refused." The field officers of the regiments wrote to Washington on 16 July that a Connecticut law "expressly exempted" the Light Horse "from Staying in Garrison, or doing duty on Foot, apart from their horses," that the troopers refused to serve otherwise, and asked to be dismissed from service. Washington's answer of the same date was brief and did not mince words:

> I can only repeat to you what I said last night, & that is, that if your Men think themselves exempt from the Common duties of a Soldier, will not mount Guard, do Garrison Duty, or the service separate from their Horse, they can be no longer of Use here, where horse cannot be brought to Action. And I do not care how soon they are Dismiss'd.[38]

This incident should not be taken as evidence that Washington underrated the value of cavalry, of which he has been accused. Quite the contrary. The following December he wrote to John Hancock, "From the Experience I have had this Campaign of the Utility of Horse, I am convinced there is no carrying on the War without them, and I would recommend the establishment of one or more Corps, (in proportion to the number of foot) in Addition to those already raised in Virginia."[39]

The Continental Company of Artificers, stationed in Boston, proved as stubborn as the Connecticut Light Horse. Artificers were skilled craftsmen, and in this particular case knew, among other things, how to make gun carriages. On 22 July Major General Artemas Ward recommended Captain Joseph Eayres's Company of Artificers: "if such a company be wanted . . . I believe a better cannot be had." Washington replied seven days later that the "Company of Artificers you mention are much wanted, would you order them on with all convenient Dispatch." Ward sent for Captain Eayres to give him his marching orders but discovered there was a problem. Captain Eayres "informs me that his men cannot go to New York unless their pay is increased to six pounds per month, and that he informed your Excellency of this before the Army left Cambridge Last Spring . . . that he is willing to march immediately, but as" for his men "he cannot induce them to march until the Establishment is made." Washington knew that he had to follow through with the pay increase, but how to do it without the word getting out and inducing jealousy in others? Read his solution to this problem:

> the consequences of raiseing their pay would be an Immediate Application from all those in Service as Artificers to be put on the same footing, if not refuse doing Duty any longer than absolutely bound.
> But these men understanding the particular branch of making Gun Carriages etc and the absolute necessity we are under for them

induces me to order them on at the Wages you mention, and to prevent the Evil abovementioned have concluded to stop them 40 or 50 Miles up the Sound and let them go on with their Business, Norwalk a town in the western part of Connecticut situated on the Sound seems a proper Station, to which place you'll please to order them as soon as possible, with their Tools compleat.[40]

Finally, let us end this litany of burdensome administrative chores that day after day, week after week, month after month, year after year for eight long years never let up, and end on a lighter note dealing with a matter of deeply traditional military protocol. It was a cherished European tradition, inherited by Americans, that on parade and in order of battle the senior regiment would stand on the right—the Post of Honor. In this particular case Colonel Thomas McKean (1734–1817) of Pennsylvania and Delaware raised a fine point that Washington was obliged to take the time to answer:

In answer to that part of your Letter of the 10th Inst. "whether, when a Brigade is drawn up, and the oldest Colonel takes the Right, his Battalion is to be on the right with him; that is, whether the Colonel gives rank to the Battalion." I shall inform you, that to the best of my Military knowledge a Regiment never looses its Rank, consequently can derive none from its Colonel, nor loose any by having the youngest Colonel in the Army appointed to the Comd of it. The oldest Regiment therefore although commanded by the youngest Colonel is placed on the Right, and the Colonel with it.[41]

That momentous matter dealt with, Washington returned to trying to figure out the age-old commander's dilemma: what was the enemy up to? Would he invade Manhattan, perhaps by landing in its northern reaches and cutting off the Rebel escape route? Would he land on Long Island and attempt to take the Rebel fortifications on Brooklyn Heights, thus dominating New York City and its dockyards? Or would he debouch into New Jersey across the narrow channel separating it from Staten Island? On 19 August Brigadier General Hugh Mercer (c. 1725– 1777) in New Jersey sent Washington intelligence he had gained from an American sea captain who had been on Staten Island and reported that the British "intended to attack Long Island first and if possible to Storm the Fort opposite the City in Order to prevent their Shippin[g] being annoy'd when the Attack is made on New York." The assault on Long

Island was to be made by the grenadiers and light infantry, but simultaneously they meant "to send the rest of their Army up the North River and Land above the Town by which means they expect to secure General Washington & the Army without firing a Shot."[42]

Two days later similar intelligence but with a twist reached him from Brigadier General William Livingston in Elizabethtown, New Jersey, who wrote, "In the utmost haste, I must inform you that very providentially, I sent a Spy last Night on Staten Island to obtain intelligence of the movements of the Enemey, as many Things apparently new was seen from our Lines." The upshot of the spy's report was that with 20,000 men "they expected to attack every Hour, he thinks this Night at farthest. It was to be on Long Island, & up the North River." Then came the twist. The spy, who put British strength at 35,000 overall, reported that the 15,000 men left on Staten Island "were to land & attack at Bergen Point, Elizabeth Town Point and at Amboy" in Jersey. On the strength of this, at 8:00 P.M. that evening Washington sent a letter enclosing a copy of Livingston's letter to Major General William Heath, commanding at Kingsbridge, at the northern end of Manhattan, urging Heath "to be as well prepared as possible for this important Event."[43]

Sir William, however, had nothing so ambitious in mind as a three-pronged attack. On the following morning, 22 August, he answered the questions everyone had been asking: When would he attack? Where would he attack?

3

"It was hard work to Die"

"The finest & most picturesque Scenes"

The night of 21 August was awful to hear and behold. "A most terrible Evening," Ambrose Serle wrote, "of Thunder, Lightning, Wind & Rain; the most vehement I ever saw, or that has been known here by the Inhabitants for many Years." In the city, an anonymous American correspondent wrote, "The thunder-storm of last evening was one of the most dreadful I ever heard; it lasted from seven to ten o'clock. Several claps struck in and about the city; many houses were damaged; several lives were lost." The symbolic effect of the storm was not lost on him. "When God speaks," he wrote, "who can but fear?"[1]

By the next day, however, the skies had cleared and the waters surrounding New York sparkled under a bright sun. Vessels from Lord Howe's fleet moved into position at dawn to cover the landing of the army at Gravesend Bay on Long Island, about a mile east of the Narrows. Facing a broad plain and without physical obstruction, the beach was a natural landing place, and in fact the Rebel general who had first commanded on Long Island, Nathanael Greene, had about a month before viewed it as such. Gathered to carry the troops across were seventy-five flatboats, eleven batteau, and two row galleys, all manned by Royal Navy seamen. At 9:00 A.M. Lieutenant General Sir Henry Clinton (1730–1795) led ashore an advance guard of splendid units: 33rd Foot, led by that intrepid regimental commander Lieutenant Colonel James Webster (d. 1781);

43

Black Watch (42nd Royal Highlanders); the entire Brigade of Grena-diers; and 3rd Battalion of Brigade of Light Infantry. More followed as the landing craft plied back and forth. The operation went like clock-work, without opposition, for there was little the Rebels could do. Lieu-tenant Colonel James Chambers (1743–1805), of Colonel Edward Hand's (1744–1802) 1st Continental Infantry, usually referred to as Pennsylva-nia riflemen, described the planned scorched-earth policy in a letter to his wife: "We marched our forces, about two hundred in number, to New Utrecht, to watch the movements of the enemy. We found it impracti-cable for so small a force to attack them on the plain, and sent Captain Hamilton with twenty men, before them to burn all the grain; which he did very cleverly, and killed a great many cattle." The adjutant general of the Hessian forces landing that day, Major Carl Leopold Baurmeister (1734–1803), described "Barns, grain stacks, and the lighthouses built here and there . . . immediately set on fire," and soon, wrote Ambrose Serle, "the Country seemed covered with smoke." By noon about 15,000 British and German regulars with artillery had landed. Colonel Cham-bers wrote that after the burnings his regiment secured its baggage and "near 12 o'clock . . . returned down the great road to Flatbush with only our small regiment, and one New England regiment sent to support us, though at a mile's distance. When in sight of Flatbush, we discovered the enemy, but not the main body; on perceiving us, they retreated down the road perhaps a mile. A party of our people commanded by Captain Miller followed them close with a design to decoy a portion of them fol-low him, whilst the rest kept in the edge of the woods alongside of Cap-tain M. But they thought better of the matter, and would not come after him though he went within two hundred yards. There they stood for a long time, and then Captain Miller turned off to us and we proceeded along their flank."[2]

Ambrose Serle went ashore after the beachhead had been secured and reported that "The soldiers and Sailors seemed as merry as in a Holi-day, and regaled themselves with the fine apples, which hung everywhere upon the Trees in great abundance." He added, "It was really diverting to see Sailors & Apples tumbling from the Trees together." Serle became rhapsodic over the sight that stretched before him, the troops formed

> upon the adjacent Plain, a Fleet of above 300 Ships and Vessels with
> their Sails spread open to dry, the Sun shining clear upon them, the
> green Hills and Meadows after the Rain, and the calm Surface of the

Water upon the contiguous Sea and up the Sound, exhibited one of the finest & most picturesque Scenes that the Imagination can fancy or the Eye behold.[3]

This helps us to set aside modern Brooklyn's teeming streets and pollution-belching traffic and consider the rugged rural topography of its eighteenth-century landscape, now to be seen only in its parks and cemeteries. The British had landed on a large, flat plain running from the ridge to the north of them southward four to six miles to the sea, and even farther eastward. On this plain running west to east and surrounded by their cultivated fields were the Dutch farming villages of New Utrecht, Gravesend, Flatbush, and Flatlands. To the north of the plain lay the British tactical problem. There loomed a natural defense that Sir William could not take lightly, especially given his experience at Bunker Hill against entrenched Rebels. Millions of years before the British landed, during the Ice Age, the land had been formed by a massive glacier that moved slowly, inexorably, over the land like a giant bulldozer, until it ended in this part of North America on Staten Island. A glacial moraine confronted the British, forming a huge, natural defensive work. Called the Heights of Guana, it formed a ridge running inland five to six miles in a northeasterly direction from Upper New York Bay. From the plain the ridge rose steeply from forty to eighty feet. The ridge and its slopes were a tangle of woods, brambles, and thickets. A Hessian officer who experienced this barrier described it as "one English mile wide . . . thickly grown with large trees . . . full of gullies and ravines, which make it impossible for even three men to walk abreast." Precisely the type of ground legends tell us where American fighting men excelled and European regulars were helpless. From east to west, this rugged topography was pierced by four passes: Martense Lane Pass joined the road running along the shore; Flatbush Pass, which led to the village of Brooklyn, and Brooklyn Heights (then called Columbia Heights); Bedford Pass, leading to the village of Bedford; and set off to the east, Jamaica Pass, from where one could head toward eastern Long Island—or west toward Brooklyn. The question facing Sir William was how and where to breach the ridge without the assault becoming a bloodbath.[4]

The Rebels, meanwhile, were not without their own problems, chief of which was a grievous loss suffered two days before the British landed at Gravesend Bay. Washington's choice as commander on Long Island,

Major General Nathanael Greene, informed his chief on 15 August "that I am confined to my Bed with a raging Fever." By the twentieth his doctor diagnosed it as "a putrid and billious fever" (typhus) and feared "his life endangered." On that same day a reluctant Washington replaced Greene with Major General John Sullivan (1740–1795) of New Hampshire, a man of unquestionable courage but no great ability. He was also unfamiliar with the countryside, which Greene had been studying since early May. Brigadier General William Alexander (1726–1783), known to his contemporaries as Lord Stirling, was given command of Sullivan's division.[5]

"German jargon"

While Washington wrestled with command problems, and Sir William reinforced his Long Island troops by 10,000 men and pondered his own problem, the British army's master of operations and tactics, Lieutenant General Sir Henry Clinton, came up with a possible solution. On 24 August Sir Henry rode with his aide-de-camp, Lieutenant Colonel Francis, Lord Rawdon (1754–1826), and Brigadier General Sir William Erskine (1728–1795) on a personal reconnaissance of the flat country stretching south and east of the Heights of Guana, and discovered that the key to attacking the Rebels in the hills lay to the east, at Jamaica Pass. In his written proposal to Sir William, Clinton succinctly described the geographical situation. "The position which the rebels occupy in our front may be turned by a gorge about six miles from us, through a country in which cavalry may make the *avant garde*. That, once possessed, gives us the island, and in a mile or two further we shall" cut the "communications with their works at Brooklyn." While the flanking movement was taking place, British and Hessian units facing the Rebels occupying the Heights of Guana should begin attacks "vigorous but not too obstinately persisted in," while the flanking force delivered from the rear an attack "which should be pushed as far as it will go." Clinton recommended a night march by a 10,000-man flanking force "so that everything may be at its ground by daybreak." He also proposed that the fleet should join in pretending that the main attack was coming from the front by making "every demonstration of forcing the enemy's batteries in the East River, without, however, committing themselves."[6]

Although it proposed a risky night march, it was an excellent plan, simple, well thought out, avoiding a costly frontal assault by taking advantage of topography, and promising that much-sought-after but rarely achieved military maneuver, a double envelopment. General Erskine, who commanded Fraser's Highlanders (71st Foot) and who was well regarded for his "military judgement," accepted the plan without reservation and the following day took it to headquarters.[7]

Where it was scorned and rejected. The old rivalry between officers who had served, like Clinton, in Germany in the Seven Years' War, and those like Howe, who fought in that conflict in America, rose with full force. A flanking movement? "German jargon," sneered Generals James Grant and James Robertson. The proposal was dismissed by Howe and his staff as "savoring too much of the German school." According to General Erskine, Howe said, "as the Rebels knew nothing of turning a flank, such a movement would have no effect." What nonsense! What could Howe have been thinking of when he made such a statement?[8]

And what could he have been thinking of the next day, 26 August, when he reversed himself and told Clinton to go ahead, take command of the flanking column's advance guard and march that night? For "In all the opinions he ever gave to me," Clinton wrote, Howe "did not expect any good from the move." Howe made only one change. Clinton had proposed that General Grant move his two brigades and 42nd Foot directly up the ridge toward the Rebel forces on the heights, but Howe changed that, for Grant to advance farther west along the shore road. Details of the flanking movement he left to Clinton, who could march "at what hour I pleased by whatever route I thought proper; and, having seized the gorge I mentioned in the plan I sent him, wait there until he joined me in the morning."[9]

"Your best men should . . . prevent the enemy's passing the wood"

On the eve of the first action in which American and British soldiers would meet in a formal, open-field engagement, let us pause and consider the combatants. As we know, on 20 August General Sullivan had replaced the desperately ill General Greene. But then that old military devil seniority intervened, and on 24 August Washington elevated over Sullivan an old Yankee warhorse, a legendary figure from the French and Indian War, fifty-eight-year-old Major General Israel Putnam (1718–1790), of whom Washington's aide, Colonel Joseph Reed, wrote, "General Putnam was made happy by obtaining leave to go over—the brave old man was quite miserable at being kept here."[10]

It was not a wise decision. Sullivan had been given at least four days to catch up and study the lay of the land. Putnam was completely ignorant of it. Washington gave him a crash course by riding the ground with him on the 25th, but Washington himself was not intimately familiar with the topography. Putnam also labored under the handicap that bedeviled all Rebel generals, described by Washington as "the want of experience to move upon a large Scale." In fact, "Old Put," as the New England men fondly called him, although suited to irregular warfare, quite simply lacked the ability to command large forces in a formal, open-field battle.

He would, however, have understood the defensive system that had been planned by Charles Lee and carried forward first by Lord Stirling and then Nathanael Greene. One and a half to three miles behind the Heights of Guana the Rebels, under the immediate direction of Colonel Rufus Putnam (1738–1824), a cousin of the "brave old man," had built a series of earthen forts and redoubts across the neck of the Brooklyn peninsula, stretching about a mile and a half from Wallabout Bay on the north to Gowanus Bay on the south. North to south, they were Redoubt Left, Fort Putnam, Oblong Redoubt, Fort Greene, and Fort Box. A system of trenches connected the forts and redoubts, and "On both wings," wrote a Hessian officer, were "zigzag trenches" that a British engineering officer, Captain John Montresor, described as extending to the marshes of Gowanus Bay on the south and the wetlands of Wallabout Bay on the north. Montresor also testified that protecting the "whole" of the fortifications and trenches was the "most formidable" abatis: a line of felled trees with sharpened branches intertwined and facing outward. This defensive complex was meant to protect Rebel fortifications built to stop the British from sailing up the East River: Fort Stirling on Brooklyn Heights, Fort Defiance at Red Hook, and Governor's Island."[11]

Although Nathanael Greene had apparently intended to keep his regiments inside the defensive works and force a siege, Washington decided that it would not do to allow the British to advance unchallenged onto the Heights of Guana and onward to besiege the Rebel works. And the high ground did suit the American talent and propensity for defensive warfare. Washington made clear to General Putnam the day after his appointment that the enemy should be met in the woods by the best troops, while the least experienced should be posted within the defensive works:

The wood next red hooks should be well attended to; put some of the most disorderly rifle men into it; The militia or most indifferent troops (those I mean which are least tutored & seen least service) will do for the interior works, whilst your best men should at all hazards prevent the enemy's passing the wood; & approaching your works; The works should be secured by abatties etc. where necessary to make the enemy's approach, as difficult as possible; Traps & ambuscades should be laid for their parties if you find they are sent out after cattle etc.

In the same letter Washington returned to a theme that dogged him daily. That the other ranks of armies try to get away with what they can, slipping now and then from the unnatural discipline so necessary to a successful army's operation, has been well known throughout the ages. But there is a big difference between that and the constant indiscipline that marked the American army at this stage in its development. In clear, unmistakable language, Washington brought Putnam's attention to the disorderliness of the American militia army, in this instance "a scattering, unmeaning & wasteful fire, from our people at the enemy," in which "every soldier conceives himself at liberty to fire when & at what he pleases." General Putnam, "without loss of time," was instructed to meet with his corps and regimental commanders and "charge them, in express and positive terms, to stop these irregularities, as they value the good of the service, their own honor, and the safety of the army." As militiamen, all civilians at heart, often wandered at will about the countryside, Washington enjoined Putnam to secure his "incampment and works," with "no person to be allowed to pass beyond the guards without special orders in writing." With an attack expected daily, men off duty "are to be compelled to remain in, or near their . . . quarters, that they may turn out at a moments warning," as nothing was "more probable than that the enemy will allow little enough time to prepare for the attack." In that judgment Washington was more prescient than he realized.

Washington was also deeply exercised over the pillaging and arson the troops had visited upon the local population. "The Officers . . . are to exert themselves to the utmost to prevent every kind of abuse to private property, or to bring every offender, to the punishment he deserves; shameful it is to find that those men, who have come hither, in defense of the rights of mankind, should turn invaders of it by destroyng the substance of their friends."

The nub of all this was expressed in a succinct paragraph toward the end of the letter that neatly summed up Washington's frustrations with the unmilitary character of his army:

> The distinction between a well regulated army, & a mob, is the good order & discipline of the first, & the licentious & disorderly behaviour of the latter; Men, therefore, who not employed as mere hirelings, but have step'd forth in defence of every thing that is dear & valuable, not only to themselves but to posterity, should take uncommon pains to conduct themselves with uncommon propriety and good order; as their honor reputation etc. call loudly upon them for it.[12]

This was all very well and certainly to be applauded, but there was an immediate problem that went beyond the good order and discipline of the army. There were only 7,000 men to man the defensive works and cover a front six miles long cut by four strategic passes. Recognizing the need for reinforcements, Washington sent more men across the East River, but it still left the Americans stretched perilously thin. And the newly raised Continentals were regulars in name only. They and the militia regiments were of a people who knew how to fight behind defensive works; how to disperse in the woods in the manner of modern infantry; how to wage war against Indians by burning their towns, fields, and food supplies. But they had never, in their history on this continent, fought a general engagement—that is, a formal, open-field battle, in which the essential parts were maneuver en masse, massive firepower delivered at short distance at the right time, if necessary followed by a bayonet charge driven home. Yet facing them on the broad sweep of flatlands at the foot of the Heights of Guana were men who knew precisely how to do those things: 25,000 British and Hessian regulars. Let us take a brief look at this formidable force before we follow Sir Henry Clinton's night march in his attempt to turn the American left flank.

On the British left, closest to the water, were two brigades consisting of eight regiments of foot reinforced by Black Watch, two companies of New York Tories, and ten guns manned by gunners of the Royal Artillery. Their mission was to advance up the shore road and give every intention of mounting a strong attack on the American lines, and at the same time extend eastward along the height of land and eventually link up with the Hessians in the center, coming by way of Flatbush Pass. But their real attack would come only after they heard a prearranged signal from Clinton's flanking force. Commanding the British left was

Major General James Grant (1720–1806), whose opinion of Americans was best expressed when he stood up in Parliament in 1775 and claimed that with 5,000 men he could march without opposition from Maine to Florida. On this occasion he commanded just over 3,100 troops.

In the center, stationed at the village of Flatbush, a little over 6,100 Hessians formed into three brigades of Jägers, grenadiers, fusiliers, and musketeers were commanded by an elderly veteran of many campaigns in the Seven Years' War, Lieutenant General Leopold Phillip von Heister (1707–1777). Their orders were to wait for the same signal that would alert General Grant's wing that the flanking force was in position and the trap sprung. Then they would march on Flatbush Pass, link up with Grant's British regiments, and push forward to hammer the rebels against Clinton's anvil coming from the rear.

If Washington had then possessed, as he did later in the war, an efficient intelligence service, events on the plain on the 26th might have alerted him to the possibility that Jamaica Pass was Sir William's key objective. For it was on that day that Cornwallis, leaving the Hessians behind and detaching Black Watch to Grant, moved the bulk of the British forces on Long Island southeast to the village of Flatlands, which lay athwart the road to Jamaica. But he lacked that information, and even when he finally realized that the main British attack was to be delivered on Long Island, he could only guess from which direction it might come, and that day on the Rebel side nobody paid much attention to Jamaica Pass.

The British flanking force numbered about 10,275 men. They were largely the cream of the army. They moved out in three divisions at staggered intervals. The advance, 5,525 strong, on whom would hinge the success of that night march, was led by the best tactician on the field that day, Lieutenant General Sir Henry Clinton, commanding King's Own (4th Foot), 27th Inniskillings, Brigade of Grenadiers, Brigade of Light Infantry, Fraser's Highlanders (71st Foot), 15th Foot, 33rd Foot, 45th Foot, 17th Light Dragoons, and Royal Artillery with fourteen guns. Lord Cornwallis commanded Clinton's reserve. The advance alone outnumbered or nearly equaled all the Rebel troops guarding all the passes.

The main force numbered 4,750 men: twelve regiments of foot, the 1,100-man Brigade of Foot Guards, and gunners of the Royal Artillery with another fourteen guns. It was commanded by Lieutenant General Hugh, Lord Percy. Sir William rode with Percy's command. The barrage train guarded by a regiment of foot brought up the rear.

This was a formidable force. Only two American regiments on the field that day could come close to matching them in stoic steadfastness, but they were stationed at the other end of the Heights of Guana. The gap in leadership was even wider. The senior British officers—Howe, Clinton, Percy, and Cornwallis—were first-rate combat commanders, all having proven themselves leading regiments in the Seven Years' War either in Europe or America. The Americans had no one present, including Washington, who could match their experience and operational and tactical abilities.

"I immediately posted a detachment there"

At 8:00 P.M. on 26 August, Sir Henry Clinton's advance moved out, he wrote, "in one column by half battalions, ranks and files close." In any age, night operations are fraught with risk. To better appreciate what the British were attempting to accomplish over 200 years ago, a bold night march around the American left flank, the reader should consider a more recent night operation by highly trained elite troops equipped with the latest in night vision and communications equipment and such sophisticated technology as reconnaissance drones, surveillance aircraft, and spy satellites. In March 2002, on a mountaintop in Afghanistan, American special operations forces suffered casualties and an initial setback due to "intelligence lapses, radio glitches and miscommunication between commanders and commandos."[13]

Undertaken before the invention of the internal combustion engine, there were none of the night noises to which we are so accustomed to mask the sounds of the British approach: the rhythmic tread of 10,000 marching feet, the crunch of wheels of the artillery. But if here and there a countryman and his spouse did hear and guessed what the muffled sounds were and what they portended, they chose to roll over and pull the covers tighter and close their eyes. Thus the regiments proceeded, unreported, unseen. Only a few miles west of the British column, a 600-man Rebel militia force under General Nathaniel Woodhull was herding cattle farther onto Long Island to forestall any British attempt to capture them. They heard nothing, and the gap between the two forces widened. Besides, what could 600 do against 10,000? Quite a lot at night, with surprise on their side and under a bold commander. At least enough noise would have resulted to alarm the American commander on the Heights of Guana. But it was not to be, and the British tramped on.

The Battle of Long Island and the Retreat from New York

Clinton had posted Fraser's Highlanders as flankers on his left "for the purpose of drowning the noise of our cannon over the stones, masking our march, and preventing the enemy's patrols from discovering it." The pace was slow, probably in another effort to advance as quietly as possible. Between eleven and midnight the sound of distant firing to his rear, which Clinton could not know were rebels to the west firing on each other, prompted him to move eastward off the road into the open fields and use the knowledge of his local Tory guides to guide him safely to his goal. The troops were halted for short breathers at intervals between one and three o'clock in the morning, when as seasoned troops they followed one of the oldest rules of soldiering: never lose an opportunity to sleep, no matter how brief the time. The column "continued our march unmolested," and it was still dark when "my guides informed me we were within a quarter of a mile of Howard's House, which was only a few hundred yards from Jamaica Pass." It was about 2:00 A.M.[14]

About an hour earlier, far to the left on the Gowanus Road, General Grant made a vigorous but limited diversionary move in his assigned mission of masking what the British were really up to. The Red Lion Inn, an American outpost guarding Martense Lane Pass, east of the shore road, was the target. It had been occupied by Colonel Edward Hand's Pennsylvania riflemen, but about midnight Hand and his men were relieved by Major Edward Burd of Pennsylvania and his "Flying Camp," which sounds formidable but was not. It was designed as a mobile reserve that could be moved quickly to trouble spots, which was a good idea, but unfortunately the force was of poor quality, and when a British regiment "with about 2 or 300 men" suddenly appeared out of the dark, the Flying Camp flew backward "without firing a gun," wrote an American officer. Either to his credit or lack of swiftness, Major Burd did not accompany his men. "I was taken prisoner on the morning of the 27th after a skirmish. . . . I was used with great civility by General Grant & admitted to my Parole, Brigadier General Agnew and Major Leslie and Major Batt also treated me with great Politeness." Burd was lucky. He was out of it, but there were other Rebel officers on the field that day who would not be treated so gently.[15]

Grant had done his job well. His sudden and forceful move convinced American commanders that at the very least a serious attack had begun: "I fully expected," wrote Colonel Samuel Atlee, commanding a Pennsylvania battalion, "as did my Officers, that the strength of the British Army was advancing in this Quarter with intention to have taken this Rout to our Lines." There was much confusion in the dark. The panic of Burd's men spread to other units behind them that joined the Flying Camp in its tumultuous retreat. Had this been the main British attack there is no telling what might have happened, but Grant followed orders and waited. By daylight Brigadier General Samuel Holden Parsons (1737–1789) had moved other troops into place and believed he had "halted their column & gave time for Lord Sterling with his forces to come up."[16]

While Grant maneuvered convincingly on the American right, Clinton on the British right had no knowledge of what lay ahead of him. Did he think it inconceivable that the pass might be unguarded? There was only one way to find out. In the darkness he sent forward a patrol from King's Own under Captain William Glanville Evelyn (1742–1776). Evelyn's patrol bumped into and took efficiently and without undue noise a five-man mounted patrol of young American officers who had been posted to the area to warn of an approaching enemy. They were brought to Sir Henry, who learned from them the astounding news that there were no Rebel units holding Jamaica Pass. It was unoccupied, unguarded, a veritable freeway for 10,000 British regulars. The five young, unseasoned American officers were the only Rebel soldiers in the area. "I immediately posted a detachment there," Clinton wrote, and "ordering parties to be distributed along the Bedford and Newtown roads, which pass through it, I waited for daylight to take possession in force."[17]

Clearly, succinctly, Clinton described his next move. "As soon as the dawn appeared, I made my disposition against any opposition I might possibly meet from the enemy, and laid hold of the pass with the whole *avant garde*." He must have still believed—and who could fault him?— that there must be American forces in the vicinity, and thus remained on guard while he waited for Percy and Howe with the main force. They arrived about two hours later. Sir William, according to Sir Henry, "In all the opinions he ever gave me, did not expect any good from the move. And during the march seemed not anxious of passing beyond the gorge." Nevertheless, the flanking column moved out upon Howe's arrival, westward on the road to Bedford, and beyond, Brooklyn. Howe could not believe the ease of their penetration of enemy country. Clinton wrote, "The Commander in Chief seemed to have some suspicion the enemy would attack us on our march, but I was persuaded that, as they neglected to oppose us at the gorge, the affair was over."[18]

The Blame Game

Surely, however, the Americans could not have made such a monumental blunder. Surely there were troops assigned to guard the Bedford Road and oppose a British flanking movement. Thus enters our tale Colonel Samuel Miles, his Pennsylvania rifle regiment, and the ensuing blame game.

East of the Bedford Road, which led from the village of Flatbush to the village of Bedford, were woods extending eastward toward Jamaica

Pass. In these woods, Brigadier General Samuel Holden Parsons wrote to John Adams, "was placed Colonel Miles with his Battalion to watch the motion of the enemy on that part, with orders to keep a party constantly reconnoitering to and across the Jamaica road." In his Journal, however, Colonel Miles claimed that it was not he who was at fault but General Sullivan. With his regiment, Miles wrote,

> I lay . . . within cannon shot of the Hessian camp for four days without receiving a single order from Gen'l Sullivan, who commanded on Long Island, out of the lines. The day before the action, he came to the camp, and I then told him the situation of the British Army; that Gen'l Howe, with the main body, lay on my left, about a mile and a-half or two miles, and I was convinced when the army moved that Gen'l Howe would fall into the Jamaica Road, and I hoped there were troops there to watch them. Nowithstanding this information, which indeed he might have obtained from his own observation, if he had attended to his duty as a General ought to have done; no steps were taken.[19]

Miles further claimed that when the Hessians formed outside Flatbush at 7:00 A.M.—another diversionary movement—and firing began, he immediately marched to the sound of the guns, a movement usually celebrated by historians but in this case it was in the wrong direction. He had not led his men more than two hundred yards when a Continental colonel senior to Miles stopped him and told him to guard the road leading from Flatbush to Bedford. Miles then continued his defense by claiming he told the colonel, "I was convinced the main body of the enemy would take the Jamaica road, that there was no probability of their coming along the road he was then guarding, and if he would not let me procede to where the firing was, I would return and endeavor to get into the Jamaica road before General Howe. To this he consented."

At this point we could ask ourselves why, if Miles was so convinced of Howe's route, he had not led his men east instead of west? To this Miles probably would have replied, I had no orders. It does seem improbable that even a general as inept as Sullivan would have failed to at least keep a small unit patrolling the Jamaica road, unless he was counting entirely on the five hapless young officers sent to watch Jamaica Pass. The testimony of General Parsons in his letter to John Adams also must be given due weight: Parsons blamed Miles, and as brigadier of the day, Parsons presumably was privy to orders of the day.

But it is time to forgo the blame game and return to the action. Miles, with one battalion numbering about 230 men, turned around and headed through the woods toward the Jamaica road. The second battalion, under Lieutenant Colonel [Daniel] Brodhead, was "some distance in the rear," Miles wrote. After marching almost two miles he came within sight of the road, "and to my great mortification I saw the main body of the enemy in full march between me and our lines, and the baggage guard just coming into the road." This meant that Howe's 10,000-man force was well on its way to enveloping the Rebel forces guarding the passes. Miles's first thought was to cut his way through the baggage train, make for Hell Gate, and there cross the East River to Manhattan. First, however, ordering his men "to remain quite still," Miles detailed a Major Williams, who was mounted, to ride back immediately to Brodhead's battalion with orders "to push on by the left of the enemy and endeavor [to] get into our lines that way."

Miles, meanwhile, with his adjutant, "crept as near the road as I though prudent" and managed to take prisoner a British grenadier who had stepped into the woods. From him he learned that the baggage train was guarded by an entire brigade. Miles then called his officers together and laid out possible courses of action, one of which entailed lying low until the baggage train passed and then making for Hell Gate and Manhattan, which Miles apparently favored because following any other course "we must lose a number of men without affecting the enemy materially." But his officers, their honor at stake, objected on the ground that "we should be blamed for not fighting at all, and perhaps charged with cowardice, which would be worse than death itself." The battalion then moved westward in an attempt "to force our way through the enemy's flank guards into our lines at Brooklyn."

There now occurred an event that clearly reveals the disability of riflemen when faced by regulars at relatively close quarters. The famed American rifle was very accurate but slow-loading and had no provision for mounting a bayonet. Read the words of Colonel Miles, whose men "had not proceeded more than half a mile when we fell in with a body of 7 or 800 light infantry, which we attacked without any hesitation, but their superiority of numbers encouraged them to march up with their bayonets, which we could not withstand, having none ourselves." Miles ordered his men to "push on towards our lines," but they shortly ran into another large body of British troops, to whom he lost several men, and from there the men undoubtedly dispersed into small groups.

Of Miles's 230-man battalion, 159 were captured. With a few men, Miles hoped to hide until night and then strike out for Hell Gate, "but about 3 o'clock in the afternoon was discovered by a party of Hessians and obliged to surrender."

"Every man was intent on his own safety"

At 9:00 A.M. two British guns boomed in Bedford Village. The pre-arranged signal to Generals Grant and von Heister was clear. The flank-ing force had successfully completed its march and was behind the Rebels. It was time for Grant and von Heister to end their pretense and launch general attacks. In the center von Heister sent his blue-coated Hessians up Flatbush Road in columns of twos, drums beating, artillery and Jägers and grenadiers ahead, firing "into the woods directly ahead of them," Major Baurmeister wrote, "followed by the several battalions, first in columns, then deployed" into line.[20]

The American center collapsed without a fight. Major Baurmeister, who had made known his opinion of "this lot of rabble which parades under the name of riflemen," claimed that "All the riflemen fled, aban-doning their strongest posts and throwing away their rifles." We know for certain that two New England regiments, 22nd Continentals and 6th Connecticut, abandoned their posts without offering resistance. Their flight was fast and furious, as witnessed by Lieutenant Colonel Daniel Brodhead, commanding the other Battalion of Pennsylvania Riflemen, who we recall had been ordered by Colonel Miles to lead his men to the Rebel lines in Brooklyn. Half of Brodhead's battalion had already become separated from him when he saw Rebel artillerymen "dragging" two field-pieces across an open field, making for the safety of some woods. With British from Howe's flanking force in front, behind, and to their right, Brodhead ordered his men to cover the gunners' retreat. But the New Englanders, "coming up with us, and running thro' our files broke them, and in the confusion many of our men run with them. I did all in my power to rally the musquetry & Riflemen, but to no purpose, so that when we came to engage the Enemy, I had not fifty men." Brodhead and his fifty delivered three rounds against the advancing British, which "caused the Enemy to retire," then made their way safely inside the Rebel fortifications at Brooklyn, "having lost," Brodhead wrote, "about one hundred men, officers included, which, as they were much scattered, must be chiefly prisoners."[21]

Lieutenant Benjamin Tallmadge (1754–1835), a Yale graduate who would go on to run successfully Washington's espionage service for most of the war, was serving that day with Colonel John Chestern's militia regiment. The experience of battle almost overwhelmed Tallmadge's emotions:

> This was the first time in my life that I had witnessed the awful scene of battle, when man was engaged to destroy his fellowman. I well remember my sensations on the occasion, for they were solemn beyond description, and hardly could I bring myself to attempt the life of a fellow creature.[22]

It was on the American right that the only respectable defense was put up. Lord Stirling, commanding Maryland and Delaware troops, was caught between Grant advancing along the shore road and Cornwallis coming up behind him. The only way to escape was to cross Gowanus Creek (now the Gowanus Canal) and its wide wetlands. Lord Stirling, commanding there, ordered most of his troops to make their escape, but to buy them time "I found it Absolutely Necesssary to Attack a Body of Troops Commanded by Lord Cornwallis . . . this I instantly did, with about half of smallwoods." Stirling was referring to Colonel William Smallwood's Maryland regiment, which, along with the Delaware regiment, was the best-trained and -disciplined American force. With about 250 of Smallwood's men, Stirling made a gallant stand, continuing his "Attack a Considerable time the Men haveing been rallied and the Attack renewed five or Six Several times" and according to Stirling were making headway when Cornwallis was reinforced. He soon "found a Considerable body of troops in my Front, and Several in pursuit of me on the Right & left & a Constant fire on me." It was the end of organized resistance by the Rebel army. Facing overwhelming numbers, the Marylanders broke and ran for safety.[23]

Eighteen-year-old Michael Graham, a six-month volunteer in the Pennsylvania's Flying Camp, "made my escape as fast as I could," and also left us a vivid description of the rout of the American army on Long Island:

> It is impossible for me to describe the confusion and horror of the scene that ensued: the artillery flying with the chains over the horses' backs, our men running in almost every direction, and run which way they would, they were almost sure to meet the British or Hessians.

Colonel Benjamin Tallmadge by John Trumbull

And the enemy huzzahing when they took prisoners made it truly a day of distress to the Americans. I escaped by getting behind the British that had been engaged with Lord Stirling and entered a swamp or marsh through which a great many of our men were retreating. Some of them were mired and calling out to their fellows for God's sake to help them out; but every man was intent on on his own safety and no assistance was rendered. At the side of the marsh was there was a pond which I took to be a millpond. Numbers as they came to this pond, jumped in, and some were drowned. . . . Of the eight men that were taken from the company to which I belonged the day before the battle on guard, I only escaped. The others were either killed or taken prisoners.[24]

For the American army in Brooklyn, it had come down to every man for himself and the devil take the hindmost, as was the case of Lieutenant Jabez Fitch and the officers and men of 17th Connecticut, which had been stationed under Lord Stirling on the American right. Lieutenant Fitch described in his diary the following events.[25]

Following several futile attempts to break out in different directions, the officers of 17th Connecticut "concluded it best, as we were Intirely Surrounded by the Enimy, to Resign our selves up to them in small Partys, & Each one Take care of himself." Lieutenant Fitch struck out downhill to the north, where he met Sergeant Ebenezer Wright, "who had his Leg Broak. I carried him some way Down the Hill, & Lay'd him in a Shade, where I Left him; I then Went up the hill to the Eastward, where I see at a Distance a party of Regulars, on which Emediately Advanc'd to them, & gave up my Arms; they Treated me with Humanity." Fitch had surrendered to troops of 57th Foot.

About five o'clock that afternoon, after other prisoners had been gathered where Lieutenant Fitch was held, they were all "March'd by the Front of several Batallions of the Hessians, where I Rec'd many insults from those Formidable Europeans." The prisoners were herded into a barn and "Confin'd with a great number of other prisoners of Different Regts." Soon after Fitch's arrival, his company commander, forty-four-year-old Captain Joseph Jewett, was carried in. Lieutenant Fitch would watch his sufferings for the next thirty-six hours. Although his diary implies that Jewett suffered his wounds in battle, seven months later he sent a statement to Jewett's wife, Lucretia Rogers Jewett, that her husband "had Rec'd two Wounds with a Bayonet after he was taken . . . one in the Brest & the other in the Belly."

While Captain Jewett "Languished & suffered great Pain," the victorious General James Grant gave the captured American officers a "Side of Mutton, & order'd his Negro to Cook it for us."

Captain Jewett "Decayed Gradually" all day on the 28th and by nightfall it was obvious that his life was in danger. "I sat with him most of the Night . . . the Capt had his senses . . . [until] about 2 in the morning, & was sensible of being near his end." Captain Jewett said more than once "that it was hard work to Die," and he asked Fitch "to see him buried with Deacence as far as our present circumstances would Admit, & write the Circumstances of his Death to his Wife; for about 2 or 3 hours before he Died, he was somewhat Delerious, & talked somewhat irrational, he was also speechless for some short time before he Expired," about five o'clock on the morning of 29 August.

At Lieutenant Fitch's request, General Grant ordered a grave dug. At 8:00 A.M. he allowed Fitch to accompany his captain's corpse to the grave, where the British had detailed a "Number of men Ready to Assist in Burying the Capt.," and about 100 yards from where he had died hard Captain Joseph Jewett of 17th Connecticut was laid to rest in an orchard.

4

The Night of the Fox

"The object was inadequate"

For Lieutenant Fitch and the other prisoners slated for the infamous prison ships in New York Harbor, the war if not the torments of slow death by disease for many of them was over. But behind the fortifications on the high ground in Brooklyn, their backs to the East River, those who had escaped the British and Hessian regulars braced for the expected assault. In the van of the victorious British army elite grenadiers and Lieutenant Colonel James Webster's crack 33rd Foot had "approached within musket shot of the enemy's lines," Sir William Howe reported to Lord Germain. In the flush of victory, momentum theirs, the troops were eager to close for the kill, as Sir William described for His Lordship:

> Without regarding the fire of cannon and small arms upon them [they] pursued numbers of the rebels that were retiring from the heights so close to their principal redoubt and with such eagerness to attack it by storm that it required repeated orders to prevail upon them to desist from the attempt. Had they been permitted to go on, it is my opinion they would have carried the redoubt, but as it was apparent the lines must have been ours at a very cheap rate by regular approaches I would not risk the loss that might have been sustained by the assault and ordered them back to a hollow way in front of the works out of the reach of musketry.[1]

Much ink and paper have been spent over the past $2\frac{1}{4}$ centuries about whether on the day of the battle the British could have stormed the Rebel works and killed or captured the rest of the American army in Brooklyn, including George Washington. Some claim that the British bloodbath at Bunker Hill, where Sir William had led the final assault, haunted him. His much-rumored affinity for Americans and conciliation has been held against him. Others believe he was merely following the slow, formal approach favored by eighteenth-century generals that spared expensive, hard-to-replace regular troops inordinate casualties, and in fact Sir William made that a major point in his defense before a later Parliamentary committee of inquiry: "the most essential duty I had to observe was, not wantonly to commit his majesty's troops, where the object was inadequate. I knew well that any considerable loss sustained by the army could not speedily, nor easily, be repaired. I also knew that one great point towards gaining the confidence of an army (and a general without it is upon the most dangerous ground) is never to expose the troops, where, as I said before, the object is inadequate."[2]

First, however, was the object "inadequate"? Most of the Continental regiments left were behind the lines. Washington was there. Initially, confusion reigned among the defeated Rebels. Howe did not know this, of course, but he also did not know that the object was inadequate, and there was only one way to find out, and that was to breach the lines and pour his troops through. He made a good point about not exposing troops needlessly, for that can severely damage morale and encourage cynicism among junior officers and the rank and file. But the testimony of some British officers strongly suggests that his restraint had just the opposite effect on the army. Major Sir Charles Stuart of 43rd Foot put it best: "This had all the eclat of a victory without any material consequences arising from it."[3]

By that evening, reported Washington's secretary, Lieutenant Colonel Robert Hanson Harrison (1745–1790), the British "appeared very numerous about the Skirts of the Woods" in front of the American lines, "where they have pitched Several Tents, and his Excellency Inclines to think they mean to attack and force us from our Lines by way of regular approaches rather than in any other manner." Regular approaches meant a siege, and we know that Washington had read Howe's dispositions correctly. The next night, 28 August, Howe's engineering officer, Captain Archibald Robertson, reported in his diary, "this night with a party of 400 men I opened ground opposite their Works and form'd a kind of

Paralel or place of Arms [where men and supplies would be gathered] 650 yards distant." On the 29th Robertson's men began preparing materials to emplace artillery to bombard the Rebel works. Once the shelling began, zigzag trenches would be dug from Robertson's "Paralel" toward the American lines so that eventually infantry could approach safely prior to an assault that would begin once the big guns had breached the lines. It was a slow but tried and true method perfected by European armies, especially the French, over the past century. Nevertheless, Washington's reaction was to defend the Brooklyn fortifications. The day after the battle, recalled Captain Alexander Graydon, his regiment, 3rd Pennsylvania, along with 5th Pennsylvania, both much reduced by dysentery, and 14th Massachusetts Continentals, commanded by the doughty Colonel John Glover (1732–1797), some 1,200 to 1,300 in all, were ferried from Manhattan to Brooklyn and took their places in the lines. On the same day, he wrote, "there was an incessant skirmishing kept up in the daytime between our riflemen and the enemy's irregulars; and the firing was sometimes so brisk, as to indicate an approaching general engagement. This was judiciously encouraged by General Washington, as it tended to restore confidence to our men, and was, besides, showing a good countenance to the foe." On the British side, Ambrose Serle agreed that "The firing was very continual & very hot, and lasted till dark night."[4]

"Men standing up to their middles in water"

Washington's determination to stand his ground on Brooklyn Heights continued to the 29th, two days after the battle. In general orders, guards stationed on Manhattan were "required to take up all soldiers coming from Long Island without passes signed by a proper officer, and send them immediately back to Long Island." That same day, however, Washington's close friend and the army's adjutant general, the handsome and influential Philadelphian Colonel Joseph Reed (1741–1785), claimed that he convinced his chief to hold an immediate council of war to assess the chances of a successful defense.

The evidence on the condition of the American works is contradictory. Recall from chapter 3 that the English engineer Captain John Montresor was impressed, especially with its "most formidable" abatis. And Lieutenant Johann Heinrich von Bardeleben of the von Donop Regiment believed that "determined troops could have held against a far stronger enemy than we were." Yet Major General James Robertson thought "they would not have stopped a foxhunter." The Americans agreed with Robertson. Lieutenant Benjamin Tallmadge claimed, "Our intrenchment was so weak, that it is most wonderful that the British General did not attempt to storm it, soon after the battle, in which his troops had been victorious." According to Captain Graydon, his colonel, the Philadelphia merchant John Shee (1740–1808), believed that "if we were not soon withdrawn . . . we should inevitably be cut to pieces." Later Reed appeared at their position, "and gave the Colonel an opportunity of conferring with him." Colonel Shee cannot have failed to voice his misgivings as well as show Reed a position described by Graydon as "low and unfavourable for defence. There was a fraised ditch in its front, but it gave little promise of security, as it was evidently commanded by the ground occupied by the enemy, who entirely enclosed the whole of our position, at the distance of but a few hundred paces."[5]

On ground that was already saturated with rain that had begun heavily on 14 August, and by night showers that continued on and off, there began on the afternoon of the 28th a cold, heavy, dispiriting rain that drenched an American army largely without shelter. Two Rebels, one a private, the other a general, vividly described conditions. Private Philip Fithian reported "that Trenches, Forts, Tents, & Camp are overflowed with water, & yet our Men must stand exposed themselves & flintlocks to it all." Brigadier General John Morin Scott (c. 1730–1784), a New York lawyer and radical patriot commanding a New York militia brigade, wrote of the lines:

> it was obvious to me we could not maintain them for any long time. . . .
> They were unfinished in several places when I arrived there, and we
> were obliged hastily to finish them, and you may imagine with very
> little perfection, particularly across the main road, the most likely for
> the approach of the enemy's heavy artillery.
>
> In this place three of my battalions were placed, the center of the
> line in ground so low that the rising ground immediately without it
> would have put it in the power of a man at 40 yards distance to fire
> under my horse's belly whenever he pleased. You may judge of our situation, subject to almost incessant rains, without baggage or tents and
> almost without victuals or drink, and in some part of the lines the men
> standing up to their middles in water.[6]

It is likely that Washington received more than one report urging him to reconsider the situation, although Reed may well have been the catalyst who prompted his chief to call a council of war on Brooklyn Heights. There it was decided without serious opposition from the seven generals present that prudence dictated a withdrawal to Manhattan. Some of the other reasons given were the great losses sustained on the day of the battle, the heavy rains that "had injured the Arms & Spoiled a great part of the Ammunition," the worn-out soldiers exposed to the elements, the lines weak in so many places, and rumors that the British might be maneuvering to place troops above Kingsbridge in northern Manhattan, thus cutting off the army's line of retreat to the hinterlands. Especially important, in my opinion, were the attempts of Lord Howe to get ships into the East River, behind the present Rebel positions, "to cut off our Communications, by which the whole Army would have been destroyed." So far the weather pattern responsible for the rains that made the army's condition miserable also had brought a storm with northerly followed by northeasterly winds that prevented British ships from beating up from the upper bay into the river. But how long would the favorable winds last? It was imperative that the army withdraw. Immediately. Not tomorrow or the next day, but now. Tonight. Accordingly, plans were quickly made and orders given.[7]

"Good God! General Mifflin, I am afraid you have ruined us"

It was the only reasonable decision Washington could have made. But if the British tumbled to what was going on and struck during the withdrawal, or if the wind changed and Lord Howe's ships were able to sail up the East River, the outcome would be catastrophic. *Quiet* was the watchword. To preserve secrecy the men and most officers were not told where they were going. As a teenage Connecticut militiaman, Private Joseph Plumb Martin, recalled:

> We were strictly enjoined not to speak, or even cough, while on the march. All orders were given from officer to officer, and communicated to the men in whispers. What such secrecy could mean we could not divine.[8]

And Lieutenant Colonel James Chambers (1743–1805) of 1st Pennsylvania Continentals wrote his wife that the withdrawal "was done with great secrecy. Very few of the officers knew it until they were on the boats, supposing an attack was intended."[9]

As for Washington, the man always knew where he belonged in a critical situation. Some commanding generals—Horatio Gates comes immediately to mind—would have left personal supervision of the withdrawal to a senior subordinate while he sought the safety of the far shore. Not Washington. To date he had shown himself to be a faulty strategist and tactician, but on this stormy night he was where he belonged, on the Brooklyn side of the river with his weary, scared, and beaten soldiers, overseeing the entire operation while Brigadier General Alexander McDougall (1732–1786), mariner, merchant, radical New York politician, supervised the loading of the boats.

Washington was fortunate to have at hand that night two splendid regiments vitally important to the evacuation: 14th and 27th Massachusetts, most of their men hardy and experienced fishermen and sailors from the Essex County towns of Marblehead, Salem, Lynn, and Danvers. Israel Hutchinson (1728–1811) commanded the 27th. The 14th was led by one of the Continental Army's finest officers, Colonel John Glover, a forty-four-year-old master mariner become an officer of infantry. Glover's regiment differed from most of the regular regiments and can be favorably compared to the men of the Maryland and Delaware Lines who had stood fast for so long on the day of the battle. For discipline had been bred into their bones from early youth. At sea, amid howling winds and mountainous waves, when split-second reaction often meant the difference between life and death, one did not question the skipper's orders. As that master historian of the oceans Samuel Eliot Morison wrote, "Instant and unquestioning obedience to the master is the rule of the sea, and your typical sea captain would make it the rule of the land if he could." Glover had. His regiment stood head and shoulders above the other Yankee regiments, as even a Pennsylvania officer, who took a dim view of his New England brethren, admitted:

> The only exception I recollect to have seen to these miserably constituted bands from New England was the regiment of Glover from Marblehead. There was an appearance of discipline in this corps; the officers seem to have mixed with the world, and to understand what belonged to their stations. Though deficient perhaps, in polish, it possessed an apparent aptitude for the purpose of its institution, and gave a confidence that myriads of its meek and lowly brethren were incompetent to inspire.[10]

Beginning at ten o'clock on the night of 29 August, stealthily, by regiments, the cold and soaked and dispirited Rebel army moved off the heights and down the hill to the ferry landing where Glover and Hutchinson and their sturdy mariners waited to begin their long night on the swift, dark waters of the East River. Boats, mostly flat-bottomed craft propelled by sweeps, had been gathered from northern Manhattan. One by one, as orders came from the shore, the regiments moved out of the line and marched to the landing. As one junior officer recalled, "the troops began to retire from the lines in such a manner that no chasm was made in the lines, but as one regiment left their station on guard, the remaining troops moved to the right and left and filled up the vacancies."[11]

Commanding the regiments that would stay in place in the lines until the last possible moment was the prominent and very radical Pennsylvania politician, Brigadier General Thomas Mifflin (1744–1800). All went smoothly until about 2:00 A.M., when the inevitable snafu occurred, endangering the entire operation. Out of the night, looking for General Mifflin, appeared Alexander Scammell (1747–1781) of New Hampshire, who was that day acting aide-de-camp to Washington. Scammell found Mifflin with one of his regimental officers, Colonel Edward Hand (1744–1802), who commanded the Pennsylvania rifle regiment. What follows, confusion culminating in a tense and undoubtedly loud confrontation in the dark between two proud men, was later reported by Colonel Hand.[12]

Scammell told Mifflin that the boats and Washington were anxiously awaiting the arrival of Mifflin's regiments. Mifflin expressed surprise. That cannot be . . . the commander in chief could not mean his command . . . it was the rear guard. Scammell insisted. He had come from the far left, ordering all the regiments he met to march for the ferry, and Mifflin should do likewise while Scammell continued on and passed the same orders to the regiments beyond. Whereupon General Mifflin ordered Colonel Hand "to call my advance picquets and sentinels, to collect and form my regiment, and to march as soon as possible, and quitted me." Hand's troops began their march, but at the Brooklyn Church he halted them to pick up the regiment's camp gear, which had been taken there earlier. But just then General Mifflin appeared, asked Hand why he had stopped, was told, and exclaimed, "Damn your pots and kettles! I wish the devil had them! March on!"

Hand resumed his march but soon met none other than the commander in chief, who said, "Is not that Colonel Hand?" Yes, replied Hand, whereupon Washington expressed surprise at finding him there, for "he did not expect I would have abandoned my post." While Hand was hastily explaining his orders, General Mifflin appeared and asked what was going on, probably ready to once again chew out Hand. But Washington struck first.

"'Good God! General Mifflin, I am afraid you have ruined us by so unseasonably withdrawing the troops from the lines.'

"General Mifflin replied with some warmth: 'I did it by your order.'

"His Excellency declared it could not be.

"General Mifflin swore: 'By God, I did,' and asked, 'Did Scammell act as aide-de-camp for the day, or did he not?'

"His Excellency acknowledged he did.

"'Then,' said Mifflin, 'I had orders through him.'

"The General replied it was a dreadful mistake, and informed him that matters were in much confusion at the ferry, and, unless we could resume our posts before the enemy discovered we had left them, in all probability the most disagreeable consequences would follow."

The incident leaves us with a question: was this the beginning of Mifflin's dislike of Washington?

There immediately followed what the rank and file of all armies learn to accept with weary cynicism: changed orders and a return to their original point of departure to hurry up and wait once again. And on this occasion the enemy was within hailing distance. But as Hand wrote, "We . . . had the good fortune to recover our former stations and keep them for some hours longer without the enemy perceiving what was going forward."

Lieutenant Tallmadge was in the rear guard that night as adjutant in his Connecticut militia regiment and went through the aborted initial evacuation and return to the lines:

It was one of the most anxious, busy nights I ever recollect, and being the third in which hardly any of us had closed our eyes in sleep, we were all greatly fatigued. As the dawn of the next day approached, those of us who remained in the trenches became very anxious for our own safety, and when the dawn appeared there were several regiments still on duty. At this time a very dense fog began to rise, and it seemed to settle in a peculiar manner over both encampments. I recollect this peculiar providential occurrence perfectly well; and so very dense was the atmosphere that I could scarcely discern a man at six yards' distance.[13]

God was indeed in his heaven that morning for the Americans. According to British sources, at four o'clock that morning a British patrol probing no-man's-land found no Rebel pickets and decided to push forward. The Redcoats entered one of the breastworks and found it empty. One historian suggests that this probably occurred during the first, mistaken, withdrawal of Mifflin's rear guard. The patrol reported back, but incredibly there was no immediate follow-up. It was not until between roughly 7:00 and 8:00 A.M. that Hessian troops entered the empty Rebel lines and advanced through the fog across Brooklyn Heights and down to the ferry landing—just in time to fire at the last Rebel boat disappearing into the mist. It may have been a boat rowed by volunteers, who had agreed to take Lieutenant Tallmadge back to get his favorite horse, which he had left tied to a post at the ferry slip.[14]

On that same day in Manhattan, a Moravian preacher, Rev. Shewkirk, observed the once-confident soldiers who had escaped from Long Island. They had, he wrote,

> thought to surround the king's troops, and make them prisoner with little trouble. The language was now otherwise; it was a surprising change, the merry tones on drums and fifes had ceased, and they were hardly heard for a couple of days. It seemed a general damp had spread; and the sight of the scattered people up and down the streets was indeed moving. Many looked sickly, emaciated, cast down, etc.; the wet clothes, tents—as many as they had brought away—and other things, were lying about before the houses and in the streets to-day; in general, everything seemed to be in confusion. Many, as it is reported for certain, went away to their respective homes.[15]

Yet a miracle had occurred. The fox and his army had escaped. Yes, the weather had certainly been on their side, and they had been given a respite by an overly cautious British commander. But in an always risky maneuver, withdrawal in the face of a victorious enemy, in this case made even riskier by the necessity of crossing a treacherous body of water, over a period of nine to ten hours about 9,000 men had been transported to safety over a notoriously difficult, swift-running tidal strait. This amateur army—in Ambrose Serle's opinion the "strangest that was ever collected: Old men of 60, Boys of 14, and Blacks of all ages, and ragged for the most part, compose a motley Crew"—these men and boys recently recruited from civilian life, led by lawyers and merchants and farmers and politicians and a Virginia planter who had boarded the last boat to Manhattan, had pulled it off like veteran soldiers. Did this give pause to Lord Howe and Sir William? A precise answer eludes us, but probably not. It certainly gave pause, however, to a British naval officer who was flabbergasted by the event. Admiral Sir George Collier wrote,

> To my inexpressible astonishment and concern the rebel army all escaped across the River to New York! how this happened is surprizing, for had our troops follow'd them close up, they must have thrown down their arms and surrendered, or had our ships attack'd the batteries, which we have been in constant expectation of being ordered to do, not a man could have escaped from Long Island. Now, I foresee they will give us trouble enough, and protract the war, Heaven knows how long.[16]

Sir William's decision not to storm the Rebel fortifications immediately on the heels of his victory had proven to be a serious error in judgment. With the Grenadiers and 33rd Foot in full cry on the heels of the fleeing Americans, he vigorously interceded and stopped them because he lacked the boldness and instinct for battle that tells the truly gifted combat commander that the time has come to strike. Closely coupled with that was the reason he gave at the parliamentary inquiry, "not wantonly to commit his majesty's troops," for in the eighteenth century the relatively small regular armies that then existed were expensive to raise, outfit, train, and replace. A prudent commander did not toy with his sovereign's army.

Once the Rebels had escaped, however, why did he not quickly pursue them? We can, I believe, speculate with reasonable certainty that had Sir William and his brother immediately, on a crash basis, collected small craft and launched a pursuit across the East River before the Rebels had recovered, the American army would have crumbled. Its morale was at rock bottom, or as Washington wrote,

> Our situation is truly distressing. The check our Detachment sustained on the 27th Ulto, has dispirited too great a proportion of our Troops, and filled their minds with apprehension and despair. The Militia

instead of calling forth their utmost efforts to a brave & manly opposition in order to repair our Losses, are dismayed, Intractable, and Impatient to return. Great numbers of them have gone off; in some Instances, almost by whole Regiments—by half Ones & by Companies at a time.[17]

Here was a perfect situation for an aggressive, victorious enemy to act immediately. Immediacy, however, seemed not to be part of Sir William's lexicon. "I know not what Mr. Washington and his army are doing," wrote Admiral Collier, "but ours have been totally inactive since the retreat of the rebels, which has occasioned universal dissatisfaction in the fleet and army." Sir William's lack of instinct to go quickly for the jugular always handicapped him, but two other factors also argue for inclusion. The irrepressible Charles Lee once described Sir William as "the most indolent of mortals." Historians have not made much of Lee's quip, and here I think they are mistaken. In the world at large, when decisions must often be made quickly without adequate information on the situation, the personal qualities of individuals, for good or ill, dramatically affect their performances. Lee's keen mind and rapier tongue and pen were often on the mark, and given Sir William's overall performance in America, Lee's words cannot be lightly dismissed.[18]

The other reason is the Howe Brothers' agenda, especially Lord Howe's continuing efforts to mend the fracture between mother country and colonies with reason instead of arms. His Lordship's need for a military breather fit his younger brother's sluggish nature. While Sir William dithered, and Washington reorganized and attempted to bring order and discipline to his motley army, Admiral Howe enlisted the services of a high-ranking prisoner of war, Major General John Sullivan, to arrange a conference between himself and a few leading congressional rebels.

"They met, they talked, they parted"

Sullivan was paroled so he might travel to Philadelphia, where Congress was in session, to deliver Lord Howe's proposal for a meeting. But was it Howe's proposal? There is no doubt that the admiral wanted to end the fighting and arrive at a peaceful conclusion of the conflict. But did he first broach the idea of a conference between himself and leading Rebels? Absolutely, if one accepts Sullivan's word. But had Sullivan meddled in a matter beyond his authority as a soldier? Had he trod on sacred civilian

turf? Absolutely, according to Lord Howe, who maintained that Sullivan had suggested that he act as Howe's agent to Congress to propose
the meeting. This, however, had followed a dinner on board *Eagle*, during which Howe had merely assured his prisoners and guests, Sullivan
and Lord Stirling, that he was authorized to go well beyond issuing pardons once the Rebels surrendered, and regaled them with talk of his
sympathy for the American positions on taxation and other issues. By
this account, the credulous Sullivan was convinced and led deftly by
Howe to propose the meeting, which Howe, under the terms of his
commission, could not do. If true, it means that Black Dick, purported
to be as grim and silent as a rock, could when the occasion arose use
words to beguile at least the likes of Sullivan.[19]

Whatever precisely transpired at their dinner, Sullivan appeared at
Washington's headquarters on Manhattan with the proposal. Although
Washington appeared to be uneasy about the affair, he did not think "It
right to withold or prevent him [Sullivan] from giving such information
as he possesses in this Instance," and therefore allowed him to proceed
to Philadelphia. There Congress, controlled by the radicals, did not welcome with open arms either the message or the messenger, and passed
a resolution directing John Hancock to inform Washington that here-
after any peace proposal from the British be in writing and addressed to
Congress "or Persons authorized by" Congress. For one thing, Sullivan
revealed that Lord Howe could not recognize Congress as an official
body; thus any delegation would have to be regarded as a private group.
This was regarded as an insult and was rejected by a resolution of Congress. But a far more serious matter was at stake. "Sullivan Says," wrote
one delegate, "that L Howe Said he was ever against Taxing of us, and
that they had no right to interfere with our internal Police, and that he
was very sure America could not be conquered, and that it was a great
pity so brave a nation should be cutting one another to pieces." This
line raised hope in the breasts of those who yearned for reconciliation
with the mother country, and placed Congress in a dilemma, as one delegate, Josiah Bartlett, described clearly to another on 3 September, the
day after Sullivan's arrival in Philadelphia:

> If the Congress should accept of the proposed Conference, only on a
> verbal message, when at the same time Lord Howe declares he can
> consider them only as private gentlemen, especially when we are cer-
> tain he can have no power to grant any terms we can possibly accept;
> this I fear will lessen the Congress in the eyes of the public, and per-

haps at this time intimidate people when they see us catching hold of
so slender a thread to bring about a settlement. On the other hand,
General Sullivan's arrival from Lord Howe with proposals of an accommodation, with 30 falsehoods in addition, are now spread over this
City, and will soon be over the continent, and if we should refuse the
conference, I fear the Tories, and moderate men, so called, will try to
represent Congress as obstinate, and so desirous of war and bloodshed
that we would not so much as hear the proposals Lord Howe had to
make, which they will represent (as they already do) to be highly
advantageous for America, even that he would consent that we should
be independent provided we should grant some advantages as to trade.
Such an idea spread among the people, especially the soldiers at this
time might be of the most fatal consequences.[20]

Congress chose three of its most influential members to meet with
Lord Howe: John Adams of Massachusetts, Benjamin Franklin of Pennsylvania, and Edward Rutledge of South Carolina. It is of interest to
note that Franklin had written to Lord Howe as early as 20 July an
uncompromising letter that went so far as to state that British actions to
date "have extinguished every spark of remaining affection for that par-
ent country we once held so dear." That and other rebuffs, however, had
not shaken Lord Howe's resolve to put conciliation to the test.[21]

On the morning of 11 September Lord Howe sent his barge from
Staten Island to Perth Amboy, New Jersey, to fetch the three Americans.
Aboard was a British officer whom Howe meant to remain in New Jersey "as an Hostage for our Security," Adams wrote. "I said to Dr. Franklin, it would be childish in Us to insist upon such a Pledge and insisted
on taking him over with Us. My Colleagues exulted in the Proposition
and . . . We told the officer . . . he must go back with us. He bowed
assent, and We all embarked in his Lordships Barge. As We Approached
the Shore his Lordship, observing Us, came down to the Waters Edge to
receive Us, and looking at the Officer, he said, Gentlemen, you make
me a very high Compliment, and you may depend upon it. I will consider it the most sacred of Things. We walked up to the House between
Lines of Guards of Grenadiers, looking as fierce as ten furies, and making all the Grimaces and Gestures and motions of their Musquets with
Bayonets fixed, which I suppose military Ettiquette requires but which
we neither understood or regarded."[22]

But they understood perfectly the constraints that bound Lord Howe,
and they had no regard for those either. Fortunately, a British member
of Parliament, Henry Strachey, was present as secretary of the peace

commission, and after Lord Howe and the Rebels had eaten a cold meal and then gotten down to business, Strachey took notes of the proceedings. His account differs in no material way from the delegation's report to Congress or their unofficial writings on the subject. It was all very civil, and when Lord Howe confessed "to the Delicacy of his Situation" in being unable to "consider the Colonies in the light of Independent States," nor to acknowledge the existence of Congress or the three Americans present "as a Committee of the Congress," Franklin, ever the diplomat, neatly solved Howe's dilemma by suggesting "that His Lordship might consider the Gentlemen present in any view he thought proper—that they were also at liberty to consider themselves in their real Character—that there was no necessity on this occasion to distinguish between Congress and Individuals—and that the Conversation might be held as amongst friends." And thus the "Conversation" ensued.[23]

We need not detain ourselves with details or pursue side issues. A few statements by the participants will tell us all we need to know. Lord Howe admitted "that his powers were, generally, to restore Peace and grant Pardons." In other words, the Rebels must submit; only then could American grievances be considered and discussions take place "upon Means of establishing a Re-Union upon Terms honorable & advantageous to the Colonies as well as to Great Britain."

The delegates were unanimous in their rejection of these terms. Franklin replied "that all former Attachment was *obliterated*—that America could not return again to the Domination of Great Britain." Adams emphasized "that it was not in their power to treat otherwise than as independent States." Rutledge said "it was impossible the People should consent to come again under the English Government."

To these Lord Howe replied "that if such were their Sentiments, he could only lament that it was not in his Power to bring about the Acommodation he wished—that he had not Authority, nor did he expect he ever should have, to treat with the Colonies as States independent of the Crown of Great Britain—and that he was sorry the Gentlemen had had the trouble of coming so far, to so little purpose—that if the Colonies would not give up the System of Independency, it was impossible for him to enter into any Negociation."

Lord Howe's civilian secretary, Ambrose Serle, summed it up admirably: "They met, they talked, they parted. And now nothing remains but to fight it out."[24]

5

Manhattan Transfer

"I would burn the City and Subburbs"

One of the men left to fight it out was exhausted following the Rebel escape to Manhattan. He was in his prime and had a strong constitution, but ceaseless tension and activity and lack of sleep had taken their toll of Washington, as he admitted to John Hancock in his report of the army's defeat and retreat:

> the extreme fatigue which myself and Family [aides-de-camp] have undergone as much from the weather since the Engagement on the 27th rendered me & them entirely unfit to take pen in hand. Since Monday [26 August] scarce any of us have been out of the Lines till our passage across the East River was effected yesterday morning & for forty Eight Hours preceding that I had hardly been off my Horse and never closed my eyes so that I was quite unfit to write or dictate until this Morning.[1]

Reading this is more evidence for questioning Sir William Howe's dilatory behavior following the Rebel withdrawal from Brooklyn. By the time Sir William and his brother got around to going to war again, Washington had recovered, although his army, reduced to fewer than 20,000 men present and fit for duty, had not. For example, the Connecticut militia alone, he wrote, had gone "from 8,000 to less than

2,000," their flight hastened not only by despair but also by the urgent needs of the harvest season.[2]

Nor were Washington, his military family, and his generals beyond criticism. One of the soundest officers in the army, Colonel John Haslet of the Delaware Line, wrote to Caesar Rodney, a member of the Continental Congress from Delaware, "The Genl I revere, his Character for Disinterestedness Patience & fortitude will be had in Everlasting Remembrances; but the vast Burthen appears too much his own. Beardless Youth, & Inexperience Regimentated are too much about him. . . . Wd to Heaven Genl Lee were here is the Language of Officers & men." It was a sentiment that would stimulate Lee's considerable ego and over the next year and a half continue to fester and spread and eventually erupt in accusations of a conspiracy to replace the commander in chief. But these events await their turn in our narrative.[3]

Following the army's escape from Long Island, Washington's dilemma, given the condition of his army and British control of the waterways, was whether to defend New York City. Throughout 1776 the Continental Congress had given every indication of wanting the city defended. As early as February, reported a New York delegate, it was "debating the fate of our City," and had called upon New Jersey and Pennsylvania to send militia units to defend New York. On 12 February John Hancock, in a letter to the New Jersey Provincial Convention, had stressed "the importance of that place to the Welfare of America, & the Necessity of throwing up a Number of Works to prevent our Enemies from Landing and Taking post there, render it necessary that a Number of Troops should immediately join General Lee." It is not surprising then that Washington, ever sensitive to the primacy of civil authority, believed that in preparing to defend New York City he was following congressional policy. This feeling was reinforced shortly after he and his army had escaped to Manhattan, when Washington flirted with the idea of scorched earth. Writing on 2 December to Hancock, after confessing to "my want of confidence in the Generality of the troops," he suggested, "If we should be obliged to abandon this Town, ought it to stand as Winter Quarters for the Enemy?" The reaction from Philadelphia was swift and unequivocal. It was resolved the following day in a committee of the whole House that "the Congress would have special Care taken, in case he should find it necessary to quit New York, that no damage be done to the said City by his Troops on their leaving it; the Congress having no doubt of being able to recover the same, tho' the Enemy should for a time obtain possession of it." Washington apparently misinterpreted this as further proof that Congress wanted New York City defended. For even though the resolution referred to the possibility of evacuation, it could be taken to mean a forced retreat in the face of a British assault.[4]

On 7 September Washington called a council of war to discuss the defense of the city, and reported the next day to Hancock that a "Majority . . . thought for the present a part of our force might be kept here and attempt to maintain the City a while longer." Those who thought otherwise "were for a total and immediate removal from the City, urging the great danger of One part of the Army being cut off before the other can support it, the Extremities being at least Sixteen miles apart." Washington's conclusion on British intentions strengthened the position of the minority. "It is now extremely obvious," he wrote, "from all intelligence—from their movements, & every other circumstance that having landed their whole army on Long Island (except about 4,000 on Staten Island) they mean to inclose us on the island of New York by taking post in our Rear, while the Shipping effectually secure the Front; and thus either . . . oblige us to fight them on their own Terms or Surrender at discretion, or by a brilliant stroke endeavour to cut this Army in peices & secure the collection of Arms & Stores which they will know we shall not be able soon to replace." Washington's opinion on British intentions was not misplaced, for a landing in the American rear was not only an obvious maneuver but also had been specifically recommended to Sir William by his deputy, Sir Henry Clinton.[5]

It is also clear in this letter that by now Washington the fighting general realized "that on our side the War should be defensive." He was now "fully persuaded that it would be presumptuous to draw our young Troops into open Ground against their superiors both in number and discipline," thus "I have never spared the Spade & Pickax." Yet he lacked at that time faith even in his army's willingness to hold strong defensive works "when the success is very doubtful and the falling into the Enemy's hands probable." Here Washington is obviously presenting an argument for evacuation. "On the other hand," he continued, "to abandon a City which has been by some deemed defensible and on whose Works much labor has been bestowed has a tendency to dispirit the Troops and enfeeble our Cause. It has also been considered a Key to the Northern Country." But he had a solution for that. The city might be abandoned, but not the entire island. The forts on Mount Washington and directly across the river on the Jersey side, combined with "Obstructions already made, & which might be improved in the Water," could secure the Hudson while improved fortifications at Kingsbridge and the heights surrounding it would make a good defensive line.[6]

Then he got to the nub of his problem. The majority of his generals, who were in favor of defending the city, were "Influenced in their opinion to whom the determn of Congress was known, against an evacuation totally, as they were led to suspect Congress wished it [New York City] to be maintained at every hazard." It had therefore been decided to divide the army into "Three Divisions, 5000 to remain for the defence of the City, 9000 to Kingsbridge & its dependencies as well as to possess and secure those posts as to be ready to attack the Enemy .... The remainder to occupy the intermediate space & support either." In other words, an army of which he was doubtful strung out for some sixteen miles to defend an island connected to the mainland by one bridge from an enemy he was convinced intended to land in his rear. It defied common sense.[7]

Matters moved quickly thereafter. Upon receipt of Washington's letter to Hancock, Congress on 10 September passed a resolution informing the general that "it was by no means the Sense of Congress in their Resolve of the third instant respecting New York that the Army or any part of it should Remain in that City a Moment longer than he shall think it proper for the publick Service that Troops be continued there." The following day seven of his generals requested that Washington hold another Council of War to reconsider the decision taken at the previous council. The ranking officer of the group was Major General Nathanael Greene, who had just recovered from his near-fatal illness. As he would prove by word and deed later in the war during his brilliant southern campaign, when necessary he could be a hard man. He had written earlier to Washington arguing that "a General and speedy Retreat is absolutely necessary," and then, ignorant of the congressional order not to destroy New York City, had added in even blunter language, "I would burn the City and Subburbs."[8]

The second council met on 12 September, and by a ten to three vote the generals recommended rescinding the decision to defend the city. But Washington had been as dilatory as Howe, taking too long to arrive at this sensible decision. On the 14th Washington wrote to Hancock, "We are now taking every method in our power to remove the Stores etc. in which we find almost insuperable difficulties. They are so great and numerous, that I fear we shall not effect the whole before we meet with some interruption." He was right. The British struck the next day.[9]

"They appeared like a large clover field in full bloom"

Early on the morning of 15 September three British ships of war, *Renown* (50 guns), *Repulse* (32 guns), and *Pearl* (32 guns), accompanied by the armed schooner *Tryal*, sailed up the Hudson River as far as Bloomingdale as a diversion to convince the Rebels that the British meant to land in their rear. And in fact Washington still believed that was Sir William's intention and the previous day had left the city for Harlem, where, he wrote, "it was supposed, or at Morisania [south Bronx] opposite to it, the principal attempt to land would be made." By then most of the Rebel army had been withdrawn to Harlem Heights, but about 5,000 men remained in the city, and five brigades of largely militia were assigned to defend against East River landings, mainly in the area of Kips Bay, stretching from present-day 32nd Street to about 38th Street. The three British ships in the Hudson prevented further evacuation of supplies and baggage by water, and very soon the already disheartened Rebels would have something far more important to protect: their lives.[10]

Sir Henry Clinton had been asked for his advice as to the next British move, and once again he favored a flanking movement and entrapment. "I took the liberty . . . to advise that we should march as soon as possible to Hell Gate . . . make every appearance to force a landing on York Island [Manhattan], and throw the troops on shore from thence at Morrisania, and move forward directly to Kings Bridge by occupying the heights of Fordham." Precisely what Washington expected and was attempting to guard against. "Had this been done without loss of time," Clinton continued, "while the Rebel army lay broken in separate corps between New York and that place, it must have suddenly crossed the North River or each part of it fallen into our power one after another." And it was highly unlikely that the Rebels could escape across the river to New Jersey, given the three warships already off Bloomingdale and the prospect of their 114 guns being reinforced by more from Admiral Howe's fleet. Yet Sir William once again rejected a Clinton plan and this time stuck to his decision.[11]

Thus on the East River side of Manhattan four British frigates joined another, *Rose* (32 guns), which had come up towing flatboats on 3 September. The frigates were *Phoenix* and *Roebuck* (44 guns each), *Orpheus*

(32 guns), and *Carysfort* (28 guns). According to fifteen-year-old Private Joseph Plumb Martin, already a combat veteran from the fighting at Brooklyn, the four frigates had come up the river on the night of 14 September, and at daybreak "The *Phoenix* lying a little quartering and her stern towards me, I could read her name distinctly under her stern." Martin and his Connecticut militia comrades were manning defensive works at Kips Bay, works described by Martin as "nothing more than a ditch dug along on the bank of the river with the dirt thrown out towards the water." Behind the ditch a large meadow provided an excellent beachhead for a landing force.[12]

The troops of that landing force had been harangued a few days before by Sir William Howe, who reminded them that in the Battle of Brooklyn they had won "by charging the Rebels with their Bayonets, even in woods where they thought themselves invincible. . . . He therefore recommends . . . an entire dependence on their Bayonets, with which they will ever Command that success which their bravery so well deserves."[13]

Four brigades of foot struck their tents at two o'clock on the morning of 15 September, loaded their baggage, and formed, Captain Frederick Mackenzie stated, "at the head of their Encampments, with their blankets and two days provisions" and awaited orders. At 4:00 A.M. the Brigade of Guards marched to Newtown and halted to await further orders. Security as to their precise destination was tight. Mackenzie wrote in his diary that "we all expected to have received orders to proceed towards Hellgate, and either to have embarked there or at some place farther to the right, in order to make a descent on that part of New York Island opposite; but were much surprized at receiving orders to march towards Bushwick."[14]

At 6:00 A.M. one column began a march from Newtown to Bushwick Point, where all arrived two hours later and began loading onto boats. Also at 6:00 A.M. the rest of the assault force began loading into sixty flatboats situated at the head of Newtown Creek. Seamen of the Royal Navy manned the oars and rowed to the mouth of the creek, where they "lay on their oars," Mackenzie wrote, "until all was ready." At 10:00 A.M. the flatboats in Newtown Creek rowed out and joined the rest of the assault force off Bushwick point. Private Joseph Plumb Martin, watching from his ditch on the Manhattan side, saw them coming. "As soon as it was fairly light, we saw their boats coming out of a creek or cove on the Long Island side of the water, filled with British soldiers. When they came to the edge of the tide, they formed their boats in line. They continued to augment their forces from the island until they appeared like a large clover field in full bloom." A little after 11:00 A.M. the big guns on the warships opened fire.[15]

"Demons of fear and disorder seemed to take full possession of all . . . that day"

Private Martin had left the ditch and was behind the lines engaged, it appears, in the very behavior that frustrated Washington, wandering off when he was supposed to be attending to duty, "when all of a sudden there came such a peal of thunder from the British shipping that I thought my head would go with the sound. I made a frog's leap for the ditch and lay as still as I possibly could and began to consider which parts of my carcass was to go first." A young British naval officer seconded Martin's reaction. Midshipman Bartholomew James, who one day would become a rear admiral, was aboard *Orpheus* and wrote in his journal, "what a tremendous fire was kept up by those five ships for only fifty-nine minutes, in which time we fired away, in the Orpheus alone, five thousand three hundred and seventy-six pounds of powder. The first broadside made a considerable breach in their works." Behind the barrage Royal Navy sailors plied their oars, carrying to the far shore about 4,000 British and German regulars.[16]

It was the end of the line for Private Martin and the Connecticut militia. They did not wait for that "large clover field" to close on them. They probably never heard the blue-coated Hessians, who "were not used to this water business," Lord Rawdon wrote, "and who conceived that it must be exceedingly uncomfortable to be shot at whilst they were quite defenceless and jammed together so close, [and] began to sing hymns immediately." The Germans need not have worried, nor the Redcoats, who "expressed their feelings as strongly in a different manner, by damning themselves and the enemy indiscriminately with wonderful fervency."[17]

For the Connecticut militia, officers and men, stampeded for the rear. Captain Mackenzie reported that the British and Hessians "landed . . . without firing or receiving a shot," and according to Midshipman James, the Rebels "in general . . . left their arms in the intrenchment." When Private Martin had gotten out of range of the British guns, "I found myself in company with one who was a neighbor of mine when at home and one other man belonging to our regiment. Where the rest of them were I knew not. We went into a house by the highway in which were two women and some small children, all crying most bitterly." Whereupon Martin and his two comrades followed the age-old custom of soldiers, even in time of peril. "We asked the women if they had any spirits in the house. They placed a case bottle of rum upon the table and bid us help ourselves. We each of us drank a glass and bidding them good-by betook ourselves to the highway again."[18]

South of Martin's brigade, another Connecticut militia brigade, commanded by Colonel William Douglas, lay in its ditch awaiting the assault when Captain Jonas Prentice hurried to Colonel Douglas and said "if I ment to Save my Self to Leave the Lines for that was the orders on the Left and that they had Left the Lines." Douglas then turned to order his men to make their way as best they could, only to find that they had anticipated him, "as I then found I had but about ten Left with me. . . . [W]e then had a Mile to Retreat Through as hot a fire as Could well be made but they mostly over shot us." Douglas's brigade was then so "Scatter'd . . . that I Could not Collect them and I found the whole Army on a Retreat."[19]

"Retreat," with its implication of orderliness, is too formal a term to describe the flight of the American army that day. Stampede is more like it, made even more frenzied by the contesting armies in places becoming mixed. Not far from the house where they drank rum, Private Martin and his comrades saw some soldiers ahead of them and tried to "overtake them, but on approaching them we found . . . they were Hessians," and the three veered off to the Post Road, which was the main route to Kingsbridge. Soon they saw ahead of them Americans, but just as they reached them British troops in a cornfield fired on them "and all was immediately in confusion again. I believe the enemy's party was small, but our people were all militia, and the demons of fear and disorder seemed to take full possession of all and everything on that day. When I came to the spot where the militia were fired upon, the ground was literally covered with arms, knapsacks, staves, coats, hats, and old oil flasks." Martin's neighbor, "having been for some time unwell was so overcome by heat, hunger, and fatigue that he became suddenly and violently sick." Private Martin carried his comrade's musket and urged him to continue. They saw a big party of Rebels, but just then another body of British troops fired on the party, who "returned but a very few shots and then scampered off as fast as their legs would carry them."

While Private Martin helped other soldiers with a wounded man, his neighbor grew impatient and kept going. When Martin followed with a few others they found their way blocked by British troops. "I immediately quitted the road and went into the fields, where there happened to be a small spot of boggy land covered with low bushes and weeds. Into these I ran and squatting down concealed myself from their sight. Several of the British came so near to me that I could see the buttons on their clothes." After they passed, Martin continued on until he found his neighbor "sitting . . . with his head between his knees." Drained by fear, illness, heat, and fatigue, his morale shattered, the man had given up. Private Martin told him to get up and come with him. "'No,' said he, at the same time regarding me with a most pitiful look, 'I must die here.' I endeavoured to argue the case with him, but all to no purpose; he insisted on dying there. I told him he should not die there nor anywhere else that day if I could help it, and at length with more persuasion and some force I succeeded in getting him upon his feet again and to moving on." Eventually Martin and the neighbor he saved found their regiment.[20]

While all of this was going on, Brigadier General Samuel Holden Parsons (1737–1789) of Connecticut had led three Continental regiments northward from Corlear's Hook in lower Manhattan to assist the troops at Kips Bay. They were marching up the west side of Murray Hill (then called Inclenberg), on the east side of Manhattan (between present-day 34th and 40th Streets), not far from the British beachhead, when they came within sight of British grenadiers marching up the east side. Whereupon the Continentals challenged the militia for the title of who could run away faster. George Washington was there and described it well:

> As soon as I heard the Firing, I road with all possible dispatch towards the place of landing when to my great surprize and Mortification I found the Troops that had been posted in the Lines retreating with the utmost precipitation and those ordered to support them, parson's & Fellows's Brigades, Flying in every direction and in the greatest confusion, nowithstanding the exertions of their Generals to form them. I used every means in my power to rally and get them into some order but my attempts were fruitless and ineffectual, and on the appearance of a small party of the Enemy, not more than Sixty or Seventy, their disorder increased and they ran away in the greatest confusion without firing a Single Shot.[21]

Stories abound about Washington striking with the flat of his sword officers and men streaming by him, throwing his hat to the ground, asking loudly if these were the troops with which he must defend America, and becoming so emotional that he refused to quit the field and was only persuaded by aides, one of whom grasped his bridle and turned his horse northward, to ride with them to Harlem and its friendly heights. None of these tales comes from eyewitness observers, but given his account to Hancock, we can certainly agree that George Washington's temper flared high that day and that he freely expressed it.[22]

And what of the 5,000 troops stationed in the city? They were commanded by General Putnam, who had been so ineffectual in Brooklyn. But given his experience, surely he could lead a retreat, and a quick one at that. Unfortunately, he could not. He had been on Manhattan since 3 April, but even after being placed in command in the city, Putnam had failed to carry out one of the most essential of the military arts: reconnaissance. Nor, apparently, had he asked people with local knowledge of an alternate road northward out of the city. He knew only the Post Road, and between Murray Hill and the city that was held by the victorious British. What to do? Listen to your aide-de-camp, that's what. Twenty-year-old Aaron Burr (1756–1836), who knew the city and its environs well, pointed out to his general that the Bloomingdale Road ran up the west side of the island. So off they went on a forced march to seek safety in the Harlem hills.

But surely Sir William Howe, who had a good map of Manhattan, had anticipated this possibility and instructed his field commander and deputy, Sir Henry Clinton, to push across the island with all possible speed and cut off the retreat of all rebels south of the Kips Bay beachhead. Alas for the British cause, such optimism was misplaced. Allowing for the traditional rivalry between sailors and soldiers, Midshipman James's conclusion rings true: "the army had landed, but, as usual, did not pursue the victory."[23]

Clinton had followed Howe's orders to seize Murray Hill and wait for the arrival of the rest of the landing force, which had to be brought over by the same boats that had taken the assault troops to Manhattan. He did not "think myself at liberty" to send troops west toward the Hudson River in an attempt to cut off Rebels trying to escape the city "before Sir William Howe joined us." Howe arrived at 2:00 P.M., but the rest of the landing force, about 5,000 strong, did not join them until about 4:00 P.M. Then the army moved northward to the Harlem plains.

According to Captain Mackenzie, Howe did not extend his lines to the Hudson until the following morning, too late to trap fleeing Rebels.[24]

Mackenzie recorded an incident that reveals just how sluggish British generals could be and how fortunate for the Americans that they were. He was brigade major under the dull-witted Brigadier General Francis Smith, of whom he wrote, "He is as brave as any man, but wants quickness of conception, and promptness in determining what should be done, and giving orders for its being carried into execution." Mackenzie's attempt to to give good advice to Smith earned him an immediate rebuke:

> As I was well acquainted with all this part of the Island, I represented to the General, that by stationing the Troops across the Island, by means of two different roads which were near him, and placing the right of the Brigade upon the road along the Shore of the North River, and the left extending towards Coerlaer's Hook . . . he would effectually prevent any of the Rebels who remained in New York, from escaping thence during the night. . . . But as he is slow, and not inclined to attend to whatever may be considered as advice, and seemed more intent upon looking out for comfortable quarters for himself, than preventing the retreat of those who might be in town, upon my urging the matter with some earnestness and undertaking to conduct and post the 22nd [Regiment] on the North River Road, he grew angry, and said I hurried him, and that he would place the brigade as he thought proper; upon which I was silent.[25]

One positive note came from the flight of the American army from Kips Bay. British failure to follow up their victory and Rebel speed afoot meant that most of the army survived to fight another day. As Benjamin Trumbull, chaplain with 1st Connecticut, recorded in his journal, "it is probable many lives were saved, and much [loss] to the army prevented, in their coming off as they did, tho' it was not honourable. It is admirable that so few men are lost."[26]

"It has given Spirits to our Men"

Mortified by the sight of his army "running away in the most disgracefull and shamefull manner," Washington entrenched on Harlem Heights, "where I should hope," he wrote to Hancock, "the Enemy would meet with a defeat in the case of an Attack." But his hope was slim, "for experience to my extreme affliction has convinced me that this is rather to be wished for than expected." The following day, however, the rash advance of British Light Infantry beyond their lines presented him with an opportunity to salvage, if not the campaign, at least a modicum of honor as well as to boost the morale of the troops.[27]

Washington was at his headquarters, Roger Morris's imposing home (modern Morris-Jumel Mansion) in present-day Washington Heights. In those days there were no obstructions southward, and Washington would have had a panoramic view looking toward the city. It was from here that he would watch almost a quarter of New York City burn on the night of 20–21 September, from Broadway to the Hudson River, destroying 493 buildings. The British believed it was the work of American arsonists, but no evidence for that has been found, and the cause remains unknown.

At about the time the dispatch rider left for Philadelphia with a letter for Hancock, Washington reported that the "Enemy appeared in several large bodies upon the plains about Two & a half miles from hence." Washington immediately mounted and rode to the American "advanced posts." Upon arrival he heard firing ahead and was informed that it was between the British advance and New England Rangers under the command of Colonel Thomas Knowlton (1740–1776), a gallant officer who had proven himself at Bunker Hill and various actions around Boston. His men consisted of about 127 volunteers from various New England regiments. Knowlton's Rangers had been sent out to reconnoiter Howe's dispositions and were attacked by British Light Infantry in the vicinity of present-day West 107th Street. Colonel Joseph Reed was with Knowlton and wrote, "our men behaved well stood & returned the Fire till overpowered by numbers they were obliged to retreat." Knowlton reported to Washington that the British Light Infantry marching on them appeard to be about 300 strong. Reed wrote that when the "Enemy appeared in open view . . . in the most insulting manner sounded their Bugle Horns as is usual after a Fox Chase. I never felt such a sensation before, it seem'd to crown our disgrace."[28]

According to Reed, Washington was then "prevailed on" to order Knowlton and his men, along with three companies from General George Weedon's Virginia Regiment under Major Andrew Leitch, to circle and get to the enemy's rear while Washington deployed other troops to engage the British in front "and thereby," Washington wrote, "draw their whole attention that way." The impetuous British light troops took the bait and surged forward into the trap being set for them. A considerable coup was in the making. Then firing began on the British flank instead of their rear. What had happened? In one letter to his wife, Colonel Reed, who was with the circling force, reported that Leitch's men "went another course; finding there was no stopping them I went with them the new Way." Six days later he gave his wife a slightly different version, claiming that the operation was "unhappily thwarted . . . by some Persons calling to the Troops & taking them out of the Road I intended."[29]

Whatever had caused the blunder, the premature attack on the British flank and the development of a firefight forced Washington to support Knowlton and Leitch. Washington committed troops from Maryland and New England, including Colonel William Douglas's Connecticut militia, the very men who had fled in terror from Kips Bay the previous day. At Harlem Heights, however, they stood and fought, and, Washington wrote, "charged the Enemy with great Intrepidity and drove them from the Wood into the plain, and were pushing them from thence, (having silenced their fire in great measure) when I judged it prudent to order a Retreat, fearing the Enemy (as I have found was really the case) were sending a large body to support their party." The aide Washington sent galloping off to recall the troops was Tench Tilghman, who reported that the advancing rebels "gave a Hurra and left the Field in good Order."[30]

This little fight is known as the Battle of Harlem Heights, but that nineteenth-century exaggeration should be laid to rest. Washington labeled the event accurately as "some smart skirmishes between some of their parties and detachments sent out by me, in which I have the pleasure to inform you our Men behaved with bravery and Intrepidity, putting them to flight when in Open Ground and forcing them from posts they had Seized Two or three times." There it was; nothing more, nothing less. Harlem Heights was not a decisive action. But it had one positive aspect. For the first time the Rebels had seen in open country the backsides of British soldiers scampering away. Colonel Reed admitted that the British defeat "will not affect their operations—but it has given Spirits to our Men that I hope they will now look the Enemy in the Face with Confidence." Later he wrote, "It hardly deserves the Name of a Battle, but as it was a Scene so different from what had happened the Day before it elevated our Troops very much & in that Respect has been of great Service." Washington agreed: "This Affair I am in hopes will be attended with many salutary consequences, as It seems to have greatly inspirited the whole of our Troops."[31]

The British now controlled all but the high ground at the northern tip of Manhattan. The Rebels on those heights continued to do what they were good at—dig. For Washington expected an attack, and he assured John Hancock that "Every disposition is making on our part for defence, and Congress can be assured that I shall do everything in my power to maintain the post so long as It shall appear practicable and conducive to the General good." Thus the combatants faced each other, their main lines about three miles apart, neither being able to learn what the other intended.

6

"This is a most unfortunate affair"

"A numerous army . . . under very little command, discipline, or order"

It will come as no surprise to the reader to learn that what Sir William intended, now that he controlled New York City and most of Manhattan, was to take his time. Instead of moving quickly and either keeping the Rebel Army on the run or trapping it, he felt the need to secure his position on the island by building a chain of redoubts from Horn's Hook (modern Carl Schurz Park) on the east side of Manhattan, about on a line with modern 91st Street, westward to Bloomingdale (between present-day West 90th and 100th Streets). This was all quite by the book, and what one would expect from a by-the-book general who had the added burden of being constrained by his brother's obsession with conciliation. So while Howe's army labors with pick and shovel instead of fighting, we will take the time to consider Washington as a field commander and the state of his army.[1]

The brilliant evacuation across the East River must not blind us to Washington's shortcomings in military operations and tactics, clearly revealed in both Brooklyn and Manhattan. To outflank an enemy must be one of war's oldest maneuvers, undoubtedly emerging during the dim centuries before writing that we call prehistory. One need not be a professional to realize its effectiveness. When I was a boy playing cowboys and Indians, it was our favorite maneuver. Yet on Long Island Washington had failed to anticipate Clinton's powerful flanking movement, and on an operational level had compounded his error by placing much of his army in jeopardy when he moved even more troops across the East River to man the lines on Brooklyn Heights. On Manhattan he had spread his forces the length of the island, despite his strong expectation of a British landing in his rear, and tarried so long before deciding to concentrate the army at the northern end of the island that he risked losing half of the army and would have, except for the sluggish nature of his foes. On both islands his expectations of militia were extravagant. Constricted as he was by the lack of well-trained, vigorously disciplined troops, with the Continentals regulars in name only and the militia unsuited to formal eighteenth-century warfare, by his deployment and actions it appears that he expected militia to face in the open the trained and disciplined regiments of Europe. But he must have known what was needed, for he knew the difference between militia and regulars. This was the man who had so admired the British regulars he had seen in the French and Indian War, despite their collapse at the Battle of Monongahela, that he had modeled his own Virginia Regiment after them. And this was the man who from the time he had taken command in Massachusetts in 1775 had understood how ill prepared his countrymen were to wage war against the world's greatest military power.

"I came to this place . . . and found a numerous army of Provencials under very little command, discipline, or order," he had written to his brother Samuel several days after arriving in Cambridge, Massachusetts, to take command of the American army. But he did not have the luxury then, or later in New York, of concentrating solely on organizing and disciplining a proper army. As he had then explained to Hancock, next to "my great Concern is to establish Order, Regularity & Discipline," he was saddled with the "more immediate & pressing Duties of putting our lines in as secure a State as possible, attending to the Movements of the Enemy, & gaining intelligence." On 3 July 1775, the day after his arrival, the Massachusetts Provincial Congress had informed him why the army was in such a state of disarray, an explanation as valid for New York as well. "The Hurry with which it was necessarily collected, and the many disadvantages, arising from a suspension of Government, under which we have raised, and endeavour'd to regulate the Forces of this Colony render'd it a work of Time."[2]

Time indeed, and it was unlikely then that most men realized how much time it would take to create a respectable army. One serious difficulty was the leveling tendency in American society, which even then was waging its own war against the ingrained Old World habit of deference to those on top of the social heap. Major General Philip Schuyler, to the manor born in one of the great landed families of the Hudson Valley, then commanding Rebel forces in northern New York State, was especially sensitive to insubordination by the lower orders, and informed Washington:

> Be assured my General that I shall use my best Endeavours to establish Order and Discipline in the Troops under my Command. I wish I could add That I had a Prospect of much Success in that Way. It is extremely difficult to introduce proper Subordination amongst a People where so little distinction is kept up.[3]

Schuyler was referring to the obstreperous Yankees in his command, whose own sensitivities were offended by the airs of the gentry. New Englanders especially were noted for this attitude, but throughout America tugging the forelock to one's alleged betters was no longer a given. Washington, who, shall we say, was genealogically compatible with his fellow landed proprietor, neatly described his own experience in this reply:

> From my own experience I can easily judge of your Difficulties to introduce Order & Discipline into troops who have from their infancy imbibed ideas of the most contrary Kind. It would be far beyond the Compass of a letter for me to describe the situation of Things here on my arrival, perhaps you will only be able to judge of it, from my assuring you that mine be a portrait at full Length of what you have had in Miniature.[4]

The Provincial Congress also had alerted Washington to another problem, which we touched on in chapter 2, about the

> General Character of the Soldiers who comprise the army . . . the greatest part of them have not before seen Service. And altho' naturally brave and of good understanding, yet for want of Experience in

military Life, have but little knowledge of divers things most essential to the preservation of Health and even of Life.

The Youth in the Army are not possess'd of the absolute Necessity of Cleanliness in their Dress, and Lodging, continual Exercise, and strict Temperance, to preserve them from Diseases frequently prevailing in Camps, especially among those who, from their Chilhood have been us'd to a laborious life.[5]

The second paragraph tells us that the soldiers came largely from the poor and working class, which should come as no great surprise, as armies generally throughout history attract people from the bottom ranks of society, not the top. It also reveals that their knowledge of personal hygiene left much to be desired, a problem that would plague Washington beyond Massachusetts and prompt several general orders on the necessity of cleanliness in camp.

The problem with militia was well and widely known. Upon the army's escape to Manhattan the following year after the Battle of Long Island, Washington wrote to Abraham Yates Jr. (1724–1796), president of the New York Convention,

It is the most intricate thing in the World Sir to know in what manner to conduct ones self with Respect to the Militia, if you do not begin many days before they are wanted to raise them, you cannot have them in time, if you do they get tired and return [home], besides being under very little Order or Government whilst in Service.[6]

In reply, the convention's Committee of Safety echoed their Massachusetts brethren:

We acknowledge the difficulty of managing the Militia so as to render them Usefull, which is in some Measure owing to their being ill appointed and unused to Camps and of Consequence suffering more than those who have got into a regular way of providing against Inconveniences.[7]

In his letter to Hancock, Washington had laid out in general terms his plan of organization and the necessity of the Continental Congress doing its part. To establish an army on paper, however, is one thing, to bring those plans to fruition quite another. The difficulties facing Washington, who had to organize and mold untutored amateurs while fighting a war, cannot be overestimated. In addition to the problems described above, it meant bringing into being an organization that had never existed in the thirteen colonies. Men had gone to war during the long struggle with the French and Indians in the seventeenth and eighteenth centuries in militia units of varying discipline, usually poor to fair, under officers whom they had elected, who were thus under the necessity of courting their favor to get elected and maintain their positions. The crux of the matter boils down to this: the Americans were a very unmilitary people, but very much a fighting people. Their militia was capable of fighting, and often fighting well, but in their own manner and when they chose, and when they did it well they produced on their own such key victories as the Battle of Bennington (1777) in upstate New York and Kings Mountain (1780) in South Carolina; or the critical Battle of Cowpens (1781), also in South Carolina, when a gifted Continental combat commander, Brigadier General Daniel Morgan, showed how to use militia in concert with regulars in a formal, open-field battle. But North and South, the rigid discipline, the unquestioning obedience, of European regulars was not their style. An observation by the very able North Carolina militia commander, Colonel William Richardson Davie (1756–1820), nailed down this truth. Recalling a successful attack in 1780 against the British outpost of Hanging Rock in South Carolina, Davie wrote,

> "In those times [it] was absolutely necessary" for the officers to explain to their men what was intended and obtain their approval, and in this case the militia "entered into the project with great spirit and cheerfulness."[8]

After the crushing defeat on Long Island, however, after the debacle at Kips Bay, it was obvious even to the Continental Congress that this approach to the war was unacceptable. Irregular troops would remain ever important to the overall war effort, and we shall give them their due when they deserve it. But big battles in the European manner that Washington intended, the endless marching and countermarching without apparent purpose to the rank and file, the long intervals in camp with its necessary but mind-numbing housekeeping duties, and the constant irritations of military life, so aptly labeled as "chickenshit" by twentieth-century American soldiers, required trained, disciplined troops inured to all of that as well as to the shocking horrors of formal warfare at close range. Of the latter, nobody ever put it better than one of Washington's favorites, Major General Nathanael Greene, who undoubtedly spoke for his chief as well as himself when he wrote in late September 1776 in clear, hard language to his brother Jacob:

> People coming from home with all the tender feelings of domestic life are not sufficiently fortified with natural courage to stand the shocking scenes of war. To march over dead men, to hear without concern the groans of the wounded, I say few men can stand such scenes unless steeled by habit or fortified by military pride.[9]

One of the problems had been Congress, which was opposed to a standing army, for that body was comprised of men who had taken in with their mothers' milk the fierce belief that a standing professional army and the sacred liberties of Englishmen, which they always considered their birthright, were incompatible. Its fears can be seen in a letter from John Jay commenting on an action by the New York Provincial Congress:

> The Resolutions of Congress restraining military officers from offering oaths by Way of Test to the Inhabitants I hope has reached you. I cant account for your Convention's submitting to this usurption on the Rights of their Constituents. To impose a Test is a sovereign Act of Legislation—and when the army becomes our Legislators, the People that moment become Slaves.[10]

Given the history of England in the seventeenth century, which they knew well, given their experience with British garrisons during the dozen years before the war, congressional fears were not unreasonable. And on the specific issue he addressed in his letter, the giving of oaths of loyalty, Jay was absolutely right. But their fears had now run up against the dire needs of the day. Was the cause for which they had laid down their lives, their fortunes, and their sacred honor to be sacrificed to uphold another dearly held principle?

In Greene's letter quoted above, he revealed his impatience with the legislators. "The policy of Congress has been the most absurd and ridiculous imaginable, pouring in militia men who come and go every month." He did not then know that Congress had finally seen the light. In a letter of 2 September to John Hancock, Washington had returned to a familiar theme and pressed his case for a standing army. He first listed the faults of the militia, who "instead of calling forth their utmost efforts to a brave & manly opposition in order to repair our Losses, are dismayed, Intractable, and Impatient to return [home]." Their "want of discipline & refusal of almost every kind of restraint & Government" had spread like an infection and become "too common to the whole." He then got to the nub of the matter:

> All these circumstances fully confirm the opinion I ever entertained, and which I more than once in my Letters took the liberty of mentioning to Congress, that no dependence could be put in a Militia or other Troops than those enlisted and embodied for a longer period than our regulations heretofore have prescribed. I am persuaded and as fully convinced, as I am of any One fact that has happened, that our Liberties must of necessity be greatly hazarded, if not entirely lost if their defense is left to any but a permanent, standing Army. I mean one to exist during the War.[11]

Upon receiving this letter, Congress on 3 September resolved itself into a committee of the whole to consider it, and on 16 September approved the raising of eighty-eight battalions to be "inlisted as soon as possible to serve during the present war." It was a promising beginning, but only a beginning, for the resolve was far easier than the doing. Provided that many men could be recruited, while the fighting was going on they would have to be trained and disciplined, and that was a major problem, for nobody in the army was capable of doing that.[12]

"Agreed that Fort Washington be retained as long as possible"

Meanwhile, the war went on. While the Rebels dug in on Harlem Heights, and the British dug in below them, Sir William had mulled things over and finally decided on his next move. A little over three weeks had passed since the Rebel rout at Kips Bay and the skirmish on Harlem Heights. Lord Howe, still pursuing his pipe dream of reconciliation, had decided to appeal directly to the people, and four days after Kips Bay had issued with his brother a declaration calling for talks to restore peace and resolve the issues that separated them. Their answer was mockery from all sides: Rebels, Tories, British officers. As a British naval officer observed, "It has long been too late for Negociation."[13]

Sir William in the meantime had decided that the Rebel positions in the hills of northern Manhattan were too strong for a direct assault and had come up with a plan to once again outflank the Rebels, and thus, as he later wrote to Lord Germain, "forcing them to quit their strongholds in the neighbourhood of Kings Bridge and if possible to bring them to action." At first the ever cautious Sir William awaited reinforcements, for he had decided that he did not have enough men to both secure Manhattan and outflank Washington. This seems a dubious proposition, but let us ignore it and get on with the story, because Sir William for some reason changed his mind and began his maneuvers a week before the reinforcement fleet dropped anchors in New York Harbor. The question was where to land his troops. Sir Henry Clinton proposed a feint toward New Jersey while marching the landing force to Whitestone in Queens and crossing Long Island Sound to either Myer's Point or New Rochelle and from there cutting the main road to New England. Admiral Howe rejected that on the ground that it lacked safe anchorage for the fleet, but then chose a tricky landing place that was too dependent on the incoming tide. His brother then accepted Sir William Erskine's proposal for a landing on a peninsula then called Frogs Neck (modern Throgs Neck), some nine miles east of Harlem Heights and about halfway between Hell Gate and Long Island Sound. From there a road ran northwest to Kingsbridge and behind Washington's main lines on Harlem Heights.[14]

On the morning of 12 October, with Admiral Lord Howe himself in command, the British fleet pulled off a neat bit of seamanship by successfully navigating Hell Gate "with a very strong tide and thick fog," wrote Captain Archibald Robertson, suffering only the loss of an artillery boat, three men, and three 6-pounders, and landed 6,500 British troops on Frogs Neck. But Frogs Neck was more of an island than a peninsula, surrounded by water at high tide, connected by a bridge and causeway to the mainland and at low tide by a ford. The British knew this, and in Sir Henry Clinton's words "pushed for the Westchester Bridge in the hopes of securing it. But the enemy had been too quick for us, having already destroyed it in their retreat." Twenty-five Pennsylvania riflemen commanded by Colonel Edward Hand had foiled Sir William's movement and were now stationed across the water behind a wall of cordwood. When Howe's advance appeared at the disabled bridge the Pennsylvanians' accurate rifle fire sent them into confused retreat. American reinforcements were rushed to the site and strong defensive works thrown up. Stymied, Sir William cast about for a solution.[15]

While one general pored over his maps, another did not have to do the same to realize that the enemy was in his rear and threatened to cut off his route of escape. Washington, however, did not at first seem too concerned. He reported Howe's landing on Frogs Neck to John Hancock in a letter of 13 October and described the measures he had taken to thwart any attempt by the British to advance off the neck. "The Grounds from Frog's point," he wrote, "are strong and defensible, being full of Stone fences both along the road & across the adjacent Feilds, which will render it difficult for Artillery or indeed a large body of Foot to advance in any regular order except thro the main Road. Our men who are posted on the passes seemed to be in good Spirits when I left 'em last night."[16]

The following day another element was thrown into the mix of personalities involved in this time of critical decisions: the return from the South of a man whose temper seemed always to be on the verge of boiling over, and during the next couple of months he would vex Washington considerably. In chapter 1 we briefly introduced the brave, eccentric, energetic, and obnoxious ex-English officer Major General Charles Lee, who had started the system of fortifications on Manhattan and Brooklyn Heights before being ordered by Congress to take command of the Southern Department in Charleston, South Carolina.

Shortly after Lee's new appointment to the South, Washington wrote a fair assessment of him: "He is the first Officer in Military knowledge and experience we have in the whole Army. He is zealously attached to the Cause—honest and well meaning, but rather fickle & violent I fear in his temper however as he possesses an uncommon share of good Sense & Spirit I congratulate my Countrymen upon his appointment to that Department."[17]

Lee's reputation was at its zenith. He had galvanized the Carolinians into efforts that culminated in a humiliating defeat for the British at the Battle of Sullivan's Island in Charleston Harbor. Yet despite Lee's major contribution to the victory, he had erred when he decided that Sullivan's Island could not be defended and strongly recommended that the garrison withdraw. John Rutledge, governor of South Carolina, overruled him. Then Lee compounded his error by deciding to sack the commander on the island, Colonel William Moultrie. Fortunately, weather intervened and prevented Lee from getting to Sullivan's Island on the day of the battle, and Moultrie's cool defense against the onslaught of a

Major General Charles Lee, designed/drawn by B. Rushbrooke;
printmaker, Alexander Hay Ritchie

British fleet made him a hero in the South. In the North, however, and among some modern historians, Lee got full credit for the victory, and with the crisis in New York facing them, Congress sent a courier South to summon Lee to Philadelphia as fast as he could ride. The members thought Washington needed the help and advice of a seasoned soldier. Which was quite true. And should anything happen to the Virginian, who was better qualified than Lee to succeed him as commander in chief? Which would have been a calamity. But Congress was enamored of its Englishman turned American patriot, and no congressman was more adoring than John Adams, who had previously written to him, "We want you at N. York—We want you at Cambridge—We want you in Virginia." Many in the army also saw him as a savior. Such hyperbole undoubtedly increased Lee's not uncommon human malady: delusions of grandeur. He was a thin man, about five feet, eight inches, with a big nose, a sarcastic manner, and dogmatic opinions. Private Simeon Alexander of the Hadley, Massachusetts, militia, who saw Lee at the siege of Boston, recalled many years later that "the soldiers used to laugh at his big nose."[18]

But Lee was not a comic figure. Impossible, of course, but intelligent, and his opinions, however undiplomatically presented, were often on the mark. For example, on the day he arrived at Harlem Heights, he wrote to Horatio Gates, "*Inter nos* the Congress seems to stumble at every step. I do not mean one or two of the Cattle, but the whole Stable. I have been very free in delivering my opinion to 'em. In my opinion General Washington is much to blame in not menacing 'em with resignation unless they refrain from unhinging the army by their absurd interference." In general, Lee was right. But Lee's style was not Washington's, whose finely honed sense of the primacy of civil authority over the long run served the Cause and the nation well.[19]

Lee was uncommonly well educated for a soldier, well versed in the classics and modern literature and proficient in six foreign languages, including Greek and Latin. During the Seven Years' War he saw action in North America and Europe and was badly wounded during Abercromby's botched assault on Fort Ticonderoga in 1758. In Portugal in 1762 he led 250 British grenadiers and fifty troopers of the 16th Light Dragoons in a surprise night attack against a Spanish camp that completely routed the enemy. The Spanish suffered heavy losses, and Lee's forces returned laden with prisoners and plunder. Between the wars he was an observer with the Russian army at war with the Turks. He had a keen sense of operations. As a strategist, however, his proposal to abandon conventional warfare and rely on a massive guerrilla war would have exposed the nation to the ravages and horrors that later racked the Carolinas and Georgia from 1780 through 1782, and almost certainly would have led to an ending far less happy than that achieved under Washington's leadership. He carried his eccentricities to such an extreme that it has laid him open to charges of madness. The violence of his speech, the savage candor of his letters, the turbulence of his emotions, his paranoia, were the stuff of legend. He had little regard for Washington's

abilities, of which Washington became well aware. But Washington respected Lee's knowledge and abilities and paid attention to his counsel.[20]

It must once more be stressed just how inexperienced the Continental and militia officers were. This partly explains the awe in which
Lee was held by many in the Rebel ranks, both military and civilian.
Here was a career officer with knowledge of all things military, a
wounded veteran of combat in the Seven Years' War, well known for his
dashing mission in Portugal, a witness to warfare between the Russian
bear and the terrible Turk. This solid professional record combined with
his strange and outsize personality and genius for self-promotion gave
him an aura that nobody else in the army possessed. Little wonder that
provincials on the fringe of the Western world saw in him the savior of
the Cause.

With Lee's arrival at headquarters, things began to move quickly.
Lee saw clearly the danger of the army being outflanked and pinned
between Howe's force and the British troops under Lord Percy facing
the American positions on Harlem Heights. Washington held a Council
of War on 16 October in, interestingly, Lee's quarters to discuss the
"Enemy's Intentions to surround us." Certainly Lee gave his opinion
with his usual rough manners and brutal candor. Lieutenant Colonel
Robert Hanson Harrison, Washington's military secretary, reported that
"Genl Lee who arrived on Monday strongly urged the absolute necessity" of withdrawing from Harlem Heights into Westchester County "so
as to outflank" Howe. "After much Consideration & Debate," the minutes read, and with only one dissent, it was decided to leave Manhattan
and retreat northward to the hills around White Plains. Lee's biographer
believed that "Lee's advice and aggressiveness may well have saved the
American army and the American republic," but this speculation rests
on flimsy evidence. It assumes that Sir William Howe would move
quickly to spring the trap, and that is a large assumption; I also find it
inconceivable that others were not also in favor of a retreat, and in fact
Tench Tilghman, a volunteer aide-de-camp of Washington's, on that
date wrote with regard to "securing a proper place of retreat beyond the
Highlands, should any accident befall the army. I cannot speak posi-
tively, but I am inclined to think the expediency of such a measure is in
deliberation before a council of war held this day at *King's Bridge*. I
know some of our ablest heads are clearly for it." But Lee's senior rank
and overwhelming reputation in the army may well have been the deciding factors. Another decision was also made at the council, in which Lee

concurred, and it would eventually reverberate through the army and Congress: "Agreed that Fort Washington be retained as long as possible."[21]

"Our Men behaved with great coolness & Intrepidity"

On 18 October the Rebel Army began its retreat fifteen miles northward, to some defensive hills overlooking the village of White Plains in Westchester County. White Plains was an obvious choice, because it was the hub for an extensive road network. The retreat was slow and laborious. Lord Stirling, recently exchanged and returned to service, was sent ahead with his brigade to take and hold the hills, arriving there on the morning of the 18th. The rest of the army began its retreat on the 21st in a series of night marches. There was a severe shortage of horses and wagons, so the artillery had to be dragged by hand. At the end of the day's march the wagons would be unloaded, then taken back to the starting point to pick up more supplies and baggage. As Washington wrote, "the want of Teams is a most dreadful misfortune." The men themselves were used as packhorses. This "March was very Tedious," wrote Colonel William Douglas, "as the men were oblige to Carry their tents & Kittles with all their own baggage," And Private Joseph Plumb Martin griped, "I was so beat out before morning with hunger and fatigue that I could hardly move one foot before the other."[22]

While all of this was going on, Sir William Howe had decided to do what he should have done in the first place. On the same day, 18 October, after finally receiving the provisions the quartermaster general was late in delivering, he moved his troops by water up the coast three miles to Pell's Point (present-day Pelham Bay Park) in Westchester County. There a smart little action took place in which a brigade of Yankees acquitted themselves with skill and honor, and since this was a rarity during these desperate months, we owe it to the memory of those men to describe their behavior against an overwhelming force.

To look for a move by Howe and take appropriate action, Washington had stationed the right man at Pell's Point: the short, stocky, redhaired Marblehead fisherman Colonel John Glover. He commanded a brigade of 750 men made up of parts of three Massachusetts regiments and his own Marblehead regiment. Three artillery pieces augmented his small force. Early on the morning of the 18th Glover climbed a hill, raised his spyglass, and saw, he wrote four days later, "the boats upwards of two hundred sail, all manned and formed in four grand divisions."

John Glover by unknown artist after John Trumbull (?)

Glover immediately marched against the enemy. But he felt overwhelmed by the responsibility. "I would have given a thousand worlds to have had General Lee or some other experienced officer present, to direct, or at least approve of what I had done." It was best, however, that Colonel Glover was left to act on his own, for he was one of those battle captains in no need of micromanagement.

As at Frogs Neck, the road leading from the coast was lined with stone walls, and in the fields on either side "high stone walls" were noted by Captain Archibald Robertson, who was with the advance of the British Light Infantry. They were made-to-order breastworks for the Rebels, and Glover took full advantage of them. After sending out a captain with an advance of fifty men to make contact with the enemy, he deployed his remaining force. On the left side of the road behind a stone wall he placed Colonel Joseph Read's 13th Massachusetts. Behind them, on the other side of the road and sheltered by their own stone wall, was Colonel William Shepard's (1737–1817) 3rd Massachusetts. Shepard, a veteran of the French and Indian War, had been wounded on Long Island. Deployed behind Shepard's regiment was 26th Massachusetts, commanded by Colonel Loammi Baldwin (1745–1807), a fruit grower whose name was given to the Baldwin apple. In the rear on the high ground were Glover's own 14th Massachusetts and the three fieldpieces.[23]

Glover's advance met British skirmishers and at fifty yards began exchanging fire with them. When five rounds had been exchanged, a few casualties suffered on both sides, and the distance between the two forces narrowed to thirty yards, Glover ordered his skirmishers to withdraw, a movement, Glover wrote, "masterly well done by the captain that commanded the party." Thereupon the British, no doubt sensing another rout, shouted and charged down the road. At thirty yards 13th Massachusetts rose from behind their stone wall, leveled some 200 muskets, and well within the accuracy range of those eighteenth-century weapons delivered a punishing volley. The British skirmishers withdrew quickly down the road whence they had come.

An hour and a half passed. Then some 4,000 British and German line infantry appeared, marching stolidly down the road, supported by six cannons, toward the 750 Americans. At fifty yards Colonel Read gave the order and the men of the 13th rose again and delivered their volley, and the enemy "returned the fire," Glover wrote, "with showers of musketry and cannon balls." Seven rounds were exchanged before Glover ordered Read's regiment to withdraw. Once again, the British and Germans thought the time for the coup de grâce had come. They came on cheering. Then from the other side of the road 3rd Massachusetts suddenly rose from behind its double stone wall and the action repeated itself. Colonel Shepard's men fired seventeen rounds into the foe, who retreated several times. According to his family tradition, at this point in the action the well-built, dark-eyed Captain William Glanville Evelyn of King's Own, who had with his mounted patrol captured the five young American officers on Long Island during Sir Henry Clinton's flank march, vaulted over a stone wall and advanced on the enemy. He had not gone far when he was wounded three times. The third round smashed his right leg above the knee, and that is literally what the big lead balls would do, tearing up flesh and bone and muscle.

Such a wound invariably meant the terrible ordeal of amputation in an age before anesthetics. But Evelyn refused the operation until it was too late. "It was then performed in vain; and after lingering for nearly three weeks he died at New York on Nov. 6, 1776." He was thirty-four, a veteran of the Seven Years' War in Europe, of Lexington and Concord, of Long Island and the fighting on Manhattan. Evelyn was of the Anglo-Irish Ascendancy, a people whose sons for centuries followed the colors to the four corners of the British Empire. Many, like Evelyn, ended their adventures in long-forgotten skirmishes, never to see home again, their corpses moldering in foreign soil, in Captain Evelyn's case, Trinity Church burial ground on lower Broadway.[24]

When the first two units had retreated behind Colonel Baldwin's 26th Massachusetts, Baldwin's men rose from behind their stone wall and fired their volleys. But the game was about up. Sir Henry Clinton wrote that he had sent Cornwallis on a flanking movement "with some battalions and cannon, with a view to getting around them," and it was the knowledge of this maneuver by the British that prompted Colonel Glover to order a general withdrawal, which was performed, Colonel Baldwin wrote to his wife, "with the greatest reluctance Immaginable though with as much good order and Regularity as ever they marched off a Publick Parade."[25]

The Rebels withdrew without incident to the hill where Glover's 14th Massachusetts waited in reserve, and for the rest of the day the two sides exchanged artillery fire. That night Glover withdrew another three miles. The Americans were not ready for a formal, stand-up fight in the open, but they had maneuvered well, fought stubbornly from behind cover, and delayed the British advance for a day. Washington's military secretary accurately described the fight to John Hancock as "a smart & close Skirmish . . . in which I have the pleasure to inform you our Men behaved with great coolness & Intrepidity." An argument has been made that Glover's day-long defense on Pell's Point saved Washington's army, for an unimpeded advance by Howe's landing force across the Bronx River would have put him in front of the slowly retreating Rebel Army. The problem with this argument is that we do not know what Sir William would have done had he not been opposed, but given his record to date, an equally strong argument can be made that he would have dillydallied. And that is precisely what he did, even though he had not been significantly checked at Pell's Point. Colonel Harrison in his letter to Hancock called it a skirmish, and Captain Archibald

Robertson's description of events ranks Pell's Point at the level of a minor action. A Scottish grenadier, Captain John Peebles, wrote, "The Advanced Troops had a skirmish with the Enemy, some kill'd & wounded, got that day to near East Chester, on the High road from N. York to Boston." Howe had driven Glover's brigade from the field. He claimed to have suffered only light casualties. Kingsbridge and the straggling American army were only six miles away. Howe could still have pushed westward to intercept Washington, or northward to beat him to White Plains. Instead, he decided to wait for the reinforcements that had finally arrived in New York Harbor on the 18th, the day he landed at Pell's Point.[26]

That reinforcement fleet had been long months at sea, which in the eighteenth century was not to be enjoyed but grimly endured. The troops consisted of 4,000 Hessians, 670 Waldeckers, and 3,700 British recruits. Some of the German troops had been on board their transports for more than four months since leaving the port of Cuxhaven on 9 June. Little wonder that one of the finest diarists of the war, a thirty-two-year-old, one-eyed Hessian Jäger, Captain Johann Ewald, wrote that "it was high time to be released from our environment, since scurvy was raging among our men so violently that in the past eight days ten men had died and almost twenty more looked forward to death, which in their misery they regarded as fortunate." Once on shore they were eager for the "fresh meat and tasty vegetables" provided them, but their stomachs rebelled. The fresh food "upset and weakened us for some time, because we had been accustomed to salted food and meager fare for so many weeks." By the 22nd, however, upset stomachs or not, the reinforcements were in flatboats on their way up the East River to join the rest of the army in Westchester County in time for Sir William's next joust with Washington. To Ambrose Serle they made a grand sight indeed, going off to battle. "They were all in high Spirits, and rowed along with Drums beating, Trumpets & Fifes sounding, and colors flying in a very gallant order. They made a fine appearance altogether."[27]

"A cannonball . . . took Taylor across the Bowels"

The main Rebel Army, 14,500 present and fit for duty, arrived at White Plains by the morning of 22 October and took up strong positions in the hills above the country village. The arrival of Lee's division on 26 October increased its strength to about 17,000. With the nightmarish march from Harlem Heights undoubtedly in mind, the first general order from White Plains emphasized the importance of logistics to the army: "The commanding Officers of regiments should, on all Marches, draw provisions for the Waggoners, who attend them, and give them all possible assistance. When their baggage is unloaded, they should have the Teams drawn up, set a Guard over them, and prevent any loss of the Horses, or abuse of the Drivers, and take care of them 'till they are ordered away."[28]

Although Washington had several days to examine the lay of the land, for some reason he neglected until the morning of the battle a commanding ridge called Chatterton Hill, which was half a mile across the Bronx River from the American right flank. It was unfortified and manned by militia levies from Massachusetts, New York, and New Jersey. Sir William, who had taken ten days to move his army seventeen miles, arrived on 28 October and had his attention drawn to Chatterton Hill by Sir Henry Clinton, who had reconnoitered ahead and spotted this weakness in the American position. Howe then ordered Hessian Lossberg Regiment to cross the river and attack, supported by 2nd British Brigade and Hessian Grenadier Regiment, with the latter assigned to a flank assault. As the British and German regiments deployed prior to going into action, two American officers were entranced by the sight, which they had probably never before seen. "The sun shone bright, their arms glittered, and perhaps troops never were shewn to more advantage than those now appeared," wrote one, while the other officer was even more expansive: "Its appearance was truly magnificent. A bright autumnal sun shed its lustre on the polished arms; and the rich array of dress and military equipage gave an imposing grandeur to the scene as they advanced in all the pomp and circumstance of war."[29]

Now on to the dirty business following the spectacle. White Plains was a tough fight in which the British and German troops once again refuted a myth that will not die: that European regulars could not match Americans in the woods and on rough ground. So let us take a brief look at it from the level of junior officers and the rank and file. The Hessian Grenadiers, reported Captain Ewald, attacked "with the bayonet without firing first," which sent the militia on the right flying for the rear. The alarm prompted Washington to send to their aid four regiments of Continentals: Colonel John Haslet's Delaware Regiment, two New York regiments under Brigadier General Alexander McDougall, and Colonel Charles Webb's 19th Connecticut. Captain Ewald described the slopes of Chatterton Hill and the British advance: "The area was intersected by hills, woods, and marshes and every field was enclosed by a stone wall." The right wing, which "was situated upon particularly steep heights, overgrown with woods, and the center was covered by a light wood that extended from the foot of the hill where the creek ran by up to the steep hill." The British and German soldiers "crossed the creek . . . and climbed up the hill occupied by the enemy, where they were exposed to very severe small arms and grapeshot fire. They drove the enemy from hill to hill through the woods, without giving him time to establish a position again." Two Jäger companies "had to work their way, under heaviest enemy cannon fire, through the ravines and marshes that lay between the two wings. Here we came upon a number of rifle-men who were hiding in these ravines, and who withdrew when they caught sight of us after sharp firing."

By six o'clock that evening, with the Americans giving "way on all sides" and the British and Germans in command of Chatterton Hill, "we could not pursue him further because of the extremely intersecting terrain. . . . Since the soldiers had climbed over nothing but hills, cliffs, and stone walls the whole day, constantly dragging their guns over all obstacles, it was impossible to ask anything more of them."[30]

It was a defeat, to be sure, but the Americans had not done badly. There had been no repeat of Kips Bay. Tench Tilghman summed it up best when he wrote, "our Troops made as good a Stand as could be expected, and did not quit the Ground till they came to push their Bay-onets." True, Colonel Haslet reported that shortly after the Delawares arrived, the second British cannon ball "wounded a militia-man in the thigh, upon which the whole regiment broke and fled immediately, and were not rallied without much difficulty." And there was backbiting afterward between McDougall of New York and Haslet of Delaware. But though another defeat it was not an inglorious performance. Consider, for example, the experience of a platoon of 19th Connecticut, the last American regiment to leave the battlefield that day. As with most rear guards, it paid a price, and one incident of battlefield mayhem was described in the homely but vivid prose of Elisha Bostwick, a musket-man in the ranks. The regiment was ordered by McDougall to

march farther down the hill [to prevent the British from outflanking them. While] Making that movement . . . a cannonball cut down Lt. Young's Platoon which was next to that of mine the first ball took the

head of [Private Nathaniel] Smith, a Stout heavy man & dash't it
open, then it took off Chilson's arm which was amputated and he
recovered, it then took [Private Joll] Taylor across the Bowels, it then
Struck Sergt. [Amasa] Garret of our Company on the hip took off the
point of the hip bone. Smith and Taylor were left on the spot. Sergt
Garret was carried but died the Same day . . . oh! what a Sight that
was to See within a distance of Six rods those men with their legs &
arms & guns & packs all in a heap. There was not a better Sergt in
the army than Sergt Garret when the Soldiers were Murmering, weary,
without Shelter cold & hungry he would Stir about among them build
fires & get them all in good humor & cheerful.[31]

Thus ended the Battle of White Plains.

"I feel mad, vext, sick, and sorry"

American casualties numbered about 134; the British and Germans,
some 250. The latter's losses were in vain, for Sir William, instead of
launching a planned coordinated attack on the main American positions, had been content to sit back and watch the action unfold on Chatterton Hill, and we must ask why. Sir William himself later provided an
answer of sorts at a parliamentary committee of inquiry when he said,
"The committee must give me credit when I assure them, that I have
political reasons, and no other, for declining to explain why that assault
was not made." But he declined to give those reasons, making it quite
clear that he would do so only if required to in court. He went on to say
that even if an assault had been made "the enemy would have got off
without much loss." Then why in the days following did he plan a second attack, against the advice of his generals, even after Washington
had moved his lines back a short distance to a stronger position? Both
sides spent the next few days digging in and strengthening their lines.
The British attack was planned for 1 November, but heavy rains intervened, and that night the fox withdrew five miles northward. The
answer to the puzzle died with Sir William Howe, and to speculate endlessly on his behavior would be fruitless.[32]

On 5 November the British withdrew from White Plains and headed
southwest for Kingsbridge and the Hudson River. The next day at a council of war Washington and his generals agreed that part of the army
should cross the river to New Jersey, in the event of a British attack on

that state. But as Washington admitted that same day, Sir William's intentions remained "a matter of much conjecture and speculation." Was it preparatory to a move against Jersey? A feint to draw rebels after him? Or did they intend to board ships and sail up the river to land above Washington and fall upon his rear? Speculation was rife. It was not until the 8th, therefore, that Washington, now convinced from intelligence reports that Howe was set on a "Penetration into Jersey," carried out the council's decision. Over the next three days troops from Virginia, Maryland, Delaware, Pennsylvania, and New Jersey crossed to the western bank, while the rest of the army stayed east of the Hudson to protect the Highlands, the route to New England, and be alert just in case Howe's movement was, after all, a feint. Washington made his purpose quite clear in several letters. To Ezekiel Cheever, the Continental Army's commissary of artillery stores: "It is unnecessary to add that the Troops under General Lee, will also cross Hudson's River, if it should be necessary in consequence of the Enemy's throwing their Force over." To his chief of artillery, Colonel Henry Knox: "It is more than probable (unless General Howe should throw his whole force into the Jerseys & bend his Course towards Philadelphia) that there will Scarce be a junction of our Troops again this Season." He continued, "It is unnecessary to add that if the Army of the enemy Should wholly or pretty generally throw themselves across the North River that General Lee is to follow."[33]

For the general Washington left in command of that part of the main army east of the river was Charles Lee, and on 10 November Washington also sent him specific written instructions that undoubtedly had been discussed by them. In light of future events, pay close attention to Washington's words. It was in the final paragraph of the letter that he got to the crucial point:

> If the Enemy should remove the whole, or the greatest part of their Force to the West side of Hudson's River, I have no doubt of your following with all possible dispatch.[34]

Farther north, at Peekskill, New York, Washington gave command of the critical Hudson Highlands to Major General William Heath, to whom he wrote, "Unnecessary it is for me to say any thing to evince the Importance of securing the Land and Water Communications through these Passes . . . of using every exertion in your power to have such

Works erected for the defence of them." To emphasize the importance Washington gave to this command, Heath recalled that "The Commander in Chief directed our General [Heath] to ride early in the morning with him to reconnoitre the grounds at the Gorge of the Highlands."[35]

Sir William in the meantime was marching toward his initial goal, the reduction of the only Rebel stronghold left on Manhattan: Fort Washington. Inside the fort were 2,900 Continentals commanded by Colonel Robert Magaw of Pennsylvania. Magaw had been ordered "to defend it to the last." Without at all meaning to denigrate the Continental Congress, whose job was not only incredibly difficult but also thankless, the affair of Fort Washington is an excellent example of congressional meddling in matters best left to field commanders. On 11 October Congress resolved "that General Washington be desired, if it be practicable, by every art, and whatever expence, to obstruct effectually the navigation of the North river, between Fort Washington and Mount Constitution [Fort Lee]." Despite the polite language of the time, and the qualification of "if it be practicable," this was an instruction. To a general like Washington, ever sensitive to congressional prerogative, they were marching orders, and he passed them on. In a letter of 21 October to another officer, he wrote, "Inform Colo. Magaw that I shall depend upon his holding the Post at Mt. Washington as long as a good Officer ought to do." Some officers would interpret that to mean to the death. Magaw told Major General Nathanael Greene that he could hold the fort until the end of the year.[36]

But what was the sense of trying to hold Fort Washington if the barriers across the Hudson were proving useless in stopping British ships from going up and down the river as they pleased? Washington made that case to Greene on 8 November:

> The late passage of the 3 Vessells up the North River . . . is so plain a proof of the inefficacy of all the Obstructions we have thrown into it that I cannot but think it will fully justify a Change in the Disposition which has been made. If we cannot prevent Vessells passing up, and the Enemy are possessed of the surrounding Country, what valuable purpose can it answer to attempt to hold a post from which the expected Benefit cannot be had. I am therefore inclined to think it will not be prudent to hazard the Men & Stores at Mount Washington, but as you are on the Spot, leave it to you to give such Orders as to evacuating Mount Washington as you judge best, and so far revoking the Order given Colo. Magaw to defend it to the last.[37]

Washington had correctly identified why Fort Washington should not be defended and without making it an order had invited Greene to evacuate the post. This letter reveals one of Washington's great strengths as a commander: his willingness to delegate authority to subordinates whose abilities and judgment he trusted. At the same time, the top commander also must know when the time has come to step in and take charge, and that moment came during the Fort Washington affair.

Greene replied the next day. Although admitting that the British ships passing upriver "is to be sure a full proof of the insufficiency of the Obstructions," he argued that the Fort Washington garrison was large enough to resist investment:

> Upon the whole I cannot help thinking the Garrison is of advantage—and I cannot conceive the Garrison to be in any great danger the men can be brought off at any time—but the stores may not be so easily removed. Yet I think they can be got off in spight of them if matters grow desperate. This Post [Fort Lee] is off no importance only in conjunction with Mount Washington. I was over there last Evening the Enemy seems to be disposing matters to besiege the place—but Col. Magaw thinks it will take them till December expires, before they can carry it out.[38]

Yet in none of the extant records were the inadequacies of Fort Washington discussed. The American had been working on it for months, all through the hot summer, finally finishing it in October. It was a five-sided earthen fort that could hold about 1,200 men, but Colonel Magaw would eventually have 2,900 men. There were bastions at each corner. There was no ditch around it, and for good reason. Mount Washington was solid granite, with only a thin covering of soil. The American talent for digging in was of no use here. The dirt for the ramparts had to be carried up the hill. It would have taken thousands of pounds of blasting powder the Rebels did not have to create a ditch, bombproof quarters for the troops, and underground food and ammunition magazines. It the event of a siege, the most fatal flaw was water: there was none on the hill. It had to be carried up from the Hudson 230 feet below.

No wonder Washington continued to worry. On the 12th, after giving General Heath his instructions at Peekskill, Washington crossed the river to the western bank and rode south to Fort Lee, arriving on the 13th, when he conferred with Greene. From there Washington wrote that "The movements and designs of the Enemy are not yet understood. Various are the opinions and reports on this head." Yet of one thing he was certain: his continuing unease over Fort Washington. But Greene remained optimistic. On the 15th Washington left Fort Lee and rode six miles west to Hackensack, where a courier reached him with a letter from Greene, enclosing a letter from Colonel Magaw. Washington's nagging concern over Fort Washington had quickly swelled to a crisis, and Sir William Howe's immediate design had been made brutally clear. Washington hurried back to Fort Lee.[39]

Magaw had that day written to Greene that the British adjutant general, James Paterson, had appeared under a flag of truce and offered Magaw

> an Alternative between surrendering at *discretion* or every man being put to the sword. He waits for an answer. I shall send a proper one. You'll I dare say do what is best. We are determined to defend the post or die.[40]

Washington arrived at Fort Lee that evening and immediately boarded a boat to take him across the river that he might personally review the situation. But on the way he met Nathanael Greene and the nominal commander in the area, Major General Israel Putnam, on their way back from Fort Washington. Greene was still optimistic. Washington wrote, "[They] informed me that the Troops were in high Spirits and would make a good Defence, and it being late at Night I returned" with them to Fort Lee. The next morning, 16 November, the three generals along with Brigadier General Hugh Mercer embarked once again for Fort Washington, "but Just at the instant we stept on board the Boat," Greene wrote, "the Enemy made their appearance on the Hill . . . and began a severe Cannonade with several field pieces." Washington had let it go too late.[41]

For Sir William Howe had determined on a course of action quite uncharacteristic of him since the British debacle at Bunker Hill. There would be no siege of Fort Washington, no slow, laborious approach. He would carry the steep, heavily wooded slope by frontal assault.

The British surrounded the hill on all but the riverside, where a rock wall plunged almost vertically to the Hudson. Four columns were readied for the assault. From the south, Lord Percy with nine battalions and a Hessian Brigade; from the east, Lord Cornwallis with the Guards,

Grenadiers, Light Infantry, and 33rd Foot; south of Cornwallis, Black Watch was to feign an attack. The main attack was delivered by the Hessian Regiments Rall and Lossberg, led in person by Lieutenant General Wilhelm, Freiherr von Knyphausen (1716–1800). A veteran of the War of the Austrian Succession and the Seven Years' War, Knyphausen was a taciturn but intelligent and skillful soldier of high reputation. Because of the heavily wooded slopes and rugged terrain the various attacks pushed forward in columns instead of the usual line formations.

The attack began at daybreak with a "violent Cannonade from all of our batteries," wrote Captain Mackenzie, who was with Lord Percy during the attack. The barrage lasted until 10:00 A.M., and during the interim the columns moved forward to their jumping-off positions. Both Percy and von Knyphausen moved forward but then had to stop because tidal conditions had delayed Cornwallis, who had to cross the Harlem River. At about 10:00 A.M. orders came to advance, and the columns pushed forward in unison. Cornwallis also ordered Black Watch to forgo their feinting maneuver and join his column in the attack. The Highlanders came under "heavy fire" while crossing the Harlem, Mackenzie reported, but upon landing they "pushed the Rebels up the precipice with great bravery . . . pursuing them across the Island with their bayonets."[42]

All of the attacking units, Guards, Grenadiers, Light Infantry, and regiments of foot, attacked with élan that day and drove all before them. But top honors must go to the Germans under von Knyphausen. Captain Mackenzie accurately reported that von Knyphausen's column, with "very difficult ground to get through . . . occupied by the principal force of the Enemy, met with considerable resistance" from Lieutenant Colonel Moses Rawlings's regiment of Maryland and Pennsylvania riflemen, who inflicted heavy casualties. Yet the Germans persevered, inspired no doubt by the gallantry of their sixty-year-old general, who led instead of followed, fighting as if he were a private in the ranks, pulling aside obstructions with his own hands, grasping bushes to haul himself up the steep slopes. Private Johannes Reuber of Rall's Regiment wrote in his diary that

> all the regiments and corps marched forward in order to clamber up
> the hills and stone cliffs. One fell down, still alive, the next one was
> shot dead. We had to pull ourselves up by grasping the wild boxtree
> bushes and could not stand upright until we finally arrived on top the
> height. As the tree and large rocks were encountered close upon one

another and [the terrain] did not become more even, Colonel Rall commanded, "All who are my grenadiers, forward march!" All the drums beat a march. The musicians played a march. Suddenly everyone still alive shouted, "Hurrah!" Then everyone was at once mixed together, Americans and Hessians were as one. No more shots were fired, but everyone ran toward the defenses.[43]

Rawlings's riflemen held out the longest, but finally, their weapons fouled by repeated firings, they retreated up the hill and into the fort, which was becoming so overcrowded with men it was impossible to mount a defense from within.

Had the Germans then stormed the fort, a massacre might have ensued. Their blood up, angry over their losses, they wanted revenge, itched to plunge their bayonets into Rebel flesh. But Sir William had given orders that the Rebels were only to be driven into the fort, which was not to be stormed by the assault troops. Colonel Johann Rall, leading his Hessian regiment in advance, sent a summons to surrender. Heavily outnumbered and surrounded on all sides, Colonel Magaw asked for terms. Von Knyphausen, Captain Mackenzie reported, demanded "surrender at discretion and they desired half an hour to consider it." Then Howe appeared and "insisted they should surrender immediately, without any other terms than a promise of their lives, and their baggage." At about 3:00 P.M. Colonel Magaw, who had vowed to fight to the death, handed over his sword to General von Knyphausen. Some on the British side were upset with Howe for not allowing the garrison to be slaughtered, which would have been in keeping with the laws of war at the time, since Magaw had originally been given the choice of either surrendering or having the garrison put to the sword. According to Captain Mackenzie, those in favor of ignoring an offer of surrender and assaulting the fort thought it "would have struck such a panic through the continent, as would have prevented Congress from being able to raise another army." Mackenzie disagreed, believing "it is right to treat our Enemies as if they might one day become our friends."[44]

It was the worst defeat suffered by the rebels until Major General Benjamin Lincoln surrendered Charleston to Sir Henry Clinton in 1780. A little over 2,800 officers and men were taken prisoner, and all of their equipment, weapons, artillery, and ammunition captured. The prisoners were a sorry lot, tormented as war prisoners of every age by the uncertain terrors that awaited them. A British officer present wrote, "The Rebel prisoners were in general but very indifferently clothed; few of them appeared to have a Second shirt, nor did they appear to have washed themselves during the Campaign. A great many of them were lads under 15; and old men: and few of them had the appearance of Soldiers. Their odd figures frequently excited the laughter of our Soldiers."[45]

One of those prisoners was Captain Alexander Graydon (1752–1818) of 3rd Pennsylvania. Upon surrendering to an officer of 42nd Royal Highlanders (Black Watch), he and some fellow officers were put in the custody of a sergeant, who was friendly but admonished them, "Young men, ye should never fight against your king." But later, gathered with forty or fifty fellow officers, he and his comrades, Graydon later wrote, "for nearly an hour sustained a series of most intolerable abuse," mainly "from the officers of the light infantry; for the most part young and insolent puppies, whose worthlessness was apparently their recommendation to a service, which placed them in the post of danger, and in the way of becoming food for powder, their most appropriate destination next to that of the gallows. The term rebel, with the epithet *damned* before it was the mildest we received. We were twenty times told, sometimes with a taunting affectation of concern, that we should every man of us be hanged." Graydon's emotions were roiled. The "indignity of being ordered about by such contemptible whipsters, for a moment unmanned me, and I was obliged to apply my handkerchief to my eyes. This was the first time in my life that I had been the victim of brutal cowardly oppression; and I was unequal to the shock; but my elasticity of mind was soon restored, and I viewed it with the indignant contempt it deserved."[46]

On the whole, however, their treatment was relatively benign while in the custody of front-line troops, and it was those troops who saved them from assault by civilians, mostly the fiercer of the species. "On the road," Graydon recalled, "as we approached the city, we were beset by a parcel of soldier's trulls and others, who came out to meet us. It was obvious, that in the calculation of this assemblage of female loyalty, the war was at an end; and that the whole of the rebel army, Washington and all, were safe in durance. Which is Washington? Which is Washington? proceeded from half a dozen mouths at once; and the guard was obliged to exert itself to keep them off." A British colonel by the name of Maxwell, "who rode along side of us . . . had enough to do to silence one of them, calling out repeatedly: 'Away with that woman! Take her way! Knock her down, the bitch! Knock her down!'" But Graydon was a lucky man. He was eventually paroled and survived the war, escaping

Major General Nathanael Greene by John Trumbull

the fate of a majority of the officers and men taken at Fort Washington. During the next eighteen months two-thirds of the some 2,800 prisoners would die in appalling conditions of captivity.[47]

Nathanael Greene underwent his own form of torment. His failure to recognize the danger to Fort Washington is usually attributed to his inexperience, and he was at that time a very inexperienced soldier. But I find his performance inexplicable, especially given his brilliant Carolina campaign (1780–1782), which set the stage for Yorktown and saved the Carolinas and Georgia for the Union. Whatever the reason for his unwarranted optimism, he was crushed. He wrote the next day to his friend Henry Knox, "I feel mad, vext, sick, and sorry. Never did I need the consoling voice of a friend more than now. Happy should I be to see you. This is a most terrible Event. Its consequences are justly to be dreaded. Pray what is said upon the occasion?"[48]

And Washington? "This is a most unfortunate affair," he wrote, "and has given me great Mortification." As well it might have. It is true that the senior officers had voted to retain the post and exuded optimism, and that group included Charles Lee, who immediately after the debacle tried to weasel out of his past support to hold the fort, claiming that "my last words to the General were—draw off the garrison, or they will be lost." It is also true that Washington in his letter of 8 November to Greene practically invited him to reconsider and withdraw the garrison. But the final responsibility was Washington's. His willingness to delegate authority and not micromanage his subordinates was admirable. But situations arise when top commanders must act firmly, decisively, and take the reins in their own hands. The debacle at Fort Washington reveals the indecision of mind that at times afflicted the Great Virginian, a trait he confessed to in a letter written three years later to Joseph Reed: "those opinions which were opposed to an evacuation caused that warfare in my mind and hesitation which ended in the loss of the Garrison."[49]

There was one glimmer of light in this debacle, probably little noted at the time, but described by a British officer. The Rebel officers taken prisoner at Fort Washington, Captain Mackenzie wrote in his diary, "are suffered to walk about in every part of town on their parole, and in their Uniforms. This gives great disgust to all the Loyalists. . . . They publickly avow their principles, and instead of appearing sensible of the crime they have committed, seem to glory in the cause in which they are engaged."[50]

For Washington, however, weighed down by responsibilities and anxiety that seemed more than one man could bear, prospects for the Cause could hardly have been darker. The New York campaign had come to an inglorious end. Defeat and retreat, crowned by the catastrophe at Fort Washington, had created an undercurrent of unease and dismay that would fester and eventually prompt second thoughts on whether the right man was commanding the Continental Army.

7

"Constant perplexities and mortifications"

"We . . . hoped to terminate the war amicably"

It was rainy on Manhattan Island on the night of 19 November, which would not have pleased the British soldiers who struck their tents and broke camp at nine o'clock. They were elite troops, some 5,000 strong under Lieutenant General Charles, 2nd Earl Cornwallis: two battalions of Light Infantry; two companies of Jägers; two battalions each of British and Hessian Grenadiers; two battalions of Guards; Cornwallis's own 33rd Foot, commanded in the field by the intrepid Lieutenant Colonel James Webster; and the Highlanders of Black Watch. By eleven o'clock, in the pitch black, the first wave was marching, its immediate destination Philipsburg in present-day Yonkers, where fifty flatboats awaited them. The boats had been brought up the Hudson from the fleet in two movements on still, dark waters under the noses of American sentinels, unseen, unheard, then hidden away on the Harlem River at Spuyten Duyvil. Beyond them British frigates rocked gently on the tidal waters of the river, guns ready if needed to cover the landing. As the first wave arrived and disembarked at the foot of the Palisades at eight o'clock the following morning, the second wave was marching to Philipsburg to meet the boats returning for them, and by 10:00 A.M. they, too, had landed in New Jersey. One of the most hazardous of military operations—crossing a large body of water into enemy territory—had so far gone off without a hitch.[1]

Only three days had elapsed since the fall of Fort Washington, yet to our surprise Sir William Howe was acting with unaccustomed vigor. His purpose, as he explained to Lord Germain, was to gain "entire command of the North River and a ready road to penetrate into Jersey." In their invasion of New Jersey, the British skill at operations was never shown to better effect. Probably guided by local Tories, the troops landed unopposed and at first unnoticed. The probable landing place was the unguarded Lower Closter Landing. Four years later the Rebel general Anthony Wayne rejected it for the movement of a large body of troops or supplies. But the British and Germans had no trouble disembarking and climbing the steep cliffs to the height of land called the Palisades that overlooked the Hudson and provided them with a magnificent view of Manhattan Island to the east. Sir William paid tribute to the men of the Royal Navy, who "distinguished themselves remarkably upon this occasion by their readiness to drag the cannon up a rocky narrow road for near half a mile to the top of a precipice which bounds the shore for some miles on the west side." It was 1:00 P.M. by the time the cannon had been wrestled to the top of the cliffs. Fort Lee was about 5 ½ miles away.[2]

The great English radical and pamphleteer Tom Paine, who was in Fort Lee, said that an American officer on patrol spotted the British column and made haste to the fort to sound the alarm. A rapid advance by Cornwallis would still have caught the Rebels, especially if he had angled southwest and cut their retreat on the road to Hackensack. In fact, Captain Ewald of the Jägers was so far in advance of the main force that "I discovered a great glitter of bayonets and a cloud of dust in the distance." He was only about two miles from New Bridge, which was about six miles northwest of Fort Lee. Upon investigating he found that it was indeed the Rebel column, which was bent on crossing the Hackensack River at New Bridge. Ewald began to skirmish with them and sent for reinforcements. Instead, "I received an order from Lord Cornwallis to return at once." When they met, Ewald reported what he had seen, whereupon Cornwallis said, "'Let them go my dear Ewald, and stay here. We do not want to lose any men. One jäger is worth more than ten rebels.'" This jibes with the claim of another Jäger officer, Lieutenant Johann Hinrichs, that Cornwallis's orders were "to capture Fort Lee, and

Lieutenant General Johann von Ewald, by C. A. Jensen
after a drawing by H. J. Aldenrath

to take up winter quarters in that part of the Jerseys situated between Elizabethtown and Amboy . . . at the same time Cornwallis had orders to follow the enemy, until they should make a stand, when he was to retire and not molest them, except in so far as the above districts were concerned."[3]

According to Ewald, it was not until 4:00 P.M. that the "entire army assembled," when it began its march to Fort Lee. Ewald, however, angled to the right of the column "in hopes of catching some baggage," and actually caught "A coach and four with several men . . . but I hardly wanted to pursue my game further, and I received new orders to keep closer to the column." From the evidence presented by Ewald and Hinrichs, and Cornwallis's movements, we can safely assume that Sir William had given strict orders to Cornwallis, and that he had not deviated from his brother's aim of conciliation. The perceptive Ewald quickly caught on and later had his insight verified. "Now I perceived what was afoot. We wanted to spare the King's subjects and hoped to terminate the war amicably, in which assumption I was strengthened the next day by several English officers."[4]

At Fort Lee Nathanael Greene was informed of the British landing by the alert Rebel officer. Only three weeks before, he had planned for supplies at the fort for 2,000 men for five months. The fall of Fort Washington having made Fort Lee useless, Washington had ordered the supplies evacuated, which Greene had begun. He wrote to Washington on 18 November, "I am sending off the Stores as fast as I can get Waggons. I have sent three Expresses to Newark for Boats but can get no return of what Boats we may expect from that place. The Stores here are large, and the transportation by land will be almost endless. The Powder and fixt ammunition I have sent off first by land as it is an article too valuable to trust upon the Water." Now it was too late to worry about supplies. The troops had to be saved. Determined not to suffer another humiliation, Greene ordered an immediate evacuation of the garrison. Washington received the news of the British landing independently at 10:00 A.M. and at once sent troops to secure the route of the garrison's retreat, including New Bridge. Washington rode to the crossroads of Liberty Pole to await Greene's column. He certainly sent a message to Greene, who later wrote, "His Excellency ordered a retreat immediately."[5]

After a hasty breakfast, the troops at Fort Lee began to straggle out of the fort and along the road to the village of Hackensack, nine miles away, where Washington had set up temporary headquarters. The evidence points to it being a slow, disorderly retreat, for the garrison of some two thousand to three thousand, Nathanael Greene wrote, "were mostly of the Flying Camp—irregular and undisciplind." Two hours after the retreat began, Greene had to return to Fort Lee, where Colonel Ezekiel Cornell "and myself got off several hundred. Yet notwithstanding all our endeavors still near a hundred remained hid above in the Woods." These men, estimated at 50 to 200, depending on the source, were in no condition to resist. An American soldier wrote, "There Was a Great many Was taken that Got Drunk With they Sutlers Liquir and nocked they heads ought of the hogsheads."[6]

The real loss at Fort Lee was eighteen pieces of artillery, flour, all of their tents, and almost all of their entrenching tools. And in the meadows between the fort and Hackensack, wrote a British officer, "The number of cattle taken . . . which had been driven from Pennsylvania and some parts of the Jerseys for the use of the grand rebel army, is truly astonishing, and amount to many thousands." Not quite the disaster of Fort Washington, but close to it. What can be more disheartening to soldiers already harried and driven than having their traveling commissary taken and sleeping night after night exposed to the elements? As they marched into the village of Hackensack they were a sorry lot. A villager watched them. "The night was dark, cold, and rainy, but I had a fair view of Greene's troops from the light of the windows as they passed on our side of the street. They marched two abreast, looked ragged, some without a shoe to their feet, and most of them were wrapped in their blankets." As desperate as the situation was, however, Nathanael Greene had not entirely disgraced himself with his unwarranted optimism on the chances of holding Fort Washington. As a result of his foresight and efforts the Rebel Army would not go hungry during its retreat. At six depots between Hackensack and Trenton, he had laid in ample supplies of flour, meat, hay, and grain.[7]

While the Rebels considered their miserable situation, at Fort Lee and vicinity the victors not only swept up the official spoils but turned greedily to the fields and homes of the bountiful Dutch farm country. Cornwallis, of course, forbade plundering, as British generals always did, and as always his troops ignored him. It was, as far as they were concerned, their right, and they made no fine distinction between Rebels or Tories. Captain Ewald wrote, "During the night all the plantations in the vicinity were plundered, and whatever the soldiers found in the houses was declared booty." Even allowing for exaggeration, Nathanael Greene's description of British and Hessian plundering rings true in a letter to his wife: "their footsteps are marked with destruction wherever they go. There is no difference between the Whigs and Tories—all fare alike. They take the Cloaths off of the Peoples back. The distress they spread wherever they go exceeds all description."[8]

Distress also afflicted the Rebel commander in chief, who had expressed his pessimism the day before the British landing in a letter to his brother:

> [I]t is impossible for me in the compass of a Letter to give you any Idea of our Situation—of my difficulties—& the constant perplexities and mortifications. . . . I am wearied almost to death with the retrograde Motions of things, and Solemnly protest that a pecuniary rewd of 20,000 Ls a year would not induce me to undergo what I do. . . . God

grant you all health and happiness—nothing in this world would contribute so much to mine as to be once more fixed among you in the peaceable enjoymt of my own vine, & fig Tree.[9]

Had one British officer—probably the young Lord Rawdon, a future governor-general of India and victor over the Gurkhas—read Washington's letter, it would have strengthened his belief that the Rebel end was near. He wrote to a friend in England,

> You see, my dear sir, that I have not been mistaken in my judgement of this people. The southern people will no more fight than the Yankees. The fact is that their army is broken all to pieces, and the spirits of their leaders and their abettors is also broken . . . one may venture to pronounce that it is well nigh over with them.[10]

"This conduct of General Lee's appeared not a little extraordinary"

Now, however, with another crisis facing him, Washington as always swept aside longings for his "vine, & fig Tree," looked at the dwindling numbers in his army, and decided he needed help, and quickly. He had present and fit for duty only about 3,700 men, and of these, some 1,600 were the Pennsylvania militia previously described by Nathanael Greene as "irregular and undisciplined." The New Jersey militia had proved craven in the face of the British invasion. The "Jersey militia," Greene wrote, "behaves scurvily and, I fear, are not deserving the freedom we are contending for." It was time, therefore, to order Charles Lee to cross the river with his some 3,400 Continentals and link up with Washington's force. The reader will recall from the previous chapter that Washington had prepared Lee for such a move in his "instructions" of 10 November. On 20 November, the day Cornwallis rode into Fort Lee, Washington put those "Instructions" into effect by having his military secretary, Lieutenant Colonel Robert Hanson Harrison, write to Lee, alerting him that the British had crossed the Hudson "in great numbers," and therefore "His Excellency thinks it would be advisable in you to remove the troops under your command on this side of the North River, & there wait farther orders." Washington himself wrote the next day, politely in deference to Lee's seniority, experience, and reputation, but also quite clearly, that Lee should cross the river. "Upon the whole . . . I am of the Opinion & the Gentlemen about me concur in it that the publick Interest requires your coming over to this Side with the Continental Troops." Then, with equal clarity as well as cogency, he described his strategy:

> My Reasons for this Measure & which I think must have weight with you are—that the Enemy are evidently changing the Seat of War to this Side of the North River—that this Country therefore will expect the Continental Army to give what Support they can & failing in this will cease to depend upon or support a Force from which no Protection is given to them. It is therefore of the utmost Importance that at least an Appearance of Force should be made to keep this Province in the Connection with the others—if that should not continue it is much to be feared that its Influence on Pennsylvania would be very considerable & more endanger our publick Interests. Unless therefore some new Event should occur, or some more cogent Reason present itself I would have you move over by the easiest & best Passage.[11]

But the last thing Lee wanted was to unite his troops with Washington's and thereafter play second fiddle to a man whose abilities he scorned. Writing on 21 November to James Bowdoin (1726–1790), president of the Massachusetts Council, he first broached his idea of two independent armies, his east of the Hudson, Washington's west of the river. Washington was worried about New Jersey, but what if the British "might alter the present direction of their operations, and attempt to open the passage of the Highlands, or enter New England"? If he crossed the river and joined Washington, New England could be lost. "We must depend on ourselves," he warned Bowdoin. To further his scheme of remaining at a distance and independent of his commander in chief, Lee inadvertently set off a dispute between himself and Major General William Heath, whom the reader will recall had been assigned by Washington to guard the Hudson Highlands. To get a good look at Lee the schemer in action, we need to look at this affair in some detail.[12]

The same day he wrote to Bowdoin, General Lee also wrote to General Heath: "I have just received a recommendation, not a positive order, from the General, to move the corps under my command to the other side of the river." Here Lee chose to interpret the polite language habitually used by Washington and his aides as only a recommendation, but it was an order, as Washington's words "& there wait farther orders" make clear. "I must desire and request," Lee continued, "that you will order 2,000 of your corps, under a Brigadier-General, to cross the river opposite the General, and wait his further orders."[13]

Heath, whose command was independent of Lee's, examined his "instructions" from Washington and on the 21st replied quite accurately that they did not "admit of moving any part of the troops from the posts assigned to me, unless it be by the express orders from his Excellency, or to support you, in case you are attacked." Lee responded two days later. "By your mode of reasoning, the General's instructions are so binding, that not a tittle must be broke through, for the salvation of the General and the army," and announced that "I intend to take 2000 of your division with me into the Jersies; so I must desire that you will have that number in readiness by the day after tomorrow, when I shall be with you early in the forenoon." Heath, however, was stubborn as well as faithful to his orders, and replied on the 24th, "Be my mode of reasoning as it may, I conceive it to be my duty to obey my instructions." Then, obviously uneasy, he wrote that same day to Washington, relating the dispute, his feelings on the matter, and enclosing copies of his exchange of correspondence with Lee. Washington replied the next day through Colonel Harrison: "In respect to the troops intended to come to this quarter, his Excellency never meant that they should be from your division. He has wrote General Lee since, so fully and explicitly upon the subject, that any misapprehensions he may have been under at first must now be done away." Washington had written to Lee the previous day after seeing a letter Lee had written to the adjutant general, Joseph Reed, in which he had given his reasons why he could not cross the Hudson "in time to answer any purpose," and had "order'd General Heath . . . to detach two thousand men." This provoked Washington to send Lee a reply that did not mince words:

> I perceive by your letter to Colo. Reed, that you have entirely mistaken my views in ordering Troops from Genl Heath's Division to this Quarter. The posts and passes in the Highlands, are of such infinite importance, that they should not be subjected to the least possible degree of risk . . . it was your division which I wanted & wish to march.[14]

That should have ended the matter. But we are dealing with the volatile Lee, who always had an excuse for not obeying Washington's orders. Their exchange of correspondence continued, with Washington ordering Lee to march and Lee promising that he would but always finding excuses why he could not come immediately. Washington's irritation is revealed again in a letter of the 27th, in which his usual courteous manner of framing orders to senior commanders was set aside. "My former letters were so full and explicit as to the necessity of your marching as early as possible, that it is unnecessary to add more on that Head. I confess I expected you would have been sooner in motion." Lee's reply on the 30th was typical: "You complain of my not being in motion sooner. I do assure you that I have done all in my power and shall explain my difficulties when We both have leisure." After committing to crossing the river on 2 December, he had the gall to add that then "I shou'd be glad to receive your instructions but I cou'd wish you wou'd bind me as little as possible—not from any opinion, I do assure you, of my own parts—but from a perswasion that detach'd Generals cannot have too great a latitude—unless they are very incompetent indeed." Here Lee confuses latitude with freewheeling independence, and is assuming that even after crossing to the Jersey side he will not be joining Washington but will continue as a detached commander. So as the reader can clearly see, our story in this regard will not end with Lee's arrival in New Jersey.[15]

At least poor Heath was off the hook. Or was he? Lee's annoyance with Heath, probably exacerbated by the thought of being under Washington's control, was made quite clear in his letter to Heath of the 26th, which began,

> I perceive that You have form'd an opinion to Yourself that shou'd General Washington remove to the Streights of Magellan, the instructions he left with You . . . have to all intents and purposes invested you with a command separate from and independant of any other superior—that General Heath and General Lee are merely two major generals, who perhaps ought to hold a friendly intercourse with each other—and, when their humor or fancied interests prompts, may afford mutual assistance but that General Heath is by no means to consider himself oblig'd to obey any orders of the Second in Ciommand.[16]

By the time Lee with his troops reached Heath's headquarters in Peekskill, New York, on 30 November, old "Boiling Water" had no doubt worked himself into a fury. Washington had specifically forbidden him to order any of Heath's command over the river, but Lee was determined to make Heath suffer for defying him, and this led to a dramatic confrontation related by General Heath. Picture the two men. Lee:

homely, skinny as a rail, with a big nose, a sarcastic manner, dogmatic opinions, and at the time a shining military reputation. Heath: stolid, unimaginative, by his own admission bald and very fat, but good at the crucial art of logistics and utterly loyal to Washington and the Cause.[17]

Lee dismounted, and Heath invited him into his headquarters and offered him a cup of tea. Lee said "he should have a good one," but before sitting down told Heath he wished to speak to him in private. When they were alone, Lee said, "In *point of law,* you are right; but in point of policy, I think you are wrong. I am going into the Jersies for the salvation of America; I wish to take with me a larger force than I now have, and request you to order 2,000 of your men to march with me." Heath said he could not spare 2,000 men. Then give me 1,000, Lee said. Heath said, "that not a single man should march from the post by *his* order." In that case, said Lee, he would give the order himself. Heath acknowledged that Lee was his senior, but Washington had made it quite clear that no troops should be taken from Heath's command. To drive his point home, Heath showed Lee the letter he had recently received from Washington. Lee's considerable ego bridled at that. "The Commander in Chief," he said, "is now at a distance and does not know what is necessary here so well as I do." By that time others had joined them. Lee asked for Heath's "return-book" (strength report), and it was handed over. Lee examined it, chose two regiments, and said to Heath's deputy adjutant general, Major Ebenezer Huntington (1754–1834), "You will order those two regiments to march early tomorrow morning to join me." Whereupon Heath, showing commendable backbone, said to Major Huntington in the dramatic fashion the occasion required, "Issue such orders at your peril!"

Having established himself as no pushover, General Heath then neatly escaped his quandary, saying to General Lee, "Sir, if you come to this post, and mean to issue orders here, which will break those positive ones which I have received, pray you to do it completely yourself, and through your own Deputy Adjutant-General, who is present, and not draw me or any of my family, in as partners in the guilt." Lee agreed. Colonel Alexander Scammell (1747–1781) issued the order, and Major Huntington transmitted it. After the intercession of Brigadier General George Clinton of New York, Lee even agreed to sign a statement absolving Heath of blame. Early the next morning, 1 December 1776, as the two regiments from Heath's command were marching toward their embarkation point on the Hudson, came the incredible outcome to what was undeniably an important matter but in the hands of Charles Lee ended in farce.

As he rode toward the river, Lee reined in at Heath's door, "and calling him" outside, said, "'Upon further consideration, I have concluded not to take the two regiments with me—you may order them to return to their former post.'"

So the end of the affair turned out to be nothing but an exercise in control, just to prove a point. Heath confessed to being nonplussed, yet he read Lee correctly: "This conduct of General Lee's appeared not a little extraordinary, and one is almost at a loss to account for it. He had been soldier from his youth, had a perfect knowledge of the service in all its branches, but was rather obstinate in his temper, and could scarcely brook being crossed in anything in the line of his profession."

Fortunately, at this time of peril for the Cause, Lee's outrageous behavior was not duplicated elsewhere, and help was on the way from other quarters. On 23 November Congress directed the Board of War to order 9th Virginia, then on the Eastern Shore, to Philadelphia, and the 8th and 12th Pennsylvania Regiments to New Brunswick, "or to join General Washington" wherever he was, all three "to March with all possible expedition." John Hancock directed Washington to order General Schuyler in the Northern Department to "immediately" transfer from his command to Washington's the regiments from Pennsylvania and New Jersey. Schuyler wrote to Robert Hanson Harrison on 3 December that he had anticipated the order and in addition to the troops requested had ordered "part of seven other Regiments . . . to join the General, the last embarked Yesterday at Albany with General Gates . . . and he writes me that he will carefully comply with the Directions contained in Your's."[18]

"No lads ever shew greater activity in retreating than we have"

Washington, meanwhile, continued to retreat, although not in haste, for Cornwallis faithfully followed Howe's orders and did not press the Rebel Army. By 21 November Washington was eight miles west of Hackensack and safely across the Passaic River at Aquakinunk (modern Passaic), "where," he wrote, "we can watch the Operations of the Enemy without danger of their surrounding us or making a Lodgment in our Rear." This is precisely what Sir Henry Clinton recommended to Sir William Howe. But Sir William had already ordered Sir Henry to take command of an expedition to capture Newport, Rhode Island, and the magnificent anchorages in Narragansett Bay. More than 6,000 troops assigned to a sideshow: one battalion of Light Infantry, one battalion of British Grenadiers, the 3rd and 5th British Brigades of Foot, and two Hessian Brigades. The reason, Sir Henry wrote, was because Lord Howe "wanted a winter station for his large ships." Sir Henry was against the Rhode Island expedition, and after Cornwallis landed in New Jersey, Clinton proposed first to Sir William, then to his brother, that "instead of going to Rhode Island Lord Percy and I should be landed at Amboy, and endeavor to intercept Washington in his retreat to the Delaware." If Sir William had meant to crush Washington and destroy his army, this was the sensible way to do it. But it must be obvious to us by this time that Sir William had no such intention. On 1 December fifty-four warships and transports hoisted sail and proceeded up the East River toward Hell Gate and Long Island Sound, bound for Newport, where the troops would remain for three years to no good purpose. Once again the British captains exhibited their superb seamanship. "The day being very clear and fine," wrote Captain Mackenzie, who was on the expedition, "the appearance of so many large ships going through such a narrow and dangerous passage, in a line ahead, with all their sails set, and with considerable velocity, afforded a grand and pleasing sight. In some places a stone might have been thrown on either shore." Grand and pleasing it must have been, but also a total waste of resources. The verdict of the British historian George Trevelyan on the Rhode Island expedition still stands firmly ninety-two years later: "For any effect which they produced upon the general result of the war, they might have been as usefully, and much more agreeably, billeted in the town of the same name in the Isle of Wight."[19]

Meanwhile, by 23 November Washington and his little army had reached Newark, twelve miles south of Hackensack.. The leisurely pace of the British pursuit, if *pursuit* is not too ambitious a word, can be gauged by Washington's stay at Newark: he did not leave until the 28th. On the day of his arrival he reported 5,140 men fit for duty. Of these, the service of 2,060 was due to expire on 1 December, and that of 950 on 1 January 1777. Nevertheless, one of Washington's aides, Lieutenant Colonel Samuel Blachley Webb, who had been wounded at White Plains, writing from Newark to Joseph Trumbull, gave further evidence of the

slowness of the British advance as well as a description of the army's
condition laced with humor,

> You ask me a true Account of our Situation; 'tis next to Impossible to
> give it to you; I can only say that no lads ever shew greater activity in
> retreating than we have since we left You. Our Soldiers are the best
> fellows in the World at this Business. Fatal necessity has obliged Us to
> give up to the Enemy much of a fine country, well Wooded, Watered
> & Stock'd; not only that, but our Cannon, Mortars, Ordinance Stores,
> etc. are mostly gone. Our whole Body did not amount to Two Thou-
> sand at the time the Enemy landed in the Jerseys, of consequence we
> had it not in our power to make a stand, 'till we arrived at this place,
> where we have collected our Force, & are not only ready, but willing,
> to Meet the Lads in blue & Red as soon as they think proper. 'Tis a
> sacred truth they never have yet ventured to Attack us but with great
> Advantages they pursue no faster than their heavy Artillery can be
> brught up. With this they Scour every piece of Wood, Stone Walls,
> etc. before they approach. If they come on soon we shall I trust give a
> good acct to our Country. This must be before ye 1st of December, as
> most of the troops on this side are then their own Masters.[20]

On the day he arrived in Newark, Washington sent the influential
Pennsylvanian Thomas Mifflin to Philadelphia with a letter and dispatches to John Hancock: "In order that you may be fully apprized of
our Weakness and of the necessity there is of our obtaining early Suc-
cours, I have by the advice of the Genl Officers here, directed Genl.
Mifflin to wait on you. He is intimately acquainted with our circumstances and will represent them better, than my hurried state will allow."
The following day he sent his trusted adjutant general, Joseph Reed,
with a brief letter to William Livingston, governor of New Jersey, on the
"Critical Situation of our affairs," and in order that Livingston might
"form a perfect Idea of what is now necessary," he referred him to Reed
for "Particulars." Concerned with what might be happening in his rear,
on that same day Washington wrote to Colonel David Forman (1745–
1797), a particularly keen foe of Tories who was then commanding a
regiment of New Jersey state levies, that he had "received information
that there is danger of an Insurrection of Tories in the County of Monmouth," and ordered Forman to march there and "apprehend all such
persons as from good Information appear to be concerned in any Plot or
Design against the Liberty or Safety of the united states." And in addi-

tion to these and all of the other matters to be dealt with at this time of peril to the cause, he was engaged in the frustrating correspondence with Charles Lee described earlier. Lee, of course, was still east of the Hudson wrangling with Heath and racking his fertile brain for reasons why he should not cooperate with his commander in chief.[21]

And while this was going on, the rich New Jersey countryside continued to suffer the ravages of contending armies. As the British army marched toward Newark, Captain Ewald wrote, "we looked upon a deplorable sight. The region is well cultivated, with very attractive plantations, but all their occupants had fled and all the houses had been or were being plundered and destroyed."[22]

Cornwallis took eight days to advance twenty-one miles against token opposition. Once he arrived in front of Newark, on 28 November, Washington retreated about twenty-five miles southwest to New Brunswick, arriving on the 29th. There, on the following day, he received a shock that hurt him deeply and, if it was possible by then, depressed him even further.

"I . . . lament with you that fatal indecision of mind"

Nine days before, Washington had written to Lee. Just before the courier left, Washington's friend and trusted adjutant general, Joseph Reed, slipped into his saddlebag his own, private, letter to Lee. It was, as we like to say today, a bombshell:

> I do not mean to to flatter, nor praise you at the Expence of any other, but I confess I do think that it is entirely owing to you that this Army & the Liberties of America so far as they are dependent on it are not totally cut off. You have Decision, a Quality often wanting in Minds otherwise valuable & I ascribe to this our Escape from York Island— from Kingsbridge & the Plains—& I have no Doubt had you been here the Garrison at Mount Washington would have composed a Part of this Army. Under all these Circumstances I confess I ardently wish to see you removed from a Place where I think there will be little Call for your Judgment & Experience to the place where they are like to be so necessary. Nor am I singular in my Opinion—every Gentleman of the Family the Officers & soldiers generally have a Confidence in you—the Enemy constantly inquire where you are, & seem to me to be less confident when you are present.

Reed then took up the disaster at Mount Washington, where

General Washington's own Judgment seconded by Representations from us, would have savd the Men & their Arms but unluckily, General Greene's Judgt was contrary. This kept the Generals Mind in a State of Suspence till the Stroke was Struck—Oh! General—an indecisive Mind is one the greatest Misfortunes that befall an Army—how often have I lamented it in this Campaign.

Reed proposed what can only be interpreted as an end run around Washington:

All Circumstances considered we are in a very awful & alarming State one that requires the utmost Wisdom & Firmness of Mind—as soon as the Season will admit I think yourself & some others should go to Congress & form the Plan of the new Army.[23]

Washington probably never saw this letter, but in Reed's absence from headquarters he opened Lee's reply of 24 November by mistake, and its tenor left little doubt as to the general nature of Reed's letter:

I receiv'd your most obliging flattering letter—lament with you that fatal indecision of mind which in war is a much greater disqualification than stupidity or even want of personal courage—accident may put a decisive Blunderer in the right—but eternal defeat and miscarriage must attend the man of best parts if curs'd with indecision.[24]

Toward the end of this letter Lee included a self-congratulatory comment that must have stung: "to confess a truth I really think our Chief will do better with me than without me."

Washington forwarded the letter to Reed with a brief note:

The inclosed was put into my hands by an Express from the White Plains. Having no Idea of its being a Private Letter, must less suspecting the tendency of the Correspondence, I opened it, as I had done all other Letters to you, from the Same place and Peekskill, upon the business of your office, as I conceived and found them to be.

This as it is the truth, must be an excuse for Seeing the Contents of a Letter, which neither inclination or intention would have prompted me to.[25]

Several months would elapse before the breach between the two men was healed.

Why "did we march so slowly"?

At 1:00 P.M. on 1 December, the British advance was sighted marching on New Brunswick. The Rebel Army had been informed that they were coming, "causing us to prepare to meet them," wrote Sergeant James McMichael of the Pennsylvania rifle regiment, but adding, "we are reduced to so small a number we have little hopes of victory." Nor did their commander in chief. About an hour later, McMichael and his comrades were ordered to withdraw toward Princeton. Nathanael Greene claimed that the evacuation of New Brunswick was forced upon Washington by "another convincing proof of the folly of short enlistments. The time for which the five months men were engaged expird at this critical period. Two Brigades left us at Brunswick notwithstanding the Enemy were within two hours march and coming on." These troops were New Jersey militia defending their own state, but when asked to extend their term of service they refused and marched for home.[26]

Before leaving New Brunswick, Washington wrote once again to Charles Lee: "The force I have with me, is infinitely inferior in number and such as cannot give or promise the least successfull opposition. It is greatly reduced by the departure of the Maryland flying Camp men and Sundry other causes. I must entreat you to hasten your march as much as possible or your arrival may be too late to answer any valuable purpose." But Lee was still on the east side of the Hudson and would not cross until the following day.[27]

According to Greene, when the army left New Brunswick, "we had not 3000 men, a very pitiful army to trust the Liberties of America upon." Washington and the main army reached Trenton on the Delaware River on 2 December. From there on 4 December, Greene wrote, "Our numbers are still small, not to exceed 5000, but dayly increasing." Greene was also "in hopes the General will give orders to advance upon the Enemy tomorrow," which tells us that Greene, a fighting general, had not yet acquired the prudence that would be one of his strengths when later in the war he matched wits with the man now following the Rebel Army: Lord Cornwallis.[28]

Haslet's Delaware Regiment was the last unit to leave New Brunswick. In command of a company was Captain Enoch Anderson, who had just reenlisted for three years or the duration of the war, whichever came first. "It was near sundown," Captain Anderson wrote, "when Colonel Haslet came to me and told me to take as many men as I thought proper, and go back and burn all the tents. 'We have no wagons,' said he, 'to carry them off, and it is better to burn them than they should fall into the hands of the enemy.' Then I went and burned them—about one hundred tents." Anderson and his men would have bitter reason to think of those tents that night:

> When we saw them reduced to ashes, it was night, and the army was far ahead. We made a double quick-step and came up with the army about eight o'clock. We encamped in the woods, with no victuals, no tents, no blankets. The night was cold and we all suffered much, especially those who had no shoes.[29]

It was probably not the first night and certainly would not be the last when Captain Anderson and his men lay on the cold, hard ground. A few nights later, on the other side of the Delaware, "we lay amongst the leaves without tents or blankets, laying down with our feet to the fire. It was very cold." And years later these dreadful experiences made him ponder on the difference between reading about war and experiencing it:

> God spared me; for throughout all the scenes and suffereings of the campaign I was not sick a day. I had read the history of Charles XII, King of Sweden, who had inured himself by degrees to the exposure of all weathers, so that he could lay down on the snow of Norway in mid-winter in sixty degrees of north latitude and take a nap! It was fun then to me. I now often thought of Charles XII.[30]

At Trenton, Washington reported to John Hancock that a "great Quantity" of "military and other Stores and Baggage" had been removed over the river to the Pennsylvania side, and "immediately upon my Arrival here, I ordered the Removal of all" the rest. "I hope to have every thing secured this Night and tomorrow if we are not disturbed. After being disincumbered of my Baggage and Stores, my future Situation will depend interely upon Circumstances." But where was Lee? "I have not heard a Word from General Lee since the 26th, which surprises me not a little, as I have dispatched daily Expresses to him desiring to know when I might look for him." Even Congress was unsettled by the eccentric Englishman's failure to either appear or communicate. General Horatio Gates had sent his aide-de-camp, Major Walter Stewart (c. 1756–1796), to Congress with dispatches, and Congress, after promoting Stewart to brevet lieutenant colonel, had directed him to ride north to Lee, "to know where and in what situation he and the army with him are." Stewart passed through Trenton, and in his letter of 3 December to Hancock, Washington wrote, "I have this Minute dispatched Colo. Stewart . . . to meet Genl. Lee and bring me an Account." He probably sent with Stewart his letter of the 3rd to Lee, directing the errant general "to give me frequent advices of your approach."[31]

But Lee, marching as always to a different drummer, had other plans. Replying to an earlier letter to Washington, he wrote from Haverstraw, New York—he was finally across the river—on 4 December that since Washington had left New Brunswick, "it is impossible to know where I can join you." But he had an idea that might be better than linking his force with Washington's. The column from the Northern Department dispatched by Schuyler to reinforce Washington

> has already advanced nearer Morris Town than I am. I shall put myself at their head tomorrow. We shall upon the whole compose an Army of five thousand good Troops in spirits. I should imagin, Dr General, that it may be of service to communicate this to the Corps immediately under your Command. It may encourage them and startle the Enemy. In fact this confidence must be risen to prodigious heighth, if They pursue you, with so formidable a Body hanging on their flank, or rear.[32]

The gall of the man. He was in direct disobedience of Washington's orders to join him. Now he meant to hijack Washington's reinforcements to augment his own force. The conceit of the man. Dear General, think of your own troops, how they would rejoice to know that they were saved. Lee has arrived!

Charles Lee was not the only character of the Revolution bloated by ego, but he was certainly the most audacious. Although much can be said for his plan to hang on the flank and rear of the British army, whether he was right or wrong is irrelevant. His duty was to join Washington. But in refusing that duty he had made his ambition quite clear. There can be no doubt that Lee wanted to succeed Washington. That fine historian and Lee's not unfriendly biographer John Alden certainly implied that when he wrote, "If Lee succeeded in breaking up the British communications and in maintaining a position at Chatham or Morristown, he would gain great credit while Washington acquired none.

Certainly such successes would render it impossible for the commander in chief to call him to account for disobedience to orders, difficult to prove in the circumstances. Indeed, Lee might well vault into the supreme command."[33]

Despite Lee's failure to join him, Washington had not given up on the possibility of making a stand in New Jersey. He blamed his inability to stop the British at river crossings, where fording places were often "knee deep only," on the failure of the New Jersey militia to turn out and reinforce his small army of Continentals, and the "want of exertion in the Principal Gentlemen of the Country." He repeated to Hancock his frequent observation that they could place "little dependance upon Militia in times of real danger" and that a larger standing army was necessary. Of the militia he wrote, "When danger is a little removed from them, they will not turn out at all. When it comes home to 'em, the well affected instead of flying to Arms to defend themselves, are busily employed removing their Families and Effects." Nevertheless, now that almost all of the army's supplies and baggage were safely across the Delaware, "I shall now . . . face about with such Troops are here fit for service, and march back to Princeton and there govern myself by circumstances and the movements of General Lee." That same day he dispatched Colonel Richard Humpton (c. 1732–1804) to find both Lee and the regiments from the Northern Department.[34]

In the meantime his opponents the Howe brothers, to further their policy of maneuver and conciliation, had five days before issued a proclamation. Throughout the war British senior commanders were very fond of issuing proclamations, none of which had any effect on the overall course of the war. In their latest effort Lord Howe and his brother promised full pardons to those who appeared before a British official within sixty days and swore allegiance to the king. Lord Howe's secretary, Ambrose Serle, issued the most trenchant criticism of the proclamation: "its Effects will only be coextensive with the Power of the Sword." The linchpin of the Revolution was the Continental Army. A swift and ruthless pursuit by Cornwallis once he had crossed the Hudson, not a proclamation, was the key to destroying that army. But as we know, the strategy of the Howe brothers was not a crushing victory but an almost benign display of British military invincibility, a maneuvering of the Rebel Army into an impossible situation in which, its morale destroyed, its prospects hopeless, it would either surrender or melt away. Then the mass of disaffected colonists and their leaders, delusions shattered, would rejoin the British family. Once again the Hessian Jäger captain Johann Ewald asked the pertinent questions. Why had they allowed the escape of the garrison at Fort Lee? Why "did we march so slowly," thus allowing the Rebels to cross rivers safely? Why did the army linger at New Brunswick for five days instead of engaging in hot pursuit? Captain Ewald answered his own questions. "One had to conclude, therefore, that we had hopes of ending the war amicably, without shedding the blood of the King's subjects in a needless way."[35]

"This is a misfortune that cannot be remedied"

On 7 December Washington began his planned advance to Princeton, but on the road he received intelligence that the British "were advancing by different Routs and attempting by One to get in the rear of our Troops," whereupon he ordered a retreat, and on the following day the army crossed the Delaware to the relative safety of Pennsylvania. Although Washington's returns were not exact because of the "disordered and moving state of the army," he estimated that he had 3,000 to 3,500 men present and fit for duty, plus about another 2,000 militia from Pennsylvania who had just joined him. According to the Rebel sergeant James McMichael, the crossing began at dawn, and the British arrived at about 4:00 P.M. Captain Ewald wrote that the Jägers "were detached immediately . . . to seize the rear guard of the enemy at the crossing, but the last boats were already leaving the shore when we were still about three hundred paces away," and the Jägers had to disperse because of "devastating fire" from Rebel artillery across the river. It was very cold that night. From the opposite shore Sergeant McMichael wrote, "Here we remained in the woods, having neither blankets or tents."[36]

Sir William himself rode into the "devastating fire," for while he had many faults, lack of courage was not one of them. Howe, Cornwallis, and three aides, including Howe's Hessian aide-de-camp, Captain Levin Friedrich Ernst von Münchhausen (1753–1795), went through Trenton, von Münchhausen wrote, to "a plain more than 200 paces wide with the Delaware to the right and a wooded valley to the left." There, "Just as we arrived, the rebels opened a terrific fire upon us with all their batteries . . . . The light infantry and jägers were forced to retreat in the greatest hurry to the valley at the left. On their way, in the blink of an eye, they lost 13 men." But in the eighteenth century it would not do for officers to seek cover, and von Münchhausen's description of the following incident brings us the flavor of war when generals of senior rank deliberately exposed themselves to enemy fire, a time when almost all officers came of a class for whom a display of fear in the face of danger would have disgraced them forever in the eyes of their entire society and was therefore worse than death itself:

> General Howe rode with us all around, stopping from time to time; he stayed there with the greatest coolness and calm for at least an hour, while the rebels kept the strongest fire going. Wherever we turned the cannonballs hit the ground, and I can hardly understand, even now, why all five of us were not crushed by the many balls, then, just as General Howe was about to move back into the town, a ball landed so close to him in soft ground that dirt splattered his body and face.
>
> A little earlier I had the honor to receive a small contusion on my knee. We were just standing still when a ball took away the hind leg of my horse, and hit some stones on the ground, one of which hit me in the knee, and caused my leg to swell up . . . my horse fell to the ground with me, with great force. . . . Afterwards General Howe gave me a superb English horse to replace mine.[37]

Meanwhile, where was Lee? In his report on the crossing to Hancock, Washington also wrote that he had "no certain intelligence of Genl Lee," but he had sent another officer, Major Robert Hoops, in search of Lee and to inform him that "I would provide Boats near a place called Alexandria" for his crossing. "I cannot account," he added, "for the slowness of his march." The day before Washington crossed the river, news had come of Lee that Washington no doubt had in hand when he wrote to Hancock. From Princeton General Greene reported that he had received intelligence that "General Lee is at the Heels of the Enimy." And on the 8th, from Morristown, the great man himself deigned to write—twice. "If I was not taught to think that your Army was considerably reinforc'd I should immediately join you, but as I am assurd you are very strong I shoud imagine We can make a better impression by hanging on their rear." But the same day, in search of Washington's phantom subordinate, Major Hoops rode into Lee's camp with another letter from the commander in chief, and upon reading it Lee hastened to reply that "I am extremely shock'd to hear that your force is so inadequate to the necessity of your situation." But he believed that Washington was in no danger of being forced to cross the Delaware, and lamented that "it will be difficult I am afraid to join you but cannot I do you more service by attacking their rear? I shall look about me tomorrow and inform you further."[38]

In fairness to Lee, we must admit that his plan to harry the British flanks and rear had merit. Cornwallis had left an entire brigade behind him at Amboy to cover his rear, which, von Münchhausen wrote a day or two after Lee arrived in New Jersey, "was most necessary since all the information we received regarding the corps of General Lee indicated that he intended to cross the Hudson River and get into the rear and right flank of our corps." On the 10th von Münchhausen wrote, "General Lee who is in our rear, makes our support line very unsafe. He often sends out raiding parties. Last night one of them captured a small escort with eight baggage wagons." And on the following day, "The support lines behind us become more and more unsafe because of General Lee, who is very audacious. He has captured several patrols and individual dragoons with letters, and has taken 700 oxen and nearly 1,000 sheep and hogs from our commissariat." There can be no doubt that von Münchhausen was expressing the common opinion among both British and Germans when he described Lee as "the only rebel general whom we had cause to fear." None of this, however, excuses his insubordination and his failure to march immediately to Washington's aid.[39]

Tomorrow came and went, but Lee stayed in Morristown until the 11th, writing to Washington that his "three thousand Men . . . are so ill shod that We have been oblig'd to halt these two days for want of shoes," an excuse he had earlier used while resisting Washington's orders that he cross the Hudson to New Jersey. Washington had directed Lee to angle to the southwest and cross the Delaware far north of Trenton, to avoid being intercepted by the British. Boats had been gathered for him. But Lee, who always knew better, also was contemplating another maneuver. If Howe's advance crossed the Delaware, he "thinks He can without great risk" cross British lines "and by a forc'd nights March make his way to the ferry below Burlington. Boats should be sent up from Philadelphia to receive him." A frustrated, exasperated Washington replied on the 14th, "I am much surprized that you should be in any doubt respecting the Route you should take after the information you have had upon that Head as well by Letter from Majr Hoops who was dispatched for the purpose. A large number of boats was procured and is still retained at Tinnicum under a strong guard to facilitate your passage across the Delaware."[40]

Lee never received Washington's final letter to him, for two nights earlier, in the language of the time, Providence had intervened on behalf of the Cause.

On 12 December Lee was a few miles southwest of Morristown. Whatever his reasons, he decided to follow Washington's orders. That night he ordered his deputy, Major General John Sullivan, to take the road to Easton, Pennsylvania, the next day. Then Lee decided not to sleep in camp that night but at a tavern owned by the widow White at Basking Ridge, three miles away. His motive is unknown, and there is no evidence for the tale that it was an assignation with a woman, although it certainly would have been in character. He took with him his aide-de-camp, Major William Bradford; Major James Wilkinson, who had arrived with dispatches from General Gates; two French officers; and his personal guard of some fifteen men.[41]

But George Washington was not the only general searching for Lee's army. So was Cornwallis. On the night Lee opted for the comforts of a tavern, Cornwallis sent out a scouting party of twenty-five men and four officers of 16th Light Dragoons, commanded by Lieutenant Colonel William Harcourt. Ironically, the 16th had served under Lee in Portugal in 1762. One of its junior officers, Cornet Banastre Tarleton (1754–1833), then twenty-two and fiercely ambitious, would later become the most feared British cavalry officer of the war. By the early morning of 13 December Harcourt was moving in the direction of Morristown when they met a Tory who told them where Lee's army was located. They were then only four or five miles from the tavern where Lee slept, but they did not then know this. Cautiously, Harcourt advanced. One mile from the tavern, two American sentries were captured. Threatened with death unless they talked, the sentries revealed Lee's location. Harcourt pondered. He was in dangerous territory with a small force, yet a glittering prize lay before him. He sent Cornet Tarleton and two privates ahead to reconnoiter. They seized an American horseman and brought him to Colonel Harcourt. Faced with a choice between the saber and his life, the horseman gave up his dispatch from Lee to Sullivan and told the British that he had just left Lee at the tavern. Harcourt conferred with his officers, then decided to strike. It was Friday, 13 December.

General Sullivan with Lee's army marched for the Delaware at 8:00 A.M., but Lee tarried at the tavern until ten that morning. He prepared a much-quoted letter to General Gates for Major Wilkinson to deliver, in which he wrote, "*entre nous*, a certain great man is damnably deficient . . . unless something which I do not expect turns up we are lost—our counsels have been weak to the last degree." That done, he was ready to leave. But precisely then Harcourt's horsemen struck from two directions. Lee's guard was totally surprised and routed. Two guards were killed, others were wounded. A fusillade poured into the house. Lee watched from an upstairs window as his little world collapsed.[42]

About fifteen minutes after the initial assault, following a British threat to fire the tavern, and the widow White's pleas to spare her property, Lee sent out word that he would surrender. The British wasted little time once Lee came out of the house. He was mounted on a horse behind a trooper, and Harcourt and his men galloped off with their prize. By that evening Lee was imprisoned in New Brunswick, New Jersey. One French officer escaped, and Major Bradford and Major Wilkinson eluded capture, the former by dressing as a servant, the latter, it is said, by hiding in the chimney.

Word spread throughout the land: Lee has been taken. Consternation swept Rebel ranks. Their savior gone, many sank into depths of despair. "This is a misfortune that cannot be remedied, as we have no officer in the army of equal experience and merit," wrote John Trumbull to his father, the governor of Connecticut. The event gave General Sullivan the "most pungent pain to inform" Washington of the "sad Stroke America must feel." Washington was more restrained in his report to John Hancock. "I will not comment on the melancholy intelligence . . . only adding that I sincerely regret Genl Lee's unhappy fate, and feel much for the loss of my Country in his Captivity."[43]

The British were elated, both in America and at home. One story has it that after Lee's arrival in New Brunswick British soldiers got "his horse drunk, while they toasted their king till they were in the same condition. A band . . . played all night." Colonel Harcourt wrote to his brother that Lee was the "most active and enterprizing of the enemy's generals," and now "it seems to be the universal opinion the rebels will no longer refuse treating upon the terms which have been offered them." When word reached England there were celebrations. There could be no doubt, many felt, that the war would soon be over. Such was the power that for a window of time Charles Lee held over the minds of many of his contemporaries.[44]

Not all, however, and there was an officer from Delaware who had a contrary opinion that is worth quoting. On 22 December Captain Thomas Rodney was with General Cadwalader of Pennsylvania, who said "everything looked very gloomy" because of Lee's capture. But Rodney wrote in his diary,

> I told him I was sorry for Gen. Lee because I knew him personally and had a regard for him, but I did not view his capture as unfavorable but as an advantage; that too much confidence had been put in General Lee, that this must have greatly embarrassed the commander in chief, as he was afraid to do anything without consulting Gen. Lee, but now he would be at liberty to exert his own talents.[45]

Rodney's insight was on the mark. There are events in history that seem alarming at the time but prove to be gifts from the gods. Thus the miserable performance of Horatio Gates at the Battle of Camden in August 1780, which removed from combat command a general unfit to command troops in battle and opened the way for Nathanael Greene to lead the Rebels to victory in the South. Or the serious wounds suffered by General Thomas Sumter of South Carolina at the Battle of Blackstocks in November 1780, thus the inability of that prima donna to take the field during the initial critical months of Greene's Carolina campaign. Charles Lee's capture at Basking Ridge falls into the same category. From the perspective of time there can be only one verdict: Good Riddance!

8

"I conclude the troops will be in perfect security"

"I think the game will be pretty well up"

Between 10 and 17 December, from the Pennsylvania side of the Delaware, "Hurried as I am and distressed by a number of perplexing circumstances," Washington wrote a gloomy letter to his cousin Lund, who was his business agent and farm manager at Mount Vernon. "I wish to Heaven it was in my power to give you a more favourable Acct of our situation than it is." The ranks were so depleted "I have no Idea of being able to make a stand, as My numbers, till joined by the Philadelphia Militia did not exceed 3000 Men fit for duty—now we may be about 5000 to oppose Howes whole army." Although "We have brought over, and destroyed, all the Boats we could lay our hands on, upon the Jersey Shore for many Miles above and below . . . it is next to impossible to guard a Shore for 60 miles with less than half the Enemys numbers; when by force or Strategem they may suddenly attempt a passage in many different places." He trembled for the safety of Philadelphia, and at the time thought that "nothing . . . can save it" except "General Lee's speedy arrival" with his army. By the time he finished the letter on the 17th, he knew of Lee's capture: "Unhappy Man! Taken by his Imprudence."

He daily expected a British assault. "Hitherto by our destruction of the Boats, and vigilance in watching the Fords of the River above the Falls (which are now rather high) [the falls were at Trenton] we have prevented them from crossing; but how long we will be able to do it, God only knows, as they are still hovering about the River." In several letters that month he mentioned the danger of the river icing over thickly enough to allow the British to march across. To make matters worse, his little army was shredded by sickness. His strongest regiment, Colonel George Weedon's (c. 1734–1793) 3rd Virginia Continentals, on paper 586 strong, by 22 December had only 134 rank and file present and fit for duty. Little wonder that Washington thought "Our only dependence now, is upon the Speedy Inlistment of a New Army; if this fails us, I think the game will be pretty well up."

Washington's appraisal of the situation was so somber that in one of the final paragraphs of this letter he prepared Lund Washington for a possible calamity:

> Matters to my view, but this I say in confidence to you, as a friend, wears so unfavourable an aspect . . . that I would look forward to unfavourable Events, & prepare Accordingly in such a manner however as to give no alarm or suspicion to any one; as one step towards it, have my Papers in such a Situation as to remove at a short notice in case an Enemy's Fleet should come up the River [Potomac]. When they are removed let them go immediately to my Brothers in Berkeley.[1]

Such was his state of mind at the time, for his brothers lived in Virginia's Back Country, near modern Charles Town, West Virginia, at the time well out of reach of the British army. It has been suggested by some that during this period Washington exaggerated the crisis, that he was a chronic complainer, that the Revolution would have gone on regardless of what happened to him and the army. But with defeat following defeat, the bulk of the army on the verge of discharge, civilian and military morale near rock bottom, can we doubt that the situation, if not desperate, was indeed dark and foreboding? If the Revolution itself was not in peril, an assertion that remains highly questionable, surely the unknown directions it could have taken if the army had been crushed or forced to flee to the Back Country should give pause to those who question Washington's deep-seated concerns. That a perilous situation existed cannot be denied.

But of all that was written by Washington and others on the string of disasters that befell the Continental Army and its commander during the late summer and fall of 1776, the homely language of Colonel William Douglas of 6th Connecticut was especially expressive and prescient. Douglas had been campaigning since the spring of 1775, first in the Northern Department, then in the fighting from Long Island to White Plains. His troops had run away in wild panic at Kips Bay but partially redeemed themselves at Harlem Heights. A few weeks before Washington wrote the foreboding letter to his cousin Lund, Douglas wrote to his wife, Hannah, words that might well have been written at any time during the war:

> america will never be Conker.d unless it is by themselves. If they would be of one hart and one mind, and even admit that the enemy Could march from one part to another, they Cant keep the Ground when they have got it, what Great things they have Done this year with the Best Army the King ever had, why they have Conker,d one Country that was their best friend but they Cant Keep but a small part of it through the winter are oblidge to Keep them-Selves Close together, I hope the Couintry will not be Discourag,d at our making some mis-steps at first, we are new but Shall be old in time as well as they.[2]

Colonel Douglas would not see his prediction come to pass. The campaigns had broken his health: "my Constitution is unsound and broke, so that I am not fit to Ingage," but "shall always Look on it as the most Honorouble Cause that ever man Serv,d in." He returned to Hannah and their four "little ones" and on 28 May 1777 died at their home in Northford, Connecticut. He was thirty-five.[3]

But in the short run the times were critical, and Washington was right in maintaining a high state of vigilance, for Howe would certainly have crossed the Delaware had there been boats. He wrote to Lord Germain on 20 December that his first plan had been to gain control of eastern New Jersey and not advance beyond New Brunswick, "but finding the advantages that might be gained by pushing on to the Delaware and the possibility of getting to Philadelphia," he had joined Cornwallis at New Brunswick on 6 December and ordered the army forward on the 7th. That he was always a few hours behind Washington is not surprising, for Sir William was a stickler for military etiquette and not a man to hurry. His Hessian aide-de-camp, Captain von Münchhausen, who had been appointed because of his fluency in English, was a devoted admirer of Howe but left in his diary and letters revealing observations of his general. In a letter to his mother he wrote, "General Howe stands for much cleanliness and properness. I have to put on a clean linen shirt in the morning. At about five to six or seven o'clock in the evening we, as well as the General, change clothes, and we all go to dinner." On the day the British left New Brunswick in pursuit of Washington, von Münchhausen entered in his diary, "The Rebels were always barely ahead of us. Since General Howe was with the vanguard, we advanced very slowly, and the Rebels had time to withdraw step by step without being engaged."[4]

This was undoubtedly one of the reasons why Lord Cornwallis's exhaustive search of the banks of the Delaware from Trenton to Coryell's Ferry (modern Lambertsville, New Jersey), fifteen miles upstream, for boats came up empty-handed. The measured pace of the pursuit—if it can be called pursuit—had given the Rebels time to carry out Washington's order that all boats on the Delaware either be destroyed or secured on the Pennsylvania side. Nor did searches downstream bear fruit.

Washington's orders had been faithfully executed, but he did not rest after the army's escape from certain disaster. He deployed his little army along the western bank of the Delaware River and kept the pressure on his brigade commanders to stay alert. "Spare no pains or expence to get intelligence of the Enemies motions and intentions," he wrote to Colonel John Cadwalader, commanding the Philadelphia militia, and added, "Keep proper Patroles going from Guard to Guard. Every piece of intelligence you Obtain worthy [of] notice send it forward by express." He was especially concerned with preventing the British from obtaining the means to cross the river. "Keep a good Guard over such Boats as are not Scuttled or rendered unfit for use. Keep a good lookout for spies—endeavor to magnify your Numbers as much as possible." In the final paragraph he repeated his concern with boats. "Be particularly attentive to the Boats & Vessels and suffer no person to pass over to the Jerseys without a permit."[5]

These orders were repeated in separate communications to other brigade commanders stationed up and down the river. To Brigadier General James Ewing he emphasized, "so much depends upon watchfulness that you cannot possibly be too much upon your Guard." To allow for speedy movements by the troops in the event of a British attempt to cross, he stressed, "Let the troops always have three Days provision

Cook'd before hand and keep them together as much as possible Night and Day—that they may be in readiness in the Shortest notice to make Head against the enemy."[6]

The latest intelligence gleaned from British prisoners came from Lord Stirling on the night of the 11th. Two captured grenadiers of 27th Foot "inform that Genls Howe, Cornwallis, Vaughn etc. with about 6000 of the flying Army were . . . waiting for Pontoons to come up with which they meant to pass the River near the blue Mounts or at Corriels [Corryell's] Ferry, they believe the latter." Washington conveyed this and other intelligence gained to John Hancock, with his opinion that "Upon the whole there can be no doubt but that Philadelphia is their object, and that they will pass the Delaware as soon as possible." Even before he wrote, Congress considered the situation so alarming that it resolved on the 11th to leave Philadelphia for the safety of Baltimore. Before leaving, it ordered the general commanding troops in Philadelphia to defend the city "to the utmost extremity against the attempts of the enemy to get possession of it."[7]

Although he had himself painted a negative picture of the military situation, Washington was not pleased with Congress's decision to leave Philadelphia, apparently considering it bad for morale. He even went so far as to inform Hancock that the matter "should not have been the Subject of a Resolve," and wrote further, "As the publication of their Resolve in my opinion will not lead to any good end, but on the contrary may be attended with some bad consequences, I shall take the liberty to decline inserting it in this days orders."[8]

Neither Washington nor Congress then knew, as we do, that at about this time Sir William had decided to follow the usual custom of eighteenth-century European armies and end the campaign of 1776. On 14 December he ordered the troops to "immediately march into winter quarters." Sir William explained to Lord Germain that "The passage of the Delaware being thus rendered impracticable" by Rebel actions denying him boats, and "the weather having become too severe to keep the field and the winter cantonments being arranged," he had established a chain of posts in New Jersey. They stretched eighty miles from Amboy to New Brunswick to Princeton and along the east bank of the Delaware from Trenton to Bordentown to Burlington. He admitted to a slight uneasiness. "The chain, I own, is rather too extensive but I was induced to occupy Burlington to cover the county of Monmouth in which there are many loyal inhabitants, and trusting to the almost general submission of the country to the southward of this chain and the strength of the corps placed in the advanced posts, I conclude the troops will be in perfect security."[9]

Having satisfied himself that all was well in Jersey, Sir William returned to the fleshpots of New York City. It was not London, not by a long shot, but there were dinners and balls and gambling, all very much to Sir William's tastes. There was also within arm's reach and closer his American consort, Elizabeth Lloyd Loring (d. 1831), beautiful, blond Betsy, wife of Joshua Loring (1744–1789), a Massachusetts Tory who held the lucrative office of commissary of prisoners. The Lorings had left Boston for Halifax with Sir William, and had come on with him to New York. Joshua evidently turned a blind eye to his wife's dalliance with Sir William, or, in the memorable language of a man who was in the city at the time, that viper-tongued New York Tory, Judge Thomas Jones, "He fingered the cash, the General enjoyed Madam."[10]

Since the fall of Fort Lee, Washington had made, for a change, all the right moves. He had carried out a successful retreat before a superior, if admittedly laggard, enemy. He had escaped Howe's clutches by putting the Delaware between them and denying Howe the means to cross that natural barrier. He had stayed on top of his commanders, demanding day-and-night vigilance and that their brigades be ready to move on short notice. Although he was pessimistic about his chances should the British attempt a crossing, he remained ever belligerent, ever the fighting general in orders to his brigadiers. March "immediately to the point of attack . . . support another without loss of time, or waiting orders from me." Meet them and fight them at the "Waters Edge."[11]

Yet his situation remained dire. Enlistments would be up on 1 January, and his present force remained ill-clothed, ill-shod, ill-fed, to European soldiers a ragtag and bobtail army. The defeats in New York, the loss of New Jersey had brought Rebel morale, civilian and soldier alike, to a low point. The threat to Philadelphia, the capital of the United States, and its possible loss haunted Washington: "you know the importance of it," he wrote to Horatio Gates, "and the fatal consequences that must attend its loss." Sir William Howe had missed another golden opportunity when he failed to destroy the Rebel Army in New Jersey, and no amount of speculation on what motivated him to let the fox escape once more can dispute that. But surely come the spring, even if a Rebel Army was then in existence, surely the game would then be up.[12]

Others were as worried as Washington. On 22 December Joseph Reed wrote to him on behalf of himself and other officers. "We are all of the Opinion my dear General that something must be attempted to revive our expiring Credit give our Cause some Degree of Reputation & prevent a total Depreciation of the Continental Money which is coming on very fast." He then asked, "Will it not be possible my dear Genl for your Troops or such Part of them as can act with Advantage to make a Diversion or something more at or about Trenton." He continued: "our Cause is desperate & hopeless if we do not take the Oppy of the Collection of Troops at present to strike some Stroke. Our affairs are hasting fast to Ruin if we do not retrieve them by some happy Event. Delay with us is now equal to total defeat."[13]

Reed obviously feared once more the indecision that had marked his commander in chief during the Fort Washington debacle. But on this occasion Washington was well ahead of Reed. He wrote on 15 December that he had "received Information that the Body of the Enemy which lay at Pennington under Lord Cornwallis, moved this Morning back towards princetown, if so, it looks as if they were going into Quarters, and this corresponds with the Account brought last Night by a prisoner, a Servant belonging to Genl Vaughns Family, who says he heard his Master talk of going soon into Winter Quarters." There were also other indications that this might be true. But the previous day, before he could be certain that Sir William had shut down his campaign, he had written three letters indicating that he had in mind an offensive stroke.[14]

To Horatio Gates, he wrote, "If we can draw our Forces together I trust under the smiles of Providence, we may yet effect an important stroke, or at least prevent Genl Howe from executing his Plan." He sent a similar message to William Heath: "if we can collect our Force speedily, I should hope we may effect something of importance, or at least give our Affairs such a turn as to make 'em assume a more promising aspect than they now have." And in a letter to Jonathan Trumbull Senior he made it even clearer that he wanted to go on the offensive. Referring to the reinforcements being brought to him from the Northern Army by General Gates, and to General Lee's force, he wrote, "Whereas by coming on they may, in conjunction with my present Forces . . . enable us to attempt a stroke upon the Forces of the Enemy, who lay a good deal scattered, and to all appearance, in a state of security. A lucky blow in this Quarter would be fatal to them, and would most certainly raise the spirits of the People, which are quite sunk by our late misfortunes."[15]

Because of the perilous situation of the army, indeed, the Revolution itself, before leaving Philadelphia for Baltimore, Congress on 12 December had given Washington "full power to order and direct all things relative to the department, and to the operations of War" until Congress resolved otherwise. Conscious, however, of the sensitivities of the delegates with regard to powers of the military, eight days later Washington brought up the matter in a long letter to Hancock, in which he reported that having "waited with much impatience" Congress's decision on his requests of October 5 and November 14, respectively, to create a Corps of Engineers and enlarge the Artillery Corps, he had acted on the authority given him under the resolution of the 12th and "ventured to order three Batallions of Artillery to be immediately recruited." To support his action, he enclosed a plan for increasing the Artillery Corps prepared by his artillery commander, Colonel Henry Knox. Drawing on his extensive readings in military history, Knox wrote in part,

> In the modern mode of carrying on a war, there is nothing which contributes more to make an Army victorious than a well regulated & well disciplined Artillery, provided with a sufficiency of Cannon & Stores. The battles which have been lately fought in Europe have generally been with cannon, and that army, which has had the most numerous & best appointed artillery, has commonly been victorious.[16]

Knox also pointed out how dependent the British were during the present campaign on superior artillery. "They scarcely or ever detach a single Regiment without two or three field pieces; the regulations of their artillery are founded upon the most convincing experience of their utility, & we shall have no reason to blush by imitating them in those particulars."

Washington felt so strongly on the issue that when he found it impossible to recruit at the old pay levels—"The pay of our Artillerists bearing no proportion with that in the English or French service"—he was "induced . . . to promise Officers & men, that their pay should be augmented 25% or that their engagements shall be null and void." He then hastened to add, "This may appear to Congress premature and unwarrantable; but Sir, if they view our situation in the light it strikes their Offices, they will be convinced of the Utility of the measure and that the execution, could not be delayed till after their meeting in Baltimore. In short, the present exigency of our Affairs will not admit of delay either in Council or the Field." Given this situation, if "every matter that in its nature is self evident, it to be referred to Congress, at the distance of 130 or 40 miles, so much time must necessarily elapse as to defeat the end in view." Therefore,

> It may be said, that this is an application for powers, that are to dangerous to be intrusted. I can only add, that desperate diseases, require desperate remedies, and with truth declare, that I have no lust for power but wish with as much fervency as any man upon this wide extended Continent for an Opportunity of turning the Sword into a Ploughshare.[17]

Washington was requesting unprecedented dictatorial powers. This had obviously been discussed with at least some of his senior commanders, especially Nathanael Greene, who wrote to Hancock in support of Washington's plea, "I can assure you that the General will not exceed his Powers altho' he may sacrifice the Cause. There never was a man that might be more safely trusted nor a Time when there was a louder Call." The verdict of almost all contemporaries who commented on this subject mirrored Greene's. One of the best statements on Washington's reverence for the primacy of civil authority came three years later from Alexandre Gerard, the first French minister of the United States, who wrote to his foreign minister,

> It is certain that if General Washington were ambitious and scheming, it would have been entirely in his power to make a revolution; but nothing on the part of the General or the Army has justified the shadow of a suspicion. The General sets forth constantly the principle that one must be a Citizen first and an officer afterwards.[18]

Congress agreed. On 27 December, "having maturely considered the present Crisis, and having perfect Reliance on the Wisdom, Vigour, and Uprightness of General Washington," it passed resolutions giving him sweeping powers for six months to reenlist soldiers through bounties and other means, establish a system of officer promotion, raise an additional sixteen battalions of infantry, 3,000 light cavalry, three artillery regiments, and a Corps of Engineers, and in addition "to take where-ever he may be, whatever he may want for the Use of the Army, if the Inhabitants will not sell it, allowing a reasonable Price for the same; to arrest and confine Persons who refuse to take the Continental Currency, or are otherwise disaffected to the American Cause."[19]

While Congress debated, however, the year 1776 was running out and with it the terms of enlistments of the Continental Army. There was little time left for the "stroke" Washington had in mind.

"No man to quit his Ranks on the pain of Death"

Washington added a postscript to his letter of the 20th to Hancock: "Genls Gates and Sullivan have this Instant come in." Reinforcements at last. Not many, to be sure, but his numbers were so few that any increase was a godsend. Sullivan had brought in Lee's command of about 2,000 men, and Gates had arrived with some 600 from the Northern Army. Sullivan stayed with the army. Gates, however, begged off. He was ill, he pleaded, he needed to get away because of his health. This at the darkest hour for the cause, Washington in need of the presence and advice of his senior commanders. "I shall not object to yr going to Philadelphia on Acct of your Health," he wrote to Gates on 23 December, "but wish it would have permitted you to have gone to Bristol [Pennsylvania] rather, in order to have conducted matters there in cooperation with what I hinted to you as having in view here." So Gates knew that battle was in the offing, but that was never an event he hankered for. In fact, during his long years of service, first in the British army, now the American, he had never led troops in battle. The spa at Bristol, with its famous bath springs, would not do for Horatio. Too ill to fight, but not too ill to lobby for himself, he hied himself off to join Congress at Baltimore. Even his sympathetic biographer found Gates's choice "odd."[20]

Washington, on the other hand, had already begun preparations to take the offensive and wage a campaign for Philadelphia, beginning with establishing supply depots in his rear. On 20 December he ordered the deputy commissary-general of the army, the Philadelphia merchant Carpenter Wharton (1747–1780), to "Seize the Mill & grain" of millers if the want of bread for the army was their fault "& employ it for the use of the Public—& if it arises from any defect in the Farmer, to take his

Grain for the Public Service, in either case paying the full Value." The following day he ordered Wharton to "Lay in Provisions for Twenty thousand men" west of Philadelphia: ten days supply at Mill Town (modern Downingtown), and four months each at York and Lancaster; other supplies on the roads from Lancaster to Winchester, Virginia; from the head of Chesapeake Bay to Alexandria, Virginia, "for the acommodation of the Troops in their march from the Southern Colonies"; and enough for six weeks for 10,000 men in Philadelphia and vicinity.[21]

Two days before Christmas he described his specific intention for the first time in writing, informing Joseph Reed that

> Christmas day at Night, one hour before day is the time fixed upon for our Attempt at Trenton. For Heaven's sake keep this to yourself, as the discovery of it may prove fatal to us, our numbers, sorry I am to say, being less than I had any conception of—but necessity, dire necessity will—nay must justify any attempt.[22]

In a postscript he added, "I have ordered our Men to be provided with three days Provisions Cook'd; with which, and their Blankets they are to March, for if we are successful which heaven grant & other Circumstances favour we may push on."

Tension built up at army headquarters. It was probably on the day before Christmas when Washington was visited by the famous Philadelphia physician and member of Congress Dr. Benjamin Rush, who recalled in his autobiography he spent "near an hour with him in private. He appeared much depressed, and lamented the ragged and dissolving state of his army in affecting terms. I gave him assurance of the disposition of Congress to support him, under his present difficulties and distresses. While I was talking to him, I observed him to play with his pen and ink upon several small pieces of paper. One of them by accident fell upon the floor near my feet. I was struck with the inscription upon it. It was 'Victory or Death.'"[23]

Washington's penchant for complicated attacks by columns operating at widely separated distances is revealed in his planning for the attack on Trenton. Brigadier General James Ewing's (1736–1806) mission was to cross the river at Trenton Ferry with 700 Pennsylvania and New Jersey militia and seize the bridge across Assunpink Creek south of Trenton, thus denying the Hessian garrison an escape route from Washington's main force, coming in from the north.

On 24 December Washington ordered Colonel John Cadwalader, commanding the Philadelphia volunteers called Associators, to cooperate with Colonel Daniel Hitchcock's (1739–1777) brigade; coordinate his movements with Washington's; cross the river much farther down, in the vicinity of Bristol, Pennsylvania; and mount a diversionary attack on the Hessian outposts south of Trenton: "let the hour of the attack be the 26th, and one hour before day (of that Morning)." Washington added, "If you should be successful (of which I have the highest hopes) move forward if possible, so as to form a junction with me, if the like good fortune should attend our Enterprize, at Trenton or Princeton." Hitchcock's brigade consisted of two Massachusetts and two Rhode Island regiments and a Rhode Island militia regiment—in all, 844 men fit for duty. Cadwalader's entire force numbered some 1,800 rank and file.[24]

Also on the 24th Brigadier General Philemon Dickinson (1739–1809), commanding officer of the New Jersey militia, whose home was near Trenton, reported to Washington that he had sent a spy across the river to gain information on where and how many sentries were posted on the roads leading to Trenton, "where the Cannon lay & what number," Hessian strength in the town, "whether any reinforcements have lately arrived, or any Troops march'd out, & such other intelligence as he can possibly procure." Upon his return in the morning he would be given a horse to report directly to Washington. Dickinson also had alarming news. He believed that the American intentions were known. An agent had arrived from across the river with reports of hearing much activity, of "Waggons going all night," and from this "tis imagined the Enemy had notice of the Boats" being brought downriver to the Rebel point of embarkation, and that the wagons were probably carrying artillery. Dickinson wrote, "they are informed of our every movement I believe."[25]

Dickinson's conjectures did not deter Washington. On Christmas Day general orders were issued for the main force's order of march to Trenton. Three days before Christmas it numbered about 5,000 men present and fit for duty. From it some 2,400 men were selected for the mission. After crossing the Delaware to the New Jersey side, the little army would proceed toward Trenton in two divisions, consisting of several brigades, "Each Brigade to be furnish'd with two good Guides."[26]

Second Division, or the left wing, would embark first, and once across was assigned to march by the Pennington road. Its three brigades were commanded by Major General Nathanael Greene. Brigadier Gen-

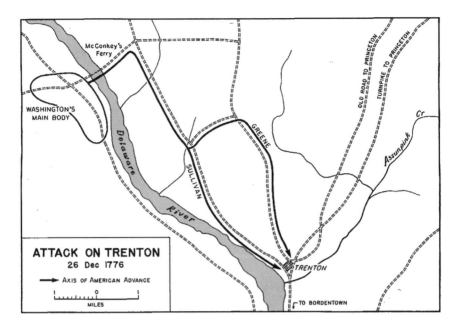

Attack on Trenton

eral Adam Stephen's brigade of three Virginia Continental regiments formed the "advanced party." Stephen had the critical mission "to attack and force the enemies Guards and seize such posts as may prevent them from forming in the streets and in case they are annoy'd from the houses to set them on fire." Stephens also had with him "a detachment of Artillery without Cannon provided with Spikes and Hammers to Spike up the enemies Cannon in case of necessity or to bring them off if it can be effected. the party to be provided with ropes for the purpose of dragging off the cannon." In support were Brigadier General Hugh Mercer's (c. 1725–1777) brigade of two Continental regiments from Massachusetts and Connecticut, respectively; a Connecticut State regiment; 1st Maryland; and the Maryland and Virginia Rifle Regiment; and in reserve Lord Stirling's brigade of two Virginia regiments, 6th Maryland, and Haslet's Delaware Regiment.

First Division, commanded by Major General John Sullivan, formed the right wing and would march by the River Road. It consisted of three brigades: Colonel John Glover's five Massachusetts Continental regiments, including his own, the 14th; Colonel Paul Dudley Sargent's (1745–1828) four Continental regiments, two from Massachusetts, two from New York, and two Connecticut State regiments; and in reserve Brigadier General Arthur St. Clair's (1737–1818) four Continental regiments.

It should come as no surprise that artillery commanded by Colonel Henry Knox formed a conspicuous part of the expedition, totaling eighteen fieldpieces: "Four pieces . . . at the head of each Column, three pieces at the head of the second Brigade of each Division, and two pieces with each of the Reserves."

A final brigade, commanded by a French volunteer, Matthias-Alexis, Chevalier de La Rochefermoy (1725–1782), was ordered to follow Greene's division and on the Jersey side to "file off" and block any British reinforcements that might come down from Princeton. Since La Rochefermoy was newly arrived and did not know the countryside, his "Guides will be the best judges of" his deployment. Like so many European volunteers, La Rochefermoy no doubt had puffed up his rank in the old country when interviewed by Congress. He probably had been a captain in the French army, but Congress thought he was a former colonel and therefore commissioned him as a brigadier general.[27]

Security was enhanced by two more measures. Captain William Washington (1752–1810) of 3rd Virginia, a big, strong six-footer, was a cousin of Washington's who would go on to command a cavalry regiment in the Carolinas, where he served with distinction. Washington and Captain John Flahaven of 1st New Jersey were detailed "with a party of 40 men each to march before the Divisions & post themselves on the road about three miles from Trenton & make prisoners of all going in or coming out of Town." General Stephen was ordered to "form a chain of sentries" out from the bridgehead while the brigades formed behind them: "This Guard not to suffer any person to go in or come out." On the approach, flanking parties would mask the marching columns, whose advance guards were to arrive at Trenton at five o'clock on the morning of 26 December.

The deadly seriousness of the enterprise was sealed with one line: "a profound silence to be enjoyn'd & no man to quit his Ranks on the pain of Death."

9

"Success of an Enterprize"

"We will go at them with the bayonet"

In Trenton were stationed three proud Hessian regiments numbering some 1,400 men: von Knyphausen, von Lossberg, and Rall. They were the victors of Fort Washington, the men who had faced galling rifle fire while hauling themselves up the steep slopes by grasping bushes, winning accolades from their British comrades for their gallantry. Their commander, Colonel Johann Gottlieb Rall, had been with them. His regiment—Rall at its head—had borne the brunt of the fighting. Rall was an inspirational commander when the shooting started. But was he up to brigade command? His Hessian superior at Bordentown, Colonel Karl Aemilius Ulrich von Donop, did not think him fit for independent command, and a subordinate, the adjutant of Regiment von Lossberg, Lieutenant Jakob Piel, wrote, "Colonel Rall was truly born to be a soldier, but not a general." Rall commanded a brigade at Trenton through the fortunes of war, namely, sickness, wounds, and death that had struck down others. Of his enemy he had total disdain. Had not he and his regiment with their bayonets driven the American militia like sheep at White Plains? Had they not attacked with élan at Fort Washington and taken a position thought to be impregnable? Sir William Howe had been much impressed by Rall's performance at Fort Washington, and on 14 December the two ate breakfast together at Trenton, and it was there that Rall talked Howe into giving him a separate brigade command at

Trenton. Lieutenant Andreas Wiederhold of von Knyphausen Regiment, who would remember "famous Trenton . . . as long as I live," referred to Rall as "our all too merry Brigadier" who "is said to have brought us by his solicitation" to Trenton; but "How well he would have done not to have solicited for it. He might perhaps have kept and preserved the un-deserved praise which was ignorantly bestowed upon him. But here it all fell into the mud."[1]

Regulations for Hessian infantry specifically instructed that

> When a Regiment or Battalion is posted in a village, which is not far from the enemy, the Chief or Commander must immediately cause a Redoubt to be erected on a chosen spot or height, or where it is in some way advantageous, which is large enough that the Regiment or Battalion has space for itself within.[2]

Yet when von Donop's engineering officer, Captain George Pauli, sent specially for the job, chose an excellent location for a redoubt for Rall's artillery, Rall neglected to build it and put his cannons in front of his headquarters. One of his officers, Major von Dechow, also proposed a redoubt for artillery "so that everything would be prepared for an unforseen event," wrote Lieutenant Wiederhold, who had twenty-four years of service behind him. Rall exclaimed contemptuously, "*Scheiszer bey Scheisz!* (Shit or by shit!) Let them come: what defenses? We will go at them with the bayonet." When Dechow pressed his argument, reports Wiederhold, Rall "repeated his previous words, laughed out loud at both of us and went off."[3]

The British and Hessians were not lacking for good intelligence from local Tories. It arrived steadily and was largely accurate. There were daily warnings of an approaching attack. But Rall's contempt for the Americans was shared by many British and Hessian officers and sol-diers, especially by Major General James Grant, who commanded all of the Jersey outposts. On 17 December he wrote to von Donop, "I can hardly believe that Washington would venture at this season of the year to pass the Delaware." And on 21 December, "I will undertake to keep the peace in Jersey with a corporal's guard."[4]

While Rall and his fellow Hessians celebrated Christmas, on the other side of the river Washington's 2,400-man strike force was formed on the afternoon of Christmas Day eight miles north of Trenton behind McConkey's Ferry (modern Washington Crossing, Pennsylvania) to "pass the Delaware." They were shielded from prying eyes along the Jersey side of the river by low hills. In the late afternoon they began moving out so that, Washington wrote, "they might begin to pass over as soon as it grew dark." Many years later Major James Wilkinson, who was standing by, recalled that the snow was "tinged here and there with blood from the feet of the men who wore broken shoes." The countersign, wrote Benjamin Rush, was "Victory or Death."[5]

The weather was foul and getting worse. On Christmas Eve and Christmas Day a great storm swept up the East Coast. More than a foot of snow fell in one location in North Carolina, two feet at Jefferson's Monticello. Had the storm's center continued on that track, a heavy snowfall such as Jefferson experienced might have dashed Washington's plans. But as sometimes happens with such storms, it moved out over the Atlantic, probably close to the North Carolina–Virginia line, and the area in which the Rebels were operating was on the edge of the storm and received a moderate snowfall. The storm, nevertheless, was severe. Snow began to fall in Philadelphia sometime after 10:00 P.M. on Christmas Day. At 11:00 P.M. snowfall commenced at McConkey's Ferry. In the wee hours of the morning, up and down the river, the storm became intense and the precipitation changed to a mixture of snow and ice. A sleet storm raged over the river valley and adjacent areas.[6]

"The night," wrote Henry Knox to his wife, "was cold and stormy; it hailed with great violence; the troops marched with the most profound silence and good order." Lower down the river, with Cadwalader's division, Thomas Rodney of Delaware described it "as severe a night as ever I saw." To add to their difficulties, wrote Knox, "The floating ice in the river made the labor almost incredible." Below-freezing temperatures had struck on the night of 18–19 December, and from then the river had begun to fill with ice. The river apparently never froze over, but there was solid ice along the shores, and the river became choked with large cakes of ice floating downstream, endangering the boats filled with troops. But the Rebels on this occasion had the right equipment and men for the job.[7]

As early as 1 December Washington had assigned Colonel Richard Humpton (c. 1732–1804), a Yorkshireman and ex-British officer who had served as a captain in 36th Foot, to gather boats on the Delaware to evacuate the army in the face of the oncoming British. In his letter of instruction to Humpton, Washington directed that "you will particularly attend to the Durham Boats which are very proper for the purpose."

The historian Alfred Hoyt Bill gave a clear description of these stout craft, which were "devised to carry iron ore and freight between Philadelphia and the northern counties of New Jersey. Ranging from forty to sixty feet in length and eight feet wide, they drew only twenty inches when fully loaded. The largest of them could carry fifteen tons and were capable of transporting the whole of some of Washington's little regiments in a single trip. They had heavy steering sweeps that could be fitted at either end and were equipped with two masts and sails and with poles to drive them against contrary winds and currents." The troops available to man them matched these splendid craft, for who better than John Glover and his Marblehead fishermen?[8]

The Durham boats made up most of the landing craft. But even with these, the passage was severe. Washington wrote that the troops "experienced the greatest fatigue in breaking a passage through the ice." He had planned to land on the Jersey side by midnight "that we might easily arrive at Trenton by five in the Morning. But the quantity of Ice, made that Night, impeded the passage of Boats so much, that it was three OClock before the Artillery could all be got over, and near four, before the Troops took up their line of march."[9]

Four hours behind schedule. Washington despaired "of surprizing the Town, as I well know that we could not reach it before the day was fairly broke." But he also felt that he could not "Retreat without being discovered, and harassed on repassing the River," so he "determined to push on at all Events." His determination carried the army forward. Had he not himself written of this operation "Victory or Death"? The long columns moved through the storm, which "continued with great violence," wrote Henry Knox, "but was in our backs, and consequently in the face of the enemy." In his journal Sergeant Samuel McCarty of 8th Virginia called it "the worst day of sleet rain that could be." About daylight, as they neared their goal, Sergeant Elisha Bostwick of 7th Connecticut heard Washington "as he was comeing on Speaking to & Encouraging the Soldiers. The words he Spoke as he pass'd by where I stood & in my hearing were these, 'Soldiers, keep by your officers for Gods Sake keep by your officers,' Spoke in a deep & Solemn voice." The "horses were then unharness'd," Bostwick added, "& the artillery men prepared," and "We marched on."[10]

Daylight came with no hint at Trenton of an attack. Because of the weather, the daily dawn patrol had been cancelled. In command of an advanced post, Lieutenant Wiederhold had detailed seven pickets during the night and "had patrols after patrols walk about, thus to protect myself from any surprises." About an hour after daybreak his "day's patrol had already returned and reported that all was quiet, and the Jägers, who stood below me had already withdrawn their night-posts." As it was daylight, "my sentinels did not keep a very sharp lookout . . . and the advance-guard did not expect the enemy" from the direction in which they appeared. "I was suddenly attacked from the side of the woods on the road to John's Ferry and had I not just stepped out of my little guard-house and seen the enemy, they might have been upon me before I had time to reach for my rifle." Lieutenant Wiederhold formed his seventeen men to give battle, believing that he was facing only skirmishers.[11]

The American coordination on this storm-driven night was superb. Captain William Hull of 19th Continentals, with Sullivan's division on the river road, wrote, "The General [Washington] gave orders that every Officer's Watch should be set by his, and the Moment of Attack was fixed." With Greene's division on the Pennington road, Major George Johnston of Virginia was one of the men Lieutenant Wiederhold faced. He wrote three days after the battle, "At 7, we halted within 500 yds of their advanced guard until the Right wing, commanded by General Sullivan . . . could get within the same distance of another of the Guards, posted on the River road. Here our two Major Gen'ls, Green . . . and Sullivan, exhibited the greatest proof of generalship by getting to their respective posts within five minutes of each other, tho' they had parted 4 miles from the Town, and took different Routes." Tench Tilghman, who was with Washington as a volunteer aide-de-camp, wrote to his father the day after the battle "that we did not reach Trenton till eight O'Clock, when the division which the general headed in person, attacked the enemy's out post. The other Division which marched the lower Road, attacked . . . within a few minutes after we began ours."[12]

"We drove them furiously," reported Sergeant McMichael of the Pennsylvania Rifle Regiment, and Lieutenant Wiederhold soon found that instead of what he had first thought to be a line of skirmishers, "I was almost surrounded by several battalions. I accordingly retreated under constant firing until I reached the Altenbockum company, which had rallied during my engagement and had taken up a position straight across the street in front of the Captain's quarters. I posted myself at their right wing and together we charged the enemy, but we were again forced to retreat in the same manner as before, so as not to be cut off from the garrison." In his report of the battle no less a participant than Washington himself gave Lieutenant Wiederhold and his comrades high marks for their performance. "The Out Guards made but small Opposition, tho', for their Numbers, they behaved very well, keeping up a constant retreating fire from behind houses."[13]

But it was for naught, as a disgusted Wiederhold testified. "Nobody came to see what was going on, no one came to our assistance with reinforcements, and yet Rall's regiment had that night its turn to be on watch." Colonel Rall, when he finally appeared, "seemed to be quite dazed," wrote Wiederhold, and this squares with the tradition that accuses Rall of drinking too much on Christmas Day and Night. Wiederhold reported what he knew of the enemy, that they were "strong in numbers" and "on both sides of" town. Rall "shouted to his regiment: 'Forward, March, Advance, Advance!' and he tottered back and forth without knowing what he was doing. Thus we lost the few favourable moments we might still have had in our hands to break through the enemy in one place or another with honour and without losses; but as it was we were surrounded before we had time to get outside of Trenton."[14]

The American onslaught carried all before it. Tench Tilghman wrote that both divisions "pushed on with so much rapidity, that the Enemy had scarce time to form, our people advanced up to the Mouths of their Field pieces, shot down their Horses and brought off the Cannon." Among the Americans who took part in this daring rush were two officers of 3rd Virginia: Washington's cousin Captain William Washington, who was wounded in the fighting; and eighteen-year-old Lieutenant James Monroe (1758–1831), who would become the fifth president of the United States. Rall's attempt to rally his regiment and attack broke down under American artillery fire. Then he attempted to move away to his left, then to his right into an apple orchard outside of town on the road to Princeton. But Washington, "perceiving their Intention, I threw a Body of Troops in their Way which immediately checked them." Lieutenant Wiederhold wrote that when Rall "was reminded, I do not know by whom, of the loss of the baggage left behind in the town, he changed his mind and with his own regiment and that of Lossberg, he attacked the city which he had just left. What madness this was! An open town which was useless to us and which he had only ten or fifteen minutes ago left of his own free will and which was now filled with three or four thousand of the enemy and then attempt to take it back again with from six to seven hundred men, bayonet in hand."

Lieutenant Colonel Scheffer described the effectiveness of the American artillery, and the weather. "It rained Cannonballs and grapeshot here, and snow, rain, and sleet came constantly into our faces. In short, none of our muskets would fire any longer." During these movements, in which Regiments Rall and Lossberg became confused and mixed to the point where neither was able to put up an effective resistance, Colonel Rall was mortally wounded. The regiments surrendered.[15]

While all this was occurring, Regiment Knyphausen, formed in tight ranks on another street and led by Rall's second in command, Major von Dechow, waited for orders, which was hardly the thing do in a perilous situation in which seconds lost could lead to catastrophe. Lieutenant Wiederhold was aghast when he and his men rejoined the regiment. "In God's name," he shouted at von Dechow, "why have we not occupied the [Assunpink] bridge?" It was too late. Von Dechow joined his colonel in receiving a mortal wound. Two American brigades, Glover's and St. Clair's, surrounded Regiment Knyphausen, whereupon the Hessians grounded their arms and surrendered.[16]

The incredible had happened. The victors of Fort Washington had been vanquished. Two Virginians described it with blunt simplicity. Sergeant McCarty wrote, "Came there about daybreak and beat the dam Hessians." Washington wrote to Hancock, "I have the pleasure of congratulating you upon the Success of an Enterprize." But the *Annual Register* of London put it best: "three old established regiments, of a people who make war their profession, had laid down their arms after inflicting only twelve casualties on the hitherto contemptible Americans." Actually, American casualties were only half that number: two officers slightly wounded, two privates killed, two wounded: a small price for one of the key American victories of the war, in which 918 Hessians were taken prisoner, 22 killed, and 84 wounded. Twenty British horsemen of the 16th Light Dragoons escaped, along with 197 Hessians.[17]

How had it happened? The official Hessian court-martial verdict laid the blame on Colonel Rall, and certainly his primary role in the defeat cannot be denied. Captain von Münchhausen put it bluntly: "To his good fortune, Colonel Rall died . . . from his wounds. I say this because he would have lost his head had he lived." His contempt for his foe, his refusal to take proper defensive measures, not taking advantage of intelligence, drinking so much on the holiday that when he was awakened he was either still drunk or too badly hung over to react effectively: all of these target Rall as the man directly responsible for the debacle.

Historians also have given other reasons, including the effects on the Hessians both physically and psychologically from a long campaign and constant harassment and patrolling, but this rings false as an important reason when one considers that the wear and tear on Washington's army far exceeded anything suffered by their enemies. The close-order ranks in which the Hessians fought certainly enabled American arms, especially artillery, to scatter and confuse the Germans. But the implication that things might have turned out differently had the Hessians deployed into open-order skirmishing formations hardly bears serious consideration, given their total surprise and the quickness of the American surge, which rendered them unable to resist effectively.[18]

Emphasis on Hessian failures tends to minimize the American successes. Trenton was one of Washington's finest accomplishments as a field commander; "his only really brilliant stroke of the war" is the sound verdict of the historian Don Higginbotham. The strategic decision to strike, the near-faultless operations in bringing his little army to the battlefield, and his active participation as a battle captain, urging his men to strike fast and hard and keep up the pressure and ordering regiments and brigades into blocking positions, reveal Washington's ability at critical moments to rise to the occasion. He had done it in New York by evacuating Brooklyn and saving the army, and now he had done it once more and breathed new life into the Revolution. As we shall see, he was still capable of major operational errors of judgment, but when the chips were down he invariably revealed himself to be a cunning opponent whom his enemies could not afford to take lightly. And in the winter of 1776–1777, he was not through.[19]

As quick as the strike had been, so was the withdrawal. The reader will recall from the previous chapter that Washington had ordered Brigadier General James Ewing with 700 men to cross the Delaware at Trenton and seize the bridge crossing Assunpink Creek, thus closing the Hessian escape route; and Colonel John Cadwalader, with 1,800 men, to cross lower down the river at Bristol and mount a diversionary action against Hessian forces south of Trenton. Both Ewing and Cadwalader failed, blaming ice conditions on the river. Ewing looked at the ice on the river and did not even try. Cadwalader managed to get two battalions of foot to the New Jersey shore, but there the landings stalled. Captain Thomas Rodney, commanding a company of Kent County, Delaware, militia, wrote to his brother Caesar, "We landed with great difficullty through the ice" but "after two battalions were landed, the storm increased so much, and the river was so full of ice, that it was impossible to get the artillery over, for we had to walk 100 yards on the ice to get on shore. Gen. Cadwalader therefore ordered the whole to retreat again, and we had to stand at least six hours under arms—first to cover the landing and till all the rest had retreated again—and, by this time, the storm of wind, hail, rain and snow, with the ice, was so bad that some of the infantry could not get back till the next day."[20]

Was the ice worse downstream? Probably not, because ice conditions usually are more severe above Trenton. Would the 100 yards of ice described by Captain Rodney have supported the weight of artillery pieces? It supported some horses, but Rodney was there and said it was impossible to get the artillery over. Should Cadwalader have done without artillery and pushed all of his infantry over the river? We could question and speculate endlessly. In his fine work *The War of the Revolution*, Christopher Ward's assessment was harsh. "One can only conclude that it took a Washington to cross the river that night, and a Ewing and Cadwalader to funk a crossing." Whatever the primary reason for their failure, without those columns carrying out their assignments Washington felt that he had no choice but to withdraw to the Pennsylvania side: "the Numbers I had with me, being inferior to theirs below me and a strong Battalion of Light Infantry being at Princetown above me, I thought it most prudent to return the same Evening, with the prisoners and the Artillery we had taken." According to Joseph Reed there was another reason. "There were great Quantities of Spirituous Liquors at Trenton of which the Soldiers drank too freely to admit of Discipline or Defense in case of attack." Washington, as was his custom, sought the counsel of his senior commanders on whether to press the advantage or withdraw. Reed wrote, "On the other hand it was argued that—Successes & brilliant strokes ought to be pursued—that History shewed how much depended upon improving such Advantages—& that a Pannick being once given no one could ascertain the beneficial Consequences which might be derived from it if it was push'd to all its Consequences." Reed failed to add that neither could one ascertain the negative consequences of a wrong decision. Washington had shown himself to be a bold commander, and fortune had been on his side. But the British still had strong forces in New Jersey, and nobody knew on the day of the victory, when a decision had to be made, how they would react. Washington had no need to push his luck. His decision, supported "in the Opinion of the Genl Officers," to withdraw was not only prudent, it was right.[21]

Ice conditions were still bad, perhaps worse, upon their recrossing of the Delaware. Sergeant Bostwick wrote, "When crossing the Deleware with the prisoners in flat bottom boats the ice Continually Stuck to the Boats driving them downstream; the boatmen endevering to clear off the ice pounded the boat, & Stamping with their feet beconed to the prisoners to do the same & they all set to jumping at once with their cues flying up and down soon Shook off the ice from the boats."[22]

"We'll go over and bag him in the morning"

The Hessian prisoners were marched to Philadelphia and paraded through the city to show the populace the fruits of the great victory, and that the much-feared Germans were not supermen. Joseph Reed claimed that he wrote to Washington on the 27th "by Express . . . urging him to cross the River again & pursue the Advantages which Providence had presented." The letter has not been found, and his claim was written at a later date. Perhaps he did, but it was not the first time that Reed claimed to have given Washington advice that the Virginian followed. On the 28th the three-man Executive Committee of Congress, which had been established on 21 December to expedite communications and decision-making between Congress and Washington, wrote that von Donop's Hessians had left their posts at Bordentown and southward and were fleeing to the north. The committee strongly suggested that if "your Victory is immediately pursued & no time allowed the enemy to recover from their surprize, you will have little difficulty in clearing the Jerseys of them." On that same date Colonel Cadwalader wrote Washington with the same information. Washington knew that Cadwalader and Ewing had finally gotten across the river, and that General Mifflin was about to follow with several Pennsylvania militia regiments. He also knew that von Donop was withdrawing from South Jersey. As with the first stroke at Trenton, it is impossible to know who first proposed another crossing, but it would not have been at all out of character for Washington to have had it in mind even as he was withdrawing. In any case, he decided "to go over myself with the whole of the Continental Troops as soon as they are refreshed and recovered of their late Fatigue." However Washington may have judged their recovery, we can be sure that his men did not greet with enthusiasm his general orders of the 29th, only two days after their great victory, ordering Greene's division to cross at Yardley's Ferry, about two miles north of Trenton, and Sullivan's division at McConkey's Ferry. Late on 29 December the boats set out once more for the Jersey shore, but ice conditions were so bad that all of the troops and their artillery did not make it until 1 January of the new year. One soldier recalled, "The horses attached to our cannon were without shoes, and when passing over the ice they would slide in every direction, and could advance only [with] the assistance of the soldiers." Conditions were succinctly but clearly described by Sergeant James McMichael:

> Having again received marching orders, we got ready at dark, and at 10 P.M. crossed at Yardley's Ferry, where we lodged. Weather very cold, snow 6 inches deep, no tents, and no houses to lodge in.[23]

By 10:00 A.M. on the 30th, McMichael and his comrades were back in Trenton.

Rebel morale soared, hyperbole reigned, and with it Washington's military reputation. The man whom many had said lacked the ability to command an army was suddenly a military genius, beside whom, the British traveler Nicholas Cresswell wrote, upon listening to his Virginia host, "Alexander, Pompey, and Hannibal were but pigmy generals." Cresswell also gave a good description of the reaction of the masses:

> The minds of the people are much altered. A few days ago they had given up the cause for lost. Their late successes have turned the scale and now they are all liberty mad again. Their recruiting parties could not get a man . . . last week, and now the men are coming by companies. Confound the turncoat scoundrels and the cowardly Hessians together. This has given them new spirits, and got them fresh succours. . . . They have recovered [from] their panic and it will not be an easy matter to throw them into confusion again.[24]

But Washington's decision to recross the Delaware and try to drive the British from Jersey or at least to its coasts quickly came up against harsh reality. For British reaction was almost as swift as their shock at the Hessian defeat. General Grant moved his headquarters southwest, from New Brunswick to Princeton. There he gathered the Hessian regiments that had abandoned the South Jersey posts. Lord Cornwallis, who had been about to take ship to England on leave, was ordered by Sir William Howe to cancel his passage and go immediately to New Jersey and take command of the army there. This was not good news for Washington. Cornwallis certainly had grave faults as a commander, which would be revealed in full later in the war in his Carolina campaign. But in action he was the opposite of Sir William.

Washington's immediate worry, however, was to keep at least part of his army together. It was the first of January 1777. Enlistments were up. The previous day Washington had deployed at Trenton on the southern side of Assunpink Creek, with "All the Artillory . . . Drawn up on the high Ground over the Bridge" and the infantry behind the artillery. North of the bridge guards were placed on roads leading into town and "patroles advanced two Milles with horse for each party." That done, on 1 January he made his pitch to the troops in a dramatic scene captured in the words of an unknown sergeant who wrote his account many years later:

> While we were at Trenton, on the last of December, 1776, the time for which I and most of my regiment had enlisted expired. At this trying time General Washington, having now but a little handful of men and many of them new recruits in which he could place but little confidence, ordered our regiment to be paraded, and personally addressed us, urging that we should stay a month longer. He alluded to our recent victory at Trenton; told us that our services were greatly needed, and that we could now do more for our country than we ever could at any future period; and in the most affectionate manner entreated us to stay. The drums beat for volunteers, but not a man turned out. The soldiers worn down with fatigue and privations, had their hearts fixed on home and the comforts of the domestic circle, and it was hard to forego the anticipated pleasures of the society of our dearest friends. The General wheeled his horse about, rode in front of the regiment, and addressing us again said, "My brave fellows, you have done all I asked you to do, and more than could be reasonably expected; but your country is at stake, your wives, your houses, and all that you hold dear. You have wore yourselves out with fatigue and hardships, but we know not how to spare you. If you will consent to stay only one month longer, you will render that service to the cause of liberty, and to your country, which you probably never can do under any other circumstances. The present is emphatically the crisis, which is to decide our destiny." The drums beat the second time. The soldiers felt the force of the appeal. One said to another, "I will remain if you will." Others

remarked, "We cannot go home under such circumstances." A few stepped forth, and their example was immediately followed by nearly all who were fit for duty in the regment, amounting to about two hundred volunteers. An officer enquired of the General if these men should be enrolled. He replied, "No! Men who will volunteer in such a case as this, need no enrollment to keep them to their duty."[25]

A modest reward was offered to those who stayed. Sergeant Bostwick of 7th Connecticut recalled that "by the pressing Solicitation of his Excellency a part of those whose time was out Consented on a ten Dollar bounty to Stay Six weeks longer & altho desirious as others to return home I engaged to Stay that time & made every exertion in my power to make as many of the Soldiers stay with me as I could & quite a number did engage with me who otherwise would have went hom." In his diary, Sergeant John Smith of the Rhode Island regiment wrote that on the 30th his brigade was paraded before General Mifflin,

> who was present with all the field Officers & after making fair promises to them he engaged them to tarey one month Longer in the Service & Almost Every man consented to stay Longer who Received 10 Doler Bounty as soon as Signed their names then the Genl with the soldiers gave three Huzzas & with Claping of hands for Joy amongst the Specttators as soon as that was over the Genl ordered us to heave a gill of Rum pr man & set out to Trenton to acquaint Genl Washington with the good success . . . we was Dismisd to Goe to our Quarters with great Applause the inhabitants & others saying we had Done honour to our Country viz New England.[26]

Another Rhode Island soldier, John Howland, said that Mifflin "did it well, although he made some promises, perhaps without the advice of Gen. Washington, which were never fulfilled; he said . . . every thing which should be taken from the enemy during the month should be the property of the men and the value of it divided among them."[27]

Despite the efforts of Washington and his officers, in the end he was left with only about 1,500 men, and his Continentals were footsore and weary. Although Cadwalader's force and Pennsylvania militia increased Washington's strength to 5,000, most of the additions were militia, and many of those inexperienced. Washington knew that Cornwallis was at Princeton, eleven miles away, with 8,000 men. Then why did he put his back to the Delaware and await Cornwallis's approach? He had done it once before, in Brooklyn, and had escaped through a combination of the weather, good planning, steady behavior by the troops, the skill of Massachusetts mariners, and good luck. But that was no reason to test his luck once more. The question remains unanswerable, and one can only conclude that Washington as a field commander showed flashes of brilliance flawed by inexplicable and serious errors of judgment.

The weather once more came to his aid. Another storm came up from the south but it brought with it rain instead of snow, and the temperatures steadily climbed until on the afternoon of New Year's Day in Philadelphia it was 51 degrees. In the countryside snow melted, the frost on the ground dissolved, and the eighteenth-century roads, nothing to boast of in good weather, became quagmires. It rained heavily through New Year's Eve, during the day, and into the night. Nevertheless, the British were on the move. Two battalions of British Grenadiers, a battalion of Guards, three regiments of foot, and a regiment of Hessian Grenadiers marched from New Brunswick at daybreak on 1 January to join General Grant in Princeton. They arrived at about 1:00 P.M. and found the troops already there under arms because of a skirmish near town between Rebels and British advanced pickets. One of our British diarists, Major Archibald Robertson, marched with the reinforcements, and in his entry of that day wrote, "In the middle of the Night Lord Cornwallis Arrived from York and superceded General Grant in his command." On that same night Captain Ewald of the Jägers began marching his command to Princeton at eleven o'clock and wrote in his diary, "since it was raining heavily the march was very unpleasant." He arrived at daybreak of the 2nd, "where I found the entire army under arms. I was ordered to draw biscuit and brandy from the depot for the men, and to continue marching." For that morning, Cornwallis had already taken the road with a 5,500-man force to Trenton, where His Lordship meant to bag the fox. To defend Princeton, he left behind three regiments of foot under Lieutenant Colonel Charles Mawhood.[28]

Both the elements and stiff resistance delayed the British march. The deep mud of the roads slowed the infantry and created a nightmare for the artillery train. Washington had sent to the village of Maidenhead (modern Lawrenceville), six miles from Trenton, a brigade commanded by the French volunteer Chevalier de La Rochefermoy to delay a British advance. La Rochefermoy unaccountably left his command and returned to Trenton, which was to the good, as the brigade was then taken over by his second, that stalwart veteran of many actions Colonel Edward Hand, whose Pennsylvania Rifle Regiment played the key role in Hand's delaying tactics. The back country and frontier riflemen kept Cornwallis's advance elements in a constant state of tension, as they slowed and on occasion temporarily stopped the British march at several points along the way, withdrawing when the British massed to overwhelm them, then from other vantage points in the woods and fields, again directing well-aimed harassing fire at the Redcoats and their Hessian allies. It was only "Toward evening," wrote Captain Ewald, that "we reached the heights" overlooking Trenton from the north, "which were occupied by the enemy with an infantry corps, some cavalry, and several guns." The British attacked, and after "slight resistance," according to Ewald, the Rebels withdrew through the town and across the bridge to Washington's position on the southern side of Assunpink Creek. Ewald claimed that the American rear guard "was so hard pressed by the Jägers and Light Infantry that the majority were either killed or captured." Henry Knox, on the other hand, in a letter to his wife, wrote that "Their retreat over the bridge was thoroughly secured by the artillery. After they had retired over the bridge, the enemy advanced within reach of our cannon, who saluted them with great vociferation and some execution." The important point among the details and different versions given by participants was that the British were repulsed at the bridge, and a Hessian attempt to ford the creek also was driven back. Sergeant Joseph White, with the American artillery, recalled the action at the bridge: "We let them come on some ways, then by a signal given, we all fired together. The enemy retreated off the bridge and formed again, and we were ready for them." The British were stubborn and kept coming, but twice more the cannons with round shot and canister swept the proud columns until, Sergeant White wrote, "such destruction it made, you cannot conceive. The bridge looked red as blood, with their killed and wounded, and their red coats."[29]

On the British side of the creek, a discussion ensued on what to do next. Cornwallis had arrived with the main force after dark. Did one push on or wait until the morning? Sir William Erskine is reputed to have said to Cornwallis, "If Washington is the general I take him to be, his army will not be found there in the morning." It was Cornwallis's decision, and it was not an easy one. The Americans were dug in, and their artillery commanded the bridge and nearby fords. Night attacks are always risky, and added to that would be another high-risk maneuver: crossing a body of water guarded by an alert, well-armed foe. Yet at Brooklyn Washington had slipped away from the British army by a night movement. His Lordship is said to have replied, "We've got the old fox safe now. We'll go over and bag him in the morning." Whatever either man actually said is unimportant, although one likes to think that Cornwallis did say what historians have been repeating over the past two centuries.

Washington, too, called a council of war and requested the advice of his senior commanders. In a famous letter written in 1814, Thomas Jefferson observed that Washington's "mind was great and powerful, without being of the very first order . . . and as far as he saw, no judgement was ever sounder. It was slow in operation, being little aided by invention or imagination, but sure in conclusion. Hence the common remark of his officers, of the advantage he derived from councils of war, where hearing all suggestions, he selected whatever was best." James Wilkinson in his memoirs gave credit to Brigadier General Arthur St. Clair (1737–1818) for the proposal to sneak away in the middle of the night and outflank Cornwallis. But Wilkinson was an unmitigated scoundrel, and his memoirs must always be used with great caution. It may well have been Washington who came up with a way out of the pickle he had gotten himself into. In 1824 John Lardner, who claimed to have been one of four light horsemen assigned to patrol the Quaker Bridge Road, wrote, "I well remember the circumstances of the Council sitting near to where the troop was station'd, on the evening of 2nd Janry, and to have heard it confidently mentioned the next day & repeatedly afterwards as the universal sentiment—that the thought of the movement that night originated entirely with Washington—solely his own manoeuvre." Whoever's idea it was, Washington wanted desperately to "avoid the appearance of a retreat," thus "destroying every dawn of hope which had begun to revive in the breasts of the Jersey Militia," and he therefore ordered the troops under Colonel Cadwalader and General Mifflin, which included large bands of militia, to join him at Trenton, "which they did by a Night march on the 1st Instt." It put them in an "exposed place," he admitted, but it also made them a part of his grand scheme.[30]

Washington's plan was simple, as most war plans are, and in the history of warfare certainly it was not the first time this particular maneuver was contemplated. The devil, of course, is in the execution, but at least fortune was smiling on Washington, for the weather had changed once more. A cold front had arrived early on 2 January, and certainly Washington took this into account when making his plans. A freeze could be expected that night, and in fact the temperature dropped below freezing after sundown. Captain Thomas Rodney of Delaware noted in his diary "the ground having been frozen firm by a keen N. West wind," and another participant observed, "the roads which the day before had been mud, snow and water, were congealed now and had become hard as pavement and solid."[31]

Washington "ordered all our Baggage to be removed silently to Burlington soon after dark." At midnight, leaving their fires burning and about 500 men behind to guard the bridge and fords and give the appearance that the entire army was still in the lines, the Rebel Army moved out to its right, the wheels of the artillery muffled by rags, to take the Quaker Bridge Road around Cornwallis's left flank. The troops moved "as silently as possible," wrote Nathanael Greene, who added, "The guards had orders to decamp three hours after our march began. No person knew where we were going except the Genl Officers." Captain Rodney confirmed the secrecy surrounding the movement: "no one knew what the Gen. meant to do." Washington explained to Hancock, "My Original plan when I set out from Trenton was to have pushed on to Brunswic" to destroy "all their stores and Magazines—taken . . . their Military Chest containing 70,000£ and put an end to the War." A large order indeed.[32]

Princeton was about sixteen miles away by the roundabout route Washington chose, avoiding the main road between Trenton and Princeton. At daybreak with 6,000 men he forded Stony Brook, about three miles southwest of Princeton, where the army was delayed while building a makeshift bridge for the artillery. There Washington sent General Sullivan ahead with his division on the byroad to Princeton. Leading the advance of General Greene's division was Brigadier General Hugh Mercer and his brigade of about 325 men. Mercer was ordered to take a side road to the left, running along Stony Brook to Worth's Mill, on the main road to Princeton, and there seize the bridge across Stony Brook, "for the double purpose," wrote James Wilkinson, "of intercepting fugitives from Princeton, and to cover our rear against Lord Cornwallis from Trenton." Washington then proceeded with the rest of General Greene's division on the byroad to Princeton.[33]

Unknown to the Americans, however, Cornwallis had ordered Lieutenant Colonel Mawhood, commanding three regiments of foot in Princeton, to bring two of them to Trenton, and Mawhood was on the march on the main road with 17th and 55th Foot. Mercer and Mawhood were on a collision course, with neither aware of the other's presence. British Light Dragoons scouting for Mawhood's column spotted Mercer's Brigade. When Washington learned of them he decided they were a reconnaissance party and left them to Mercer to deal with. Upon being informed of Mercer's approach, Mawhood turned his regiments around and prepared for battle, while Mercer, unaware that two regiments of foot were ahead of him, marched on. Captain Thomas Rodney, with his Delaware militia company, covered Mercer's flank and left the following account in his diary. The 17th Foot

> posted themselves behind a long string of buildings and an orchard [and Mercer] never discovered the enemy until he was turning the buildings they were posted behind, and then they were not more than fifty yards off. He immediately formed his men, with great courage, and poured a heavy fire in upon the the enemy, but they being greatly superior in number returned the fire and charged bayonets, and their onset was so fierce that General Mercer fell mortally wounded and many of his officers were killed, and the brigade being effectually broken, began a disorderly flight. Col. Haslet retired some small distance behind the buildings and endeavored to rally them, but receiving a bullet through his head, dropt dead on the spot and the whole brigade fled in confusion.[34]

The Pennsylvania rifleman Sergeant McMichael, who was in the thick of the fighting, described the moment of truth:

> Gen. Mercer with 100 Pennsylvania riflemen and 20 Virginians, were detached to the front to bring on the attack. The enemy then consisting of 500, paraded in an open field in battle array. We boldly marched to within 25 yards of them, and then commenced the attack, which was very hot. We kept up an incessant fire until it came time to pushing bayonets, when we were ordered to retreat.[35]

Thus was exhibited once again the vulnerability of riflemen unsupported by regulars armed with quick-loading muskets and trained to fight with bayonets. Bayonets could not be attached to rifles, and rifles were slow-loading. If indeed the Pennsylvanians advanced to within twenty-five yards of 17th Foot, it was foolhardy, for British infantry "pushing bayonets" could cover the gap between them far faster than the riflemen could reload, and the "retreat" must have been what Captain Rodney called it: "a disorderly flight."

It appeared that the Rebels were in for another drubbing. But the British were too few, and Washington was determined to carry the day. The sounds of the guns had brought him and Greene's division hurrying to the scene. Colonel Cadwalader's brigade of about 1,100 men was first on the field and began to deploy from column, but the fire was so hot that the men in front broke twice and sowed confusion among those behind. "At this moment," a soldier recalled, Washington rode "in front of the American army" with his usual contempt for death and attempted to bring order out of chaos and has been given credit for changing the course of the fight. Yet according to Colonel Cadwalader Washington "exposed himself very much, but expostulated to no purpose." Cadwalader said he suggested that his brigade re-form 100 yards to the rear and that Washington agreed. Whatever happened, the two men, joined by General Greene, organized a counterattack by Cadwalader's brigade, to which Washington added Colonel Daniel Hitchcock's New England Brigade and Colonel Edward Hand's Pennsylvania riflemen. The artist Charles Willson Peale, then Lieutenant Peale of the Philadelphia militia, was in the fight, and in his journal entry of that day wrote, "I must here give the New England Troops their due. They were the first who regularly formed, and stood the fire, without regarding the balls, which whistled their thousand notes around our heads." The Americans advanced, took heavy British fire, but continued on until, according to Cadwalader, "I pressed my party forward, huzzaed, and cried out, They fly, the day is our own." The British, reported Cadwalader, "flew with the utmost precipitation, and we pursued with great eagerness." The British did indeed break, and Nathanael Greene, who was not usually given to praising militia, was unstinting in his description of the behavior of Cadwalader's Philadelphia Associators. "Great credit is due to the Philadelphia Militia who were in the Princeton action and who behaved exceeding well considering they were never in action before."[36]

The scene of carnage on the recovered ground was recalled several years later by a Rebel sergeant:

O, the barbarity of man! On our retreat we left a comrade of ours whose name was Loomis from Lebanon, Ct., whose leg was broken by a musket ball, under a cart in a yard; but on our return he was dead, having received several wounds from a British bayonet. My old associates were scattered about groaning, dying and dead. One officer who was shot from his horse lay in a hollow place in the ground rolling and writhing in his blood, unconscious of anything around him. The ground was frozen and all the blood which was shed remained on the surface, which added to the horror of this scene of carnage.[37]

The British survivors fled toward Trenton and Princeton, depending where they were when they were broken. The official British casualty return showed 18 dead, 58 wounded, and 200 missing, of whom many were prisoners. The Americans lost some 23 killed and about 20 wounded. Two of the British wounded were carried into a private home in Princeton. The owner of the house, who referred to the British soldiers as "Regulars," described the scene:

> Almost as soon as the firing was over our house was filled and surrounded with Genl Washington's Men, and himself on horseback at the door. They brought in with them on their Shoulders two Wounded Regulars, one of them was shot at his hip and the bullet lodged in his groin, and the other was shot through his body Just below his short ribs he was in very great pain and bled much out of both sides, and often desired to be removed from once place to another, which was done Accordingly and he dyed about three o'clock in the afternoon. They was both Used very Tenderly by the Rebels (as they call them). The other also bled much and they put a Cloth dipt in vinegar to the wound to Stop it and three of them Stay'd with the wounded men near an hour after the Others were gone, the man that lived was left at our house above two days and one night With his Wound not drest, before the Regulars that was left to take care of the sick and wounded would take him away.[38]

The dead British regular was lucky in contrast to Washington's old friend General Mercer, who also must have been in great agony in the ten days it took him to die. Dr. Benjamin Rush tended him, and on 7 January wrote to Richard Henry Lee that Mercer "is wounded in seven places with a bayonet. One of these wounds is in his forehead, but the most alarming of them are in his belly."[39]

"Never . . . despise any Enemy two much"

Meanwhile, what of Cornwallis at Trenton that morning? He awakened to the astonishing news that the fox had vanished. The answer to his whereabouts was soon apparent, "which surprised everyone," Captain Ewald admitted. At "about 8 o'clock," wrote Major Archibald Robertson, "a very Brisk fire of Small Arms and Smart Cannonading was heard in our rear towards Prince Town, upon which the Guards and Grena-

Hugh Mercer Jr. (Study for *The Death of General Mercer at the Battle of Princeton, January 3, 1777*) by John Trumbull

diers British had orders to go back as quick as possible and the Light Infantry and Hessian Grenadiers to follow." Alas, "before we got there the affair was over." Captain Ewald described the "entire field of action . . . covered with corpses." The shock was such, said Ewald, "that it was completely forgotten even to obtain information about where the Americans had gone." Thus the race went on because Cornwallis feared for the British supplies at New Brunswick, "as it was said," wrote Major Robertson, "they intended the same Coup upon Brunswick."[40]

The Rebel Army, however, was at the end of its tether. In action or on the march almost constantly in harsh weather since 26 December, the troops could not sustain a grueling seventeen-mile march followed by almost certain battle, for Cornwallis was not Sir William Howe. Mortified at being hoodwinked, the rich stores in New Brunswick apparently in danger, he would not dillydally. Washington conferred with his officers, a quick council on horseback, and decided that "the harrased State of our own Troops (many of them having had no rest for two nights & a day) and the danger of loosing the advantage we had gained by aiming at too much induced me by the advice of my Officers to relinquish the attempt." The army left the New Brunswick road, angled to the left, and marched about ten miles to Pluckemin in the hill country, where Washington was "obliged to encamp," wrote Captain Rodney, "and await the coming up of nearly 1000 men who were not able through fatigue and hunger to keep up with the main body . . . as all our baggage had been left at Trenton the army in this situation was obliged to encamp on the bleak mountains whose tops were covered with snow, without even blankets to cover them." Lieutenant Peale was there and noted in his diary that "Many of the men, in their hard march on an icy road, were entirely barefooted." Washington also testified to the state to which his little army had been reduced and paid a rare tribute to the militia. He doubted that the Philadelphia Associators "will scarcely submit to the hardships of a winter campaign much longer, especially as they very unluckily sent their Blankets with their baggage to Burlington. I must do them justice, however, to add, that they have undergone more fatigue and hardships than I expected Militia (especially Citizens) would have done at this inclement Season. I am just moving to Morris town where I shall endeavour to put them under the best cover I can. hitherto we have been without any and many of our poor Soldiers quite bear foot & ill clad in other respects."[41]

At 9:00 A.M. on 6 January the army resumed its march, the goal safety in the rugged hill country around Morristown, where it arrived at 5:00 P.M. Despite its fatigue and ragged condition, it was a victorious army, which was made quite clear by the people who watched them go by. One of the marchers recalled that "The inhabitants manifested very different feelings towards us, from those exhibited a few weeks before, and were now ready to take up arms against the British."[42]

Given the condition of his army, however, Washington's decision to disengage was wise, for Cornwallis had set out from Princeton at about 4:30 P.M. on the 3rd, "and after a most fatiguing forced march all night long in frost and ice," wrote Major Robertson, "we reached Brunswick about 6 in the morning the 4th." Speaking for many in the British army with regard to the startling events of the past ten days, the Major added, "we . . . must hope it wll serve as a lesson in future never to despise any Enemy two much."[43]

10

"Harrass their troops to death"

"They are now become a formidable enemy"

The psychological impact of the Trenton–Princeton campaign on Americans, Britons, and highly interested European onlookers was immeasurable. To Captain Ewald of the Jägers "This brilliant coup which Washington performed against Lord Cornwallis, which raised so much hubbub and sensation in the world . . . gave Washington the reputation of an excellent general." Of Washington's despised ragtag and bobtail army, Colonel William Harcourt, who had captured Charles Lee, wrote to his father, "though it was once the fashion of this army to treat them in the most contemptible light, they are now become a formidable enemy."[1]

It also appeared that even Sir William Howe had given up on his brother's dream of reconciliation through sweet talk, proclamations, and the carefully measured application of force. "I do not now see," he wrote to Lord Germain on 20 January, "a prospect of terminating the war but by a general action, and I am aware of the difficulties in our way to obtain it, as the Enemy moves with so much more celerity than we possibly can with our foreign troops who are too much attached to their baggage." How like a frustrated general to blame troubles of his own making on somebody else, in this case his German allies. Had they not suffered enough humiliation at Trenton? Must they now take full blame for the failed policy of the brothers Howe? How interesting that Sir William, who had planned just such an action before his brother's arrival, had come full circle. Now, however, the man he faced was not the George Washington of Long Island, Manhattan, and Fort Washington. The bitter experiences of those debacles had been largely, if not wholly, absorbed by the Virginian and he came out of them a far wiser and cunning commander.[2]

While the British abandoned most of New Jersey to the Rebels, maintaining bases only at South Amboy and New Brunswick, Washington led his victorious but scarecrow army to the rugged hill country surrounding Morristown for his first but not last winter encampment in this haven from British attack. He wrote to General Putnam that he meant to stay only a few days while the troops recovered from their ordeal; and later to John Hancock, "as soon as the purposes are answered for which we came, I think to remove, though I confess, I do not know how we shall procure covering for our Men elsewhere." As it turned out, the army would not leave until May. On 7 January Sergeant McMichael "secured good quarters, where I lived happily while we remained at Morristown, with very agreeable people." Although the sergeant described the town as "devoid of beauty, both in its form and location," he found its "inhabitants very hospitable, all professors of the Presbyterian religion, which renders them to me very agreeable."[3]

New Jersey's landscape has been so altered by nineteenth- and twentieth-century industry and faceless suburban sprawl that one does not associate rugged hill country with this now heavily populated state. In 1777, however, it was easy to see why Washington chose Morristown as his winter encampment. It rested on a high plateau protected on the east by a range of hills that allowed passage only by narrow passes that could be easily defended. On the west a ridge pierced by passes for escape overlooked the plateau. Although it was on the main post road between the Hudson and Delaware Rivers, the road network in the region was sparse, giving Sir William Howe few choices for approach. Morristown was about thirty miles from what was then New York City, thirty-six miles from the British post at South Amboy, and forty miles from the main British post in Jersey, at New Brunswick. The Tories, who had been in the ascendancy during Washington's miserable retreat through the state, had either fled or were keeping their heads down, cowed by now-active local Rebel militia units. While the New Jersey militia did what eastern militia was very good at when the regular army was nearby—maintaining control over the populace and harassing British foraging parties—Washington was in an excellent position to keep a close eye on Sir William Howe. From Morristown it was but a short march northward to the Hudson Valley and an almost equally short march southward to the Rebel capital of Philadelphia, by which he set such great store.

Even before setting out from Pluckemin to Morristown, Washington hoped to set in motion operations designed to help clear the British from New Jersey and keep them on the defensive elsewhere. He ordered General Heath, still in the Hudson Highlands, to "move down towards New York with a Considerable force as if you had a design upon the city— that being an object of great importance, the Enemy will be reduced to the necessity of withdrawing a Considerable part of their force from the Jerseys if not the whole to Secure the City. I shall draw the force on this Side of the North River together at Morristown—where I shall watch the motions of the Enemy & avail myself of every circumstance." On the same day he wrote to Major General Israel Putnam, who was then in Bristol, Pennsylvania, with about 600 men, "to march the Troops under your command to Crosswix [Crosswicks, New Jersey, about fifteen miles northeast of Burlington] and keep a strick watch on the Enemy upon that quarter." He warned Putnam to be alert "lest you meet with a surprise. As we have made two successful Attacks upon the Enemy—by way of surprise—they will be pointed with resentment and if there is any possibility of retaliating will Attempt it." He then became even more specific: "You will keep as many Spies out as You will See proper, a number of horsemen in the dress of the Country must be Constantly Kept going backwards & forwards for this purpose." And if Putnam had dependable intelligence of any major movement, "Let me be informed thereof as soon as possible by Express." Early on he also approved of Brigadier General William Winds (1727–1789) of the New Jersey militia waylaying British movements on the "Roads between-Brunswick and Amboy."[4]

General Heath followed his orders and marched on the advanced British position near Kingsbridge, in what is now the Bronx. Howe's Hessian aide, Captain von Münchhausen, wrote that "General Washington gave us a good scare from the side of Kingsbridge near Fort Knyphausen." It was on this occasion that von Münchhausen left us a good impression of Sir William's priorities. As the young German told it,

Howe could not personally attend to Heath's threat as "There was to be a big festival because of the Queen's birthday, during which ceremony my General was to receive the Order of Bath from Admiral Howe, in the name of the King." Von Münchhausen accompanied General Knyphausen with a small force of Hessians and Tories to counter Heath's movement. It must be admitted that Howe's presence was not needed. Heath sent a summons to surrender, it was rejected, and after an exchange of artillery fire Heath withdrew. Von Münchhausen then returned to New York City, arriving "in time to see a superb fireworks and to have the pleasure of attending the ball. A crazy life it is, just having been under serious fire, and then seeing fireworks of joy and to dance."[5]

Although Heath's attack, if it can be described as such, was feeble, it made Sir William nervous. Von Münchhausen wrote, "Since General Washington continues to harass us in Jersey, as well as at Kingsbridge, orders have been sent to Rhode Island for six English battalions to return here."[6]

"Shabby ill managed occasions"

It has been written by a leading historian of the war that "except for . . . sporadic skirmishes, there was no military activity in the Jerseys that winter." And John Adams, ever vigilant for military shortcomings real or imaginary, wrote to General Sullivan, "Are we to go on forever this way, maintaining vast armies in idleness, and losing completely the fairest opportunity that ever was offered of destroying an enemy completely in our power?" The historian was referring to the absence of major battles. As for John Adams, did he temporarily take leave of his senses? His vision of "vast armies" was certainly an incredible figment of his imagination. To understand what happened in Jersey we would do best to turn to British and Hessian sources, for the historian's statement, and Adams's pipe dreams, would have come as great surprises to such men as Captain Johann Ewald of the Jägers, or Major Archibald Robertson of the Royal Engineers, or the Scottish grenadier Captain John Peebles (1739–1823) of the Black Watch (42nd Royal Highland Regiment). While Sir William partied in New York City, there occurred in the winter of 1777 a nasty partisan war that kept the British and Hessian garrisons at Amboy, New Brunswick, and vicinities in a constant state of activity. It had started in a small way during General Lee's stay at Morristown in late 1776 but now began in earnest. Washington was clear in his purpose: "harrass their troops to death," he wrote to General Heath, describing the general nature of operations in New Jersey, where "We have found the advantage of such practices . . . for by keeping four or five hundred men far advanced, we not only oblige them to forage with parties of 1500 and 2000 to cover, but every now and then give them a smart Brush." Weeks earlier he had written to Joseph Reed that in Jersey "I would not suffer a Man to stir beyond their Lines, nor suffer them to have the least Intercourse with the Country." In a letter of 7 January to Hancock, Washington reported a militia victory over fifty Waldeck soldiers who had been on a raid with British cavalry to intercept a party of Rebels. But the force was almost cut off itself and retreated. Twelve British troopers of the 17th Light Dragoons and the Waldeckers later were attacked by about the same number of Rebel militia. The dragoons escaped, but none of the Waldeckers returned. Washington reported eight to ten killed and wounded and the remainder taken prisoner.[7]

The men on the receiving end of the partisan campaign were not happy troops at the beginning of 1777. We have focused to now on the privations endured by Washington's army, and there can be no doubt that they were prolonged and severe. But the enemy soldiers also felt much used and abused, and in the time-honored manner of men at war, let their feelings be known. Upon taking up winter quarters in a house near New Brunswick, Captain Ewald of the Hessian Jägers described the conditions endured by the British and Hessians.

> After a very exhausting campaign, these quarters, where the soldier could not even get straw for his bedding, were to serve for refreshing the troops. For this whole region had been completely sacked during the army's march in the past autumn, and had been abandoned by all the inhabitants. The entire army had been stripped bare of shoes and stockings by the constant marching during the bad weather. Uniforms were torn and the officers, especially those of the jäger companies, had almost no clothing on their bodies. The winter now began to set in very severely, for snow had fallen for several days over a half-man deep.[8]

On 9 January Lord Cornwallis visited the Jäger positions, and Ewald reported that "when he saw that the men were very cheerful despite their ragged clothing and hard duty, he ordered me to assure the jägers that plentiful provisions would arrive any day, and that each jäger would be clothed at his expense." His Lordship was true to his word, and by the middle of the month, Ewald reported, "everything necessary for the men was arriving in abundance from New York," and on the 23rd arrived the "promised gift . . . of a complete uniform for each man." But their situation remained far from pleasant. The American positions "were less than one hour's march away." Skirmishing that Ewald called "teasing" occurred daily, "and when they did not visit us, we rendered the honors to the Americans." A constant state of readiness was demanded of the troops. "Not only did the men have to stay dressed day and night, but they had to be kept together, the horses constantly saddled, and everything packed."[9]

Ewald's mention of horses alerts us to a daily need of eighteenth-century armies. Instead of gasoline, oil, and spare parts so vital to modern armies, forage for horses was critical, and getting it was dangerous, as our Jäger captain pointed out:

> the horses also had to be fed, and the little fodder which we found in this area could not last long. For this reason foraging had to be undertaken, and since the Americans were close on our necks, we could not procure any forage without shedding blood.[10]

Major Robertson of the Royal Engineers reported that on 20 January part of a foraging party of 500 men "was attacked by Rebels, which occasion'd such disorder Amongst the Waggon Drivers that 42 Waggons were left behind." The Rebel force of 400 New Jersey militia and about fifty Pennsylvania riflemen were commanded by Major General Philemon Dickinson (1739–1809) of the Jersey militia, who often took the field and was especially active in supporting the Continental Army in that busy winter of 1777. The wagon drivers had good reason to become disordered, as George Washington made clear in a somewhat more detailed account of the action in a letter to John Hancock. He claimed that "The enemy retreated with so much precipitation, that General Dickinson was able to take only nine prisoners," and the British "were observed to carry off a good many dead and wounded in light Waggons." Prevented from crossing Millstone River on the bridge, which was covered by three British cannons, Dickinson had led his troops downstream and plunged into the river through the ice. Washington was unstinting in his praise:

> Genl Dickinsons behaviour reflects the highest honour upon him, for tho' his Troops were all raw, he lead them thro' the River, middle

deep, and gave the enemy so severe a charge, that, altho' supported by three feild pieces, they gave way and left their Convoy.[11]

On 23 January a British convoy left from New Brunswick to Amboy with an escort of two regiments of foot to collect provisions. About 400 Rebels attacked but, wrote Major Robertson, were "drove off." Yet this minor skirmish cost the British fourteen men and one officer "Killed and Wounded."[12]

Major Robertson joined an expedition on 1 February of "upwards of 1,000" troops, Brigadier General Sir William Erskine commanding. At about 2:30 P.M., forage collected and the wagons nearly loaded, they were attacked by 400 to 500 Rebels. After a hot firefight of about ten minutes, Erskine ordered a battalion of Hessian grenadiers "to advance towards the Rear and Flank of the Rebels," who showed great good sense and "immediately gave way and ran." The British and Germans pursued, but suddenly another Rebel force "appeared within 250 Yards" and "began to form with great Steadiness," but they also "run away" under artillery and musket fire. Simultaneously two more Rebel columns appeared, but "they very soon disspersed and run except poping from behind Rails." Robertson estimated the total number of Rebels at 2,000 and claimed that they left "between 30 and 40 dead on the spot besides a Number of Wounded they had taken away." Later accounts received by the British led Robertson to estimate that in total 180 Rebels had been killed or wounded, although the casualty estimates of both sides with regard to the enemy should be taken with a large grain of salt. Robertson admitted to "Our loss" at "30 Killed and Wounded.[13]

A major expedition of about 2000 men under the personal command of Lord Cornwallis marched at daybreak on 8 February. The intrepid Captain Ewald and 50 Jägers led the way. All the way the column marched through woods "in which three devastated plantations were situated," and at the first plantation American riflemen only "withdrew after stubborn resistance." As the Americans withdrew "several were killed and captured," but that did not discourage the survivors or their comrades. The village of Quibbletown was the British target. A creek in a ravine wound through the town, and there the British and Hessians found more American riflemen on both sides of the ravine, behind stone garden walls, and in the houses. Their stubborn resistance did not end until artillery was brought forward and they were bombarded. Even then, however, they retreated only as far as "the nearest wood on the other side of the village." The mission was completed at 3:00 P.M., and Captain Ewald was ordered to withdraw:

> I had hardly begun the movement when I was so heavily attacked from all sides by a vast swarm of riflemen that only a miracle of bravery by my men could save me. Nevertheless, I reached the village, where the crossings over the bridges were covered by the battery.
>
> The enemy took possession of the outlying houses on the other side and erected cannon behind stone walls, whereupon a stubborn fight occurred and many brave men were lost. I received orders here to form the rear guard and two companies of light infantry joined me. The road was not more than five to six hundred paces from the village up to the wood, where several cannon had been placed to cover my retreat, but I was left on my own through the wood.
>
> The enemy hung on our rear until we reached our outposts.[14]

Captain Ewald, an exemplary officer and small-unit combat commander, had done well, and Lord Cornwallis "honored me by publishing an order expressing his satisfaction with me and my courageous men, and each jäger received a gift of one piaster." But the good captain also admitted that "Since the army would have been gradually destroyed through this foraging, from here on the forage was procured from New York." But Ewald also felt that "these encounters were very beneficial for the army, for a renewed spirit entered the hearts of the soldiers, who had become completely disheartened by the disasters of Trenton and Princeton."[15]

Some local foraging did continue, and one expedition was described by Captain John Peebles of the Black Watch. It was a "fine clear frosty morng" on the Sabbath, 23 February, when troops who had returned from Rhode Island, including Peebles' regiment, went ashore at Amboy and marched into the countryside. Peebles and twenty of his men joined a detachment of 400 to 500 grenadiers "to make a sweep." Peebles and his company were in advance when Americans appeared and a firefight developed. The ensuing action was not handled well by the British command. Following a series of movements, Peebles had maneuvered to a fence line at the edge of some woods. He now had fourteen or fifteen men left. Reinforcements came to their support but fired at too great a distance to do damage and "soon found themselves gall'd by a fire on their right" and were in danger of being outflanked. In this

Situation the men are dropping down fast when they . . . are given orders to retire which I hear'd nothing off. I remained at my post till I had not one man left near me except Jno. Carr lying wounded, & fired away all my Cartridges, when seeing the rascals coming pretty close up I took to my heels and ran back to the Compy. under a heavy fire which thank God I escaped, as I fortunately did all the rest of the day.[16]

Peebles admitted "in this affair we had the worst of it," because of contradictory orders given by Colonel Campbell and Colonel Charles Mawhood. The British gathered their wounded and loaded them into wagons. When the Rebels saw that the British were marching back they immediately gathered for the attack and had to be discouraged by "a counter march to oppose them," whereupon the Rebels retired immediately. The British soldiers were "much fatigued & harrassed a great many of them quite knock'd up," and their travail had not ended. On the main road the Americans "appear'd in our rear & rear flanks & harrass'd the Grenadrs. that formed the rear guard very much. We were at last obliged to halt & fire some Cannon amongst them which sent them a scampering." Then more Rebels appeared in front of the column and they, too, had to be dispersed. The British got into Amboy "between 7 & 8 oclock much fatigued." Peebles gave their loss at "69 killed & wounded & 6 missing." The next day he

went ashore in Eveng & saw the wounded men several of them in a very dangerous way poor fellows, what pity it is to throw away such men as these on such shabby ill managed occasions.[17]

"We are distressed beyond measure for Cloathing"

Daily alarms continued throughout the winter, and "Scarcely a day passed," wrote Captain Ewald, "when we did not have to stand under arms for hours in the deepest snow." Yet there were, he admitted, compensations, for Cornwallis's earlier largesse had not been a one-shot affair:

But the men lacked nothing, for the most excellent provisions of salted beef and pork, peas, butter, rice, and flour for bread, along with the best English beer, were commonly supplied durng this time. Indeed the concerns of the English nation for its soldiers went so far that twenty overcoats of the finest English material were furnished free to each company, which were distributed to the sentries and the sick.[18]

Contrast that with the situation of Washington's much-diminished army at Morristown. There would be none of the "best English beer" and "finest English" cloth for the likes of them. The subject of logistics, which is the technical term for maintaining and transporting an army, is a largely thankless job that has none of the glamour of battlefield feats, which is why during the Revolution field commanders anxious for glory tried in every way possible to squirm out of the job of supplying the army. Yet the vital nature of logistics was succinctly described by that primary icon of eighteenth-century warriors, Frederick the Great of Prussia, who complained, "It is not I who commands the army, but flour and forage who are the masters." And of history's greatest field commander, Alexander the Great, Peter Green wrote in his brilliant biography, "One of the crucial factors behind Alexander's continuous and unbroken success was the unparalleled efficiency of his supply and transport commands." Applying this to the Continental Army's situation, one might say that one of the crucial factors behind the near-breakdown of the war effort on more than one occasion was the unparalleled inefficiency of its supply system.[19]

Writing on 10 January, Washington revealed that "We are distressed beyond measure for Cloathing, (Shoes & Stockings particularly) & for want of some person whose business it is to attend to this department, those articles which have been sent from Philadelphia have either been lost—or misapplied, to the extreame prejudice of the Service." Misapplied supplies was a common occurrence. In the case of a big shipment of clothing procured by Congress in New England and bound for Morristown via Fishkill, New York, near the east bank of the Hudson, Washington had become concerned with the shipment's unaccountable delay when he was informed by the quartermaster general that New York State, without a by-your-leave, had appropriated twenty-six bales of the shipment. Washington wrote with much agitation to William Duer (1747–1794), a member of New York's Committee of Safety, "This I look upon as a most extraordinary peice of Conduct" that placed him "in the greatest difficulties, for depending upon that Cloathing, I have not applied elsewhere." He insisted that the balance of the shipment be forwarded immediately. "I don't doubt," he ended, "but your Troops were in want of Cloathing, but consider they were in comfortable Barracks while ours are marching over Frost and Snow many without a shoe Stocking or Blanket." The New York Committee of Safety wrote a long letter of explanation and apology, assured Washington that "if we have erred it was from an anxiety to promote the public service," and promised never to do it again.[20]

Whatever the Committee's promise was worth, it did not apply to two Continental officers, Major General Israel Putnam and Major General John Sullivan. The following July Putnam ordered part of another shipment of clothing at Fishkill destined for Washington's troops distributed to his needy soldiers, and once the balance of the shipment had crossed the river and was wending its way southward, Sullivan intercepted it and did the same. This practice by Continental offices detached from the main army continued throughout the war, and Washington protested in vain, as he did against states that regularly appropriated clothing, other supplies, and sometimes food passing through their respective jurisdictions on their way to the Continental Army. Even militia officers on their own authority got in the game. In June an increasingly frustrated Washington, realizing that he could not stop the practice, directed one of his aides-de-camp, Alexander Hamilton, to inform Putnam that "His Excellency desires you will not open or distribute the Cloathing stopped at your post, 'till a Deputy Cloathier comes up to take Charge of it, who will be with you without Loss of time." Washington wrote to Putnam in greater detail the following day: "Some Regiments not content with a compleat suit of Uniform have drawn a Frock, waistcoat and over alls, by which means they are doubly clad while others are perishing. This must not be allowed." While he was dictating this letter, Putnam's letter of 8 June came to hand, which informed Washington that General Gates, commanding the Northern Department with headquarters at Albany, also had hijacked a shipment of clothing sent to him by mistake. Washington found it "very extraordinary that Genl Gates should undertake to stop the Cloathing of those Regs. that are at peekskill. that accounts for the deficiency." These are only a few examples of the correspondence concerning clothing and other supplies that took up so much of Washington's time. But with that enormous capacity for detail—without, we hasten to add, neglecting all of his other responsibilities as well as the big picture—he persevered. This attention to duty was one of his great strengths as a commander.[21]

Clothing was important, food more so. Provisions were almost always short, and sometimes absent. The food supplies of the Continental Army at Morristown rarely equaled the cornucopia described by Captain Ewald. Writing on 3 February, Washington reported that "The present State of the Commissary's department in this quarter, makes me fearful . . . that the Army will in a little while want Supplies of every kind." Washington and other officers, especially Nathanael Greene, often importuned Congress to adequately supply the army, and to regale readers continually with their pleas would only tax their patience. Readers may take it as a given that throughout the war the Continental Army was often ill fed, ill clothed, ill supplied. In our time of the bountiful PX it may be difficult for some to realize just how bad the situation was. The hardships the troops suffered were incredible. It was largely an infantry army, and the soldiers therefore depended on their feet to get wherever they were ordered to go. Yet lack of good shoes was chronic, and clear evidence exists that the tales of bloody footprints in the snow are not myth. They often were without tents in foul weather and lay down to sleep, if sleep were possible, on sodden ground or snow. Bellies often were empty, bodies more often than not exposed to wind and rain, sleet and snow, because of the tattered condition of the soldiers' clothing. It is remarkable that they persevered, and not at all unremarkable that many left the army when their terms of service were up and never reenlisted. A European regular army of the time would not have put up with such conditions.[22]

The fault for this state of affairs rested with Congress, which insisted on depending on the states to supply the army. In addition to Congress's inexperience in military matters and pipe dreams of quickly winning the war, this arrangement was in keeping with an American political culture that placed high value on decentralization of authority and local initiative, strains still deeply embedded in American political thought and clearly revealed in the speech and actions of many current politicians. It was accompanied by a deep-seated distrust of standing professional armies. In 1778, having seen the error of its ways, Congress attempted to centralize logistics. But the spirit of localism defeated the effort. State and local officials at all levels continually exerted their authority and seriously interfered with the collection and transfer of supplies to the Continental Army, until finally Congress gave up and left it to the legislatures of the states to feed the army. In the words of the historian E. Wayne Carp, "Real Whig ideology, with its conspiratorial fear of power, suspicion of corruption, hatred of standing armies, and idealization of republican virtue" prevailed, even in the face of the obvious and gross inefficiency of the logistical system. It was irrational, but when has irrational thinking stopped humans from making wrong decisions? This political attitude, not battlefield defeats, almost lost the war. As Washington struggled with the never-ending headache of logistics and attempted to keep unrelenting pressure on Sir William, a grave problem that had been lurking since Washington had taken command of the Continental Army at Boston came to a head and demanded a decision, for failure to deal with it could destroy the army, and with it the Revolution.[23]

"Dont conclude . . . that I think inoculation a light matter"

A sergeant in Washington's army recalled more than a half century later, "At Morristown I was sick of the small-pox and many of our little army died there of that disease."[24]

One of the eighteenth century's scourges was the highly contagious disease of smallpox. Americans born in the first half of the twentieth century can connect it to a great fear of parents when I was growing up: polio. People feared smallpox as they did the plague, as they had for nearly three thousand years. Perhaps today's readers can appreciate this grave health problem more than other diseases of the past because of recent fears of its spread by biological warfare, and as I write, the continuing controversy in the United States over whether to vaccinate all health workers. In 1775 a smallpox epidemic struck North America from deepest Mexico to the Arctic. It did not end until 1782—one year shy of lasting throughout the Revolutionary War. In an age of small population levels—the Thirteen Colonies then had only about 2.5 million people—it killed more than 100,000 and left countless others scarred for life, some with the loss of sight in one or both eyes, many covered over their bodies with loathsome, stinking pustules. Vaccination was not available, for it was not until 1796 that the English physician Edward Jenner discovered vaccination, which he published in 1798 in his famous *An Inquiry into the Causes and Effects of the Variola Vaccinae*. Before vaccination one could flee the place of outbreak, or the victims or potential victims could be quarantined. But flight meant the possibility of infected people spreading the disease. Charleston quarantined all immigrants on Sullivan's Island, in the harbor, for months. In each case, however, people were still susceptible to catching smallpox at another time. For in prevaccination years there was only way to become immune to smallpox: to catch it and survive. Once that happened, you were immune for life. And there was a way to make that happen with a fair chance of not coming down with a full-blown case of smallpox. It was called inoculation. But it was risky.[25]

Inoculation had been practiced for centuries in parts of Africa and Asia but did not become known in Europe until the early eighteenth century, one of the sources being the Massachusetts preacher Cotton Mather, who had learned of it from his African slave. From a smallpox patient a doctor took pus containing the smallpox virus. Then he made an incision, usually in the hand or arm, of the person to be inoculated and placed the pus inside the incision. A different method was used in Asia, where the scabs of a victim were ground up and inhaled through the nose. In the case of the incision method, John Adams, who underwent inoculation along with his brother in 1764 during a smallpox outbreak in Boston, left a description of the procedure. "They took their Launcetts and with their Points divided the skin for about a Quarter of an Inch and just suffering the Blood to appear, buried a thread . . . in the Channell." The thread contained the virus. John Adams came through it with only eight or ten pockmarks, and his wife, Abigail, who put off the procedure until 1776, also survived with only a mild case.[26]

John Adams became a fervent champion of inoculation, writing to Abigail in the summer of 1776, "The small Pox! The small Pox! What shall We do with it? I could almost wish that an innoculating Hospital was opened, in every Town in New England." Yet he was also well aware of the danger involved. One could die from inoculation. Adams had written in 1764 to Abigail, then his fiancé, "Dont conclude from any Thing I have written that I think Inoculation a light matter," which may be why she delayed her own inoculation for twelve years. But Adams felt the risk worth the chance of attaining immunity from the dread pestilence. In the same letter to Abigail he maintained "who would not cheerfully submit . . . rather than pass his whole Life in continual Fears, in subjection, under Bondage."[27]

The answer: many people. Inoculation was an extremely controversial procedure. It was new, therefore it was feared. But people also properly objected to the often unregulated nature of inoculation. Those inoculated against the disease could spread it as quickly as patients who had taken sick naturally, and it was absolutely necessary to keep them in isolation until they had fully recovered. Yet inoculated patients often displayed scandalous irresponsibility in this regard, including Abigail Adams, who repeatedly attended church services during her recovery period. The danger presented by inoculated patients sometimes provoked violent responses. During an outbreak of smallpox in Boston in 1721, Cotton Mather talked Dr. Zabdiel Boylston into an inoculation program that ended when a mob firebombed Mather's home. In 1738 Charleston outlawed inoculation within two miles of the city, and in 1747 it was forbidden within the city and county of New York. In Norfolk, Virginia, in 1768 a mob set fire to the house of a doctor who had inoculated patients inside. They fled into the rain. Riots and tarring and feathering erupted in Salem and Marblehead in 1774, and an inoculation hospital was destroyed. In fact, the fiercest resistance against inoculation was in New England, and it was there, one year after the mobs in Salem and Marblehead ran amok that the War of the Revolution began, and George Washington was faced with a decision on what to do about this pestilence, which could destroy an army faster and more terribly than any human foe.[28]

Smallpox struck Boston in the summer of 1775. By that fall the British army cooped up within the besieged city had inoculated the relatively few troops who had not had the disease. Washington, however, was hesitant to order inoculation of the Continental Army, which had far greater numbers in danger of contracting smallpox. It could not be done all at once or the army would be immobilized in the face of a possible British attack. And there was always the danger in such an undisciplined horde of inoculated men evading isolation and starting an epidemic among the entire army as well as the surrounding civilian population. Left unsaid but no doubt weighing upon Washington's mind was the strong New England feeling against inoculation, for at that time the army was largely comprised of New England men. He decided against inoculation in favor of quarantine, isolation, and continuing, he wrote to John Hancock, "the utmost Vigilance against this most dangerous enemy." He continued this vigilance the day after he arrived in New York City. In his first general order from New York he directed that "All persons infected with the Small-Pox are to be immediately removed to a secure place to be provided by the Qr Mr General, who will consult the magistrates of the City, thereupon. A proper Guard, to be composed of men, who have had that disorder, to be fixed at this Hospital, to prevent any intercourse but such as the manager shall license."[29]

But in Morristown in January and February 1777 the threat became so dangerous to the army that Washington had a change of heart. New recruits to the army were coming via Philadelphia, the smallpox capital of America, and he had already seen at long distance what the virus could do to an army. The American army retreating from Canada had been decimated by the pox. He could not stand by and allow that to

happen to the main army, even as small and exhausted as it was. Without inoculation, he wrote, "the Army . . . would otherwise become a
Hospital of the most loathsome kind," and "should the disorder infect
the Army in the natural way and rage with its usual virulence we should
have more to dread from it than from the Sword of the Enemy." Yet for
a little while he vacillated, for to inoculate the entire army was a tremendous undertaking. By 5 February, however, he wrote to John Hancock that

> The small pox had made such Head in every Quarter that I find it
> impossible to keep it from spreading thro' the whole army in the natu-
> ral way. I have therefore determined, not only to innoculate all the
> Troops now here, that have not had it, but shall order Docr Shippen
> to innoculate the Recruits as fast as they come in to Philadelphia.
> They will lose no time, because they will go thro' the disorder while
> their cloathing Arms and accoutrements are getting ready.[30]

He also warned Dr. Shippen to "keep the matter as secret as possible,"
and repeated the warning to Governor Nicholas Cooke (1717–1782) of
Rhode Island: "I need not mention the necessity of as much secrecy as
the nature of the Subject will admit of, it being beyond doubt, that the
Enemy will avail themselves of the event as far as they can." He also
requested that Cooke forward the Rhode Island troops for inoculation to
Brigadier General Samuel Holden Parsons in Connecticut, who was gath-
ering that state's regiments and whom Washington had ordered, "You
will . . . give orders for the Innoculating the Connecticut Troops . . . and
the Rhode Island Troops." To Colonel George Baylor, who was recruit-
ing the 3rd Continental Dragoons in Virginia, he wrote, "I must desire
that you will innoculate your Men as fast as they are inlisted."[31]

During February and early March susceptible troops at Morristown
underwent inoculation, and throughout the country that year thousands
of soldiers were inoculated, which brings the return to our tale of Joseph
Plumb Martin, who gives us a good look at the army's inoculation procedure. He had taken his discharge from a Connecticut state regiment
in December 1776 and reenlisted on 12 April 1777, this time as a regular in 8th Connecticut Continentals, which was assigned to the Hudson
Highlands. There Martin was ordered

> in company with about four hundred others of the Connecticut forces,
> to a set of old barracks, a mile or two distant in the Highlands, to be

inoculated with the smallpox. We . . . cleaned out the barracks, and after two or three days received the infection, which was on the last day of May. We had a guard of Massachusetts troops to attend us.[32]

A nearby farmer's house caught fire, but only the guard was allowed to fight it, because "Our officers would not let any of the inoculated men go near the fire." Private Plumb "had the smallpox favorably as did the rest, generally. We lost none." He "left the hospital on the sixteenth day after I was inoculated, and soon after joined the regiment." But he admitted that it was "more by good luck . . . than by my good conduct that I escaped with life." During his quarantine Plumb and a friend left the barracks "the very day on which the pock began to turn upon me," evaded the guard, and went up a brook until they were out of sight and went fishing for "three or four hours" by stripping and wading into the waters up to their shoulders "to catch suckers by means of a fishook fastened to the end of a rod." They had not only put their health in jeopardy but also had risked spreading the disease.

Civilians in regular contact with the army also had to undergo inoculation. As spring approached, officers' wives, including Martha Washington, came to Morristown to take up temporary quarters with their husbands. Martha Daingerfield Bland described her ordeal. She "was for four weeks very ill," and the pox marked her face. "I shall be pitied with them," yet "every face almost keeps me in countenance. Here are few smooth faces and no beauties, so that one does very well to pass."[33]

The risk involved also affected civilians in other ways. On 12 February twenty-three citizens of Hanover, Pennsylvania, a village about twenty miles southwest of York, well out of the war zone, sent a petition to Washington imploring him not to use their village as an inoculation center. Their plea also serves to remind us of the impact of the war on noncombatants:

Request that no Continental soldiers be inoculated in their town as Comparitively Verry fiew in Our Town has had that infectius Disorder and For the reasons as Follows.

1st It must be Verry Distressing to the Inhabitance at this Season of the Year When our Provisions Such as Fowls and Every other Nessesary Fit for that Disorder is already Exhausted by armies Passing and Repassing and Many of them being sick and Billitted so long amoungst us

2nd Our grain is almost spent and Numbers of Familyes has none but what they buy at a Verry Dear Rate and that from what they Earn by their Dayly Labour and be at the Expence of Fetching it 20 or 30 miles.

3rd Many of Our Labouring men being out in the Militia—thereby many Families is Left with onely a Woman and a Number of Small Children and is at Present for Want of Firewood and many other Comforts of Life Put to Greate Difficulty.

4th Our Young men being so many them Out in service and Laybourers being so Exceedingly scarce that Every man left at home has Enough to do to get Fireood and Take Care of his Stock which the Latter must be attended to with the Greatest Prudence & care to bing them throug the Winter as much of Our hay has been taken to supply the Army.[34]

The travails of the good citizens of Hanover may be taken as common to civilians in many parts of the country, but there was nothing that Washington could do for them. They must suffer, as the army suffered, so the newborn republic could survive.

The smallpox danger hovered during the war as new recruits enlisted, and the inoculation program would continue.

"Fatal infatuation!"

Meanwhile, the war went on. Sir William Howe came to New Brunswick on 21 February to get a feel for what was going on in New Jersey, and upon setting out on his return to New York on 5 March he got a close-up taste when, Major Robertson reported, his "escort had a Skirmish with the Rebels" on the way to Amboy "in which we had about 12 men killed and Wounded." In between balls and dinners and gambling and dancing, Sir William had given much thought to the upcoming campaign of 1777, and had decided to proceed to Philadelphia. For he apparently believed what he had been told by Tory refugees in New York, that the majority in Pennsylvania were loyal to Britain. Thus he was afflicted by a malady common to other British generals and the ministers in London: the strong belief that the Rebels were a minority and that hordes of American Loyalists throughout the land were waiting for British arms to appear, when they would rise and smite their dastardly tormentors. One British general, Charles O'Hara, later in the war labeled it accurately as a "Fatal infatuation!"[35]

There was also another general in the field in North America who had come up with his own plan, which had been approved by the king. General John Burgoyne proposed to advance with an army of British and German regulars, Tories, and Indians from Canada southward down the classic invasion route via Lake Champlain to Albany, where he would cooperate with Sir William and his army coming up the Hudson. But Sir William never agreed to go as far as Albany, only to send a detachment as far as the Hudson Highlands while he concentrated on taking the Rebel capital, Philadelphia. Instead of demanding that Sir William coordinate his movements with Burgoyne's, Lord Germain in London approved Howe's Pennsylvania offensive. In the words of a keen student of the war, the ministers in London, "preoccupied with personalities, politics, and economics . . . was unable to provide the comprehensive direction—or the reinforcements—that were now essential to victory in America."[36]

But before invading Pennsylvania, Sir William had unfinished business to attend to in New Jersey, where an upstart general had not only humiliated him in the winter snows of Trenton and Princeton but also had made life miserable for his troops in the months that followed. By the end of March, Captain Ewald wrote, "we watched the snow disappear, and everything was green in a few days," which meant that the campaign season was near, and with it the decisive battle with the Continental Army, now long overdue. Sir William was in no hurry, though. He was seldom in a hurry, but his countrymen and Rebels alike were still puzzled by his inactivity. In the meantime,the vicious partisan warfare in Jersey continued into the spring while friend and foe alike waited for Sir William to act. On 15 April Major Robertson reported that "the Rebels surprised our Piquet at Bonheim Town and carried off a Sergeant and 12 men." There was heavy fighting involving large bodies of men on both sides in April and May, and during this time Sir William busied himself with activities that left compatriots and Rebels guessing. He had told Lord Germain in early April that he intended to go to Pennsylvania by sea, which meant a major naval movement down the coast to Delaware Bay and up the Delaware River, or to Chesapeake Bay to its head. To further such a movement Admiral Lord Howe prepared provisions for three months for the troop transports and made other preparations that indicated a movement by sea. At the same time, however, Sir William had a bridge built across the Raritan at New Brunswick, pontoon bridges built for a river crossing, and twenty flatboats mounted on carriages for movement overland. Surely Sir William meant to march to the Delaware and cross it.

Or did he?

11

"The American Fabius"?

*Howe's delay "seemed to create
a general astonishment"*

Washington spent those winter and early spring months directing the operations meant to "harrass their troops to death" and striving to recruit a new army. While that was going on, nothing too grand could be risked. When Major General Joseph Spencer (1714–1789) of Connecticut wrote to him in March that he had made all of the necessary logistical preparations necessary to attack British forces in Rhode Island but had been forced to call it off for lack of men, Washington's reply described what he was about:

> I . . . think you were right in not putting any thing to the risque of a miscarriage, for until we get our new army properly established, it is our Business to play a certain game, and not depend upon Militia for anything capital.[1]

For the main army that he led in 1776 had largely disappeared. He had gone to Morristown with probably under 1,400 men. For several months the state of the army remained so uncertain that the first full monthly strength report of the main army would not appear until May. On 19 January Washington admitted to Hancock that the army was "composed cheifly of Militia," which "bids fair to reduce us to the Situation in which we were some little time ago, that is of scarce having any army at all." At that time the New England Continental troops numbered about 800, with the enlistments of some up at the end of January and the rest the middle of February. "The five Virginia Regiments are reduced to a handful of Men, as are Colo. Hands, Smallwood and the German Battn." Washington neatly summed up his predicament: "Thus you have a Sketch of our present Army, with which we are obliged to keep up Appearances." Since "Militia must be our dependance, till we can get the new Army raised and properly arranged," he implored Hancock to continue his efforts to get Pennsylvania, Maryland, and Virginia to raise every man possible, and added a detail that may seem piffling but that vexed American regular and militia commanders throughout the Revolution and for several decades beyond. He wanted militia recruited for more than their usual time, but if they insisted on joining for a "Month or any limited time, it should commence from the time they actually join the Army, and not from the time they leave their homes, otherwise the marching backwards and forwards consumes the term of engagement."[2]

Serious manpower problems continued during the following months, and the evidence of how many men Washington actually had during the period is contradictory. He wrote the governor of Connecticut that by 15 March "I shall be left with the remains of five Virginia Regiments, not amounting to more than as many hundred Men, and parts of two or three more Continental Battalions—all very weak. The remainder of the Army will be composed of small parties of Militia from this State and Pennsylvania, on whom little dependance can be put, as they come and go When they please." In a letter of 14 March to Hancock he estimated his numbers at "under Three Thousand" throughout New Jersey, of which only 981 were Continentals, the balance militia, and they "stand engaged only till the last of this month." In addition, about 1,000 of those men, including the troops guarding them, had been inoculated. Yet on 15 March a return of Continental troops under Washington's command at various posts in New Jersey reported 2,543, but of that number 571 men of six Virginia regiments were temporarily unfit for duty, as they had recently been inoculated, leaving a total fit for duty at 1,972. In the same return, militiamen were given a total number of 976. Of that number, 240 were scheduled to leave when their terms of service expired in April. In addition, there were 300 to 400 other militia under arms, but their time would expire on 28 March. All of which leaves us as confused as Washington with regard to his actual strength.[3]

Of some things, however, we can be certain. Whatever the true figures—and they must have swung wildly—Washington certainly never had more than 3,000 Continentals and militia spread over New Jersey. Not until late April and May would the new Continental Army begin to grow with new recruits. But the new Continental Army was quite different in its makeup than the army of 1775–1776. For the most part the yeomen of the middle class had lost their enthusiasm for the miseries of war and were content to let working-class youths, the poor and the desperate, blacks both slave and free, and British and Hessian deserters take over the nasty business of fighting and dying.[4]

Meanwhile, although Washington's position at Morristown was strong, it was not impregnable. Surely in that winter and spring of 1777 the time was ripe for a stroke by the British, and in fact Washington could not understand why Howe did not strike. On 12 January Washington wrote to Colonel Robert Hanson Harrison,

> With great truth I can add, that heaven alone knows upon what principle they (the Enemy) act, or by what Means, they are kept quiet. That we are not able to make the least Stand, if they move, is as clear as the sun in its' meridian Brightness. . . . We have scarce enough to mount the common guard.[5]

We can excuse Sir William his failure to act during the winter months, for he was very much an eighteenth-century general, and winter campaigns in the Northern Hemisphere were then not the norm. One buttoned up in the winter and turned out in the spring. But no one understood then, nor does anyone understand now, why Sir William Howe lolled in New York during the spring of 1777. April, May, and the first half of June, all good campaigning months wasted, while the new Continental Army began to grow in numbers. Yet Sir William dithered and dallied. Captain Peebles of the Black Watch observed that on 9 April "the weather was uncommonly warm for the season & the spring begins to appear in Vegetation," yet the following day he tells us that officers coming from New York "all agree that there's nothing going on there but Luxury & dissipation, of all kinds." Was Sir William waiting for the grass to grow high to gather fodder for the army's horses? His brother's secretary, Ambrose Serle, thought so. Or was it waiting for tents and supplies from Britain that kept him idle? Perhaps, but no one was sure.

Or was it, as Charles Lee would insist, an indolent character that explains Sir William's lack of action? Whatever the reasons, the delay "seemed to create a general astonishment," wrote his brother's good friend Captain Andrew Snape Hamond, master of HMS *Roebuck*. The closest student of Sir William's thinking and activities during his command in America, the historian Ira Gruber, believes the American victory at Trenton, having ruined the brothers' plans for reconciliation, "immobilized him." That may well be true, but in the end Sir William's actions, or lack of them, remain a mystery.[6]

By 21 May, Washington's first strength report for 1777 reported 10,000 Continentals, of whom 7,363 were present and fit for duty. It seemed that Sir William had let another opportunity slip by. Perhaps it could be redeemed, however, for on 29 May Washington left his secure fastness of Morristown and moved his headquarters some fifteen miles southwest, to Middlebrook, behind the first range of the Watchung Mountains. Here he was in a protected position but only about eight miles from New Brunswick and in a position to act should Sir William decide to march for Philadelphia. Defensive positions were prepared as insurance against a British attack on the army. Two days after the move Washington's acting adjutant general, Colonel George Weedon (c. 1734–1793), wrote a letter describing the "new army":

> The Army is now drawn together at this place, at least that part of it, which have been Cantoned all Winter in this state. The whole of them [are] now Encamped in Comfortable Tents on a Valley covered in front and rear by ridges which affords us security. His excellency our good Old General has also spread his Tent, and lives amongst us. Every Department of the army is properly Arranged and strictly Attended to—so different in our situation in every respect, to what it was last Campaign, that a friendly heart cannot help being highly elated on Reflection. Our men all happily over the small pox, and remarkably healthy, well Armed, well Cloathed, and from our Commander in Chief down, to the private Centinal, in the highest spirits. Was our Difficencies but completed and sent on we would hang heavy on Sir Williams hands go where he would.[7]

Washington believed that the British "will shortly push for Philadelphia by water," and he ordered General Sullivan to organize an intelligence operation "to keep a careful eye upon them, and communicate the minutest proceeding" by horsemen "with all speed to me." Sullivan was instructed to use area "inhabitants, whose attachment you can be sure," and will "know the country better than" light horsemen of the army, for "I am informed a great part of Col. Moylan's men have been raised in Philadelphia, and are foreigners, and of the most vagrant kind. These men should not be employed for special purposes, where their fidelity would be eminently required."[8]

Despite the growing tension centering on what Sir William Howe might be up to, the administration of the army also demanded daily attention, as, for example, when Nathanael Greene devoted most of a letter to Washington on the subject of vinegar. What was then called camp fever had begun to threaten the army's health. Greene as a young man had devoured military texts, and had read in the *Memoirs* of the great seventeenth-century French soldier Marshal Saxe that vinegar in drinking water had been used in the Roman army to promote health and drunk to excellent purpose in the French army. "Nothing," Greene wrote, "will correct this evil like the free use of vinegar" in such amounts "as to allow the men a Gill if not half Pinte a day. If cyder Vinegar cannot be had in such plenty as the State of the Army requires, Vinegar can be made with Molasses, Water and a little flour to produce a fermentation. One Hogshead of Molasses and one Barrel of Rum will make Ten hogs-heads of Vinegar." Washington paid immediate attention to the problem. Three days later Greene wrote to the commissary general, Colonel Joseph Trumbull, that the commander in chief was anxious to supply vinegar to the troops and therefore Trumbull should act at once on the matter.[9]

Another matter that came to a head at this inopportune time, not as serious as the army's health, but nonetheless vexing to all concerned and a threat to the morale of the officer corps, was the flood of foreign volunteers, mostly French, who had come to America in a manner that became time-honored, to attain positions well above their European ranks and, if they were really lucky, fame and fortune. There were, to be sure, European officers whose contributions to the Cause are beyond measure. Lafayette and von Steuben come immediately to mind. Some, such as Casimir Pulaski and the Hungarian Michaël Kôváts de Fabricy, fought bravely, if at times foolishly, and paid the ultimate price. But scores had nothing to offer but vanity and puffed-up résumés and were nothing but trouble. Washington asked his friend and member of Congress Richard Henry Lee (1732–1794) "what Congress expects I am to do with the many Foreigners they have, at different times, promoted to the Rank of Field Officers? and by the last resolve, two to that of colonels." He continued,

Marquis de Lafayette by Charles Willson Peale

These Men have no attachment or tyes to the Country, further than Interest binds them—they have no influence—and are ignorant of the language they are to receive and give orders in, consequently great trouble or much confusion must follow: but this is not the worst, they have not the smallest chance to recruit others, and our Officers thinks it exceedingly hard, after they have toild in this Service, & probably sustaind many losses to have Strangers put over them, whose merit perhaps is not equal to their own; but whose effrontery will take no denial.[10]

At its most serious, the arrival of foreign officers and the possibility of some outranking senior American officers led to Henry Knox's threat to resign and a bitter exchange that ended the friendship between Nathanael Greene and John Adams.[11]

The main problem at hand, however, was Sir William Howe's intentions. Since the debacle on Long Island, Washington's intelligence network had much improved and included a spy in New York City in what we would today call deep cover, "a person of Veracity," Washington told John Hancock, "and one who is much in the confidence of the Enemy." On 29 May the spy reported that "This Morning two Brigades" had left New York for Amboy, and that 300 wagons had been sent there from Long Island. The British, he said, "are determined to make a sudden and violent attack on our camp," for "They have determined the destruction of Genl Washington's Army." Washington sent the report to John Hancock and confirmed that "These accounts are corraborated by information of the same kind from several different Quarters." Yet he did not believe the key piece of information. "But I do not place so much dependance upon the account of the intended attack upon this place, because I think if such a matter was really in agitation, it would be kept a profound secret." Washington's volunteer aide, Tench Tilghman, sent another copy of the spy's report to General Sullivan, commanding at Princeton, and wrote in his covering letter, "Although there is no doubt that he has been informed of all that he reports, yet it is more than probable that it is thrown out to cover some other designs. Perhaps they may think that while they amuse us by threatening an attack upon our camp they may find an opportunity of making a hasty march to Delaware [River] through your quarters." Washington was sure of Sir William's goal: "I can see no other object but Philadelphia." Thus is laid out for us the age-old problem of the interpretation of intelligence. And in this instance the well-placed American spy was right.[12]

"General Washington . . . neither moved nor let himself be lured out"

For Washington's shift in position had whetted Howe's appetite for a major action when, if everything went right, he would finally accomplish what he and his brother's policies had denied him the previous year: the destruction of the Continental Army. He therefore assembled most of his combat arm in that narrow corridor between Amboy and New Brunswick. But Washington knew that Howe had gathered his force in New Jersey, and in general orders dated 8 June placed the army on alert, "in constant readiness to move at a moments warning; and for that purpose they are to be always furnished with three days provisions, ready cooked." The following day, Sir William himself left New York for Amboy to take command of the British army in Jersey. On the wet morning of the 12th, he marched from Amboy to join the British troops already at New Brunswick, and between 10:00 P.M. and midnight, 13 June, he answered the question on Washington's mind. Some 16,000 strong, the British army headed straight for the American camp, in the hope of bringing the fox to bay.[13]

In two columns, one commanded by Lord Cornwallis, the other by Major General John Vaughan (c. 1731–1795), who was accompanied by Sir William Howe, the British Army advanced along the Raritan River. It was an army aching to bring the Rebels to battle. Sir William's Hessian aide Friedrich von Münchhausen spoke for all: "Everyone in our army wishes that the rebels would do us the favor to take their chance in a regular battle. We would surely defeat them." Earlier that year, after a successful American raid, he had written, "Once the campaign has started, we will again be respected by them, because they will have to learn running again, which they seem to have forgotten some time ago." But as the British and Hessians marched up the valley of the Raritan to seek battle, the young German also put his finger on the most critical military problem that faced the King's forces throughout the war: "This force is strong enough to chase the Rebels, but is far from strong enough to penetrate deep into the country, leaving behind garrisons and ways of communication."[14]

On the day Sir William headed in his direction, Washington ordered the brilliant Rebel battle captain Colonel Daniel Morgan (c.1735–1802) to hover with "very small scouting parties" on the left flank of the British army, and "In case of any movement of the Enemy you are instantly to fall upon their flanks and gall them as much as possible, taking especial Care not to be surrounded, or have your Retreat to the Army cut off." To lessen the vulnerability of Morgan's Corps of Rangers, who were armed with very accurate but slow-loading rifles, Washington also informed him that "I have sent for Spears which I expect shortly to receive and deliver to you, as a defense against Horse. Till you are funished with these, take care not to be caught in such a Situation as to give them any advantage over you." Seven days later the spears arrived. But with that attention to detail he was capable of even at moments of peril and stress, Washington wrote to the secretary of the Board of War that "they would be more conveniently carried if they had a sling fixed to them, they should also have a spike in the But end to fix them in the Ground. . . . The Iron plates which fix the Spear Head to the shaft should be at least eighteen inches long to prevent the shaft from being cut through with the stroke of a Horsemens Sword." With or without spears, Morgan and his riflemen skillfully carried out their mission. On one occasion a 200-man detachment of rangers skirmished for half an hour with Cornwallis's corps of 6,000, then, reported Captain von Münchhausen, "retreated in good order out of the woods." The young Hessian officer also reported that when Sir William reconnoitered with other officers and staff, "General Howe was exposed to several rifle shots from the Rebels who were hidden in the bushes."[15]

The following day Washington ordered the army "to be in readiness to march . . . tents be immediately struck; the baggage and camp equipage loaded," horses hitched, "and all men paraded . . . ready to move [at] a moment's warning." The order of march was spelled out in detail, with all precautions taken against surprise:

> The Vanguard to consist of 40 Light horse and one brigade of foot . . . to advance about 2½ Miles in front of the army—to march about an hour before the troops are order'd to be in readiness. Reconnoitering parties to be sent some distance in front and upon the flanks to examine all the roads and Suspected places where ambushes may be concealed. The pioneers to march between the light parties in front of the Vanguard and to make such repairs in the Bridges and roads as are necessary to afford an easy and safe passage to the army.

Another brigade formed the rear guard, with a quarter of that force

> to march in the rear of the rest about half a mile to pick up straglers. A detachment of 30 light dragoons to form a part of the rear guard. Colonel Morgan's light infantry to cover the left flank of the army, exclusive of which, Each Brigade to furnish a party of 90 men properly officered to keep on the enemy's flank.[16]

The order stressed that "Great attention must be paid, in passing difficult defiles, that the men may pass them briskly . . . the head of the collumn to move slow, as soon as they have passed the defile, untill the rear has gain'd it also."

All arrangements made, ready to withdraw if the British attacked his stronghold, or follow them should they march for the Delaware, Washington watched and waited, and also made sure that General Sullivan in Princeton was not cut off from the main body, which von Münchhausen said the British meant to do. On the same day that he issued his general orders, he admitted to Sullivan, "I am uneasy at hear-

ing nothing from you." That evening he wrote to Sullivan again, ordering him to leave Princeton, pass in front of the British army, and "get
upon their right Flank," then "you can always form a junction with this
army." By the next day Sullivan had safely reached a forward position
where he could immediately notify Washington of British movements,
whether "they are determined to push forward," to head for the Delaware, or "back to Brunswic," and at the same time harass them.[17]

As for the British and Hessians, they were as confused as Washington as to Sir William's intention, and it turned out that Washington's
stance had confused the British. "I believe," Major Archibald Robertson
wrote, "it was generaly imagined upon our Armys making the Aforesaid
Move, He [Washington] would have quitted his stronghold and retreated
towards the Delaware. However it proved otherwise. He stood firm."
And the British had no intelligence of what the Rebel general might
do. So while both armies waited, Sir William ordered redoubts built,
and what Europeans called *petite guerre* ("little war") continued. Captain
Ewald of the Jägers, confirming Major Robertson's observation, wrote in
his diary that "General Washington, who neither moved nor let himself
be lured out of his strong position by this demonstration, sent out several detachments daily which observed and harassed our army, whereby
constant skirmishing ensued." The road behind them to New Brunswick,
whence supplies came, "is completely unsafe," von Münchhausen wrote.
On 17 June he and a favorite comrade, Captain Henry Knight, went on
a reconnaissance mission to "gain intelligence of Washington's advantageous mountain position" and for their trouble were almost taken by
aggressive American dragoons who got so close that von Münchhausen
shot one at three paces when the dragoon "was striking at me with his
sword."[18]

By 19 June Sir William decided that Washington would not give
battle and ordered the army to return to New Brunswick. The troops,
who had been harassed and sniped at incessantly, took out their frustration on civilians along the way. "On this march," wrote Captain Ewald,
"all the plantations of the disloyal inhabitants, numbering perhaps some
fifty persons, were sacrificed to fire and devastation." At 9:00 P.M. on
21 June, the army received orders to march to Amboy and prepare to
embark, and by 4:00 A.M. the regiments were on the move. It has been
claimed that Washington was so surprised by Sir William's withdrawal
that the enemy columns got off almost without disturbance. But Washington informed Hancock that he "detached three Brigades under the

command of Majr Gen; Green to fall upon their rear, and kept the main Body of the army paraded upon the Heights to support them if there should be occasion." The diaries of von Münchhausen and Ewald confirm Washington's report. The flank patrols on the left of Cornwallis's command were "so fiercely attacked by about 800 riflemen," von Münchhausen wrote, "that they started to retreat toward our main column." Sir William personally led two regiments against them and about a half hour of skirmishing ensued that ended only when Howe "brought up two cannon and fired several grape shot at them, whereupon they retreated." The British lost about thirty men killed and wounded, and captured one Rebel captain. Captain Ewald and his Jägers met incessant opposition. "On the 21st and 22d all our outposts were alarmed and harassed by the enemy, both day and night." Between New Brunswick and Amboy on the 23rd "a great number of riflemen, supported by light cavalry and guns, followed us so closely that we had to withdraw under constant skirmishing up to the vicinity of Bonhamtown. The Queens Rangers . . . had strayed too far from the army, and was attacked so severely by a superior force that half the corps was killed or wounded. During this retreat the detachment under Captain Wreden [Jägers] also suffered very much." Stung by incessant sniping, harassed on the march, discouraged by retreat, the troops, von Münchhausen reported, "looked quite sullen because of the march back," and in their black mood they took out their frustrations on the civilian population. Traveling with the army was an English civilian, Nicholas Cresswell, who wrote in his journal, "All the Country houses were in flames as far as we could see. The Soldiers are so much enraged that they will set them on fire in spite of all the Officers can do to prevent it."[19]

Washington admitted that the British were in such strength that "it was impossible to check them," and "fearing they might be led on too far from the main Body," Greene's pursuing brigades "returned to Brunswic." By the testimony of von Münchhausen and Ewald, the Americans had acquitted themselves well in harassing actions, which were never meant to result in major engagements. Nathanael Greene was especially proud of two of his units, as reported to Hancock by Washington. "Genl Green desires me to make mention of the Conduct and Bravery of Genl [Anthony] Wayne and Colo [Daniel] Morgan and of their officers and men upon this occasion, as they constantly advanced upon an Enemy far superior to them in numbers and well secured behind strong redoubts."

According to an intelligence report received by Washington, in New York City the entire afternoon of 22 June was "employ'd," the informer wrote, "in removing the wounded soldiers from the docks to the Hospitals there, said to amount to five Hundd Men by a Lieutenant wounded in the arm." Other accounts received by Washington claimed that British "Officers were heard to say, they had not suffered so severly since the affair at prince town."[20]

On the 24th Washington descended with the main army from his mountain stronghold to the flat country, where he "would be nearer the Enemy and might act according to circumstances." He detached light troops to lay "close on the Enemy's Lines to watch their motions." Lord Stirling's division was placed in advance about five miles northeast of New Brunswick to take advantage of any opportunity that might present itself. But Washington made it quite clear to Hancock that he was not seeking a major battle: "the Idea of forcing their Lines or bringing on a General Engagement on their Own Grounds is Universally held incompatible with our Interest."[21]

Washington's descent from his lair was reported to Sir William. Sensing an opportunity to finally engage the Rebel Army on level terrain, he continued to embark men on vessels while at the same time planning a stroke to catch Washington napping. The men aboard vessels were recalled, troops brought from Staten Island, and at 6:00 P.M. on 25 June, tents were struck and baggage left within British lines, and the troops rested on their arms and waited for the order to march. Early on 26 June the army set out in two columns, sweeping northward to come around Washington's left flank and block a retreat to the Watchung Mountains. Washington with the main force got away to the mountain passes without loss as soon as he heard firing to his front, but the rapid march of the British and Hessians caught up with the light troops and Lord Stirling's division. A sharp action ensued, and Stirling had a close call. Captain Ewald wrote, "The enemy was attacked with the bayonet and driven back, whereby Colonel Minnigerode and his grenadier battalion greatly distinguished themselves, taking from the enemy three Hessian guns which had been captured at Trenton." Cornwallis pursued Stirling, but the awful heat of the day finally forced Cornwallis to stop, whereupon Stirling was able to extricate himself and gain the mountains with a loss, in addition to the guns, of an estimated thirty killed and fifty captured. The artist/soldier Lieutenant Charles Willson Peale watched

Charles Willson Peale, *Self-Portrait in Uniform*

the skirmishing from high above the Raritan and described the view for us in his diary, and while there received a visitor:

> I went to [a] Rock which afforded one of the most sublime prospects I have ever seen—overlooking the country as far as my Eyes could see—Brunswick Amboy and Statten Island—and even beyond the bay at Amboy. The Enemy burnt 3 Houses in their progress and I could also distinguish their Course by the Dust. and we soon see that there was some engagement at about six miles distance. This I have since understood was Genl. Stirlings Brigade which had like to have been surrounded. . . . I had been but a short time here before Genl. Washington came to this spot and where I spent the whole day. I made a Slite sketch with my pencil of the View on the Back leaf of this Book. Genl. Washington gave me an Invitation to Dine with him the Next Day.[22]

*The Artist (?) and General Washington Overlooking the Raritan River
and the Advance of the British Army* by Charles Willson Peale

The British withdrew the following day, and on 28 June, reported
Captain Ewald, "the army marched back in two columns to its former
encampment at Amboy. On this march an enemy party followed our
rear guard, but it was constantly repelled by the jägers." The weather
had not only halted Cornwallis's pursuit of Stirling, it also had taken a
toll of the troops. "Since it was extremely hot, especially on the 26th,
some twenty men died marching, among whom were seven jägers of the
troop, who had make this march on foot burdened with their hussar
boots and great hussar sabers." Captain Peebles reported that "in the
course of this excursion several men died from the excessive heat,
fatigue & drinking water." Two days later, 30 June 1777, the last units of
the British army in New Jersey embarked on vessels for the short sail
across the Kill van Kull to Staten Island, their efforts of the past eight
months for naught. The opponents were right back where they had
started the previous November, and the effects on the British army were
ominous: the other ranks sullen, the officers in despair, Sir William
Howe's reputation in tatters. It was still a superb professional organization, the rank and file as tough and skilled and brave as any army that
ever marched to war. It could and would win battles. The question was,

given its leadership to date, could it win the war? Writing two months later with regard to the June campaign in New Jersey, Ambrose Serle told Lord Dartmouth, "I can scarce hear a Man speak on the Subject but in Passion or Despair."[23]

"Passion must give way to reason"

The New Jersey campaign of 1776–1777 was one of the most important of the war. It went from patriot despair at Washington's miserable retreat through the length of the state in 1776, to passionate joy over the victories at Trenton and Princeton. But the partisan campaign in the winter and spring of 1777 and Washington's refusal to be drawn into battle have received few accolades, although they combined to foil Sir William and drive his army to distraction. In the minds of many, however, glamour trumps. Partisan warfare is nasty, vicious, often anonymous, and succeeds, if it succeeds, in dribs and drabs, a sentry killed here, a few foragers captured there, perhaps half a dozen casualties in the course of a week. Partisan war nibbles the enemy to death, which is not exciting enough for those who yearn for grand engagements of armies. And generals who avoid battles always try the patience of their masters. We need, therefore, to take a closer look at Washington's strategy at that time, its historical background, and the reasoning behind it.

Washington's policy of avoiding a major engagement in favor of harassing the British army with limited surprise offensives, as he had done at Trenton and Princeton, and partisan warfare had drawn notice in both America and Europe. With reference to Trenton and Princeton, London's *Annual Register* for 1777 commented,

> These actions, and the sudden recovery from the lowest state of weakness and distress, to become a formidable enemy in the field, raised the character of General Washington as a commander, very high, both in Europe and America, and with his preceding and subsequent conduct serve, to give a sanction to that appelation which is now pretty generally applied to him, of the American Fabius.[24]

The reference at the end of the quotation was to the Roman general Quintus Fabius Maximus (c. 266–203 B.C.), whose nickname Cunctator means the "delayer." The Fabian strategy of maneuver, attrition, and refusal to be tempted into major battle was used brilliantly by Fabius against the great Carthaginian Hannibal during the Second Punic War

(219–202 B.C.). Upper-class eighteenth-century Americans knew their classical history, and Washington's maneuvers against an increasingly frustrated Sir William Howe were not an example of reinventing the wheel. He knew what his precursor had done and what he himself was about, and the word *Fabian* was commonly used by Rebels, British, and European observers to describe his strategy. An Italian, Domenico Bertini of Florence, was so carried away by the American Fabius that in his enthusiasm he wrote a sonnet and sent it to Washington. The relevant line read, "Illustrious Rome shall see with wonder, that Fabiuses can yet be born among us, worthy to be adorned with wreaths of the Triumphal Oak." By June even the often critical and constantly irritable John Adams had come around to accepting the strategy, writing to Abigail, "We are under no more Apprehensions here than if the British Army was in the Crimea. Our Fabius will be slow but sure."[25]

His cousin Sam Adams thought differently. In May, in a letter to Nathanael Greene, he gave the general an unsolicited history lesson on a subject Greene was already familiar with, in which Adams contrasted the situations facing Fabius and Washington and asked if Fabius were facing Howe, would he "Pursue the method he took with the Carthaginian General? Would he not rather attend to [present?] Circumstances, and by destroying the Army in Brunswick prevent as much as possible the Enemy increasing in Strength even if reinforcements should arrive, or putting a total end to the Campaign if they shoud not?" Destroying Howe's army was, of course, another pipe dream, and Adams admitted that our own "Circumstances have been such, thro' the Winter past, as to make it impracticable to attempt anything," yet he persisted with the "hope we are or shall be very soon in a Condition to take a decisive part." The following month he wrote to his close friend James Warren (1726–1808), "I confess I have always been so wrong headed as not to be over well pleased, with what is called the Fabian War in America. I conceive a great Difference between the Scituations of the Carthaginians and the British Generals. But I have no Judgement in Military Matters, and therefore will leave the Subject to be discussed as it certainly will be, by those who are masters of it." Adams's assessment of himself was quite accurate, and in fact masters of "Military Matters" in Europe were discussing Washington's generalship, as revealed by the congressional agent Arthur Lee (1740–1792) in a letter of 15 June to Washington from Berlin: "I have the pleasure of assuring you that your conduct against General Howe has been highly approved, by the principal military Men here and in France. that approbation has been increased in those to whom I have had the Opportunity of Stating the great inferiority of the troops you commanded to those of the Enemy in number & in every necessary provision for war." Yet Sam Adams longed, as many did, for a climactic battle that would end it all with final victory for America. Which is precisely what many Romans longed for, and when Fabius was out of power and his tactics abandoned they got their great battle—the Roman disaster at Cannae in 216 B.C., in which a Roman army was literally destroyed. Rome survived Cannae, but it is highly doubtful that the Revolution would have survived an American Cannae. Yet the doubters carped and quibbled and complained. Sam Adams was a brilliant politician whose contributions to furthering the Cause were indispensible. But in matters military a wiser head than the fifty-five-year-old Adams's rested on the shoulders of twenty-two-year-old Alexander Hamilton, then an aide-de-camp to Washington, who penned one of the best contemporary descriptions of American strategy at the time and the principles behind it:

> I know the comments that some people will make on our Fabian conduct. It will be imputed either to cowardice or to weakness; But the more discerning, I trust, will not find it difficult to conceive that it proceeds from the truest policy, and is an argument neither of the one nor the other. The liberties of America are an infinite stake. We should not play a desperate game for it or put it upon the issue of a single cast of the die. The loss of one general engagement may effectually ruin us, and it would certainly be folly to hazard it, unless our resources for keeping up an army were at an end, and some decisive blow was absolutely necessary; or unless our strength was so great as to give certainty of success. Neither is the case.

Hamilton then claimed that "America can in all probability maintain its army for years," whereas "no great reinforcements are to be expected to the British army in America. It is therefore Howe's business to make the most of his present strength, and as he is not numerous enough to conquer and garrison as he goes, his only hope lies in fighting us and giving a general defeat in one blow." He then summed up in one sentence the strategy of the campaign during the first half of 1777: "Our business then is to avoid a General engagement and waste the enemy away by constantly goading their sides, in a desultory, teazing way." Finally, Hamilton admitted that

In the meantime it is painful to leave a part of the inhabitants a prey to their depredations; and it is wounding to the feelings of a soldier, to see the enemy parading before him, and daring him to a fight which he is obliged to decline. But a part must be sacrificed to the whole, and passion must give way to reason.

Nevertheless, another question confronts us. Did Washington intend to continue his Fabian strategy indefinitely? Did he believe the war could be won by refusing to engage in a major way, by bringing the British to their knees by a process of attrition? Hamilton's letter provides a clue that we should keep in mind as our story progresses:

On our part, we are continually strengthening our political springs in Europe, and may every day look for more effectual aids than we have yet received. Our own army is continually growing stronger in men arms and discipline. We shall soon have an important addition of Artillery, now in its way to join us. We can maintain our present numbers good at least by enlistments, while the enemy must dwindle away; and at the end of the summer the disparity between us will be infinitely great, and facilitate any exertions that may be made to settle the business with them.[26]

In other words, we will soon be stronger than the British, and then the time will come to "settle the business" between us.

"I could not help expressing my Surprize"

Sir William also sought to "settle the business," but he went about it in a strange way. On 21 June, while Sir William was trying to tempt Washington into battle, General John Burgoyne and his nearly 8,000-man British and Hessian army, supplemented by Canadians and Indians, sailed onto the sparkling waters of Lake Champlain, following that old corridor of armies into the vastness of the northern New York Back Country. Washington, watching from New Jersey, was aware of the northern expedition, and by 1 July he received intelligence from General Schuyler, commanding the Northern Department, that British forces had reached the vicinity of the American-held Fort Ticonderoga, at the southern end of Lake Champlain. This prompted Washington to write, "it appears almost certain to me, that Genl Howe & Genl Burgoyne design if possible to unite their attacks & form a junction of their two Armies." For the rest of the month and beyond, this belief was at the core of Washington's thinking. But he always kept the potential threat to Philadelphia in mind while he waited for more intelligence on British activities and intentions. If Burgoyne's entire army was approaching Ticonderoga, he wrote, "I should not hesitate a Moment in concluding that it is in consequence of a preconcerted plan with Genl Howe," who would take his army up the Hudson and first seize the Highland passes. But what if British forces spotted on Lake Champlain represented a "feint—calculated to amuse and distract" and draw Washington with the main army northward, leaving Philadelphia open for Sir William to march in? Washington had decided, therefore, to sit tight "till we have further proof of his Intentions, and that our conduct must be governed by his." He added, "Our situation is truly delicate and embarrassing."[27]

It is ironic that Washington's thoughts on cooperation between Howe and Burgoyne mirrored Lord George Germain's in London. Sir William, however, had other ideas, and Germain failed to either properly evaluate Howe's plans or give him explicit orders to cooperate with Burgoyne. Although Germain had approved Sir William's plan to invade Pennsylvania, he also expected Howe to closely cooperate with Burgoyne, which was "highly necessary" to win the war, and he meant it to be won in the campaign of 1777. Sir William knew this, yet he persisted in the primacy of his own plan. Germain did send to Howe a copy of Burgoyne's instructions and a copy of a letter to General Carleton in Canada that expressed Germain's clear intention that the two armies should join. But he never wrote directly to Sir William with instructions to carry out this plan. He apparently assumed that Howe understood it and would act on it, and that in the course of 1777 he could invade Pennsylvania, capture Philadelphia, and take his army up the Hudson in time to cooperate with Burgoyne. And Sir William for his part continued to act as if he and Burgoyne were fighting different wars. This strategic sloppiness, these delusions in administration and thinking in England and America are breathtaking, and one can only conclude that the American Rebels were indeed fortunate that Britain at the time was so ill served by its politicians and generals.[28]

For the sake of argument, however, let us suppose that Burgoyne and Sir William had cooperated in an attempt to establish control of the Hudson River Valley between New York and Albany. As we discussed in chapter 1, conventional wisdom for many at the time held that whoever controlled this line could cut off New England from the rest of the country. Since important Continental Army supply lines ran southward from the Rebel stronghold of New England, this would so strangle the American war effort that they would have to either give up or risk a major engagement to reopen the line. This supposes, however, that Britain had the thousands of troops necessary to guard the line and prevent supplies, reinforcements, and communications from moving. Once again the brilliant, precocious Alexander Hamilton cut to the core of the British problem:

> And as to the notion of forming a junction with the northern army, and cutting off the communications between the Northern and Southern States, I apprehend it will do better in speculation than in practice. Unless the Geography of the Country is far different from any thing I can conceive, to effect this would required a chain of posts and such a number of men at each as would never be practicable or maintainable but to any immense army. In their progress, by hanging upon their rear and seizing every opportunity of Skirmishing, their Situation might be rendered insupportably uneasy.[29]

All quite moot, however, since Howe had no intention of cooperating with Burgoyne.

Sir William's movement began on 4 July 1777, when the British and Hessian soldiers on Staten Island began embarking on troop transports. This took six days, and the troops spent the next ten days waiting for something to happen, which certainly annoyed them but would not have surprised them, for such is the way of armies in all ages and climes. On 19 July 225 transports, carrying some 14,000 British and Hessian soldiers and escorted by 25 warships, weighed anchor and began the ever-tricky job of getting out of New York Harbor. The winds not cooperating, the fleet got nowhere that day, but the next morning half of the ships made it through the Narrows and on to Sandy Hook, and on the 21st all ships but the big men-of-war joined them. There was little wind the next day, but on the 23rd a fair wind filled the sails, the men-of-war joined the fleet, and with a frigate leading the way and men-of-war hugging the flanks and rear, the tall ships cleared Sandy Hook and stood out to sea until the land disappeared and the white sails were lost to the view of watchers who desperately wished to know their destination.[30]

On 18 July, the day before the fleet first weighed anchor off Staten Island, Washington had received an intelligence report that the pilots recruited for the British fleet were not well acquainted with the waters southward along the Jersey coast and that "many of the Horses were in Sloops from the Sizes unfit for Sea & in several not even a compass." This led the writer and others to the conclusion that the British fleet was bound for either the Hudson or East Rivers, their targets either "Connecticut or a Junction with their Northern Army & not the least Conjectures of their going to the southward." Although judging the validity of intelligence reports is certainly one of the most perplexing responsibilities of a commander, this certainly must have strengthened Washington's firm belief that Sir William meant to advance up the Hudson and join Burgoyne. In fact, about a week earlier he had written to the governor of New Jersey that there was "little room to doubt, that their intentions are to form a Junction up the North River. I have therefore thought proper to March that way," since the British advantage of going by water made "it necessary that we should be advanced before them." By 15 July he had moved his headquarters northward to Smith's Clove, which was an important pass in the Ramapo Mountains connecting northern New Jersey and the Hudson Highlands. On 23 July the light horse commander, Colonel Stephen Moylan (1737–1811), reported the fleet putting out to sea from Sandy Hook, but he was unable to precisely ascertain its direction. Washington speculated that Delaware was its "most probable place of their destination" and began moving the army southward.[31]

On 30 July the British fleet raised Cape Henlopen, at the mouth of Delaware Bay, and there HMS *Roebuck*, Captain Andrew Snape Hamond commanding, came out to meet Howe. Hamond had been on the Virginia and Delaware station since March 1776 and had intimate knowledge of the river approaches to Philadelphia. There was no doubt in his mind before he even spoke to Sir William that the army would land and proceed forthwith to the Rebel capital. But at a meeting of senior army and naval officers aboard Lord Howe's flagship, HMS *Eagle*, Sir William astounded many when he announced that he would not land at the Delaware but proceed to Chesapeake Bay and disembark the army at its head. Among the reasons given were that the enemy would be taken by surprise; the landing would be unopposed, whereas he expected "great opposition" on the Delaware; and they would be closer to the Rebel supply magazines at York and Carlisle, which he meant to destroy before proceeding toward Philadelphia.[32]

Captain Hamond was nonplussed. He wrote in his diary, "I could not help expressing my Surprize at the bare mention of Chesapeake Bay," and proceeded to point out that he had "made some preparations for the guidance of the Fleet up the River," and he "could not help contending for the proposition of pushing up as far as they might go with perfect safety from anything that was to be apprehended from the enemy." "Even Sir William's brother," Hamond wrote, "seemed to incline to the Delaware, but the General saying 'he was from the beginning for making the landing in Chesapeake Bay,'" and the quartermaster general reporting fourteen days forage left, "the resolution was accordingly taken." Admiral Howe's secretary, Ambrose Serle, expressed the general reaction: "The Hearts of all Men were struck with this Business, every one apprehending the worst." He ended his lamentation with, "I can write no more: my Heart is full." The fleet sailed the next day. Before leaving, Sir William paid lip service to his responsibility toward Burgoyne's expedition by writing to Sir Henry Clinton, commanding in New York City, "if you can make any diversion in favour of General Burgoyne's approaching Albany, with security to King's-Bridge, I need not point out the utility of such a measure."[33]

Washington, in the meantime, was as baffled as Captain Hamond. The fleet was at sea, its destination unknown, and Washington's fear amounting to an obsession that Sir William meant to link up with Burgoyne haunted him. By 29 July he was at Coryell's Ferry on the Delaware River, two days' march from Philadelphia, where his doubts as to Howe's destination convinced him "to halt the Army at this place, Howell's Ferry and Trenton, at least, till the Fleet actually enter the Bay and put the matter beyond a doubt." So uneasy was he that he had ordered General Sullivan to wait with his division at Morristown, within easy striking distance of the Hudson Highlands. Lord Germain in London would have agreed with Washington that "Genl Howe's . . . abandoning Genl Burgoyne, is so unaccountable a matter, that till I am fully assured it is so, I cannot help casting my Eyes continually behind me." He alerted General Gates to keep a sharp eye out for the appearance of the fleet and to send word of its approach immediately. On the same day that Sir William astonished Captain Hamond with his decision to go up Chesapeake Bay, Washington wrote to Hancock that from his present position, if Howe's "expedition to Sea only means a deep feint and should turn his attention again to the North River," he could reinforce General Putnam in the Hudson Highlands "more expeditiously, than if we were farther advanced."[34]

At nine-thirty on the morning of 31 July, Washington got word that the fleet had arrived the day before at the mouth of Delaware Bay. He

Sir Andrew Snape Hamond, artist and present location unknown

immediately put the army in motion for Philadelphia and ordered General Putnam, who had succeeded General Heath as commander in the Hudson Highlands, to order two brigades to cross the Hudson and march for Philadelphia. But on the following day came the report that the fleet had once more disappeared to sea, in an easterly direction. Express riders galloped out of headquarters with orders to the generals to turn their troops around again and head for the Hudson Highlands. To the officer commanding the two brigades just dispatched by General Putnam went an order to "return immediately to Peeks kill," and General George Clinton was requested to "immediately call in every Man of the Militia that you possibly can to strengthen the Highland posts." Washington feared that the "Enemy's movements will be extremely rapid, in order if possible, to carry the Highlands by a sudden stroke." On the night of

2 August, however, he received intelligence that the fleet had once again been sighted, and "some people conclude that their going off, was to gain more sea Room to weather the Shoals of Cape May; and that they will still come up Delaware." Because of the uncertainty of British intentions and the heat of the season, he wrote to General Sullivan, "it is terrible to march and counter-march the Troops," and he therefore ordered Sullivan to halt. But if he received dependable intelligence that the fleet was sighted off Sandy Hook or the coast of New England he was to immediately march northward and cross the Hudson at Peekskill.[35]

This yo-yo-like movement of the army not only was distressing to the troops, it also led Washington to issue general orders with regard to a phenomenon that attended eighteenth-century armies:

> In the present marching state of the army, every incumbrance proves greatly prejudicial to the service; the multitude of women in particular, especially those who are pregnant, or have children, are a clog upon every movement. The Commander in Chief therefore earnestly recommends it, to the officers commanding brigades and corps, to use every reasonable method in their power, to get rid of all such as are not absolutely necessary, and the admission or continuance of any, who shall, or may have come to the army since its arrival in Pennsylvania, is positively forbidden; to which point the officers will give particular attention.[36]

Washington's language makes it clear that this was a delicate situation, not to be dealt with dictatorially, except for the women newly arrived in camp since the army entered Pennsylvania. Camp followers, as they are traditionally called, have often been portrayed as nothing but harlots. Many, however, were wives and other family members of the soldiers, and they provided invaluable services: cooking, washing, nursing, and the comfort that men engaged in hazardous duty take from the presence of women. They can truly be called eighteenth-century support troops to the combat arms, and Washington obviously realized that they could not be lightly dismissed.

Meanwhile, British movements continued to vex the Rebel commander in chief, for as he wrote, "The advantages they derive from having the command of the Water are immense. At the same time, that they are transporting themselves from One place to another with the utmost facility and convenience, they keep our Immaginations constantly in the feild of conjecture, as to the point of Attack. . . . their conduct is really so mysterious, that you cannot reason upon it." That is one of the best descriptions ever penned of Sir William Howe's behavior. The advice given by Washington's generals was contradictory. "Some imagining that they are gone to the Southward, whilst a majority (in whose opinion upon this occasion I concur) are satisfied they are gone to the Eastward." And while the high command debated, "the Troops under my Command have been More harassed by Marching, & Counter Marching, than by any thing that has happen'd to them in the course of the campaign." He added, "The fatigue . . . & injury, which men must Sustain by long Marches in such extreme heat as we have felt for the last five days, must keep us quiet till we hear something of the destination of the enemy."[37]

Sightings of the fleet as it proceeded southward down the coast even led Washington and his generals at a Council of War on 21 August to conclude that "Charles Town [Charleston, South Carolina], from a view of All circumstances, is the most probable object of their attention." What should they do? August in the South was not only unhealthy, the army could not get to Charleston in time to oppose the enemy. That possibility was rejected, which led them to the following decision: "The Army should move immediately to the North River." Orders were issued for the army to march the next day. But those orders were canceled shortly after they were given, for on the afternoon of the day the council met, John Hancock wrote that the fleet had been seen on 14 August "standing in" for the Capes of Virginia. Washington immediately replied that although "I cannot yet think that Genl Howe seriously intends to go into Chesapeake," he decided that "I shall in consequence of this information halt upon my present ground till I hear something further." That came on the afternoon of the 22nd, when Hancock wrote, "This moment an Express is arriv'd from Maryland with an accott of near Two hundred Sail of Mr. Howe's Fleet being at Anchor in Chesapeake Bay."[38]

That sealed it. Sir William's mysterious design was finally clear. Philadelphia was the goal. It did not make sense to Washington, but at last he could make definite plans. Express riders rode out of headquarters on 22 August with new orders to detached units to "join this Army . . . as speedily as possible." As for the main army, "I have issued orders for all the Troops here to be in motion to morrow morning very early, with intention to march them towards Philadelphia—and onwards."

12

"Come boys, we shall do better another time"

"A single traitor could have betrayed him"

On 24 August the new Continental Army, 15,000 strong, twelve deep in parade formation, took more than two hours to pass through Philadelphia. Washington, the finest horseman of his age, led the march, the marquis de Lafayette at his side. The Great Virginian, whose gift for high drama is not widely appreciated, meant to present in the capital city a rousing spectacle of men at arms, with the hope "that it may have some influence on the minds of the disaffected there and others who are Dupes to their artifices & opinions." To that end he issued precise instructions the day before. The order of march, the appearance of the soldiers, pioneers with axes on their shoulders, distance between units, all were spelled out. He "expected that every officer, without exception, will keep his post in passing thro' the city, and under no pretence whatsoever leave it, and if any soldier shall dare to quit his ranks, he shall receive Thirty-nine Lashes at the first halting place afterwards." The baggage train was banned from the parade. As were women. "Not a woman belonging to the army is to be seen with the troops on their march thro' the city." Parades, of course, require music. "The drums and fifes of each brigade are to be collected in the center of it; and a tune for the quick step played, but with such moderation that the men may step to it with ease; and without *dancing* along, or totally disregarding the music, as too often has been the case." The troops evidently paid attention to the beat and forsook dancing along, for a congressman wrote that they marched "with a lively smart Step," and Richard Henry Lee told Thomas Jefferson that "they made a fine appearance."[1]

John Adams found the soldiers to be "extreamly well armed, pretty well clothed, and tolerably disciplined." But he felt that much improvement was required:

> Our soldiers have not yet, quite the Air of Soldiers. They dont step exactly in Time. They dont hold up their Heads, quite erect, Nor turn out their Toes, so exactly as they ought. They dont all of them cock their Hats—and such as do, dont all wear them the same Way.[2]

Adams's observations were hardly surprising, since the new army was largely made up of fresh recruits, mostly young and poor, which, given the history of armies in general, also should not be surprising, although writers of an ideological bent read more into that than is merited. It is also worth observing that American soldiers, at least during my lifetime, have never marched with the panache of other armies. In general, spit and polish have never been our forte. The test would come, as it always does, on the battlefield. Opinions differ on whether a cadre from the 1776 army existed. I suspect it did, but either opinion would be very difficult to prove.

Whatever the state of the army, however, Washington meant to defend the capital city. The man the world was calling "the American Fabius" was prepared to give Sir William the battle he desired. What choice had Washington? Congress and patriots everywhere expected Philadelphia to be defended. Militarily, it made no more sense than it had to defend New York City. Politically, it was essential. And, of course, it fit Washington's essential nature as a soldier. A Fabian strategy had been forced on him the previous winter because of the army's small size and condition. But now, the army strong once more, if still to a large degree amateurish, Washington had a renewal of confidence that would lead him again to battle.

Reunited with its baggage train and women and children, the army camped that night about five miles beyond Philadelphia, where Washington immediately gave orders for the divisions of Generals Greene and Adam Stephen to march the following day toward Wilmington, Delaware. Tents were struck at 3:00 A.M., the march began an hour later, and at 2:00 P.M. on the 25th Greene's division made camp five miles from Wilmington. The divisions of Lord Stirling and General Wayne followed the next day. Stirling and Wayne were enjoined to prevent straggling of their troops from camp and "to prevent an inundation of bad women from Philadelphia."[3]

It was also about this time that Washington received good news from northern New York. General Burgoyne had sent a detachment eastward toward New England "to disconcert the Councils of the enemy . . . and obtain large Supplies of Cattle, Horses and Carriages." The 750-man force, comprised largely of dismounted Brunswick dragoons and commanded by Major Friedrich Baum, on 16 August was shattered and overrun, and a supporting column routed, by New York and New England militia reinforced by 150 Continentals. Major Baum was mortally wounded, 696 enemy soldiers captured and perhaps 200 killed, although a Rebel who was there said, "we do not know how many we have killed, our scouts daily find them in the woods."[4]

From another quarter, however, came disturbing news. General Sullivan, then with his command in New Jersey, decided, before joining Washington, to raid British-held Staten Island in reprisal for a British raid into Jersey. Sullivan botched the operation and lost 13 killed and 172 captured, although Sir Henry Clinton claimed that his forces took 259 prisoners. Neither Washington nor Congress was pleased. Washington wrote to Sullivan with barely veiled criticism, "I am not sufficiently acquainted with circumstances to form a certain judgement of what might have been expected from this expedition, but from the view I have of them, and from your own representation of the matter, the situation of the enemy seems to have been such as afforded an opportunity of reaping much more decisive advantages than were in fact gained." Congress believed that Sullivan's "Conduct was not altogether free from Censure," although that language was stricken from Hancock's letter to Washington directing that a court of enquiry be held. The court, which was held in October, acquitted Sullivan. The New Hampshire general was a brave officer and ever faithful to the American cause, but his competence in action usually left much to be desired.[5]

A more pressing matter then intervened, which was why Sullivan's court-martial was put off until mid-October. On 25 August, the day after Sullivan's debacle, British and Hessian troops began landing at Elk Ferry on the Elk River, eight miles from where the river flowed into

Chesapeake Bay. Admiral Lord Howe had led the tall ships in by taking "soundings himself in a boat at the head of the fleet," Captain Ewald reported, and two days before the landing, Lord Howe and Sir William personally reconnoitered possible landing places, approaching within gunshot range of armed Americans on Turkey Point, at the mouth of the Elk River. Between two and three o'clock on the morning of the 25th, flatboats for the first wave came alongside the transports carrying elite troops: Jägers and British light infantry, grenadiers and guards. Both Howe brothers joined the first wave and led the way in HMS *Vigilant,* which carried the admiral's flag. They landed between 10:00 and 11:00 A.M. The Jägers, Ewald wrote, "immediately moved forward a half an hour into the country through a pathless region which was cut through with brushwood and steep rocks" and "took post in a wood where we found the highway to" the village of Head of Elk. Sir William, who always knew where he belonged on an operation, went with them. The countryside was virtually empty of people, for tales of the army's plundering and burning in New Jersey had preceded them, and the people had fled with most of their belongings. The Jägers found "oxen, sheep, turkeys, and all kinds of wild fowl," and "Since we did not find any of the enemy, we skirmished with these animals, of which so many were killed that the entire Corps was provided with fresh provisions." Strict orders had been issued against plundering, but many troops carried on as usual, for which Sir William "sentenced some to be hanged on the spot and others to be flogged within an inch of their lives," a German officer reported. It was intensely hot and that afternoon "several jagers fell down dead" from the heat. Violent thunderstorms came up toward evening, and the troops were drenched in downpours that continued into the morning of the 27th. The storms increased the heat "to such a degree that we believed we would suffocate in the fiery air." Behind the first wave the rest of the fleet anchored, and waves of troops came ashore and advanced some 2½ miles beyond the ferry. Most of Sir William's army landed on the 25th "without the least Opposition," Major Robertson wrote, "every thing being conducted with the utmost regularity." This should not surprise us, for Sir William and his brother and their fellow army and naval officers down to the Ewalds and Robertsons and Peebles were very good at operations, everything being carried out with an expertise that had been gleaned from past generations of soldiers and honed over decades of personal experience.[6]

Most of the British army was probably ashore when the news was reported to Washington at 6:00 P.M. on the 25th. He immediately ordered Generals Greene and Stephens to join him at Wilmington with their divisions. The next morning he set out on a personal reconnaissance mission that brought him so perilously close to the enemy that it reminded his officers of how Charles Lee had been captured. He and his party, including Alexander Hamilton and Lafayette, proceeded to Head of Elk, described by a British officer as "a pretty Village." From high ground northeast of the village he surveyed at least some of the British activities. What he discovered, a "few Tents . . . to be seen" from their vantage point, was not worth the risk he took. Two months later he explained to a friend that although "It is not my wish to avoid any danger which duty requires me to encounter I can as confidently add, that it is not my intention to run unnecessary risques. In the instance given by you, I was acting precisely in the line of my duty, but not in the dangerous situation you have been led to believe. I was reconnoitring, but I had a strong party of Horse with me. I was, as (I afterwards found) in a disaffected House at the head of Elk, but I was equally guarded agt friend and Foe. the information of danger then, came not from me." I beg to differ with Washington's estimation of the danger he was in. The storms described by Ewald forced him to take shelter, with Nathanael Greene and Lafayette, in the house of a Tory, and there he insisted on spending the night. The next morning he admitted to Lafayette that "a single traitor could have betrayed him." Consider the potential disaster: Washington, the truly indispensable man, a prisoner; with him Nathanael Greene, whose brilliant Carolina campaign played a key role in bringing Cornwallis to bay at Yorktown in 1781; and the marquis de Lafayette, symbol of the future Franco-American alliance, without which events would have turned out far differently than they did. No, General, you made an unwise decision that night, and you were lucky to get away with it.[7]

"One bold stroke will free the land"

The British began probes northward on 28 August. "Since the region here is heavily wooded and cut up with ravines, we marched very slowly and carefully," reported Captain von Münchhausen. On the hills northeast of Head of Elk they could see Rebel officers observing "us with their glasses as carefully as we observed them," and von Münchhausen claimed that British officers present "who know Washington well, maintained that the man in the plain coat was Washington." But that cannot be, since Washington had already carried out his reconnaissance and returned to Wilmington on the 27th. It would not be the last time during the Pennsylvania campaign that British officers thought they saw Washington in the field.[8]

On that same day General Horatio Gates, in the Northern Department, wrote a letter to Washington describing another Burgoyne setback. Washington would receive it on 1 September. Burgoyne's plan included a column of Tory regulars and Iroquois commanded by Lieutenant Colonel Barry St. Leger to make its way from Canada to Fort Oswego in north-central New York State, then take Rebel-held Fort Stanwix (modern Rome, New York) on the portage route between the Mohawk River and Lake Ontario, and advance along the Mohawk Valley toward Albany. But Benedict Arnold, commanding the Rebel relief column, reported to Gates that the siege of the fort had been abandoned by St. Leger, who had retreated in great haste, "leaving their Tents standing, their Provisions, Ammunition, etc., etc. which have fallen into our hands."[9]

In Sir William's army, individuals were falling into Rebel hands, and the fate of some was gruesome. Almost as soon as he heard of the British landing, Washington wrote to the Philadelphia militia officer General John Cadwalader that he thought "many important advantages would be derived from the Militias hanging on his Rear or Right Flank, after he leaves Elk, while he is opposed by this Army in Front or in such Other way as shall seem most adviseable from circumstances." But he admitted that he was unfamiliar with the militia organizations and officers of the area and requested Cadwalader's "Good Offices and interest in assisting to assemble—spirit up and forward them . . . towards the Head of the Bay, that they may be in a situation to annoy the Enemy." But some Rebels near Head of Elk had obviously taken matters into their own hands before anything official was done at the levels of Washington and Cadwalader to mobilize and deploy them. At 9:00 A.M. on the 29th, Captain Ewald wrote, "the army was alarmed on all sides by enemy parties," and "A few foot jagers and infantrymen were killed and wounded, since our sentries beyond the two highways could scarcely see over twenty paces in front of themselves because of the thick wood." Despite the danger, British and Hessian troops, master plunderers, never

allowed general orders, lashings, or the enemy's proximity to stand between them and loot. Captain John André reported an amusing example when "Some Hessians belonging to a baggage guard demolished a
whole flock of sheep which the owners were voluntarily driving to us."
But some plunderers paid with either their freedom or their lives. The
day after Washington wrote to Cadwalader, Captain von Münchhausen
wrote, "Because of increasing acts of pillage . . . last night we lost several men who had advanced too far and were captured," and on the following day, "more pillaging troops captured." Captain Peebles's diary
entry for the 29th reads, "Moroding [marauding] to shamefull degree,
expecially among the Hessians—above 40 soldiers of ye army missing,
supposed to be taken or deserted." And on 1 September, "2 men of 71st
[Fraser's Highlanders] found in the wood yesterday with their throats
cut, & 2 Grrs. [grenadiers] hang'd by the Rebels with the plunder on
their backs."[10]

On the 30th Washington reminded Colonel Theodorick Bland
(1742–1790), commanding a regiment of Continental Light Horse, to
maintain "constant patrols, both of horse and foot, on the flanks and in
front of the enemy, as near to them as prudence will permit, so that
they cannot possibly move any way, without your having information of
it. I shall expect to have immediate notice of every matter of importance which comes to your knowledge." That same day Washington
appointed Brigadier General William Maxwell (c. 1733–1796) of New
Jersey commander of a corps of Light Infantry that was established by
taking 100 men from each brigade, to a total of about 700 men. This
corps was meant to replace Colonel Daniel Morgan's rifle regiment,
which had performed so well earlier in the year in New Jersey, and which
Washington had reluctantly sent to reinforce Gates's army in northern
New York. Maxwell's light troops were assigned to harass Howe's advance.
Maxwell, however, was no Morgan. Washington on one occasion rebuked
Maxwell for failing to intercept a British raiding party and found it necessary to write to him often with detailed instructions and in general to
"be prepared to give them as much trouble as you possibly can." But
when the main British advance on the road to Philadelphia began on
3 September, Maxwell's men did offer resistance, and a running fight
began.[11]

At daybreak Captain Ewald took a patrol of six dragoons forward
"not . . . a hundred paces from the advanced guard when I received fire
from a hedge, through which these six men were either all killed or

wounded." Ewald's horse, "normally . . . well used to fire, reared so high several times that I expected it would throw me. I cried out, 'Foot jägers forward!' and advanced with them" and "ran into another enemy party, with which I became heavily engaged." Captain von Münchhausen also was in action that day and "saw several rebels behind trees, firing at our advancing jägers, then retreating about 20 yards behind the next tree, then firing again." According to von Münchhausen, the Rebels "can run so fast one can not catch them without taking a chance of being cut off." But running, as long as it was controlled, was a favored tactic of light troops charged with delaying an enemy superior in numbers, and by Ewald's testimony it was a heavy fight that day. The Hessians could see Iron Mountain, 325 feet high and "overgrown with woods, rising up like an amphitheater and occupied by enemy troops." Sir William himself came forward and ordered Lieutenant Colonel Ludwig Johann Adolph von Wurmb, commanding the Jäger corps, to clear the mountain. At the same time a battalion of British Light Infantry under Lieutenant Colonel Robert Abercromby (1740–1827), who sixteen years later would succeed Lord Cornwallis as commander in chief in India, was ordered to work its way to the rear of Maxwell's force and cut it off. But Abercromby could not get across a marsh that blocked his way. It was up to the Jägers, and they responded splendidly.[12]

"The charge was sounded," wrote Ewald, the Jägers attacked with "spirit" and "came to close quarters with the enemy, and the hunting sword was used as much as the rifle." Following "a seven hour engagement," the Rebels were driven from the mountain. Von Münchhausen wrote that the Jägers "finished the whole affair themselves, driving the Rebels through the thick woods, then across the barren hill and the Christiana Creek Bridge, which led them across a second creek and a deep ravine." Thus ended the so-called Battle of Cooch's Bridge. As usual, casualty figures are contradictory. Washington reported about forty Americans killed and wounded and thought Maxwell's men had done more damage to the British. But von Münchhausen claimed that the British buried forty-one Rebel dead, "among them several officers," and that British and Hessian losses were three dead and twenty-three wounded, whereas Sir William reported to Germain that the Rebel loss "was not less than fifty killed and many more wounded." Captain Ewald admitted to eleven Jägers dead and forty-five wounded. The following day Sir William rightly paid tribute in writing to the Jäger corps as deserving the "the highest praise and the fullest acknowledgement of the Commander in Chief, and has attracted the greatest admiration of the entire army." But Maxwell's light troops also had carried out their assignment of harassing the enemy and delaying his advance, in this case by at least a day.[13]

Washington felt that the time was fast approaching when the two main armies would meet for a decisive contest, and he felt confident:

> If they are overthrown, they are utterly undone—the war is at an end. Now then is the time for our most strenuous exertions. One bold stroke will free the land from rapine, devastations & burnings, and female innocence from brutal lust and violence.

After describing the successes of Rebel forces in the Northern Department, "who can forbear," he wrote, "to emulate their noble spirit." He reminded the soldiers of the great difficulties encountered over the past two years, but noted that "the prospect has since brightened, and our affairs put on a better face. Now is the time to reap the fruits of all our toils and dangers!"

> If we behave like men, this third Campaign will be our last. Ours is the main army; to us our country looks for protection. The eyes of all America, and of Europe are turned upon us. . . . And the General assures his countrymen and fellow soldiers, that he believes the critical, the most important moment is at hand, which demands their most spirited exertions in the field. There glory waits to crown the brave— and peace—and freedom and happiness will be the rewards of victory.[14]

Another pep talk, modern cynics might note. Another harangue, as it was then called. But such writings and exhortations were then commonly directed to troops at critical moments and cannot be judged by modern standards. Besides, there are phrases in it that tell us much about Washington—not Washington the Fabian, but the true Washington, the fighting general. "One bold stroke . . . they are utterly undone . . . this third campaign will be our last." He truly was out to end it all, and he thought he could do it.

Shortly thereafter Washington learned that the "enemy have disincumbered themselves of all their baggage, that their movements may be quick and easy." Thereupon he strictly forbade the Rebel wagonmasters to turn their horses loose in the fields at night to graze, but to keep them hitched to the wagons, to graze them only by day, and then to stay close to them with tackle ready, and to always be ready to march "at a moment's warning." Washington and his senior officers guessed that Sir William would now advance on Philadelphia on the main road via Wilmington, Delaware, and therefore on 8 September deployed his forces accordingly. Some of Sir William's aides guessed the same, for Captain von Münchhausen wrote, "to our great surprise, instead of taking the road by way of Christiana Bridge to Wilmington as expected, we went to our left by way of White Clay Creek and Newark [Delaware]." And on that road the Rebels missed a grand opportunity to do some real damage to Howe's army, as described by Captain Ewald. The army passed through Newark "and toward morning on the 8th crossed the White Clay Creek, which was surrounded on both sides by steep, rocky heights that formed a most frightful defile half an hour in length." These heights rose from 100 to 200 feet, and Ewald never understood why the Rebels

> abandoned this position, where a hundred riflemen could have held up the army a whole day and killed many men. My hair stood on end as we crammed into the defile, and I imagined nothing more certain than an unexpected attack at the moment when we would have barely stuck our nose out of the defile. For the precipitous rocks on both sides of the creek and along the defile were so steep that no one could scale them.[15]

The British and Hessians marched on unopposed. When Howe's route became clear, Washington moved quickly, for he feared that Sir William aimed at getting "between us and Philada and cut us off from that City." The army received its orders at 4:00 A.M. on 9 September and by hard marching crossed Brandywine Creek that evening to a strong defensive post, "upon the High Grounds near Chad's Ford," Washington wrote, where Lieutenant McMichael described the army arriving "extremely fatigued for want of rest and severe marching." A British officer left a more precise description of Washington's position, which had "every advantage . . . that nature could well afford. The ground is extremely broken and the risings from the creek (some of very considerable height) most happily disposed for defence—flanking the vallies between them, and covereing a morass in their front." General Maxwell and his light infantry were positioned on the high ground on the west bank of the Brandywine, their mission to patrol aggressively to gather intelligence as to British intentions. The following day, 10 September,

Howe's army marched into Kennett Square, Pennsylvania, about thirty-three miles from Philadelphia, some eight miles from Chadds Ford. Washington, standing in Sir William's way, determined to protect Philadelphia, showed no signs of shifting position.[16]

"Most assuredly it was not General Washington"

In view of the intentions of both commanders to seek battle, we should now briefly consider the topography of Brandywine Valley. It was best described for us in 1846, when it was much closer to its appearance in 1777:

> The whole country abounded in forests, interspersed with plantations, more or less detached. To the east of the Brandywine it was more open, but both banks of the creek were pretty densely covered with woods. The country is undulating, the larger hills usually skirting the creek separated by flats now forming beautiful and luxuriant meadows, but then doubtless covered with the primitive forest. So dense and impenetrable were the wood and undergrowth upon these flats that a part of them above Painter's Bridge on the street road bears to this day the name of Dungeon Bottom.[17]

Over this fertile, bucolic landscape occurred scenes that have become all too familiar to us from television images, as frightened civilians tried to get out of the way of maneuvering armies. "The Enemy plunder most amazeingly," General Nathanael Greene wrote. But the Rebel soldiers were almost surely the equals of their British and Hessian counterparts, their behavior wringing passionate language from Washington:

> Nowithstanding all the cautions—the earnest requests, and the positive orders of the Commander in Chief, to prevent *our own army* from plundering *our own friends* and *fellow citizens*, yet to his astonishment and grief, fresh complaints are made to him, that so wicked, infamous and cruel a practice is still continued—and that too in circumstances most distressing—where the wretched inhabitants, dreading the enemy's vengeance for their adherence to our cause, have left all and fled to us for refuge![18]

That is only a small part of a long paragraph, ending with the threat "that he will have no mercy on offenders against these orders; their lives shall pay the forfeit of their crimes." The transgressions of the opposing armies led Greene to describe to his wife "some of the most distressing scenes imaginable. The inhabitants generally desert their homes, furniture moveing, Cattle driving and women and children traveling off on foot. The country all resounds with the cries of the people." But orders, exhortations, threats, lashings, and hangings, whether coming from Washington or Sir William, would not deter the troops. As repelled as one is by such behavior, one can only shrug and say with the French, *C'est la guerre*.[19]

According to Captain Ewald, the British army moved out from Kennett Square on 11 September at two o'clock in the morning. A thick fog masked its movements during the early morning. Sir William had divided the army into two columns. One column, commanded by the skilled and experienced Hessian, Lieutenant General von Knyphausen, headed for Chadds Ford with about 6,800 men. On point were Captain Patrick Ferguson's (1744–1780) seventy-odd picked British soldiers, each armed with the famous breech-loading rifle that Ferguson erroneously claimed to have invented; and Tory regulars of the Queen's Rangers. Behind them were two British Brigades, a Hessian Brigade, part of the 16th Light Dragoons, and two Brigades of artillery followed by more artillery and as a rear guard the three battalions of Fraser's Highlanders (71st Foot). Von Knyphausen's mission was to advance to Chadds Ford and make a demonstration as if he meant to engage the Rebel Army.[20]

The destination of the second column is where the Battle of Brandywine gets interesting. Commanded by Lieutenant General Charles, 2nd Earl Cornwallis, with Sir William by his side, it was about 8,200 strong and made up of the cream of the army: the Jäger corps, two battalions of British Light Infantry, two battalions of Guards, two battalions of British Grenadiers, three battalions of Hessian Grenadiers, two Brigades of British infantry, the rest of the Light Dragoons, and field artillery. Soon after leaving Kennett Square the column turned sharply left and marched away from Chadds Ford, up the Great Valley Road toward the upper fords across Brandywine Creek. Sir William's purpose was to cross the creek at a ford several miles above Chadds Ford, then turn back and come crashing down on Washington's right flank. In other words, an approximate repeat of the Battle of Long Island.[21]

While Sir William's column disappeared into the heavy morning fog, von Knyphausen carried out the diversionary movement meant to pin the American army at Chadds Ford. Three miles east of Kennett Square, at a place called Welch's Tavern, von Knyphausen's point units,

Ferguson's riflemen and Queen's Rangers, made first contact with Maxwell's patrols, and the skirmishing was quite constant from then. By 10:30 A.M. Maxwell had been driven off the high ground and back to the other side of the Brandywine. Major Baurmeister wrote that "the small arms fire ceased entirely, although our cannon fired from time to time, each shot being answered by the enemy. The purpose of the gunfire, however, was only to advise the second column of our position."

It was probably during this phase of the fighting that an incident took place that is still accepted as gospel by some and heralded as one of the great "what ifs" of American history. Captain Ferguson and his riflemen were lying on the ground at the edge of some woods "whenn a Rebel officer remarkable by a hussar dress passed . . . within 100 yards of my right flank, not perceiving us. He was followed by another dressed in dark green or blue mounted on a very good bay horse with a remarkable large high cock'd hat." Ferguson, a crack shot, could easily have hit the second officer, probably killed him, "but it was not pleasant for me to fire at the back of an unoffending individual . . . so I let him alone." The next day, however, he was told "Genl Washington was all the morning with the Light Troops, generally in their front and only attended by a French officer in a huzzar Dress, he himself mounted and dressed as above directed." Ferguson went to his grave convinced that he had spared the indispensable man, thus missing his chance to change the course of history.[22]

Two men disputed the story. Captain Alexander Graydon of 3rd Pennsylvania, who had seen Washington often before being captured at Fort Washington, in his memoirs claimed that "most assuredly it was not General Washington." Graydon was adamant that "no one acquainted with the style of General Washington's costume during the war, or any other time, can suppose it to have been him. . . . The General's uniform . . . was blue and buff, which . . . he never varied, at least to an entire change of colours: neither was he ever seen in a hat of the description given in the letter. It is true, he wore a cocked hat, but, of a moderate size."[23]

The second man offers even harder evidence that Ferguson was mistaken. A prominent New York Tory, James P. de Lancey, was Ferguson's second in command and present that day, and he always insisted on a different version. De Lancey's daughter married James Fenimore Cooper, who many years later wrote a letter to the *New-York Mirror* specifically to refute Ferguson's version. Ferguson had never seen Washington, but de Lancey had met, conversed, and dined with him in Philadelphia in 1774. De Lancey, Cooper wrote, "to whom the person of Washington was so necessarily well known, constantly affirmed that his commander was mistaken. I have often heard Mr. De Lancey relate these circumstances, and though he never pretended to be sure of the person of the unknown horseman, it was his opinion from some particulars of dress and stature that it was the Count Pulaski." And so another good story almost certainly bites the dust.[24]

"I had no orders to Take any Care above Buffentons Ford"

The fords of the Brandywine were key to the battle, and there were several that are germane to our story. A little ways downstream of Chadds Ford was Gibson's Ford. It was guarded by two brigades of Pennsylvania militia. Upstream from Chadds Ford six miles to the junction of the east and west branches, forming the Brandywine proper, there were four fords, also well guarded. Traveling upstream they were Brinton's Ford, Painter's Ford, Jones's Ford, and finally Buffington's Ford, where the east and west branches meet. The right wing of the Rebel Army was assigned to guard the four upstream fords. That wing was commanded by Major General John Sullivan, whose main force was astride Brinton's Ford. Sullivan sent Colonel David Hall's (1752–1817) Delaware Regiment to guard Painter's Ford, and Colonel Moses Hazen's (1733–1803) 2nd Canadian Regiment to guard Jones's and Buffington's, the latter a mile above Jones's. From these assignments and more evidence given below, Washington cannot, as some writers have averred, be charged with neglecting his flanks, especially his right flank. The problem was that Sir William and Lord Cornwallis and their 8,200 regulars were headed for none of these fords. They had with them the well-known Philadelphia Tory Joseph Galloway (c. 1731–1803), who had strongly supported American rights within the empire but balked at independence and in 1776 had gone over to the British. He had brought with him local Tories who were well acquainted with the area, its roads and fords. They knew of a ford called Jeffries on the west branch of the Brandywine about a mile above the fork, and about a mile and a half above Jeffries Ford was Taylor's Ford. According to General Sullivan, writing to Washington about a month and a half after the battle, and feeling very defensive if not downright paranoid about the attacks on his performance,

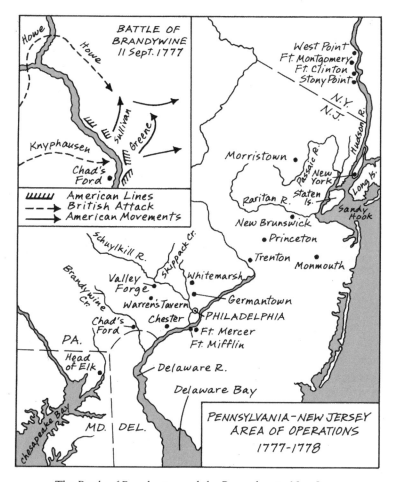

The Battle of Brandywine and the Pennsylvania–New Jersey
Area of Operations

Upon my asking whether there were no fords higher up [above Buffington's] I was Informed in presence of yr Excellencey That There was
none within Twelve miles to Cross at which the Enemy must make a
Long Circuit Through a very Bad Road & that all the Light Horse of
the Army were ordered to the Right to watch the Enemys motions on
that Quarter. I had no orders to Take any Care above Buffentons Ford
nor had Light Troops or Light Horse for the purpose.

I see no reason to disbelieve Sullivan, and in fact Washington agreed in
his reply that only the fords above Chadds Ford to the forks of the river
were assigned to Sullivan's division, and then added, "we were led to

believe by those whom we had reason to think well acquainted with the Country that no ford above our picquets could be passed, without making a circuitious march." Washington, however, had been misinformed, while Sir William's intelligence on the lay of the land was right on the mark. Captain Ewald, who led Cornwallis's advance guard, was expansive on the excellence of British intelligence:

> Lord Cornwallis had sent me a guide who was a real geographical chart and almost a general by nature. During the entire march I often spoke with him regarding the area which was beyond the horizon. He constantly judged so correctly that I always found the enemy there where he presumed him to be. His description was so good that I was often amazed at the knowledge that this man possessed of the country.

The guide was probably Joseph Galloway himself, given Ewald's observation that the man was "almost a general by nature," for Galloway, born to wealth, had married wealth, before Independence a member of Pennsylvania's power structure, was described by the historian John Ferling as "aloof, overbearing, even imperious." We should add, however, that a local farmer named Curtis Lewis claimed to have guided the British army and after the war submitted a claim to the British government.[25]

But despite Washington's defective intelligence report on the location of distant fords, he was not unmindful of possible danger above the forks. So began, on 11 September 1777, a long day of tension and indecision at Washington's headquarters at Chadds Ford as he and his staff tried to unravel Sir William's intention.

"Colo. Hazen's Information must be wrong"

8:45 A.M., *Chadds Ford*. Washington's aide, Lieutenant Colonel Robert Hanson Harrison, wrote to John Hancock that "The Enemy are advancing. Their present appearance indicates a disposition to pursue this route," which means that von Knyphausen's diversion was up to this time succeeding.

In the meantime, Lord Cornwallis's column on the Great Valley Road was marching through prime ambush country. Captain Ewald had been "ordered to march as slowly as possible, and to use all caution in order not to fall into an ambuscade, as the area was traversed by hills, woodlands, marshes, and the steepest defiles."

9:00 A.M., *Brinton's Ford*. Major John Jameson (1752–1837) of Virginia, 1st Continental Dragoons, told General Sullivan that "he came from the Right of the Army & I might Depend there was no Enemy there." Sullivan then ordered Jameson "to Send an officer over to the Lancaster Road," which was about two miles north of Buffington's Ford, and that officer "Returned & Said no Enemy had passed that way."

11:00 A.M., *Great Valley Road*. Lieutenant Colonel James Ross (1752–1808) of 8th Pennsylvania was scouting with "about 70 men" when he spotted "close in their rear" Cornwallis's flanking column and immediately dispatched a note to Washington: "A large body of the enemy—from every account 5000, with 16 or 18 field pieces, marched along this Road just now. this Road lead to Taylor's and Jeffries ferries on the Brandy wine." Ross confirmed that Sir William and Galloway were with the British column, "as Joseph Galloway is here Known by the inhabitants, with many of whom he spoke, and told them that Genl Howe was with him." Ross also reported that Captain [Michael?] Simpson and twenty men had fired three rounds at the column. Captain Ewald also reported fighting on the road: "I ran into a warning post of the enemy, five to six hundred men strong, who withdrew from one favorable position to another under constant skirmishing until around noon time." There seems to be no evidence that the noise of these skirmishing actions raised the curiosity of Rebel commanders.

About 11:00 A.M. Cornwallis's column begins crossing Trimble's Ford on the East branch of the Brandywine, two miles above the fork and three miles from Jeffries Ford on the West Branch. The column halted until all units were across, then pushed on toward Jeffries Ford.

About 11:20 A.M., *Chadds Ford*. At some point during the morning, before Washington received Colonel Ross's report, Colonel Moses Hazen, one of whose battalions was guarding Buffington's Ford, reported to Sullivan that British troops had been seen at the forks of the Brandywine. Sullivan passed this information on to Washington, who immediately wrote to Colonel Bland, commanding the Light Horse, whose responsibility was to scout the country above the Forks. "In a particular manner, I wish you to gain satisfactory information of a body confidently reported to have gone up to a Ford Seven or Eight miles above this. It is said the fact is certain. You will send up an intelligent—sensible Officer immediately with a party to find out the truth. What number It consists of, and the Road they are now on. be particular in these matters."

About noon, Chadds Ford. Washington probably received Colonel Ross's dispatch reporting Cornwallis's column on the Great Valley Road. Washington now had two reports, Ross's and Hazen's, of a sizable British force on the Great Valley Road and at the Forks of the Brandywine. These reports apparently led him to order an attack on von Knyphausen. Sullivan was ordered to cross the creek and attack von Knyphausen's left while the rest of the army crossed over, against the enemy's right. But just as the attack was getting under way, the picture changed drastically.

About noon to 1:00 P.M., Brinton's Ford. General Sullivan sent a dispatch to Washington reporting the arrival in his camp of Major Joseph Spear of the Chester County militia, a local man who knew the country well. Spear "Came this morning from a Tavern called Martins on the Forks of the Brandywine . . . & heard nothing of the Enemy about the Forks of the Brandywine & is confident they are not in that Quarter so that Colo. Hazen's Information must be wrong." Major Spear also told Sullivan that Washington himself "had sent him out for the purpose of discovering whether the enemy were in that Quarter." Sullivan later told John Hancock that he doubted Spear's report but felt he must pass it on lest he be blamed for withholding information that might be correct. But if he doubted Spear, why cast doubt on Colonel Hazen's information in his letter to Washington? Sullivan's desperate after-action wrigglings to defend himself do not lend themselves to a sympathetic reception, then or now.

As for Washington, he was betwixt and between. If Spear was right, was the entire British army just across the creek from Chadds Ford? Was he being drawn into a trap? Writing forty-three years after the event, Colonel Charles Cotesworth Pinckney (1745–1825) of South Carolina, who was at Chadds Ford, said that Washington was convinced by Spear's report "to suppose that the [flanking] movement of the enemy was a feint, & that they were returning to reinforce Knyphausen at Chad's Ford." The attack was canceled and the troops withdrawn to their positions on the east bank. Washington would later label Spear's erroneous intelligence "a most unfortunate circumstance."

1:15 P.M., Above the Forks of the Brandywine. Colonel Bland of the Light Horse finally reported to Washington that he had "discovered a party of the Enemy on the Heights Just on the Right of two Widow davis's, who live close together on the Road called the fork Road, about half a mile to the Right of the meeting house (Birmingham)." This report put Cornwallis over Jeffries Ford.

About 2:00 P.M., Jeffries Ford. There is a discrepancy in time here, between Bland's report in the previous paragraph and Captain Ewald claiming that he crossed Jeffries Ford at about 2:00 P.M. But that is of little consequence. The important thing is that Cornwallis and Howe crossed the West Branch of the Brandywine in the early afternoon and outflanked Washington. And here is where we have more evidence of Washington's real failure that day. We know that he did not ignore the possibility of a flanking movement and tried to guard against it. But he did fail to properly reconnoiter the countryside. He probably did not have time to do it personally. But certainly a senior officer other than the hapless Sullivan should have had that responsibility. For proper reconnaissance of the countryside along the West Branch could have led to a defense that might well have defeated Howe's plan. Read Captain Ewald's description of the topography after he had crossed at Jeffries Ford: "the road ran up along a deep and winding precipice." After halting at this defile to confer with his guide and Lord Cornwallis, who had come forward, Ewald

> took twelve jägers and let them pass the defile by twos, two paces apart, with instructions to take post as soon as all twelve were across and had reached a point where they could see around. But as soon as the van of the enemy was encountered, they were to retreat by twos.
>
> I was astonished when I had safely reached the end of this terrible defile, which was over a thousand paces long, and could discover nothing of the enemy a good half hour away. Lord Cornwallis, who had followed me, was surprised himself and could not understand why the warning post with which I had fought from morning until around noon was not stationed here. The pass had been left wide open for us, where a hundred men could have held up either army the whole day.

2:00 P.M., Brinton's Ford. General Sullivan sent Washington the following message: "Colo. Bland has this moment sent me Word that the Enemy are in the Rear of my Right about two miles Coming Down. there is he Says about two Brigades of them."

Although the size of the flanking force was much larger than Colonel Bland's estimate, there could now be no doubt of Sir William's intention.

Washington reacted quickly, sending the divisions of Lord Stirling and General Adam Stephen to confront Cornwallis and Howe about two miles north of Chadds Ford and ordering Sullivan to join them with his division and take command. While on the march Sullivan met Colonel Hazen and discovered that the British force was far larger than two brigades.

The British flanking force, meanwhile, had arrived on a hill described by Captain von Münchhausen as a "steep, barren height, where we formed in lines by brigades." From this commanding height, called Osborne's Hill, the British could see the Americans under Lord Stirling and General Stephen formed opposite them on Birmingham Hill and Birmingham Meeting House. Stephen's division was on the right, Lord Stirling's in the center. Upon his arrival on the field, General Sullivan's division would deploy on the left while under fire. The British had marched seventeen miles that day and forded two creeks in water up to three feet. The morning fog had given way to intense heat, and the final climb had been steep and arduous. "Here we paused for a long hour to give the men some rest and to enable the last of the battalions to come up," von Münchhausen wrote. A British officer noted that "Sir William Howe with the most cheerful countenance conversed with his Officers and invited several to a light refreshment provided on the grass." A picnic on the hill before the slaughter.

"Their arms and bayonets . . . shone as bright as silver"

4:00 P.M., *Osborne Hill.* The British and Hessians formed for the advance in columns. On the left, British Light Infantry and Jägers with 4th English Brigade behind them. In the center, British Grenadiers backed up by Hessian Grenadiers. The right wing, the post of honor, went to the Household Guards. In reserve was 3rd English Brigade, and near Sir William and his staff the two squadrons of 16th Light Dragoons awaited orders as circumstances might require. Eighty-two hundred fighting men decked out in the full panoply of war. It must have been a stirring sight, and there was a local Quaker lad, twenty-one-year-old Joseph Townsend, there to describe the army's approach to Osborne Hill, there forming for battle, and its advance into the maelstrom:

> Possessed of curiosity and fond of new things, my brother William Townsend and myself with some others, rode along the Brandywine some

distance, to discover the approach of the British army . . . our eyes
were caught . . . by the appearance of the army coming out of the
woods . . . on the west side of the creek above the fording place. In a
few minutes the fields were literally covered with them, and they were
hastening toward us. Their arms and bayonets being raised, shone as
bright as silver, there being a clear sky and the day exceedingly warm.

Anxious for the safety of their farm, the brothers went home, but
when the British did not appear, their curiosity got the better of them
again and they set out once more and met Sarah Boake, wife of Abel,

who had been as curious as ourselves, and had been among the soldiers as they marched along. [Sarah] encouraged our going amongst
them, at the same time admiring their appearance, and saying what
fine looking fellows they were, and to use her own expression, "they
were something like an army."

When Joseph and William were challenged by a flanking party they
told the officer in charge "we wished to see the army," and he allowed
them to proceed and soon they were in the middle of marching men.
They spoke with officers and men, all of whom wanted to know where
the Rebels were and "where Mr. Washington was to be found." An officer told Joseph, "you have got a hell of a fine country here, which we
have found to be the case ever since we landed at head of Elk."
They saw Lord Cornwallis passing by.

He was on horseback, appeared tall and sat very erect. His rich scarlet
clothing, loaded with gold lace, epaulets, etc., occasioned to make a
brilliant and martial appearance. [For Joseph's description of Sir William Howe, whom he also saw, see chapter 1.]

Joseph left an interesting observation about the British officers to
whom he spoke:

It may be observed that most or all of the officers who conversed with
us, were of the first rank, and were rather short, portly men, were well
dressed and of genteel appearance, and did not look as if they had
ever been exposed to any hardship; their skins being as white and delicate as is customary for females who were brought up in large cities
or towns.

Walking on ahead of the army, Joseph and William soon had the opportunity to see the deadlier side of the pageant spread out before them:

> On turning our faces back, we had a grand view of the army as they advanced over and down the south side of Osborne's Hill and the lands of James Carter, scarce a vacant place left. While we were amusing ourselves with the wonderful curiosity before us, to our great astonishment and surprise, the firing of the musketry took place, the advanced guard . . . fired upon by a company of Americans in an orchard.

The battle began between 3:30 and 4:00 P.M. The Americans from General Stephen's division had fired on the Jägers. Joseph said that "The Germans immediately returned fire from a fence line running alongside the road." Joseph now retired from the immediate vicinity, "finding that my inconsiderate curiosity had prompted me to exceed the bounds of providence." He slipped away to a hill where he mingled with other local civilians, probably other Quaker neutrals, to observe the British high command and their aides confer as the battle "commenced in earnest."

If the British expected the Rebels to fold quickly, as they had on the American left flank at Long Island, or at Kips Bay in Manhattan, they were in for a rude shock. Captain von Münchhausen, who had a ringside view of the action, wrote, "When we got close to the rebels, they fired their cannons; they did not fire their small arms till we were within 40 paces of them, at which time they fired whole volleys and sustained a very heavy fire." The British Grenadiers, however, were undeterred. Accompanied by their band playing "British Grenadier," von Münchhausen watched as they "advanced fearlessly and very quickly; fired a volley, and then ran furiously at the rebels with fixed bayonets." The division Sullivan had brought to support Lord Stirling and General Stephen had not been deployed properly by him when he assumed overall command upon arrival, with a gap between his division and the units in place. The Grenadiers' charge drove the division off the field. But Sullivan claimed that five times the British drove the Americans from the hill and five times the Americans regained their positions. His account is not supported by other sources, but that is the nature of battles and eyewitnesses to them, with their different vantage points, prejudices, and agendas. In both military and civilian circles Sullivan was widely blamed for what happened before and during the battle, and his reaction, quite naturally, was defensive. Some of the best evidence on battles can be praise given to one's foe, and at Brandywine von Münchhausen paid tribute to the American right wing. "By six o'clock our left wing still had not been able to advance. Here the Rebels fought very bravely and did not retreat until they heard in their rear General von Knyphausen's fire coming nearer." And along the entire line Captain Ewald described "a steady, stubborn fight from hill to hill and from wall to wall." Throughout the battle Sir William was true to the code of the British officer class, as described by Captain von Münchhausen: "As usual, the General exposed himself fearlessly on this occasion. He quickly rushed to each spot where he heard the strongest fire. Cannon balls and bullets passed close to him in numbers today."

"Push along, old man"

Washington in the meantime was at Chadds Ford, watching Knyphausen in front of him while listening to the increasing noise of battle behind him. Deciding to reinforce Sullivan, he ordered General Greene to immediately march his division to the fighting in the rear. Greene had under him two Virginia Brigades commanded by Brigadier General George Weedon (c. 1734–1793) and Brigadier General John Peter Gabriel Muhlenberg (1746–1807), a Lutheran preacher turned soldier. Weedon's Brigade in the lead, accompanied by Greene, literally raced to the battlefield. Washington also was on his way, having turned over command at Chadds Ford to Brigadier General Anthony Wayne (1745–1796) of Pennsylvania. A secondhand account written sixty-eight years later stated that Washington dragooned an elderly local farmer, Joseph Brown, to guide him and his staff to the battlefield by the "shortest and speediest route." At a gallop Washington and his aides rode cross-country, leaping fences as he had done in his fox hunting days. Joseph Brown told the man who repeated the story that "The head of Washington's horse . . . was constantly at the flank of the one on which he was mounted, and the General was continually repeating to him, *Push along, old man—Push along, old man.*"

When Washington arrived, the rout was on. Although Washington tried mightily, he could not stop it. British and Hessian bayonets had finally proved too much. The outnumbered Rebels were fleeing in disarray. But Weedon's Virginians were undismayed, and under their brigadier general and Greene they stood like rocks against the onrushing enemy. Almost a year later a somewhat bitter Nathanael Greene described to a friend what happened at the end of the day, when Weedon's Brigade formed, opened its ranks to allow fleeing survivors through, then closed them against the foe:

> I marched one brigade of my division . . . between three and four miles in forty-five minutes. When I came upon the ground I found the whole of the troops routed and retreating precipitately, and in the most broken and confused manner. I was ordered to cover the retreat, which I effected in such a manner as to save hundreds of our people from falling into the enemy's hands. Almost all of the park of artillery had an opportunity to get off, which must have fallen into their hands; and the left wing posted at Chadsford, got off by the seasonable check I gave [the] enemy. We were engaged an hour and a quarter and lost upwards of an hundred men killed and wounded. I maintained the ground until dark, and then drew off the troops in good order. We had the whole British force to contend with, that had just before routed our whole right wing. This brigade was commanded by General Weedon, and, unfortunately for their own interests, happened to be all Virginians. They being the general's countrymen, and I thought to be one of his favorites, prevented his ever mentioning a single circumstance of the affair.

In his diary entry of that day our old friend Lieutenant McMichael confirmed Greene's version of events:

> We took the front and attacked the enemy at 5:30 p.m., and being engaged with their grand army, we at first were obliged to retreat a few yards and form in an open field, when we fought without givng way on either side until dark. Our ammunition almost expended, firing ceased on both sides, when we received orders to march to Chester. We marched all night until we neared the town, where we halted, but not to sleep. This day for a severe and successive engagement exceeded all I ever saw. Our regiment fought at one stand about an hour under incessant fire, and yet the loss was less than at Long Island; neither were we so near to each other as at Princeton, our common distance being about 50 yards.

As Greene implied, Knyphausen also had attacked and sent his regiments across Chadds Ford, and after some close fighting had driven off

Wayne, who retreated toward Chester, Pennsylvania. Knyphausen and Sir William joined up at Dilworth village, near where Weedon's Brigade had made its gallant stand. The Rebels were now in full retreat, but pursuit was out of the question. The British flanking column had marched seventeen miles and had fought hard in hilly, broken country for up to three hours. "Night and the fatigue the Soldiers had undergone prevented any pursuit," Captain André wrote, and von Münchhausen agreed in that assessment. The Hessian also wrote, "If daylight had lasted a few hours longer, I dare say that this day would have brought an end to the war." That, however, is a big leap, although the American army's adjutant general, Colonel Timothy Pickering (1745–1829), agreed in his journal entry on Brandywine that "It was fortunate for us that the night came on, for under its cover the fatigued stragglers and some wounded made their escape."

It had been a bloodbath. A modern estimate of losses put Rebel casualties at 200 killed, 500 wounded, and 400 captured. The official British casualty return listed 89 killed, 488 wounded, and 6 missing. For the wounded of both sides, especially those needing amputation, all the horrors of surgery in a preanesthetic age awaited. The surgeons now came into their own, and young Joseph Townsend, who helped carry wounded into a house being used as a hospital, noted that "divers of them were busily employed."[26]

Washington's official report to John Hancock was written at midnight, and he put as good a face as possible on defeat. He regretted "that in this day's engagement we have been obliged to leave the enemy masters of the field." But his final assessment was not really off the mark. "Notwithstanding the misfortune of the day, I am happy to find the troops in good spirits; and I hope another time we shall compensate for the losses now sustained." If we can accept the *Recollections* of Captain Enoch Anderson of Maryland as an accurate assessment of the mood of the troops once the shooting stopped, then Washington's words are not those of a beaten general ascribing false emotions to his soldiers.

Anderson was franker than his general. "Here then we experienced another drubbing," he wrote many years later to his nephew, Alexander Anderson, but then added,

> Through all these trying times, I saw not a despairing look nor did I
> hear a despairing word. We had our solacing words always ready for
> each other. "Come boys, we shall do better another time," sounded

throughout our little army. Had any man suggested, merely hinted the idea of giving up, of relinquishing further opposition, he would have been knocked down, and if killed it would have been considered as no murder! Such was the spirit of the times—such were the ideas of us "poor ragamuffins" (as the British called us)—such were my views, your father's, and thousands of others.

13

"Perplexing Maneuvres"

"Driping wet and shivering with cold"

Young Joseph Townsend and his fellow Quakers witnessed the aftermath of battle. Joseph persuaded some friends to go down to the "field of battle and take a view of the dead and wounded, as we might never have such an opportunity. . . . We hastened thither and awful was the scene to behold—such a number of fellow beings lying together severely wounded, and some mortally—a few dead, but a small proportion of them considering the immense quantity of powder and ball that had been discharged. It was now time for the surgeons to exert themselves."

The ground occupied by the British army also was ravaged, and Joseph explored it after Sir William and his troops marched on. Joseph said it was "left in a desolate condition, exhibited a sense of destruction and waste." Those who lived there "had their stock of cattle destroyed for the use of the army. Their houses taken away, and their household furniture, bedding, etc, wantonly wasted and burned. It was not uncommon to see heaps of feathers laying about the farms, the ticks having been stripped off and made use of and the remains of small pieces of valuable furniture which lay about their fireplaces in the fields unconsumed, when there was no want of timber, and fence rails that might have been used for their cooking, etc.; but being in an enemy's country, inhabited by rebels, there was no restraint on the soldiery and rabble who accompanied them."[1]

The day following the battle Washington issued orders for the army to "march on in good order" to a camp near Germantown, about six miles northwest of Philadelphia; for each brigade commander to send out officers to collect stragglers "and bring them on"; for "A gill of rum or whiskey . . . to be served out to each man who has not already received that allowance"; and for officers "without loss of time to see that their men are completed with ammunition—that their arms are in the best order, the inside of them washed clean and well dried—the touchholes picked and a good flint in each gun." With regard to the latter, he expected that the "strictest attention . . . will be paid to this order as the officers must be sensible their own honor, the safety of the soldier, and success of the cause depends absolutely upon a careful execution of it." Washington and the army may have been beaten once again, but for Washington it was business as usual, for he was poised to get between Sir William and Philadelphia. Washington meant to continue to defend the Rebel capital, and he looked forward to renewed battle.[2]

His determination to defend the city was made clear in letters of 13 September to Thomas Wharton Jr. (1735–1778), president of Pennsylvania's supreme executive council, and to John Hancock. Wharton had written to Washington the previous day expressing the council's concern with the "unguarded Condition" of the forts on the Delaware River below Philadelphia, since the council had not the "means to reinforce them." Washington replied that he could not afford to release troops to complete the forts, for unless "General Howe can be checked upon land the obstructions in the River will be of little avail." He wrote Hancock in the same vein, even after receiving from him a congressional resolution directing Washington to complete the defensive works on the river and to use "such Officers, engineers and troops as he shall think proper." At the same time he wrote Wharton that "As I am well apprized of the importance of Philadelphia you may rest assured that I shall take every measure in my power to defend it, and I hope you will agree with me that the only effectual Method will be to oppose General Howe with our whole united Force."[3]

To assist in the campaign Washington urged General Smallwood to use his militia forces to fall "on the Enemy's Rear . . . attacking and harrassing them, as Often as possible." On both sides throughout the war there was the feeling, or at least the hope, that by one brilliant stroke the war could be brought to a speedy conclusion, and Washington was no exception. "No Exertion can be too great at this Time," he wrote to

Smallwood, "and a spirited Effort by the people would in all probability put a happy & speedy end to the present contest."[4]

In another general order issued on the 13th, he congratulated the officers and soldiers who had "bravely fought in their country and its cause," chided those "whose conduct reflects dishonour upon soldiership" and left "them to reflect, how much they have injured their country," and assured the troops that he had "full confidence that in another Appeal to Heaven (with the blessing of providence, which it becomes every officer and soldier humbly to supplicate) we shall prove successful." Of far more interest to the army, however, was his announcement that Congress, "in consideration of the gallant behaviour of the troops," had been "pleased to order thirty hogsheads of rum to be distributed among them," and Washington ordered it passed out "to each officer and soldier, one gill per day, while it lasts."[5]

Congress at this critical time should have limited itself to passing out rum to the troops, but its penchant for meddling got the better of it over General Sullivan's performance at Brandywine, and on the 14th it passed a resolution that Sullivan be "recalled from the army until the enquiry theretofore ordered into his conduct shall be duly made." That this irritated Washington is probably an understatement. He wrote to Hancock the following day requesting that he be allowed to defer action, since "Our situation at this time is critical and delicate, and nothing should be done to add to its embarrassments. We are now probably on the point of Another Action, and to derange the Army by withdrawing so many Genl Officers from it, may & must be attended with many disagreeable, if not ruinous, consequences." Congress acceded to his request, but his time could have been used to better purpose.[6]

As for Sir William's activities, he cannot be faulted for not pursuing the beaten Americans on the day of the battle. His flanking force was exhausted from the long march and the hard fighting that followed, and pursuit at night, as with any night operation, is a highly risky business for any military force in any age. But why did he not set out with the entire army early the next morning? Why did he wait another four days before breaking camp and marching? As is clear from von Münchhausen's defense of his general, some of his officers were as puzzled as we, and quite critical. "Some stupid people are dwelling on the fact that our general does not quickly follow Washington with his whole force. Of course this would be a good thing if it were possible," but von Münchhausen claimed that the wagons normally used for the army's provisions and baggage were needed to send away the sick and wounded, and "It is not possible to procure enough wagons here to do both at the same time." Despite his faithful Hessian aide's defense, a precise answer to Howe's delay eludes us, and we must fall back on the quite valid observation that Sir William was rarely a general to be quick off the mark.[7]

There followed in the ensuing weeks a series of maneuvers in which Washington tried to prevent Sir William from marching on Philadelphia and Sir William attempted first to bring Washington once again to battle and then to outwit him. But we will only concern ourselves with the main events.

Finally, on 16 September, Sir William aroused himself and moved out, looking for Washington, who at the same time was looking for Sir William. For Washington had left Germantown "with a determination to meet the Enemy and give them Battle whenever a convenient opportunity should be found." Rain fell intermittently as the two armies approached each other. The British were in two columns, one commanded by Lord Cornwallis, the other by General von Knyphausen. A battalion of Light Infantry in advance of Howe's column met a Rebel advance unit about 300 strong. The British advanced "very briskly," whereupon the Rebels "gave us one fire and run away," wrote Lieutenant Henry Stirke of the Light Infantry. Or as an American officer put it, "Shamefully fled at the first fire." The action turned out differently at the head of von Knyphausen's column and caused some levity among the Jägers. The Hessian colonel von Donop led foot and mounted Jägers on a reconnaissance mission and impetuously pursued an American advance party too far, which allowed another Rebel unit to get between him and the main army. Under what Captain Ewald described as "sustained rifle fire," the colonel "got off with his skin," but Ewald, who had not been along, criticized von Donop's inexperience in partisan operations. "That is not a trade for one to follow who has no knowledge of it. We all laughed secretly over this partisan trick."[8]

Just as the armies were about to get down to the serious business of a major engagement, a northeaster that had been brewing struck, accompanied by what Captain Ewald called an "extraordinary thunderstorm." Nevertheless, he reported that he was ordered to attack a Rebel force situated in a "thick wood." Ewald advanced "several hundred paces" across an open field through "heavy rain," which greatly diminished Rebel fire as weapons and powder began to get wet. Jäger rifles also misfired because of the rain, and Ewald ordered his men to draw their short hunting swords. "I reached the wood at top speed and came to close quarters with the enemy, who during the furious attack forgot that he had bayonets and quit the field." So ended what has been mis-named the Battle of the Clouds, which was not a battle at all but a series of skirmishes by advance units of both armies. Further fighting was prevented by the storm, and almost all sources agree on its violence. "I wish I could give you a description of the downpour which began dur-ing the engagement and continued until the next morning," Major Baur-meister wrote. "It came down so hard that in a few moments we were drenched and sank in mud up to our calves." The "rain poured down vehemently," Colonel Timothy Pickering wrote in his journal, and "fell in torrents for eighteen hours," Lieutenant McMichael confided to his diary. Sir William reported to Lord Germain that an attack was "imprac-ticable" because of "a most violent fall of rain . . . continuing the whole day and night without intermission." By midafternoon the Schuylkill River behind Washington was rising fast, and by 6:00 P.M. Colonel Joseph Reed reported that it had "swelled so much that it is now impassable & from the best Accounts and Opinions it will be 24 Hours before it will be fordable for Footmen." Washington also found it impossible to con-tinue, for the army's ammunition was ruined, and the Continentals were not yet bayonet fighters. Major Samuel Shaw of Massachusetts wrote to his father that Washington chose "to avoid an action in which the dis-cipline of the enemy in the use of their bayonets (the only weapon that could then be of any service, and which we were by no means generally supplied with) would give them too great a superiority." So began another slow, slogging retreat. A thirteen-year-old artilleryman, Jacob Nagle, recalled that "small runs of water were overflowed by the rain, that the foot soldiers could scarcely get a cross without swimming in several dif-ferent places." Young Jacob, on horseback behind an ammunition wagon, was "driping wet and shivering with cold."[9]

Washington had no choice but to retreat, for "Upon examining the State of our ammunition I find it so generally hurt by the Rain that we are not in a Condition to make a stand." He need not have worried, for true to form Sir William let three days elapse before making a serious move. Washington could not know this, of course, and decided to put the Schuylkill River between him and the British. There began on the 19th and ended on the 20th, over roads that had become quagmires, a grueling thirty-six-mile march during which, Lieutenant McMichael wrote, "we had to strip to wade" the Schuylkill, which was running "deep and rapid," wrote Washington. An onlooker, the well-known Lutheran preacher Henry Melchior Muhlenberg (1711–1787), witnessed their passage:

> The passage of the troops lasted through the night, and we had all kinds of visitors, officers, etc. To get wet up to one's chest and then to march in the cold, foggy night while enduring hunger thirst, etc. is hard for the poor men. It takes courage, health, etc. But instead of prayers, what one hears from many of them is the horrible national vice: cursing. [10]

The situation throughout the area was enough to make civilians curse, too, which also would have horrified Pastor Muhlenberg. In another passage in his journals he claimed that it made no sense to flee to seek safety elsewhere, "for no place is safe. Where the two armies do not go, one finds thieves, robbers, and murderers who are taking advantage of the present times and conditions." There were also camp followers to contend with, "the marauders," he called them, "who are following the American army are still stopping in to complain of hunger and thirst, etc."[11]

"I believe he knows Nothing of my Situation"

This move put Washington with the main force on the left bank of the Schuylkill, temporarily safe from attack and in a position to contest an attempt by Sir William to cross the river. To further embarrass Howe, Washington had ordered Brigadier General Anthony Wayne to keep his troops on the right bank of the river, follow the British army, and harass their rear. He sent similar orders to General Maxwell, who was expected to assist Wayne with his light infantry. But Washington warned Wayne to "take care of Ambuscades." And Lieutenant Colonel John Fitzgerald, an aide-de-camp to Washington, sent an undated letter to Wayne that accompanied Washington's first letter and read in part, "He is fully satisfied you will do everything in your power to Harrass & Distress them on their March, without suffering yourself to be reduc'd to any disagreeable situation."[12]

It had been a neat bit of maneuvering by Washington that on the face of it left Sir William boxed in. But General Wayne was in an offensive mood, as suited his temperament, and wrote on the early morning of the 19th to Washington that Howe was lying supinely, and "There never was—nor never will be a fairer Opportunity of giving the Enemy a fatal Blow than the present, for God sake push on as fast as possible." Thus once again we observe that will-o'-the-wisp of the Revolution: settling the issue once and for all with a brilliant stroke. A few hours later he wrote Washington again, reporting that he momentarily expected General Maxwell on the British left, "and as I lay on their Right, we only want you in their Rear—to Complete Mr. Howes business." Wayne's confidence extended to the security of his position:

> I believe he knows Nothing of my Situation—as I have taken every precaution to prevent any Intelligence getting to him—at the same time keeping a Watchful Eye on his Front Flanks & Rear.[13]

Wayne, however, was self-deceived. British intelligence was excellent, as revealed in Captain von Münchhausen's diary. On the night of 19 September Sir William received a report "that General Wayne had been detached by General Washington with 800 men [Wayne actually had about 1,500] to make the region behind us insecure." In his diary entry of the 20th, von Münchhausen spelled out Sir William's detailed knowledge of Washington's plans and the location of Rebel forces:

> Washington, having achieved his aim by his forced marches . . . has now gained our left flank. He has controlled access to supplies as well as a route of retreat to the lower provinces. He himself is positioned behind the Schuylkill with a strong force in the region. . . .
> It is said that he intends to prevent our crossing of the Schuylkill, which is wider and deeper than the Brandywine. In order to achieve this more effectively, he has detached 4,000 men to this side of the Schuylkill, 2,000 of whom are on our left flank and 2,000 are close behind us, under the command of General Wayne. Both Corps have orders to attack us if we march again, and particularly if we try to cross the Schuylkill River.[14]

Washington has often been praised, and rightly, for his efficient intelligence service, but in this instance praise is due the British. They often exhibited an abysmal knowledge of the conditions and mood of the country, but in this instance their military intelligence was amazingly precise. And knowing what Washington was up to, Sir William decided to do something about it. On 20 September he ordered Major

Brigadier General Anthony Wayne
by John Trumbull

General Charles Grey (1729–1807), who had entered the army as an ensign when he was fourteen years old, to conduct a surprise night attack on Wayne's command. Grey took with him 2nd Battalion Light Infantry, Black Watch, and 44th Foot. In support was Lieutenant Colonel Thomas Musgrave, with two regiments of foot. His assignment was to act as a blocking force. Grey's entire command numbered about 2,000 men, with the assault force totaling about 1,500. Grey marched at 10:00 P.M., Musgrave an hour later. General Grey gave a specific order to the troops of both columns, as described by Captain John André, who was with Grey's column: "No soldier was suffered to load; those who could not draw [unload] their pieces took out the flints." Silence was the objective, the mission to be accomplished with the bayonet.[15]

Wayne's command was camped at the present site of Paoli, Pennsylvania, which took its name from the nearby eighteenth-century General

Paoli Tavern, named after the Corsican patriot General Pasquale Paoli. Anthony Wayne (1745–1796) was the son of affluent local farmers who had become a surveyor as well as a farmer himself. He had been an ardent patriot during the events leading to armed revolt and a member of the provincial assembly. Although he had no military education or experience, in 1776 he was commissioned a colonel in the Continental Army. Aggressive, an iron-handed disciplinarian, he distinguished himself in the Canadian campaign. In February 1777 he was promoted to brigadier general. He did not acquire his famous nickname "Mad Anthony" until 1781, when a soldier who considered him insane applied it to him; but his troops honored him by adopting it because of his impetuous nature.

"Altogether the most dreadful scene I ever beheld"

Ample warning had come to Wayne of an impending action by the British against him, and in fact one informant said "they would attack Genl Wayne's Party that Night." Given the warnings, why did Wayne stay where he was? It is true that he was expecting General Smallwood to join him shortly with a large force of Maryland militia and feared that if he moved Smallwood might not find him; and Wayne later testified that "I had the fullest and Clearest Advice that the Enemy would March that Morning at 2 OClock for the River Schuylkill." That advice may have been full and clear but it was wrong. There also was a lack of communication between Wayne and his subordinate officers. But there appeared to be enough pickets—six positions each, consisting of one junior officer and eighteen enlisted men—stationed on the approaches between half a mile and a mile from camp.[16]

General Grey's column did not achieve complete surprise. Two alert videttes (mounted pickets or sentries) fired on the British advance, then galloped off. One of them rode straight to Wayne's headquarters. Upon receiving his report, General Wayne immediately ordered his division to arms, which was accomplished in under five minutes, whereupon Wayne gave the order to evacuate the camp. But the regiments were held up by artillery and twenty-five or more ammunition and supply wagons that went first.[17]

Meanwhile, the British marched on in grim silence. Pickets close to the camp were alert and fired on the foe at very short range, but the English riflemen and Light Infantry were not to be denied and made short work of the Rebels with short swords and bayonets. General Grey himself rode up and shouted, "Dash, Light Infantry," and silently those elite troops ran through the woods. A Light Infantry officer, Lieutenant Richard St. George, wrote that they "received a smart fire from another unfortunate Picquet—as the first instantly massacred." Captain John André described the scene as the British came within sight of Wayne's camp. "On approaching the right of the Camp we perceived the line of fires, and the Light Infantry being ordered to form to the front, rushed along the line putting to the bayonet all they came up with, and overtaking the main herd of fugitives, stabbed great numbers." By the "main herd" André was referring to the regiments in column waiting for the way before them to be unclogged. The Light Infantry hit them in the rear and flank. One of the British officers was Lieutenant Martin Hunter, who in a long military career became a general and served under Lord Cornwallis in India. Yet near the end of his life Hunter wrote that the bayoneting, "with the cries of the wounded formed altogether the most dreadful scene I ever beheld. Every man that fired was immediately put to death."

Suddenly a second wave burst out of the woods. The 16th (Queen's Own) Light Dragoons swept into the camp, their nearly three-foot sabers raised high, and began slashing and cutting, causing, Lieutenant St. George wrote, "a dreadful scene of Havock . . . the Shrieks, Groans, Shouting, imprecations, deprecations The Clashing of Swords and bayonets . . . was more expressive of Horror than all the thunder of the artillery etc. on the Day of action." If that were not enough, on the heels of the dragoon horses, 44th Foot, 500 strong, bayonets fixed, poured out of the woods. Pandemonium ensued as they came upon the already mauled rear and flank of Wayne's stalled column. The noise was tremendous, and this intimidated many Rebel soldiers.

In the camp proper, confusion reigned. Attackers were chasing fugitives, bayoneting them. Some Rebels hid in the woods, others in a nearby swamp, where one officer, thinking he was alone, in the morning found fifty-five other fugitives around him, proving how quiet men can be when in mortal fear for the lives. Some no doubt ran over hill and dale until they could run no more.

There now occurred what might be called the pièce de résistance of that terrible night. Still poised in the woods, in two ranks 600 Highlanders of Black Watch were given the order Charge Bayonet! On they came, joining Light Infantry and 44th Foot in the killing and burning.

The huts of the Rebel soldiers burned brightly. Flames leaped high, and ghastly shadows danced across the campground. One source claimed that those still alive inside the huts chose death by fire rather than suffer cold steel.

General Wayne and others—officers and sergeants and probably lowly privates with initiative—finally managed to get the column moving. A rear guard was formed, and most of Wayne's command escaped with their lives. In the meantime, General Smallwood was approaching with his Maryland militia. Yet out there in the dark elite British Light Infantry, victorious, their blood up, were wandering, searching for fresh prey. They were responsible for the first shots fired by the British, and the big lead balls were directed at the Maryland militia. The effect was described with amusing understatement by a Rebel militia officer, Colonel Mordecai Gist: "You will readily conclude that Militia unused to an Attack especially in the Night, must be thrown into some confusion." How much confusion? Their commander, General Smallwood, was brutally candid: "many flung down their Guns & run off, & have not been heard of since, whilst the Artillery men & Waggoners cutting their horses loose and running off with them." Unable to rally those who did not run to present a proper front to resist attack, Smallwood ordered a retreat of about five miles and admitted that "this was the only well executed Order of the Night."

The action that night of 20 September 1777 is called the Paoli Massacre. We should observe, however, that the escape of most of Wayne's command means that it was not a massacre. Nor was it a full-scale battle. Action at Paoli would be a better description. American casualty figures are difficult to ascertain, for if an official return was made it has never surfaced, and the numbers we have from the American side did not come from participants. The standard source for casualties during the Revolutionary War lists 200 American dead and 200 wounded, but the author of this careful study notes that these are estimates and not official returns. They are also far closer to British than American estimates; and all participants, British and American, throughout the war consistently exaggerated the enemy's losses. The closest student of the battle finds the most reliable figure to be fifty-three Americans, all killed by cold steel, buried on the battlefield, but he admits it is uncertain whether others died and were buried elsewhere. Hundreds must have been wounded. Captain André reported "Near 200 must have been killed" and seventy-one prisoners taken, "forty of them badly wounded were left at different houses on the road." He claimed one British officer and one or two enlisted men killed, and four or five wounded. To attempt to go beyond this would be a futile discussion.[18]

General Charles Grey has come down in history as "No Flint" Grey, and he continued to have a good war, leading successful raids in New England in 1778 as well as pulling off another surprise bayonet attack in the same year, this time in New Jersey against Colonel George Baylor's 3rd Continental Light Dragoons, during which Baylor was seriously wounded and many American cavalrymen killed. Grey went home to England in 1778 and never returned to America. He was promoted to lieutenant general and knighted in 1782, became a peer of the realm in 1801, and in 1806 was created the first Earl Grey. Did he, however, fail to restrain his men? In 1783 a British historian delivered this verdict:

> General Grey conducted this enterprize with equal ability and success though perhaps not without that humanity which is so conspicuous in his character. . . . A severe and horrible execution ensued. . . . The British troops as well as the officer that commanded them gained but little honour by this midnight slaughter. It shewed rather desperate cruelty than real valour.[19]

Perhaps. According to American participants, British soldiers were heard to call out "No quarter," but no evidence has been found that General Grey or other officers gave such an order, and the prisoners taken argue against it. But we can argue that the mere order to either unload weapons or remove flints and rely solely on swords and bayonets invited unnecessary killing, because when soldiers come to close quarters the instinct for survival magnifies and creates an uncontrollable frenzy to kill before you are killed. Yet the British army was in a delicate situation, with enemies in front and behind. Grey's mission was critical to remove the danger behind, secrecy and silence were absolutely necessary, and the possibility that careless soldiers could compromise the mission was real. The argument could go on and on. "War is hell," Sherman said. It always will be.

"Oh, Heaven! Grant Us one great Soul!"

Criticism of Wayne was rife in the army and Congress, which led to the general demanding a court-martial, which was convened in mid-October and which, of course, duly acquitted him. But in the opinion of many he remained guilty of negligence. One of the most interesting comments came from an important congressman, Henry Laurens of South Carolina, who wrote on 6 October that Sullivan's "blunder" at Brandywine and Wayne's "unpardonable negligence" at Paoli "have reduced the American States to the present dilemma." Taking him at his word, Laurens actually believed that except for their mistakes "we [would not] have heard any more of General Howe but his hurrying fragments of Regiments & Men on board his fleet." What utter nonsense: chasing the chimera of instant victory. Such are the tricks that self-delusion plays on otherwise intelligent minds.[20]

With regard to Wayne, no matter what the true figures of his casualties, his command was in shock and temporarily unfit for action. Sir William's rear was therefore secure, whereupon he began moving northwest along the west bank of the Schuylkill in the direction of Reading, fifty miles upriver from Philadelphia. At a Council of War held on 23 September, Washington explained why he had marched in the same direction on the opposite side of the river. As the British army "appeared to be in motion, and from our own observation and the accounts of our reconnoitering parties were marching rapidly up the Reading Road this induced us to move up likewise to hinder them from crossing above us and by getting between us and Reading take the opportunity of destroying a large collection of military Stores deposited there." Late on the night of 21 September the American army "encamped near Pottsgrove [Pottstown]" on the road to Reading. The next day Washington wrote to Brigadier General Alexander McDougall, who was on the march with his command from Peekskill, New York, to "proceed on the most direct Rout leading to Pots' Grove." Washington was now above Sir William's advance units, his right flank for the time being out of danger, the American army ready to contest a British advance on Reading. Which was all well and good, except Sir William had something entirely different in mind.[21]

Late on the evening of 22 September the British army began crossing the Schuylkill at Flatland Ford, about twelve miles below Washington's position. It took several hours, as the river was wide at that point, the ford three feet deep. Captain von Münchhausen wrote that the "men had to walk about 300 paces in the water owing to a bend in the ford." As each regiment reached the opposite bank "they formed into line some 100 paces from the water, and lighted big fires to dry their clothes." Major Robertson reported that the crossing was completed by

6:00 A.M. on the 23rd, but von Münchhausen said the last unit did not
cross "till four in the afternoon." This detail is unimportant. Of signifi-
cance were the positions of the two armies. Sir William had outwitted
Washington and placed himself between the Rebel Army and Philadelphia, to which Sir William headed that very day. In his Council of War,
held after he discovered that the British had crossed the Schuylkill,
Washington put the obvious question to his senior officers: should the
army march and engage the enemy before he could reach Philadelphia?
No, was the unanimous opinion. Given the "present state of the Army
it would not be adviseable to advance upon the Enemy, but remain upon
this Ground or in the Neighbourhood till the detachments [Wayne and
Maxwell] and the expected Reinforcements come up." Washington's
explanation of the situation to Hancock as much as admitted that he
had been outmaneuvered by the Englishman:

> The Enemy, by a variety of perplexing Maneuvres thro' a Country
> from which I could not derive the least intelligence being to a man
> disaffected, contrived to pass the Schuylkill last Night at the Flat land
> and other fords in the Neighbourhood of it. They marched immedi-
> ately towards Philada and I imagine their advanced parties will be
> near that City to Night.[22]

Washington thought it impossible to come up with Sir William's
"Rear with troops as harrassed as ours had been with constant marching
since the Battle of Brandywine." He would march in the morning toward
Philadelphia, not in hopes of catching Howe, but "to form a junction
with the Continental Troops under Genl McDougal from Peekskill and
the Jersey Militia under General Dickenson. . . . I am also obliged to
wait for Genl Wayne and Genl Smallwood who were left on the other
Side of Schuylkill in hopes of falling upon the Enemy's Rear, but they
have eluded them as well as us." He admitted to Hancock that he had
thought the British goal was to gain the Rebel Army's right flank and
from there "detach parties to Reading." Instead, Sir William had gained
Washington's left flank and now had the Rebel capital within his grasp.
In this letter Washington revealed the wretched condition of the troops:

> [T]he strongest Reason against being able to make a forced march is
> the want of Shoes. Messrs Carroll, Chase and Penn [members of Con-
> gress] who were some days with the Army can inform Congress in how

deplorable a Situation the Troops are for want of that necessary Article, at least one thousand Men are bare footed and have performed the marches in that condition.

"God Save Great George Our King" the fifers played on the bright morning of 26 September as 3,000 British and Hessians under Lord Cornwallis marched into Philadelphia. Drums rolled, regimental bands played, burnished arms gleamed in the sunlight. These men looked like real soldiers. Sixteen-year-old Robert Morton, a quaker of Tory sympathies, announced in his diary that their entrance into the city was "to the great relief of the inhabitants who have too long suffered the yoke of arbitrary Power; and who testified their approbation of the arrival of the troops by the loudest acclamations of joy."[23]

The conqueror, Sir William Howe, entered the city two days later. He had achieved his goal. He had both defeated and outmaneuvered Washington, and the archtraitors who made up the Continental Congress had fled westward, to Lancaster, Pennsylvania. But now that he had the Rebel capital in his power, what was he going to do with it? He had captured New York City, but that victory had not ended the Revolution. He had taken control of New Jersey and then lost it. Now he had Philadelphia, but the American army, footsore, weary, and ragged, still lurked in the neighborhood, beaten but unbowed and ready again to contest for the Cause. So the question remains: what was he going to do with his victory? We must admit that John Adams would have rejected our argument. Even before Sir William had crossed the Schuylkill and taken Philadelphia, Adams had worked himself into a state of near hysteria and expressed his feelings about Washington in one of his wonderful hyperbolic tirades:

Oh, Heaven! Grant Us one great Soul! One leading Mind would extricate the best Cause, from that Ruin which seems to await it. . . . One active masterly Capacity would bring order out of this Confusion and save this Country.[24]

14

"Our army is in higher spirits than ever"

"I wish soon to receive the most pleasing
Accounts from you"

The familiar phrase "fog of war" is apt for the events that took place on the morning of 4 October about six miles northwest of Philadelphia, in Germantown, where Sir William Howe's advance was posted. Fog ruled the early hours from the end of September through early October and generally did not dissipate until midmorning. Through these mists an attacking force could come to within thirty to a hundred yards of an enemy before being discovered. Fog also made all but certain that eventually confusion would reign among both attackers and defenders. For Washington, however, the situation presented an opportunity to once more pull off a brilliant stroke. Twice he had surprised the enemy at Trenton, first the Hessians, then Lord Cornwallis himself. Now it would be Sir William's turn to experience the cunning of the fox. How did this come about?

Washington's reaction to Sir William's crossing of the Schuylkill was a combination of defense and offense. Upon receiving news that the British had crossed the Schuylkill, he immediately, if belatedly, turned his attention to the American defenses on the Delaware River below Philadelphia, especially Fort Mifflin on Mud Island (also called Fort Island), whose guns commanded the river's upper approaches to the city, and Fort Mercer, on the New Jersey side of the river. "It is of the utmost importance," he wrote, "to prevent the Enemy's Land Forces and Fleet from forming a junction . . . by seizing on Fort Island . . . and thereby gain the Navigation of the Delaware by weighing and removing the Chivaux Defrize [Chevaux-de-Frise], which have been sunk for that purpose." Washington was referring to underwater devices designed by Robert Smith, a Philadelphia architect and carpenter, to prevent ships from sailing up the river. A modern authority on the Chevaux-de-Frise in the Delaware described them as cribs usually thirty feet wide made of "twenty-five or thirty logs varying in length from forty to sixty-five feet, twelve to twenty-six inches thick." The cribs were anchored to the river bottom with twenty to forty tons of stone, depending on their size. Smith made a machine to lower the stones into the cribs. Extending obliquely downstream from each crib were two or three huge iron-tipped spears whose points "had to be no more than six feet below the surface of the river at low tide. At this depth they would rip open the bottom of any eighteenth century wooden ship that accidentally sailed upon them." Only ten of the most skillful and trusted river pilots knew the locations of the cribs. Chevaux-de-Frise—literally Horse of Friesland, a province of northern Holland—were first used there in streams as defense against cavalry.[1]

Washington appointed a veteran of the Prussian army, Colonel Heinrich, Baron d'Arendt, to command on Mud Island, but the good baron was prone to accidents. Earlier he had fallen off his horse during a skirmish, and at Fort Mifflin he fell off a parapet. Because of his injuries he served as commander for only a few days in late October, and the command for most of the period devolved upon his second, Lieutenant Colonel Samuel Smith (1752–1839) of Maryland, whom Washington ordered to Fort Mifflin with about 200 Continentals. Smith's men were not, in his words, "properly chosen for such an expedition," for "Few of them have Shoes or Stockings, many of them without Coats or Blankets & scarce any who have more than one shirt," and thirty-six of his men could march no farther. Nevertheless, on the 27th, four days after receiving his orders, Smith and most of his command were in Fort Mifflin. At the same time Washington, in a letter in which he explained his plan for offensive and defensive warfare, urged Commodore John Hazelwood (c.1726–1800), who commanded the Pennsylvania navy, to cooperate with Continental forces to defend the river:

> If we can stop the Enemy's fleet from coming up & prevent them from getting Possession of the Mud fort, & they take Possession of the City & our Army moves down upon the back of it, it will be the most effectual method of ruining General Howe's Army that ever Fortune Favor'd us with.[2]

He asked of Hazelwood, "Let us Join our Force & Operations both by Land & Water in such a manner as will most effectually work the Ruin of the common Enemy, without confining ourselves to any particular department." Pennsylvania had neglected the river's defenses, and Washington's attention to them was overdue, but with proper cooperation between the Continental Army and the state forces of Pennsylvania and New Jersey, perhaps it was not too late. As it turned out, the garrisons of both forts experienced ferocious fighting and put up valiant defenses until forced to evacuate Fort Mifflin on the night of 15–16 November and Fort Mercer on 21 November. Thereafter the river approaches to Philadelphia were clear for British shipping.

Washington also wrote to Major General Putnam, then commanding in the Hudson Highlands, expressing surprise that General McDougall had brought only 911 Continentals with him, and ordered Putnam, "without a Moments loss of time," to send more reinforcements to bring the total number from the highlands to 2,500 rank and file and noncommissioned officers. Putnam would have to make do with what he had to protect the highlands, and if threatened "you must get what aid you can from the militia." Haste was paramount. The detachment must march "without the least possible delay." This was one of the few times when Washington dispensed with his usual courteous language that at times made orders seem like requests. "That you may not hesitate about complying with this order, you are to consider it as peremptory and not to be dispensed with." This letter is more evidence of his belief that he could be on the verge of a stroke against the British that would turn the campaign around. He also wrote to General Gates, whose army had clashed with Burgoyne's a few days before in the first Battle of Saratoga, to send back to him if possible Colonel Daniel Morgan and his rifle regiment. Washington did not then know of the first action at Saratoga.[3]

As always, militia was needed, for rarely were there enough Continentals to meet the British in formal battle without militia auxiliaries in support. But the turnout in Pennsylvania and the surrounding states was poor. "The conduct of the militia is much to be regretted," Washington wrote. "In many instances, they are not to be roused, and in others they come into the field with all possible indifference, and, to all appearance, entirely unimpressed with the importance of the cause in which we are engaged. Hence proceeds a total inattention to order and to discipline, and too often a disgraceful departure from the army at the instant their aid is most wanted." His adjutant general, Colonel Timothy Pickering, had even harsher language for the militia, in the course of which he revealed his Yankee bias:

> No militia can be more contemptible than those of Pennsylvania and Delaware . . . none can be spoken of more contemptuously than they are by their own countrymen. And how astonishing is it, that not a man is roused to action when the enemy is in the heart of the country, and within twelve miles of their grand capitol, of so much importance to them, and the Continent! How amazing, that Howe should march from the Head of Elk to the Schuylkill, a space of sixty miles, without opposition from the people of the country, except a small band of militia just around Elk! Such events would not have happened in New England.[4]

From northern New York, however, on 27 September came good news. Although the information had not come through official channels and could not be regarded as "authentic as I could wish," it was reported that General Burgoyne had attacked General Gates's army, only to be repulsed. Actually, the intelligence of the first action at Saratoga (the Battle of Freeman's Farm) was accurate, but General Gates, instead of notifying his commander in chief, had sent official notice by an aide-de-camp to John Hancock, president of the Continental Congress, who on 30 September forwarded to Washington copies of letters from Gates and others. In his letter of transmittal Hancock also placed a monkey on Washington's back: "I wish soon to receive the most pleasing Accounts from you, we are in daily expectation of agreeable tidings, & that genl Howe is totally reduced."[5]

Yet in a Council of War held two days before, to discuss whether the army should "make a general & vigorous attack upon the Enemy" or await reinforcements, the senior commanders were unanimous against an "immediate Attack." Instead, they recommended that the army move to within twelve miles of Sir William's main force, then encamped at Germantown, "and there wait for a further Reinforcement, or be in readiness to take advantage of any favourable Opportunity that may offer for making an Attack."

But the situation changed quickly. On 1 October Washington wrote,

> a little time and perseverance will give us an opportunity of making amends for our late ill fortune, and putting our affairs in a more flourishing condition than at present. Our army has now had the rest and refreshment it stood in need of—and our men are in very good spirits.[6]

The next day the army left its camp near the Schuylkill to get closer to Howe's main force at Germantown, a move that affords us another opportunity to briefly observe the effects of war on a civilian population. After the army left, the Reverend Henry Melchior Muhlenberg wrote, "It looks as if a swarm of locusts had been here. Bad policing. If the fences or rails around the farmers' fields and meadows are burned and their limited woodlands are cut and ruined, food for men and cattle will be reduced and starvation must follow. Before this I bought ten acres of woodland near the church; they have now been laid waste, etc." Such has always been the way of armies, and it did no good that both Washington and Sir William railed against excesses. Besides, action was pending, and officers had more important things on their minds than punishing troops for laying waste to civilian property.[7]

"For shame, Light Infantry!"

The army marched to within about fifteen miles of the enemy's positions at Germantown. This was not the British advance, as some writers have suggested. It was the main force under Sir William Howe, although it had been weakened by the siphoning off of detachments for duty elsewhere. All of the British and Hessian Grenadiers and two squadrons of the Light Dragoons were with Cornwallis in Philadelphia, about five miles away, and two regiments of British foot had been detached to attack one of the Rebel forts on the Delaware. Since the British were blocked from getting supplies up the Delaware, other troops had been assigned to escort wagon trains from Head of Elk. Washington knew of the detachments from intercepted letters and communicated this intelligence to his senior commanders, who agreed that an attack on Sir William's troops at Germantown was warranted. Washington's numbers at the time were about 8,000 Continentals and 3,000 militia.[8]

On the morning of 3 October orders were issued that were to be carried out that day. The veteran junior officer Lieutenant McMichael described troop preparation:

Early this morning orders were issued for the troops to be furnished with two days cooked provisions, and each man served with forty rounds of ammunition. At noon the sick were sent to Bethlehem, which indicates that a sudden attack is intended. At six P.M. the whole army marched, with General Greene's division in the advance.[9]

Packs and blankets were left behind. Men who had haversacks could carry their provisions in them; men who did not could carry them in "any other manner least inconvenient."

Celebrated far and wide as a Fabian, Washington the fighting general would once more offer Sir William a major battle, and this time instead of waiting to receive an attack he was going to deliver it. As with the Christmas march against Trenton the previous year, his plan revealed his penchant for complex night marches that would tax the best-trained and best-disciplined troops, and this march was not only more complicated, it also involved on both sides many thousands more men than at Trenton.

Four columns would converge on Germantown. Two divisions under General Sullivan, his own and General Wayne's, formed the right wing and marched down Skippack Road and on to Germantown Pike, which led through the village to Philadelphia. Sullivan had about fourteen miles to go before meeting British pickets north of the village. Preceding this column was a brigade assigned to overcome those pickets and then move to the right of Sullivan and attack the British left flank. The brigade was commanded by Brigadier General Thomas Conway (1733–1795), who was Irish-born but had served in the French army for more than twenty-five years and had become a colonel in that service. To the right of Sullivan's command, at least a mile away, the well-experienced Brigadier General John Armstrong (1717–1795) and his division of Pennsylvania militia marched down Manatawny Road along the Schuylkill. After dealing with British pickets its mission was to attack the enemy's far left flank and rear. In reserve behind Sullivan were General Maxwell's light infantry brigade and Brigadier General Francis Nash's North Carolina brigade. Sullivan's command probably numbered about 3,000 men. Washington accompanied Sullivan.[10]

The American left wing, under Major General Nathanael Greene, was comprised of his division and General McDougall's division, with General Adam Stephen's division in reserve. Greene had marched about an hour earlier than Sullivan, as Greene had several miles farther to go on a circuitous route until he headed south on Lime Kiln Road toward the British lines. To Greene's left, marching on a fourth road, were General Smallwood's Maryland militia and Colonel David Forman's (1745–1797) New Jersey militia, whose mission was to attack the British right flank and rear. Since neither man knew the area, directions were included in Washington's general orders:

> Smallwood and Forman to pass down the road by a mill formerly Danl Morris' and Jacob Edges mill into the White marsh road at the Sandy run: thence to white marsh Church, where take the left-hand road, which leads to Jenkin's tavern on the old york road, below Armitages, beyond the seven mile stone half a mile from which [a road] turns off short to the right hand, fenced on both sides, which leads through the enemy's encampment to German town market house.

Concise it may have been. Clear it was not.

General orders were quite specific for an attack on the British army early on the morning of 4 October. All four columns were expected to "get within two miles of the enemy's pickets on their respective routs by two OClock [A.M.] and there halt 'till four and make the dispositions for attacking." The attacks were to be delivered "precisely at five OClock with charged bayonets and without firing, and the columns to move on to the attack as soon as possible." Yet a mile or more separated each column, and the militia columns on each flank were seven miles apart. Light horsemen were assigned to keep the columns in touch with each other, but given the dark and the rough country, this proved impossible. So we have some 11,000 soldiers, half-trained and half-disciplined at best, marching at night on four parallel roads, out of touch with each other, and expected to arrive at their jump-off points at the same time and attack together. It leaves one speechless.

The British were not without at least one warning that something big was up. British pickets had been driven in by aggressive American patrols for several nights prior to the 4th. On the 3rd Captain Ewald was approached by an American whom he had befriended who described himself as a "friend of the States and no friend of the English government," but Ewald had shown him "that humanity which each soldier should not lose sight of." He told Ewald, "You stand in a corps which is hourly threatened by the danger of the first attack when the enemy approaches. Friend, God bless your person! The success of your arms I cannot wish. Friend! General Washington has marched up to Norriton today! Adieu! Adieu!" He then went off toward Philadelphia without another word. The editor of Ewald's diary speculates that the man was "probably" a well-known minister and teacher, the Reverend Dr. William Smith, first provost of the Academy and College of Philadelphia, which in 1779 became the University of Pennsylvania.

Ewald was shocked, standing for "quite a while as if turned to stone." He then hurried to his superior, Colonel von Wurmb, and repeated what he had been told. Von Wurmb immediately mounted and rode to General von Knyphausen with the report. Von Knyphausen just as quickly took it to General Howe, who was unimpressed. According to Ewald, Sir William dismissed the intelligence with, "That cannot be!" Major André supported the general nature of Ewald's diary entry in a notation in his own diary: "Some intimations had been received the 3d of the designs of the Rebels to attack us, which were very little credited." We may safely speculate that Sir William could not believe that a general he had soundly defeated three weeks earlier, and prior to that on every occasion they had met, would dare to attack him, or that the army he led was in any condition to take the offensive.

Howe's force at Germantown—perhaps seven to eight thousand—was less than Washington's, although a Hessian report stated that "our army . . . did not consist of more than 5000 combatants . . . for twelve of the strongest battalions were detached." Topography, however, favored Sir William. Ravines, hills, and streams confronted any attacker. Adding to these natural barriers, Germantown was full of stone houses that made for strong defensive posts, and fields and pastures were partitioned by many hedges, fences, and walls. The presence of these man-made features was undoubtedly known to Washington, for one of his orders stated that "All the Pioneers of each Regt & Division who are fit to march are to move in front of their respective divisions with all the Axes they can muster."

Howe's main line of defense lay on the southern edge of Germantown just southeast of the village square, where market days were held, and crossed Germantown Road. The British camp was not far behind this line, and Sir William's headquarters were half a mile behind the line. Facing Sullivan's column as he advanced down Germantown Road was General von Knyphausen's left wing, which extended from Germantown Road to the Schuylkill. Beyond Howe's main defense line, just outside the northern edge of the village, Lieutenant Colonel Thomas Musgrave's 40th Foot was camped near a big stone house, the Chew mansion, also known as Cliveden, which was the country estate of Benjamin Chew, chief justice of Philadelphia. Beyond 40th Foot, about two miles from Market Square, 2nd Light Infantry, which had done such damage to Wayne's Pennsylvanians at Paoli, was posted athwart Germantown Road on a slight eminence called Mount Pleasant. Their pickets were stationed just to the north, on Mount Airy.

The right wing, commanded by General Grant, extended northeastward beyond Lime Kiln Road, down which Greene's column would be marching. The 1st Light Infantry Battalion, with its pickets, was posted on Lime Kiln Road a few miles north of Grant.

Captain Ewald was duty officer in his sector on von Knyphausen's left wing. Although Sir William had dismissed the warning of an American attack, the Hessians apparently had not, for Colonel von Wurmb ordered the pickets doubled and Ewald "to patrol steadily both roads near the Schuylkill and the highway to Norriton. I did this unceasingly."

As the Americans neared their jump-off points, Captain André said that patrols of 1st Light Infantry took some Rebel prisoners and learned that Washington's "whole army . . . was within a very small distance and was to begin his attack immediately." As with most intelligence, however, it had to be delivered up the chain of command—in the eighteenth century by foot or horseback—discussed, mulled over, digested, and then either dismissed as groundless or acted upon.

Captain von Münchhausen had risen very early to ride to Philadelphia and at 5:30 A.M. "heard cannon shots behind me. I immediately rushed to Lord Cornwallis' quarters and asked one of his aides to report the firing to his lordship, who was still asleep. . . . I then rushed back to my general," to find that Sir William had been suddenly awakened by American cannonballs striking his headquarters.

The Americans were running late. By daybreak they were still about four miles from the British main line of defense. The militia columns on the far flanks never arrived, never took part in the battle. The sun had risen by the time the advance attacked the British pickets. But word of a possible American attack had not reached the pickets, and the Americans were not spotted until the last minute. The light infantrymen on picket duty fired their muskets, and two signal cannons boomed to alert the army. Wayne's Pennsylvanians, bayonets fixed, thirsting for revenge, led the way. The pickets fell back on their light infantry colleagues, who did not panic but with a shout attacked. Lieutenant Richard St. George, who had been with the light infantry at Paoli, was hit in the head by a

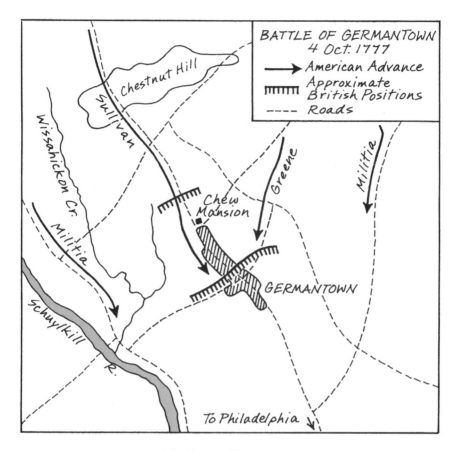

The Battle of Germantown

musket ball and carried from the field by an enlisted man. For a short time the fighting seesawed with charge and countercharge until Sullivan brought more units into play and the light infantry was in danger of being outflanked. Another light infantry veteran of Paoli, Lieutenant Martin Hunter, said the battalion "was so reduced by killed and wounded that the bugle was sounded to retreat; indeed, had we not retreated at the very time we did, we should all have been taken or killed."

Probably not taken. General Wayne wrote, "Our People Remembering the Action of the Night of the 20th Sepr . . . pushed on with their Bayonets—and took ample vengeance for that night's work." His officers "Exerted themselves to save many of the Poor Wretches who were Crying for Mercy," but the "Rage and fury of the Soldiers was not to be Restrained for some time—at least not until Great Numbers of the

Enemy fell by our Bayonets." The fury of the American attack broke the light infantry, and there occurred a rare sight in the Revolutionary War: British regulars showing their backsides as they fled the field in wild disorder. Lieutenant Loftus Cliffe of 46th Foot saw "them quite broke, flying like Devils," but expected they would rally when he heard the shout "Stop, L Infantry, Stop!," which had no effect, and then "a Devil of a fire upon our front & flank came ding dong about us, we had but 60 men, could not cope, were obliged to fly, for the first time ever I saw the 46 turn, but alas it was not the last that Day."

Sir William could not believe what he saw. He had ridden, as Captain von Münchhausen expected, "in the direction of the heaviest fire, and there I found him." Nor could von Münchhausen believe what *he* saw. He "was astounded to see something I had never before seen, namely, the English in full flight." Lieutenant Hunter of light infantry wrote that Sir William "got into a great passion, and exclaimed, 'For shame, Light Infantry! I never saw you retreat before. Form! Form! it is only a scouting party.'" Just after that Sullivan's forces appeared, and grapeshot hit a chestnut tree near Sir William. Lieutenant Hunter wrote,

> I think I never saw people enjoy a discharge of grape before, but really all the officers of the 2nd Battalion appeared pleased to see the enemy make such an appearance, and to hear the grape rattle about the Commander-in-Chief's ears, after he had accused us of running away from a scouting party. He rode off immediately at full speed.

"Almost an unspeakable fatigue"

Sullivan's division overran the camp of 40th Foot near the Chew mansion and kept going, flowing around the big stone building and fighting their way into town along Germantown Pike. The going was not easy. Light Infantry had rallied, other troops had come forward. The Americans found themselves fighting for "every yard House & Hedge," Sullivan wrote, as the British conducted a fighting retreat.

Behind the American brigades that had pushed on, Lieutenant Colonel Thomas Musgrave of 40th Foot, finding himself beleaguered on all sides, dashed into the Chew mansion with 120 men. The shutters on the downstairs windows were closed, the doors barred, and the best marksmen assigned to the upstairs windows. Musgrave told his men that the Americans were giving no quarter so they must fight it out until the rest of the army came up. There General Maxwell's brigade halted. Initial attempts to take the stone house failed. The ground before the house began to be littered with Rebel bodies. The fighting became fierce as the Americans persisted in their efforts to either storm the house or set it afire. The men of 40th Foot, feeling they had nothing to lose, responded as fiercely. By that time the morning fog had rolled in. Depending on where one was, visibility decreased from thirty to one hundred yards and would play an important role in the battle.

Officers gathered to discuss what to do about the big stone house in their way. Washington, Sullivan, chief of artillery Henry Knox, and many others were there. The discussion centered on whether to bypass the Chew mansion or call for its surrender. General Knox argued vigorously for a summons to surrender. Besides, he added, "it would be unmilitary to leave a castle in our rear." The adjutant general, Timothy Pickering, said, "Doubtless that is a correct general maxim, but it does not apply in this case." Pickering claimed that he argued to leave a "small regiment" behind to contain Musgrave's force inside the mansion and to press forward with the rest of the troops: "We are now in the midst of the battle; and its issue is unknown." Captain Henry (Light Horse Harry) Lee (1756–1818), who also was there, recalled that many junior officers and Alexander Hamilton "urged with zeal the propriety of passing the house." But Knox prevailed, and Pickering's assistant, Lieutenant Colonel William Smith of Virginia, volunteered to carry a flag forward to summon Musgrave's surrender. But the British did what Pickering had predicted. Smith was shot and mortally wounded as he went forward. Knox was a good officer, and a competent, self-taught artillery commander, but before the war he had owned a bookshop in Boston, where his favorite reading was military treatises and history, and now he drew upon his wide theoretical knowledge to convince Washington that an army should never leave a "castle" in its rear. He would reduce it with artillery. Colonel Benjamin Tallmadge said he "distinctly heard" General Knox persuade Washington to permit "him to bring his field artillery to bear upon it." For an hour, perhaps more, cannonballs pummeled the stone walls, to no avail. The walls could not be broken down. The artillery did blow out the downstairs doors and shutters, but the British were ready to deal with that.

The fight at the Chew mansion was not just a gross error of judgment by Knox and Washington, it also became a slaughterhouse for 6th Pennsylvania and 1st and 3rd New Jersey. "To do them justice," a

British officer wrote, "they attacked with great intrepidity, but were received with no less firmness; the fire from the upper windows was well directed and continued; the rebels nevertheless advanced, and several of them were killed with bayonets getting in at the windows and upon the steps, attempting to force their way in at the door." Some managed to get inside before being killed.

While all of this was going on, what of Greene's column? He had farther to go, and his guide had misguided him onto a wrong road. He was half an hour late as he finally neared the enemy lines. One of his subordinates, Brigadier General Adam Stephen, hearing the sound of battle around the Chew mansion, left the line of march with his brigade and headed for the sound of the guns, a type of movement often celebrated in the history of war but in his case a disastrous decision. General Stephen not only did this in direct contravention of Greene's orders, he never told Greene what he was doing. Why did he do it? As we will see, he may have been drunk.

In the meantime General Wayne, fighting in the village, also had heard the sounds of battle behind him and according to Sullivan feared that Sullivan's division, which was actually abreast of his on the other side of Germantown Pike, was in trouble behind him, so he turned his division around to go to the rescue. This brought him back just in time to bump into General Stephen's errant brigade. In the thick fog that old devil friendly fire reared once more. Stephen's brigade fired on Wayne's division, Wayne's men fired back. Then British units from General Grant's right wing advanced against them. The Americans, Stephen's and Wayne's men, now disorganized and confused, panicked and together fled.

General Greene, ignorant of what was going on to his right, spread his units to either side of Lime Kiln Road and attacked. He had lost General Stephen's brigade, of course, and General McDougall's brigade to the east of the road never got into the fight. But General Muhlenberg's brigade followed by General Weedon's brigade forged ahead, swept aside 1st Light Infantry, and penetrated the British right wing. One regiment, 9th Virginia, Colonel George Matthews commanding, went so fast it lost contact with its brigade and soon was near the far side of Germantown, well behind British lines. During his exhilarating advance, Matthews had taken 100 prisoners. But Wayne was no longer in the village, Sullivan's division also was in trouble, and Matthews soon found himself alone, surrounded, and forced to surrender. He lost his prisoners, his liberty, and his regiment. Another Virginia regiment from Muhlenberg's brigade, Colonel Walter Stewart commanding, almost got into the same predicament, but retreated in time and got away with three British cannons to boot.

The problem with Sullivan's division, which had no knowledge of Wayne's retreat, was lack of ammunition. Their forty rounds per man was gone or almost gone, and they chose not to carry on with the bayonet. According to our old friend Private Joseph Plumb Martin, "Some of the men unadvisedly calling out that their ammunition was spent, the enemy were so near that they overheard them" and attacked. General Sullivan wrote that his division "retired with as much precipitation as they had before advanced against every effort of their officers to rally them." In an effort to stop the rout and get the men to turn around and return to the assault, Washington spurred into the thick of it. "I cannot help observing," Sullivan wrote to a friend,

> That with great Concern I saw our brave Commander Exposing himself to the hottest fire of the Enemy in such a manner that regard to my Country oblidged me to ride to him & beg him to retire—he to gratify me & some others withdrew a Small Distance but his anxiety for the fate of the Day Soon brought him up again where he remained until our Troops had retreated.

On the American left Greene's division could not carry on alone. In a very confused situation in which it is impossible to precisely track events, with the smoke of battle added to the dense fog, Greene got out in the nick of time and at about 10:00 A.M. retreated down Lime Kiln Road. General Grant pursued Greene for four or five miles but never caught up and gave up the chase. Lieutenant McMichael was there and left us his opinion on what happened, and from his narration it seems that Greene's retreat was orderly:

> We drove the enemy for near 3 miles with the utmost precipitation, but the Maryland militia under the command of Gen. Smallwood, not coming to flank us in proper time, together with the cowardice of the 13th Virginia regiment, gave the enemy an opportunity of coming round our left flank. When their main body attacked our left, we advanced into a field and put every party to retreat that attacked us in front; but by this time we sustained a fire from front, left, and part to the rear, when Gen Stephen ordered Colonel Stewart to evacuate the

ground. . . . It was disagreeable to have to leave the field, when we had almost made a conquest, if the Virginians had stood to our aid. Agreeably to orders, we retreated regularly a short distance, but the enemy taking a different route, we were obliged to march the road from whence we came, in order to head them, but did not fall in with any part of them afterwards. We then marched up the Skippack Road to Pennybecker's [Pennypacker's] Mill, where we betook ourselves to rest at 9 P.M.

Cornwallis arrived from Philadelphia with reinforcements and for a while followed the Americans but never made contact. Washington chose to lead the army past its starting point the night before to Penny-packer's Mill (present-day Schwenksville), about thirty miles from Germantown. This meant that in a little over twenty-four hours Washington and his army had marched forty-five miles and fought a three- to four-hour battle during which they were almost constantly on the move. Greene's column, in fact, had marched closer to fifty miles. Little wonder that Lieutenant McMichael wrote,

I had previously undergone many fatigues, but never any that so much overdone me as this. Had it not been for the fear of being taken prisoner, I should have remained on the road all night. I had marched in twenty four hours 45 miles, and in that time fought four hours, during which we advanced so furiously thro' buckwheat fields that it was almost an unspeakable fatigue.

"We are in high spirits"

Lieutenant McMichael considered the Battle of Germantown a far tougher action than Brandywine, which "was not in any measure such a general attack, neither was the loss at that place any way equivalent." Depending on the source, there are various numbers for Rebels killed at the Chew mansion, but Captain Ewald walked the ground and through the house after the battle. "I counted seventy-five dead Americans, some of who lay stretched in the doorways, under the tables and chairs, and under the windows, among whom were seven officers. The rooms of the house were riddled by cannonballs, and looked like a slaughterhouse because of the blood spattered around." The British lost 4 killed, 29 wounded, and 3 missing.

American casualties for the entire battle numbered 152 killed, 521 wounded, about 400 captured or missing. The British casualties were about half that number. Two generals were killed: Francis Nash of North Carolina and James Agnew of 4th British Brigade. A different type of casualty was General Adam Stephen of Virginia, who was found drunk and sleeping in a barn. He was court-martialed, convicted, and thrown out of the army. It was a sad end for a brave officer ever loyal to the Cause.

It had been an audacious attack by Washington. He had caught the British by surprise and initially sent them running. In the end, however, it was another American defeat. Many reasons have been given, and most have merit. Officers on both sides agreed that the unnecessary delay at the Chew mansion was a factor, and that the dense fog had caused confusion among the attackers. It is also true that Sullivan's brigades deployed slowly. Greene was an least half an hour late arriving on the field. Confusion and panic were spread by friendly fire. Sullivan's division ran out of ammunition. But a few years later an eighteenth-century European soldier put his finger on the root cause of the American defeat.

The Marquis de Chastellux was a major general in the French army and came to America with the French expeditionary force under Comte de Rochambeau. During his travels in various part of the United States, the marquis took the opportunity to examine the field of Germantown and talk to a few of the participants, and he spotted the flaw in Washington's plan:

> Military men who shall view the ground, or have before them an accurate plan, will, I imagine, be of the opinion, that the extensiveness of the object occasioned the failure of this enterprise. The project of first beating the advanced corps, then the army, and afterwards of becoming masters of Philadelphia, was absolutely chimerical.[11]

In the vernacular, Washington bit off more than he could chew. The plan would have been daunting to well-trained, well-disciplined troops. Leaving aside the notion that all four columns would arrive at their jump-off positions at the same time, the American army was not capable of performing quickly and efficiently the maneuvers necessary for formal battle. Marching in column to their assigned positions, regular armies then spread into long lines two, sometimes three, deep to bring their firepower to bear. But as Chastellux noted, "they had no instruction, and were so ill-disciplined, that they could neither preserve good order in marching in a column, nor spread themselves when it became necessary." In short, the American army was just not up to the complex marching and maneuvering called for in Washington's plan, a view supported by Light Horse Harry Lee, who wrote in his memoirs of "the yet imperfect discipline of the American army" and "the inexperience of the tribe of generals." Combined with everything else that went wrong, especially the fog, Greene's late arrival on the battlefield, and the blunder at the Chew mansion, there should be no surprise that at Germantown the Americans were once again defeated.[12]

Yet they also had done remarkably well, and if the plan had just called for overrunning the British advance and giving them a good pummeling, taking the town, and then withdrawing by plan, the action might have ended as an American victory similar to those at Trenton and Princeton. For the army of 1777, the army that fought at Brandywine and Germantown, was not the army of 1776 at Long Island, Kips Bay, and Fort Washington. This was a much tougher, more capable army. It has even been suggested that it was a better army than the one that triumphed at Trenton and Princeton, although I think that an exaggeration. Wayne's Pennsylvanians, humiliated at Paoli, dreamed of vengeance and got it at Germantown. The officers were more experienced than in 1776, although they were still capable of appalling blunders, such as Washington's reconnaissance failure at Brandywine and Knox's stubbornness, backed by Washington, at the Chew mansion. But despite the defeat, and as flawed as the plan was, Washington's audacity in launching a major attack on Sir William and getting away scathed but with the army largely intact had positive results.

Even Chastellux admitted that "One is at a loss whether most to extol the sage intrepidity of the chief, or the resolution displayed by his army in making an attack on the same troops whose shock they were unable to sustain a month before." Although like a typical eighteenth-century general Chastellux believed the action was "too bloody for any advantage derived from it," he also felt

> The capacity he [Washington] had just displayed on this occasion, the
> confidence he had inspired into an army they [the British] thought
> disheartened, and which, like the Hydra of the fable, re-appeared with

a more threatening head, astonished the English, and kept them in awe, till the defeat of Burgoyne changed the aspect of affairs.[13]

This also was the reaction at home and abroad. Congress passed a resolution thanking "General Washington, for his wise and well concerted attack upon the enemy's army," and also praised officers and men "for their brave exertions." Confident that "the best designs and boldest efforts may sometimes fail by unforseen incidents," Congress ordered a medal to be struck and presented to Washington. This enthusiasm would not last, especially after Burgoyne was defeated at the second Battle of Saratoga (Bemis Heights) and subsequently surrendered to General Gates, who then became the darling of many congressmen.

The American army was satisfied with its performance and not disheartened by defeat. The troops and their officers thought they had won. General Weedon of Virginia said that "though the enterprise miscarried, it was worth the undertaking." Hyperbole got the better of General Wayne of Pennsylvania: "Upon the whole it was a glorious day." Private Joseph Plumb Martin, 8th Connecticut, described his role in the battle in a very matter-of-fact fashion, never giving way to either the elation of temporary victory or the despair of defeat. His main complaint is typical of soldiers of all ages: "I had eaten nothing since noon of the preceding day, nor did I eat a morsel till the forenoon of the next day, and I needed rest as much as victuals." Lieutenant Colonel William Heth of 3rd Virginia was convinced that "Tho' we gave away a complete victory, we have learned this valuable truth: [that we are able] to beat them by vigorous exertion, and that we are far superior [in] point of swiftness. We are in high spirits. Every action [gives] our troops fresh vigor and a greater opinion of their own strength. Another bout or two must make their [the British] situation very disagreeable."[14]

Colonel Heth's assessment and that of Major Henry Miller (1751–1824), 2nd Pennsylvania, reveal how far the army had come from those depressing months in the summer, fall, and early winter of 1776. Six days after the battle, on 10 October 1777, Major Miller wrote to his family,

> Our army is in higher spirits than ever, being convinced from the first officer to the soldier, that our quitting the field must be ascribed to other causes than the force of the enemy: for even they acknowledged that we fled from victory. We hope to meet them soon again, and, with the assistance of Providence, to restore our suffering citizens to their possessions and homes.[15]

That much of their optimism was misplaced, that the valiant defense by 40th Foot of the Chew mansion, and that the reinforcements from the main British camp and Cornwallis's Philadelphia garrison had much to do with their defeat were irrelevant. It is what they believed that was important. The American army came out of Germantown believing in itself. Despised by its enemy as ragtag and bobtail, not yet a finished product, the army had to a great extent come of age.

15

"We . . . took post near the Valley Forge"

"You must forage the Country naked"

Nineteen December 1777. "Wind cold & piercing," general orders reported. At 10:00 A.M., following some 2½ months of marching and countermarching, false alarms and skirmishing, Lieutenant McMichael wrote, "We marched from Gulph [Mill] and took post near the Valley Forge, where our ground was laid for cantonments." By 7 February 1778, Brigadier General James Mitchell Varnum of Rhode Island would write, "We are situated in a Place that abounds with nothing but poverty and Wretchedness."[1]

When we ask what manner of soldiers they were who marched to Valley Forge, these lads from eighteenth-century working-class America, we would be close to the truth if we recall the exchange between the Byzantine emperor Justinian and his great general Count Belisarius:

> "What sort of recruits do you want?" Justinian asked. Belisarius replied, "Give me men who can drink foul water and eat carrion."[2]

It has long been known that the travail of the Continental Army at Valley Forge, about twenty miles northwest of Philadelphia, was not primarily due to weather. The winter of 1778–1779 was relatively mild.

The army suffered far more from weather at Morristown during the severe winter of 1779–1780, with its bitter cold and deep snows, although sickness and death were far less than at Valley Forge. Nor were its sufferings due to Valley Forge being far from sources of supply. Copious supplies of food were nearby. Gristmills abounded. The fertile limestone soils of southeastern Pennsylvania supported prosperous family farms that supplied not only the entire area but also exported grain far and wide in the Atlantic world. And the harvest had been abundant that year. At Valley Forge the problem was the all-important logistical system. It broke down. It was broken by the time Lieutenant McMichael and his comrades "took post near the Valley Forge," and it was still broken when General Varnum penned his bitter description of the encampment. Its fixing did not begin until Nathanael Greene was appointed quartermaster general in March 1778 and with ruthless efficiency undertook a job he wanted no part of. For as he wrote, "No body ever heard of a quarter Master in History." He served in that position for 2½ years, before going on to win immortality in his brilliant Carolina campaign.[3]

The tone was set for Valley Forge the day after Lieutenant McMichael and his comrades arrived, when three officers appointed as a committee to inspect beef for Brigadier General Ebenezer Learned's (1728–1801) Massachusetts Brigade reported to Washington that "we have examined the Beaf and Judge it not fit for the use of human beings, unwholesome & destructive to nature for any person to make use of Such fude." When the beef was edible it often contained such little fat and so much bone that it left men with the dispiriting pangs of hunger.[4]

That the Morristown winter of 1779–1780 was far more severe, that food was relatively near at hand if it only could be transported, should not blind us to the real sufferings of the soldiers at Valley Forge. For they were real, and as we contemplate Valley Forge from our comfortable armchairs any suggestion that descriptions of their travail is mere romanticism smacks of revisionism for the sake of being different. Washington has been accused of exaggerating the army's plight. But when he wrote with regard to the army's commissary department to Henry Laurens of South Carolina, who was the new president of the Congress, that "unless more vigorous exertions and better regulations take place in that line and immediately, This Army must dissolve," he was only carrying out his responsibility as commander in chief. There was a real danger that the army would fall apart. Many officers and civilians alike believed it to be imminent. That it did not dissolve must remain today as then a tribute to the common soldiers in the ranks, whatever their various reasons may have been for sticking it out.[5]

For make no mistake about it. The army almost perished at Valley Forge. A mild winter, yes, but winter is still winter, and no time to be poorly clothed and poorly fed. The breakdown of the logistical system is highlighted in a famous passage from the diary of the Connecticut surgeon Albigence Waldo. Tasteless water and dough cooked over a campfire were too often the soldiers' fare. "What have you for dinner, boys? 'Nothing but fire cake and water, Sir.' At night. 'Gentlemen, the supper is ready.' What is your supper, lads? 'Fire cake and water, Sir.' The Lord send that our Commissary of Purchases may live [on] fire cake and water until their glutted guts are turned to pasteboard."[6]

The food supply remained sporadic throughout the winter, at times approaching a feast-or-famine regimen, and it proved impossible to stanch the flow of food from the rich farms of the area into Philadelphia. When British raiding parties did not take what they wanted, they paid hard cash—gold—and Pennsylvania farmers, whether Rebel, Tory, or neutral, were not about to pass up that rare commodity. On 19 December Major John Clark Jr. (1751–1819) of Pennsylvania, who was running spies into Philadelphia, wrote, "I must again tell your Excellency, that the Country People carry in provision" to Philadelphia; "a number went to Day." If the farmers did not go to the city, the city dwellers went to them. At the end of the month Major John Jameson (1752–1837) of 1st Continental Light Dragoons was stationed east of the Schuylkill at Whitemarsh. He reported that it was going to be very difficult to prevent Philadelphians from getting food from the countryside, since "they mostly walk out and when they are going in enquire what time the Horse leave the lines and so remain at some House til they see them and then slip off. . . . I believe there are not less than two hundred a day that come out with bags for a Quarter of Flower or Meal etc."[7]

As the winter progressed and the situation grew worse, Washington was driven to put into effect the power Congress had given him to seize supplies from civilians. He knew this might alienate the people, which was why he took so long to do it, but the army's precarious condition drove him to it. In mid-February, during the army's worst time, Washington received intelligence that the British were about to launch a foraging expedition on a grand scale. To counter it he sent Anthony Wayne, Lighthorse Harry Lee, and his most gifted subordinate, Major General Nathanael Greene, to deny the British the largesse of the countryside

"as well as to supply the present Emergencies of the American Army."
Wayne was assigned to New Jersey, Lee to Delaware, Greene to Pennsylvania. Greene was "to take, Carry off and secure all such Horses as
are suitable for Cavalry or for Draft and all Cattle and Sheep fit for
Slaughter together with every kind of Forage." Certificates were to be
given to the owners that they might apply for payment from commis-
saries and the quartermaster general. And good luck to them.[8]

This was no mission for the tenderhearted. Greene wrote to one of
his officers,

> You must forage the Country naked, and to prevent their complaints of
> the want of Forage we must take all their Cattle, Sheep and Horses fit
> for the use of the Army. Let us hear from you and know how you go on.[9]

That Greene the well-read and thoughtful man was also one of the
hard men when necessity dictated is also revealed in one of his reports
to Washington, in which he admitted that

> the Country is very much draind. The Inhabitants cry out and beset
> me from all quarters. but like Pharoh I harden my heart. Two men
> were taken up carrying provisions into the Enemy yesterday morning.
> I gave them an hundred [lashes] each by way of Example. I have sent
> of[f] all the Cattle Sheep and Horses. I will send on the forage and all
> further collections that may be made as fast as possible. I am determin
> to forage the Country very bare. nothing shall be left unattempted.[10]

"Bare footed, bare leg'd, bare breech'd"

If the food supply was erratic and at times desperate, it was surpassed as
a problem by the lack of proper clothing. Letter after letter raises the
specter of half-clothed soldiers in a wintry environment. "To see our poor
brave Fellows living in Tents, bare footed, bare leg'd, bare breech'd, etc.
etc. in Snow, in Rain, or March, in Camp, & on duty without being able
to supply their wants is really distressing," wrote Lieutenant Colonel
John Brooks of 8th Massachusetts on 5 January 1778. He asked, "'is
there not some chosen curse' reserved for those who are the cause of so
much misery." By then most of the troops were housed in fourteen-by-
sixteen log huts they had been set to building in December, and soon all
would occupy such quarters, twelve men to a hut. But 2½ weeks later

Brigadier General Enoch Poor of New Hampshire reported to his governor that "the present situation of your soldiers, with respect to clothing, near one half of them destitute of any kind of shoes or stockings to their feet, and I may add many without either Breeches shirts or blankets exposed as they are unavoidably obliged to be to all the inclemencies of the cold season living in log huts without doors or floors." Second Lieutenant Archelaus Lewis of 1st Massachusetts voiced similar complaints and concluded, "Really my dear friend this is the case with the greatest part of our army."[11]

The very worst time was during the middle of February, when Colonel Richard Butler of 9th Pennsylvania wrote since there was "not a blanket to Seven men, I have been obliged to Retain the tents as substitutes for Blankets." Colonel Philip Van Cortlandt, commanding 2nd New York, reported about thirty men "fit for duty, the Rest Sick or lame, and God knows it wont be long before they will all be laid up, as the poor Fellows are obliged to fitch wood and water on their Backs, half a mile with bare legs in Snow or mud." By 23 February, in a Massachusetts brigade of 756 other ranks present, its brigadier claimed that 450 were "unfit for Duty for want of shoes and other clothing."[12]

Sergeant John Gibbs of 1st New Hampshire blamed the large Quaker population for food shortages, insisting that they were "No friends to the Cause we are engaged in but on the Contrary which Causes us to suffer much . . . that sometimes we have ben Obliged to go . . . and take their Provision by Force allowing them a reasonable price." In referring to the Cause, Sergeant Gibbs gave voice to the mostly anonymous other ranks. Despite their sufferings, he continued, "it is verry Remarkable that our Troops amidst all their hardship which they Suffer Still keep a Steady Solid Fortitude of Mind." What the historian Charles Royster has called a "mixture of patriotism, resentment, and fatalism" imbued the soldiers with a spirit that kept the army largely together during a terrible time. This was the poetry of the Revolution that must not be lost sight of amid all of the material explanations of what kept men in the field under miserable conditions. A European regular army of the time would not have put up with such conditions. But the American army was a revolutionary force, and like all such armies it knew how to suffer, certainly not in silence, for during the worst time they let their officers know of their feelings: "No meat, no meat," or "No bread, no soldiers." Through it all, however, the Cause burned brightly among them and in large part made them forsake home and loved ones. Lieutenant Colonel John Cropper of 11th Virginia tried to explain it to his dear Peggy:

> My dear! Excuse your husband for doing what he thinks is Right! Excuse in him an overfondness for his Country's Cause! Don't think him insensible for a *husband's* affections, or the distress of an absent *wife:* I know the whole, but the interest of my Country, my wife, my angel inphant . . . united and jointly call upon Me, to struggle in this cause of Virtue, Justice, millions & Posterity.[13]

"The whole amounts to little more than tittle tattle"

The burdens that Washington labored under at Valley Forge were not restricted to the supply problem and the suffering troops. Many in the officer corps did not allow the army's dire situation to prevent them from importuning him incessantly on the subject of promotions desired, promotions refused, promotions unfairly given to others—so the allegations claimed. What a bunch of whiners many were. Hundreds resigned, many others begged leave to go home to assist their ailing families, not to mention escaping the hell of Valley Forge. Although rank-and-file desertions were high, they were lower than in previous periods, and by and large the other ranks behaved better than the officer corps. But another crisis, partly of Washington's own making, throughout the winter loomed even larger in his estimation.

"We want a General," the attorney general of Pennsylvania, Jonathan Dickinson Sergeant (1746–1793), wrote to Washington's most adamant congressional critic, James Lovell (1737–1814) of Connecticut, and continued,

> Thousands of Lives & Millions of Property are yearly sacrificed to the Insufficiency of our Commander in Chief. Two Battles he has lost for us by two such Blunders as might have disgraced a Soldier of three Months Standing, and yet we are so attached to this Man that I fear we shall sink with him than throw him off our Shoulders. And sink we must under his Management.[14]

Strong stuff, but based to a considerable degree on unrealistic expectations. Lovell himself exhibited the malady in a letter of the following day. "I have reason to think the battle of Germantown was *the* day of salvation offered by Heaven to us, and that such another is not to be looked for in ten Campaigns." Such sentiments, from Jonathan Sergeant's extremism to James Lovell's dashed hopes, were in the air that winter, written about, discussed privately between friends, colleagues, a few comrades in arms. It was impossible to keep the talk, the whispers, the missives secret. And it can come as no surprise that the wagging tongues and poison pens created a reaction. At army headquarters, then, and during the long years of the nineteenth century and for almost half of the twentieth, it was received wisdom that during the late fall and winter of 1777–1778, George Washington was the target of a conspiracy to replace him as commander in chief, specifically with the Hero of Saratoga, Major General Horatio Gates. It became known as the Conway Cabal.[15]

The background goes straight to the Rebel belief that this would be a short war. Many had fallen prey to it. Washington, John Adams, Alexander Hamilton, Elbridge Gerry, and others believed, or at least hoped, that a "brilliant stroke" would suddenly end it all, or as James Lovell had put it, "salvation offered by Heaven to us." But the war had already lasted some 2½ years. If somebody had told Congress and the army that it would go on another five years that person probably would have been accused of having taken leave of his senses. On top of the war weariness this vain hope of a short war had helped produce was the bitter disappointment over Washington's defeats at Brandywine and Germantown and the loss of Philadelphia. This in dramatic contrast to Horatio Gates's great victory over Burgoyne at Saratoga. That the loss of Philadelphia got the British no closer to quelling the rebellion, that the Continental Army came out of both defeats with a grim determination to do better next time, that Gates's contribution to victory at Saratoga consisted of taking a strong defensive position, letting Burgoyne come to him, and not doing anything foolish while sending out better men to do the fighting—all of that is irrelevant. It is what men believed at the time that is important, and some did not hesitate to engage in the age-old sport of armchair generalship.

James Lovell thought

The Spirit of Enterprize is a Stranger in the main Army. You may expect so long as the War continues that 3 times more men will be lost in the *main* army by marching and countermarching over hills and thro' rivers than in *battles*. I should deceive you greatly if I lead you to look for any Thing favourable from the *main* army.[16]

Although a vociferous critic of Washington and a proponent of his replacement, Lovell belonged to a tiny minority. But his "Spirit of Enterprize" statement mirrored congressional desire. One of the most important members of Congress, Elbridge Gerry (1744–1814) of Massachusetts, was by no means an enemy of Washington, but even he preached for a winter offensive. "In some of the Officers," he wrote, "there seems to be an irresistible Desire of going into Winter Quarters but others are averse to it, as are Congress unanimously." Gerry was a member of a three-man committee sent by Congress to Washington's headquarters at Whitemarsh, prior to the march to Valley Forge, to urge the commander in chief to mount a winter offensive. He also echoed the need for an "enterprizing spirit," and persisted in the fallacy that "one vigorous Effort" might "subdue the Enemy."[17]

The only other major Washington critic among important leaders of the Revolution, the explosive Dr. Benjamin Rush, wrote to John Adams, "Be not decieved, my friend. Our army is no better than it was two years ago." This was patently untrue, a ludicrous falsehood, yet there can be no doubt that Rush sincerely believed it. His hero, his savior, was Horatio Gates. "I have heard," he wrote Adams about a week later, "several officers who have served under General Gates compare his army to a well-regulated family. The same gentlemen have compared General Washington's imitation of an army to an uniformed mob." His hyperbole reached such heights that he maintained "Gates has saved Pennsylvania in the State of New York just as much as Pitt conquered America in Germany."[18]

Criticism was not restricted to civilians or to obvious malcontents in the army. Had Washington seen the letter of a prominent foreign volunteer, who 2½ years later would suffer a gallant death for the Cause, he would have been shocked and probably mortified. Major General Johann, Baron de Kalb, wrote,

> he is too slow, even lazy, much too weak, and not without his dose of vanity and presumption. My opinion is that if he does anything sensational he will owe it more to his good luck or to his adversary's mistakes than to his own ability. [19]

With the exceptions of being lazy, which was not true, and weak, by which de Kalb probably meant Washington's predilection for holding councils of war and giving full consideration to the opinions of his senior commanders, this is not an unfair assessment, although when it comes to luck one must always keep in mind the dictum of the hardbitten Jäger, Captain Johann Hinrichs: "Luck is the main thing in war." What is relevant, however, is that if honorable and experienced soldiers such as de Kalb, who never intrigued against his chief, had such thoughts, is it any wonder that civilians without experience in war, nourished by their delusions of how easy it would be to defeat the British and drive them from Philadelphia, gave vent to their bitter disappointments? They refused to accept the reality that at this stage of the contest the British army was a better tactical force than the American army.[20]

Even such a level-headed man as Henry Laurens, who did not then know Washington well, wrote to his son John, an aide-de-camp to the Great Virginian, that although he abhorred tattletales, "Nevertheless I am afraid there may be some ground for some of these remarks."[21]

Into this mix of dashed expectations, euphoria over Burgoyne's surrender, and delusions among both soldiers and civilians as to Horatio Gates's character and ability stepped a bilingual Irish-born French soldier of fortune by the name of Thomas Conway (1733–1795). Conway had been a soldier in the French army for thirty years and by 1772 had reached the rank of colonel. He arrived in America in the spring of 1777, was appointed by Congress a brigadier general the following month, and on 19 May Washington gave him command of a Pennsylvania brigade in Lord Stirling's division. Even before the controversy broke out, Washington had second thoughts about Conway. The Franco-Irish soldier served with distinction in New Jersey and at the Battle of Brandywine, and his brigade became known as the best-drilled in the army. Some thought his brigade had behaved very well at Germantown, although General Cadwalader accused Conway of cowardice at that action, and they later fought a duel over it. But Conway's real difficulty was not whether he shrank from the fighting at Germantown. His oversized ego and big mouth, his open contempt for many senior officers, even in council, did not endear him to his American fellow officers, especially when he began lobbying Congress in October 1777 for promotion to major general, which would have catapulted him over many officers senior to him in American service. Washington made clear his feelings on the matter in a letter of 16 October to Congressman Richard Henry Lee (1732–1794):

General Conways' merit then, as an officer, and his importance in this Army, exists more in his own imagination than in reality, for it is a maxim with him to leave no service of his own untold nor to want any thing which is to be obtained by importunity.[22]

A crisis was brewing, and its explosive nature was soon revealed.

A little over a week later Horatio Gates's aide-de-camp, that chronic liar, intriguer, and scoundrel of the Revolution and the early republic, Major James Wilkinson (1757–1825), on his way to Congress to deliver news of his commander's victory at Saratoga, stopped at Lord Stirling's headquarters and told Stirling's aide, Major William McWilliams, about the contents of a letter Conway had written to Gates. McWilliams repeated this tidbit to his boss. There was no love lost between Stirling and Conway, and on 3 November Stirling passed on the gossip to Washington. Instead of checking first with Gates, who had the letter, Washington reacted immediately in a short, two-sentence letter to Conway:

> Sir, a letter which I received last Night contained the following paragraph. In a letter from Genl Conway to Genl Gates he says—"Heaven has been determined to save your Country, or a weak General and bad Councellors would have ruined it." I am Sr Yr Hble Sert.[23]

Conway just as quickly replied, admitting that in his letter to Gates he had "found fault with several Measures pursued in this army," but denying, truthfully, that he had written the specific passage passed on to Washington. After praising Washington as a man of courage, honesty, patriotism, and "great sense," he added,

> your modesty is such, that although your advice in council is commonly sound and proper, you have often been influenc'd by men who Were not equal to you in point of experience, Knowledge or judgement.[24]

In other words, Washington lacked the strength of character and judgment to spurn bad advice given by his senior commanders and staff. Conway had a knack for insulting people he was trying to placate. Washington never saw Conway's original letter to Gates. According to Henry Laurens, who did, Wilkinson's gossip is not what the letter stated. Laurens copied an extract from the letter and sent it to Washington via an aide-de-camp in mid-February 1778. The extract read,

> What pity there is but one General Gates! but the more I see of this Army the less I think it fit for general Action under its actual Chiefs & actual discipline. I speak [to] you sincerely & wish I could serve under you.[25]

Major General Horatio Gates by John Trumbull

This was almost as bad as Wilkinson's gossipy version. As for Gates, his relations with Washington had been deteriorating since his failure to directly inform his commander in chief of the victory at Saratoga, preferring to deal with Congress, and his resistance to sending reinforcements to the main army. Nor could Washington have forgotten his disappointment when Gates declined to take part in the Trenton expedition of 1776, once again preferring to ingratiate himself with Congress by following them to their retreat in Baltimore. Now Gates's reaction to the tempest over Conway only deepened Washington's suspicions of this wily character. Thomas Mifflin informed Gates of what had happened. Gates then wrote to Washington, not to pledge support, not to disavow Conway's criticism, but to complain bitterly about the rifling of his correspondence. "Those letters have been stealingly copied; but, which of them, when, or by whom, is to me, as yet, an unfathomable Secret." He told Washington that he was sending a copy of his letter to President Laurens, "that the Congress may, in concert with your Excellency, obtain, as soon as possible, a Discovery, which so deeply affects the Safety of the States. Crimes of that Magnitude ought not to remain unpunished." Washington's chilly reply of 4 January 1778 revealed Wilkinson as the culprit and repeated what Wilkinson had told McWilliams and his own letter to Conway. But he was greatly surprised that Gates had sent a copy of his letter

> to Congress—for what reason, I find myself unable to acct; but, as some end doubtless was intended to be answered by it, I am laid under the disagreeable necessity of returning my answer through the same channel, lest any member of that honble body, should harbour an unfavourable suspicion of my having practiced some indirect means, to come at the contents of the confidential Letters between you & General Conway.[26]

The tone of subsequent correspondence between Washington and Gates did not improve. Conway also had unwisely admitted in his letter to Washington that he had expressed his reservations about the main army to another man Washington distrusted, Thomas Mifflin. Going from bad to worse in Washington's view was the congressional action on 13 December appointing Conway inspector general with the rank of major general and the mission, among other things, of instructing the troops. The appointment and promotion were not meant to embarrass or antagonize Washington, but of course they did, and then in the same bumbling way Congress reorganized the Board of War, made Gates its president and selected Washington's enemy Thomas Mifflin to serve on it along with Colonel Timothy Pickering, who was critical of the senior commanders and aides-de-camp surrounding Washington. And who was appointed secretary of the board? None other than Major James Wilkinson. The makeup of the board and Wilkinson's appointment would have made anybody suspicious.

The flames were fanned by Washington's friends, who warned of a conspiracy to replace him, and these warnings came not only from his supporters in the army, men such as Nathanael Greene and Henry Knox. One of Washington's closest civilian friends, Dr. James Craik (1730–

1814), had been visiting him at Valley Forge, and on 6 January wrote from his home in Port Tobacco, Maryland:

> Notwithstanding your unwearied diligence And the unparalleled Sacrifice of Domestic happiness and ease of mind which you have made for the good of your Country yet you are not wanting in Secret enemies who would Rob you of the great and truely deserved esteem your Country has for you. Base and Villainous men tho' Chagrin, Envy, or Ambition, are endeavouring to lessn you in the minds of the people and taking underhanded methods to traduce your Character. The morning I left Camp I was informed by a Gentleman, who I believe to be a true Friend of yours, that a strong Faction was forming Against you in the New board of war and in the Congress.

If Craik's tale had rested only on the testimony of one unnamed individual, one would hope that Washington would have taken it as a piece of evidence awaiting verification. But there was more. Craik had deferred writing until he reached home in case he heard more such stories on the way. And indeed he had:

> At my arrival in Bethlehem I was told of it there, and was told that I should hear more of it on my way down I did so, for at Lancaster I was Still assured of it. All the way down I heard it, and I beleive it is pretty general over the Country. no one would pretend to affix it on particulars, yet all Seemed to beleive it, it was Said some of the Eastern and Southern Members were at the bottom of it, particularly one who has been Said to be your Enemy before, but denied it, R. H. L. [Richard Henry Lee] and that G_____ M_____ [Thomas Mifflin] in the New Board of War was a very Active person.

Craik then got down to the details of the alleged plot:

> The Method they are taking is by holding up General G_____s [Horatio Gates] to the people and making them beleive that you have had three or four times the number of the Enemy, and have done nothing. that Philadelphia was given up by your Mismanagement and that you have missed many opportunities of defeating the Enemy, and many other things as ungenerous & unjust. These are low Artifices they are making use of. It is said they dare not appear openly as your Enemy, but that the new Board of War is Composed of Such leading men as will throw such obstacles and difficulties in your way as to force you to

Resign. Had I not been assured of those things from such Authority as I cannot doubt it, I should have not troubled you with this.[27]

Washington has been criticized by many historians—with the benefit of hindsight, of course—for taking seriously talk of a conspiracy and reacting with open hostility against those he believed were involved. Before we leap to this judgment, however, we must ask ourselves a question. If one of us were in a position of authority and received such a letter from a close friend, on top of all the similar messages sent by other friends and trusted army comrades, is it not conceivable that we might fall prey to deep suspicions that a cabal was conspiring against us? Especially if we were as thin-skinned as Washington, which may not be a admirable character trait, but he was stuck with it. He was also very much a man of his age, which believed strongly in conspiracies and looked upon factions in public affairs as inherently evil. Can we then really blame Washington for reacting as he did? A much-defeated general who had first lost New York and then the nation's capital, desperately weary, harassed from all sides, burdened by a logistical system that was a joke and states that failed to pull their weight—is it any wonder that he believed the tales, especially when Congress established a bureaucratic oversight system that on the surface seemed to be part of a conspiracy?

His paranoia, if that is not going too far, was certainly strengthened by the ravings of Dr. Benjamin Rush, a former member of Congress, one of the most eminent physicians of his time, and eventually the leading American medical doctor and teacher. Rush was a zealot, of a temperament that needed a bright cause in which to believe, a God who would not fail him. He was brilliant, belligerent, and reckless with tongue and pen. *Moderation* and *compromise* were words foreign to Benjamin Rush. He went from an early, ardent admirer of Washington to an implacable foe who delivered thundering broadsides against the Virginian in almost every letter he wrote. One of those letters tarnished Rush's reputation then and into our own time. On 12 January he wrote an unsigned letter to Patrick Henry, who immediately recognized his handwriting, as Rush undoubtedly knew he would. Three sentences stood out:

The northern army has shown us what Americans are capable of doing with a GENERAL at their head. The spirit of the southern army is no ways inferior to the spirit of the northern. A Gates, a Lee, or a Conway would in a few weeks render them an irresistible body of men.[28]

This reveals an incredible lack of judgment and misreading of the characters and abilities of those three men as well as the capabilities of the British army by an otherwise very intelligent man.

Henry forwarded the letter to Washington, who also recognized the handwriting. By the time Washington received the letter, however, the so-called conspiracy had pretty much run its course, and Washington was approaching untouchable status. On the same date, 12 January, that Dr. Rush wrote his inflammatory letter, Henry Laurens wrote to Lafayette,

> I think the friends of our brave & virtuous general, may rest assured that he is out of reach of his Enemies, if he has an Enemy, a fact which I am in doubt of. I beleive I hear most that is said & know the outlines of almost all that has been attempted, but the whole amounts to little more than tittle tattle, which would be too much honoured by repeating it.

Laurens admitted that

> I am not insensible that General Washington has been in several Instances extremely Ill used by the neglect of those who ought to be his grand support & to prevent every cause of complaint on his part, but if I were with him half an hour & could persuade myself he wanted information, it would be very easy to convince him there has not any thing been *designedly* done or omitted to affront him. I speak of so large a majority as 9 in 10.[29]

More scathing observations on Washington and his senior commanders would circulate, including the anonymous "Thoughts of a Freeman" letter, which was found on 26 January by a congressman on the stairs in the building in York, Pennsylvania, in which Congress was meeting, and delivered to Henry Laurens, who forwarded it to Washington. The letter is quite interesting, not so much for its specific but familiar criticisms of military shortcomings but for reminding us that, among a people who knew well their classical history and the fate of the Roman republic, a standing army was inimical to their liberties, a danger only enhanced when its leader was placed on a pinnacle. The unknown writer maintained "That the liberties of America are safe only in the hands of the Militia," and ended his tract with a blast at the godlike George:

> That the people of America have been guilty of Idolatry by making a man their god—and that the God of Heaven and Earth will convince

them by woefull experience that he is only a man. That no good may
be expected from a standing Army untill Baal [Washington] & his
worshipers are banished from the Camp—I beleive that. Verte.[30]

Many of Washington's critics, including Benjamin Rush, agreed with
whoever wrote "Thoughts of a Freeman." John Adams, who was not in
favor of replacing Washington, nevertheless inveighed throughout the
war and into his very old age against Washington's status as a demigod,
and, being a vain man himself and not unaware of his own considerable
contribution to the Cause, the very idea that the Great Virginian was
indispensable drove him to bitter frustration.

In the case of the Conway Cabal, however, other prominent men
capable of taking the pulse of Congress agreed with Laurens. Elbridge
Gerry (1744–1814) of Massachusetts wrote to Henry Knox in early February that he could find no evidence of a plot against Washington, and
Elephalet Dyer (1721–1807) of Connecticut, who was well versed on
military matters, wrote in March, "Be assured there is not the most distant thought of removing Genll Washington, nor ever an expression in
Congress looking that way." Which takes us back to the good Dr. Craik,
who, the reader will recall, despite his dire warnings to his old friend,
specifically stated that "no one would pretend to affix it on particulars,
yet all Seemed to beleive it." Without meaning to, Dr. Craik pretty
much summed up the affair. Much talk, a lot of smoke, but no blaze, no
hard evidence of a conspiracy to replace George Washington as commander in chief.[31]

But Washington always believed that there had been a plot. In
1794, five years before his death, he mentioned Benjamin Rush's letter
and his gratitude to Patrick Henry for sending it to him, in a letter to
Lighthorse Harry Lee, in which he referred to "the opposition that was
forming against me at that time." It was a puny opposition, however,
and never gained the strength of a full-scale conspiracy. But even this
puny opposition, as vitriolic as it often was and therefore stinging to a
man of Washington's pride, strengthened his position, for its utter failure to accomplish its aims thereafter made absurd any suggestion that a
new direction and a new chief were needed. There was nobody left to
challenge the indispensable man.[32]

The intriguer who provided the spark that set off the mythical Conway Cabal, Major James Wilkinson (1757–1825), was not only promoted to colonel and elected secretary of the Board of War but also

given by Congress the brevet (temporary) rank of brigadier general. This put so many noses out of joint in the army that he resigned his brevet rank in early March 1778. Then he got into such a quarrel with his former patron, Horatio Gates, that at the end of the month he resigned as secretary of the board. But Wilkinson always managed to land on his feet, and Congress appointed him Continental clothier general, a position he held until March 1781, when problems with his accounts led to his resignation. As reprehensible as his conduct had been during the Revolution, it was after the war that he came into his own as a villain. Shady business and political dealings, including treasonous behavior, marked his postwar career. He rejoined the army as a lieutenant colonel in 1791; was promoted to brigadier general in 1792; and, quite incredibly, in 1796 succeeded to Washington's old position as commander in chief of the American army. If that is not enough to digest in one sitting, at the same time he was receiving payment in gold as Secret Agent No. 13 of the Spanish government, which still held the Gulf Coast and was contending with the United States for the Mississippi Valley. He later entered into the famous intrigue with Aaron Burr that probably aimed at detaching at least part of the trans-Appalachian West from the Union, but when the conspiracy began to unravel he betrayed Burr, was eventually court-martialed, acquitted, and restored to his command. He failed miserably as a field commander in the northern theater during the War of 1812, but of course in 1815 was honorably discharged from the army. The following year he published in three volumes *Memoirs of My Own Time*. It is a pity that they are quite unreliable, for the man was an eyewitness observer to many famous events: Arnold's march to Quebec, the Trenton-Princeton campaign, Saratoga, Anthony Wayne's victory over the Indians at Fallen Timbers in 1794, and the tumultuous history of the Old Southwest and the Gulf Coast during the early years of the republic. Seeking fresh opportunities, he went to Mexico City in hopes of obtaining a land grant. There he was also, if one can believe this, agent for the American Bible Society. The gods finally caught up with James Wilkinson, however, and it was in Mexico City in 1825 that he died a long and painful death from dysentery.

Benjamin Rush's heroes Thomas Conway, Horatio Gates, and Charles Lee either left the scene or in one case revealed his incapacity to lead men in battle. Conway fought a duel with General Cadwalader and received a serious wound in his face. From his sickbed he wrote a letter of apology to Washington. Conway then returned to France, reentered the army, and in 1781 went to Pondicherry in India to command a regiment. In 1787 he was appointed governor general of French India. He was back in France in 1793, but as a royalist had to flee, and shortly thereafter died in exile. Thomas Conway was a very competent soldier whose talents were outweighed in America by his arrogance. Charles Lee, whose abilities were vastly exaggerated by his contemporaries, was later court-martialed, separated from service, and died in obscurity, but more of that later. In 1780 Congress rewarded the Hero of Saratoga, Horatio Gates, with command of the Southern Department. Ignoring Charles Lee's advice to beware of exchanging his Northern Laurels for Southern Willows, Gates committed a major error of deployment against Lord Cornwallis at the Battle of Camden, safely positioned himself too far behind his main line of defense to see what was happening, and when his militia fled the field he went with them, leaving his regulars to fight on alone. Can one imagine George Washington behaving that way? Toward the end of the war Gates became second in command of the army, but he never again led troops in the field.

"Lieutt Genl in the King of Prussia's Service"

While all of this was being played out, and while Washington and others struggled with the logistical system, there arrived at Valley Forge an unemployed European soldier who would make a significant contribution to the Continental Army. He had never gained such exalted rank as "Lieutt Genl in the King of Prussia's Service," but Benjamin Franklin, who introduced him with that title by letter to Washington, was not above gilding the lily when it came to opening doors that needed to be opened. He had been a captain on Frederick the Great's staff during the Seven Years' War. Once that war ended, many staff officers became redundant and were thrown out of work. Having little if any private means, and burdened by debt due to his love of the gaming table, he had to work, but employment in his chosen field was hard to come by anywhere in Europe after the war. He ended up as chamberlain in the minor court of the Prince of Hohenzollern-Hechingen in southwestern Germany. The prince made him a *Freiherr* (baron), and he also became a Knight of the Margrave of Baden's Order of Fidelity. This elevation into the minor aristocracy was apparently based on an "erroneous lineage" created by his father, but to my knowledge there is no evidence that he was ever stripped of his titles for giving false evidence. His grandfather had added *von* to the family name in 1708, but that was twenty-two years before he was born, and von it remained until some historians recently began calling him simply Frederick Steuben.[33]

How nitpicking of them. How cruel to deprive one of the important players in the Revolution of honors that were obviously important to him. Besides, many foreign volunteers of unquestionably authentic titles of aristocracy gained by the accident of birth proved worthless. Not so the man named by his parents Friedrich Wilhelm August Heinrich Ferdinand, who became in America Major General Friedrich Wilhelm von Steuben (1730–1794).

His Prussian rank of mere captain should not fool us. And we should set aside his comic reputation, which stemmed from his problems with the English language and led him to swear at the troops in German and French, with an occasional "Goddamn!" thrown in, which the Continentals found hilarious. But he was far from the stage German so beloved of television situation comedies. Von Steuben was a hardbitten professional soldier who had learned his trade well as a Prussian staff officer under the Great Captain of the age, Frederick the Great of Prussia. A scholar who has closely studied von Steuben's career wrote of his "impeccable credentials as a soldier," and he became in America the leading expert on the military arts. Of vital importance, he got along with Washington, the aides-de-camp, and the officer corps.[34]

Von Steuben arrived at Valley Forge on 24 February 1778. Three days later Washington wrote Henry Laurens that "he appears to be much of a Gentleman, and as far as I have had an opportunity of judging, a man of military knowledge and acquainted with the World." He was right on all counts. The following month, von Steuben went to work with the army.[35]

Again we must remind ourselves that the Continental Army at Valley Forge was not the mob pictured by Washington's enemies. Poorly clothed and shod, yes, and hungry often. Its equipment and uniform problems were constant, its food supply sporadic. Von Steuben was candid when he met with a committee of officers on 27 February and gave "The impression which our Camp has made upon" upon him. The minutes of the meeting are explicit:

> Our arms are in horrible condition, covered with rust, half of them without bayonets, many from which not a single shot can be fired. The pouches are quite as bad as the arms. A great many of the men

have tin boxes instead of pouches, others have cowhorns; and muskets, carbines, fowling pieces and rifles are to be seen in the same
Company. His description of our dress is not easily repeated: our men
are literally naked, some to the fullest extent of the word. Officers
have mounted Guard at the Grand Parade in a sort of dressing gown
made of old blankets or woolen bed covers.[36]

Nor was there a uniform drill system throughout the army. "Each
Col," the minutes read, "seems to have had his own system, one according to the English, Muhlenberg's according to the Prussian, and some
according to the French style. Only one thing in the Army has been
uniform, our way of marching, all having adopted the files used by the
Indians." This is precisely what Chastellux was criticizing when he noted
that the Continentals could not march "in column to their assigned positions" and then quickly spread into lines to bring their firepower to bear.[37]

But as the Prussian recognized, it was a tough, dedicated, seasoned
force lacking only the attention to its arms and accoutrements and the
drill and discipline of the parade ground that would turn it into a finished product. That was von Steuben's job, and he knew how to do it.
Captain Benjamin Walker, who spoke French, offered to translate, swear-
ing and all, and slowly, awkwardly, a transformation began. Von Steuben
started with a model company and gradually reached out to the entire
army. Every day, day after day, week after week, fair weather and foul,
von Steuben, Walker, and the troops practiced close-order drill and all
the maneuvers that an eighteenth-century Western army needed to know.
American officers, accustomed to the British method of sergeants drill-
ing troops, were amazed. Von Steuben taught officers and men not only
how to maneuver on a battlefield from column to line and back again
with ease, but also how to march compactly and arrive on the field as a
tightly knit force instead of in long, straggling files, thus losing precious
time in forming to fight. He turned the army Chastellux had described
as having "no instruction, and were so ill-disciplined, that they could
neither preserve good order in marching in a column, nor spread themselves when it became necessary," into a force trained and disciplined in
the European manner, as had always been Washington's dream.

It remained, however, very much an American army. Von Steuben's
insight told him not to insist on transferring Prussian drill and manual
of arms wholesale. He adapted them to the men and conditions he
found. Nor did he attempt to instill fear as a motivating factor for either
drill or fighting, for he had quickly learned to gauge the American tem-

per. He wrote to a European friend, "the genius of this nation is not in the least to be compared with that of the Prussians, or Austrian, or French. You say to your soldier, 'Do this,' and he doeth it; but I am obliged to say, 'This is the reason why you ought to do that'; and then he does it." Washington's aide-de-camp Colonel John Laurens confirmed von Steuben's assertion, informing his father that the Prussian "seems to understand what our Soldiers are capable of, and is not so starch a Systemist as to be averse from adapting established forms to stubborn circumstances." As he went along, von Steuben wrote out what he taught on the parade ground, and produced *Regulations for the Order and Discipline of the Troops of the United States*. It went through seventy editions and was used until the War of 1812.[38]

Washington was so impressed by what von Steuben had accomplished that at the end of April he recommended to Congress that von Steuben be appointed inspector general, with the rank of major general, and Congress agreed.

Recently, however, the historian Wayne Bodle has questioned whether von Steuben's reforms and teachings bore fruit on the battlefield. On 28 June 1778, following the British evacuation of Philadelphia, the first major battle after Germantown took place at Monmouth, New Jersey, while the British army under its new commander in chief, Sir Henry Clinton, was withdrawing across the state to Sandy Hook to take ship to New York City. Monmouth was the battle in which Washington's old tormentor Charles Lee, who had been exchanged and was once again serving the Cause, infuriated Washington for retreating during the opening stage of the fight. It produced one of Washington's rare public displays of his volcanic temper. Without getting bogged down in the merits, which is not our purpose, Lee demanded a court-martial, got it, and was convicted and suspended from service for one year. Later he wrote such an offensive letter to Congress that he was dismissed from service. He died in 1782 in Philadelphia, barely remembered by those who once toasted his alleged genius.[39]

Monmouth was a long, hotly contested battle that is best described as a draw. American artillery played a major role and may have been the deciding factor, but the infantry of both armies clashed often during the battle. Alexander Hamilton, who was there and watched the American and British regiments in action, said that until then he had never "known or conceived the value of military discipline." But Bodle suggests that "Hamilton's role as one of Washington's main apologists puts his reliability into a problematic light." I must confess that I find it puzzling why Hamilton's opinion on military discipline should be suspect because he took Washington's side in the dispute with Lee. Hamilton continued, "Our troops, after the first impulse from mismanagement, behaved with more spirit and moved with greater order than the British troops." Here, it is true, Hamilton is charging that Charles Lee mismanaged the beginning of the battle. But Hamilton claimed to be objective, adding, "You know my way of thinking about our army, and that I am not apt to flatter it. I assure you I never was more pleased with them before this day." Frankly, I accept Hamilton at his word. Another participant, Nathanael Greene, said that "our troops behaved with the greatest bravery," and Colonel Joseph Cilley "did himself imortal Honor" when he and 1st New Hampshire launched a bayonet charge that drove back British Grenadiers and Black Watch with heavy losses.[40]

Wayne Bodle feels that because of the Lee-Washington controversy the particulars of the battle became so politicized that it cannot be used as a gauge of what was accomplished at Valley Forge. He writes, "The Battle of Monmouth on June 28 was not decisive enough to prove the transformative effects of Friedrich Steuben's work with the Continental army." I respectfully disagree. He also notes that this was the last major engagement in the North and adds, "the army never did enough fighting in the north after June 1778 to test Steuben's efforts on the battlefield," thus "the long-term dynamics of the war may have deprived the army of a chance to prove its mettle in conventional combat situations." He does credit von Steuben's training with giving "the soldiers a deeper identification with and pride in their craft," which is quite true. But then he pushes his analysis to an erroneous conclusion, maintaining that von Steuben's efforts made the soldiers "better able to withstand the rigors of military routine rather than the terrors of the British bayonet charge." This totally ignores the major engagements fought in the South in 1780–1781, which is not surprising given the short shrift the Carolina campaign has in general received from historians.[41]

The Battle of Camden (16 August 1780), South Carolina, was a major American defeat in which Horatio Gates proved once and for all that he was not the great captain he and others thought he was. Lord Cornwallis's regulars so terrified the Virginia and North Carolina militia that with the exception of one regiment, they fled the field in wild panic. This left the rest of the American army, 900 regulars of the 1st and 2nd Maryland Brigades and the Delaware Regiment, alone to face 1,700 high-quality British regulars who were under superb combat leadership. In the old days the Continentals probably would have fled when they saw the militia desert them. But at Camden those grim veterans under the gallant Major General Johann de Kalb first drove the British line before them, then stood fast and fought it out, volley for volley, bayonet to bayonet, as the British surrounded them with foot and horse. That astute observer Colonel Otho Holland Williams of Maryland was there and wrote, "The regular troops, who had the keen edge of sensibility rubbed off by strict discipline and hard service, saw the confusion with but little emotion." Abandoned by the militia and General Gates, they fought on until de Kalb was mortally wounded and their ranks were broken by cavalry in full charge crashing down on their rear, whereupon those who could get away did, individually and in small groups, to fight on other days on other fields.[42]

The Battle of Cowpens (17 January 1781), South Carolina, Daniel Morgan's tactical masterpiece of the Revolutionary War, is another excellent example of the results of training, discipline, and hard service. The British commander was the dreaded cavalry leader Lieutenant Colonel Banastre Tarleton. Following Morgan's planned withdrawal of his advanced militia line after it had delivered at least one or two volleys to soften up the British infantry, the British marched against Morgan's main line of defense, which was made up of 1st Maryland, the Delaware Company, and discharged Virginia Continentals serving as militia. Due to a misunderstood order, the American regulars about-faced and marched for the rear with drill field precision. The British regulars misinterpreted the withdrawal, smelled victory, and came on in a wild rush. Morgan, alarmed, rode up to the commander of the American regulars, Lieutenant Colonel John Eager Howard (1752–1827), of Maryland, and asked if he was beaten. Howard pointed at his disciplined lines and observed that "men were not beaten who retreated in that order." For their withdrawal followed precisely von Steuben's manual, and as the historian Lawrence Babits has pointed out, Colonel Howard's postwar description of their movement "virtually quoted von Steuben." Morgan then chose a spot for the Continentals to turn and face the rapidly closing enemy. Once again they about-faced. Upon Colonel Howard's command, at a distance estimated by participants at ten to thirty yards, they fired a volley into the onrushing British that stopped them in their tracks.

"Charge bayonets!" Colonel Howard then cried, and the American regulars sprang forward with glistening steel extended, a charge that ended with British regulars running away or dropping their muskets and begging for mercy. With the exception of one company guarding the wagon train, Colonel Tarleton lost his entire infantry force: 822 men killed or captured. I know of no evidence showing that American regulars maneuvered like that during battle prior to von Steuben's reforms.[43]

Our final example occurred during the Battle of Guilford Courthouse (15 March 1781), North Carolina, fought between Nathanael Greene and Lord Cornwallis, technically won by the British, since they retained the field of battle, but a Pyrrhic victory as it completed the ruin of Cornwallis's army. During the final stages of the battle, 1st Maryland and two Delaware companies were attacked by three crack units: 33rd Foot, Guards Light Infantry, and Jägers, all under that superb combat commander Lieutenant Colonel James Webster (d. 1781). Grim, silent, the Continentals held their fire until Webster and his men were within 100 feet, then shattered them with a thunderous volley and repulsed them in disorder. A little while later 1st Maryland counterattacked 2nd Guards Battalion and engaged those elite troops in a desperate hand-to-hand struggle. The Guards wavered, bent, seemed to be on the verge of breaking when to avert defeat Cornwallis unleashed his artillery, firing grapeshot into the wild melee, which sent both units scattering for cover and effectively ending the battle.[44]

Summing up, I believe that the training received from and the discipline inculcated at Valley Forge by Baron von Steuben, passed on to recruits by officers and sergeants and privates who had been there, lay at the root of the achievement of the regulars in formal combat situations in the South.

"Many patriotic toasts were drank"

While Nathanael Greene, now quartermaster general, scoured the land for food and other supplies and labored to fix the broken logistical system, and von Steuben drilled and disciplined the army, spring arrived at Valley Forge, and with it not only the rejuvenation of spirits that always attends the rapid retreat of winter, but also the arrival of news that meant the United States was no longer alone on the planet to face the world's foremost military power. Our hardy and faithful veteran Lieutenant James McMichael described the celebration that occurred. On 6 May 1778 the entire army was paraded at 9:00 A.M., whereupon each brigade received a discourse by chaplains. At 10:00 A.M. a cannon roared, signaling "the whole army to load and ground arms." At 11:30 A.M. another cannon boomed, and all marched to their alarm posts, where General Washington rode their lines and inspected them.

> Attended by all of his aids and guards, he then took post upon an eminence to the right in rear. Immediately afterwards a signal was given for a feu de joy [feu di joie, or musket fire, one man after another firing a round into the air in a continual roar], when a discharge of 13 pieces of cannon followed by a running fire of infantry from right to left of the front line and continuing to the left with a like discharge from left to right of the rear, were performed. Then a signal for three cheers. This was followed by a discharge of 13 pieces of artillery, with the same ceremonies as in the former fire. We afterwards retired by brigades to our encampment, when all the officers in general were desired to dine with his Excellency Genl Washington and spent the afternoon enjoying all desirable mirth and jollity. Many patriotic toasts were drank, and at evening we returned to our quarters.[45]

The occasion was the celebration of an event that proved to be the grand turning point in the War of the Revolution: the signing on 6 February 1778 of the Treaty of Alliance between the United States and France. In our time it is well to remember and honor that alliance, for France was as important to us in the eighteenth century as we were to France in the twentieth century. But it was not an elixir for immediately turning the war around. Another five hard years of struggle remained. The collapse of the currency in 1779–1780 was considered by Washington to be the most serious crisis of the war. At the same time the growing French financial crisis, that nation's warweariness, and the receptive attitude of the French foreign office toward partition of North America threatened the viability of the union of all thirteen states. A reinvigorated Congress and the efforts of a great merchant and the superintendent of finance, Robert Morris (1734–1806) of Pennsylvania, to restore the nation's credit saw the country through the financial crisis, while Nathanael Greene's campaign in the Carolinas and the great Franco-American victory at Yorktown averted partition and effectively marked the end of the first British Empire.

The years between the British assault on New York in the summer of 1776 and the emergence of the army from Valley Forge in the early summer of 1778 were the critical years of the Revolution. We must admit that major strategic errors as well as operational sluggishness by the British commanders played significant roles in the Continental Army's survival. We also know that on more than one occasion Washington, the army, and the Revolution teetered on the brink of disaster. Yet with grim determination, the army and its commander persevered through defeat and travail. Washington survived, the army survived, and with them the Cause.

Epilogue

The Brothers Howe

Black Dick resigned in late 1777, soon after his brother, but emerged with his military reputation largely intact and did much better after the war than Sir William. Black Dick refused to serve in any capacity under the ministry of Lord North, but when it left office he reentered the service and became commander in chief in the English Channel. In the fall of 1782 he came by deft maneuver and seamanship to the relief of Gibraltar, during which he outwitted the combined Franco-Spanish fleet, for which he was praised at home and abroad.[1]

In January 1783 he was named first lord of the Admiralty, and, with a brief interlude, served in that position until 1788, and made many technical improvements, especially in signals, for which Nelson later complimented him. Black Dick made enemies during his tenure, and he was described by one writer in a pamphlet dripping with venom as "a man universally acknowledged to be unfeeling in his nature, ungracious in his manner, and who, upon all occasions, discovers a wonderful attachment to the dictates of his own perverse, impenetrable disposition." Two years later he was once again given the Channel command, and on 1 June 1794, in the first naval engagement of the French Revolutionary Wars, won an overwhelming victory over a French squadron in the Battle of the Glorious First of June, for which the king conferred upon him the Order of the Garter.

His last official act as a sailor was at the behest of George III. Sailors at the big British naval station at Spithead had mutinied because of poor pay, rations, and provisions for their wives and children. The sailors trusted Black Dick, who had always been "temperate, gentle and indulgent to the men under his command," and the mutiny ended when he went to Spithead, spoke to them, and gave them his assurances. He died two years later. Given his postwar exploits, it seems a reasonable judgment that during the Revolutionary War Admiral Richard, Lord Howe should have left high policy to others and stuck to fighting.

Sir William did not fare as well. General John Burgoyne surrendered his army to General Horatio Gates at Saratoga on 17 September 1777. Burgoyne's surrender and the guilt it engendered in Howe for failing to cooperate with the Canadian army, the emptiness of his conquest of Philadelphia, sharp criticism of his Pennsylvania campaign by the ministry, and deep unhappiness among his officers for everything gone wrong, meant the collapse of Sir William's position as commander in chief. He resigned in October. But communications being what they were then, it was not until May of the following year that he learned that his resignation had been accepted. Incredibly, on 18 May 1778, he allowed his officers to stage a celebration worthy only of a triumphant commander. It was called a *mischianza,* or "medley of pleasures," as one of his biographers describes it. It was beyond extravagance; it was bizarre. Major Baurmeister and Captain von Münchhausen were among those who described it for us.[2]

Seven hundred fifty people were invited. For dancing and dining "a great salon was built and decorated with mirrors and candelabra and chandeliers." At 3:30 in the afternoon the guests gathered, "attended by 108 oboists," and were taken a few miles down the Delaware in galleys and other boats. Baurmeister reported that the sloop bearing the Howe brothers was given a nineteen-gun salute by HMS *Roebuck,* although von Münchhausen said "The warships fired a salute of 21 guns as we sailed past." When the ladies and gentlemen landed, they "passed though a corridor of cavalry and infantry displaying all the flags and standards of our entire corps, then we proceeded to a place arranged in the form of a square where two contingents of" Knights of the White Rose and the Burning Mountain "with their armor-bearers fought with lances and swords in the style of Don Quixot and Sanchopancha, their Dulcineas sitting on elevated thrones, watching the knights who fought for them."

From the knightly tournament they went to the "center of the great lawn," which extended down to the Delaware, and passed through "a very beautiful triumphal arch" to the salon, where tea was served. They then danced until nine and gambled against a bank of 2,000 guineas. At 10:00 P.M. fireworks in front of the salon were set off, which lasted for two hours. "Thereupon we dined in the very large luxurious hall, which was illuminated by 1,200 candles, the 108 oboists playing all that time." Major Baurmeister reported that "The finest fruit that can be obtained here and in the West Indies in the spring was served." After dining they danced until six in the morning. Major Baurmeister thought "It was a spectacle one will never forget," and Captain von Münchhausen wrote that "everything was as splendid and magnificent as possible, and all, even those who have been in Paris and London, agree that they never had seen such a luxurious fete." The staff officers paid 3,000 to 4,000 guineas for the fete, and the Philadelphia shop of Coffin and Andreson was paid 12,000 pounds sterling "for silk goods and other fine materials, which shows how elegantly the ladies were dressed."

Totally bizarre. But perhaps fitting, given the strange campaigns waged by the Brothers Howe, who sought peace but only guaranteed a long and bitter war.

One week later, Sir William sailed for England. He requested an inquiry by a committee of the whole House of Commons, as he and his brother thought that their performance in America had been "unjustly impugned by the ministry." The inquiry, however, came to nothing, trailing off inconclusively. Sir William consistently denied that he had allowed his preference for conciliation to interfere with military operations, but we know otherwise. Although he was appointed lieutenant general of ordnance, was promoted to full general, and held the important command of England's eastern district after the French overran the Netherlands, he never again served abroad, never again led troops into battle. He lived a long time after the war, with plenty of time to think about what went wrong, what might have been. His final illness was long and painful, until his death in Plymouth in 1813.

Sir William Howe was an excellent eighteenth-century example of the twentieth-century Peter Principle, which states that "In a hierarchy every employee tends to rise to his level of incompetence." In 1969 the historian John Alden gave the best estimate of Sir William Howe as commander in chief: "He had failed to fulfill the promise of his youth. As a young man he had performed splendidly under direction. In his middle age he would have been a brave and useful colonel."[3]

The Great Virginian

Of Alexander, Caesar, Napoleon, we can agree: each was a great captain, and Alexander was history's greatest field commander. Each was brilliant, possessing those razor-sharp minds that penetrate the mists of uncertainty, the fog of war, into which others peer in vain. Can we say the same of Washington? I fear not. He was not a brilliant man. He arrived at conclusions slowly. He often hesitated to make decisions that required a quick decisiveness. He never won a major open-field battle. His two victories were critical to the Cause, but Trenton was really a large-scale raid, and his triumph at Princeton was over Cornwallis's heavily outnumbered rear guard. Monmouth was a draw. Yorktown sealed his victory, but it would not have been possible without a French fleet and a French army. Yet in his own way he became a great captain. How did this come about?

It has to be apparent to all of us by now that he was lucky in his opponents. Was England ever as badly served by its generals as in the War of the American Revolution? The Crimean War immediately comes to mind, but not as much was at stake, for in America the British lost an empire. He was, therefore, a lucky general, and luck, as we have observed, is a key requirement for all successful generals.

And it was well that fortune was on his side, for as a commander in the field Washington never displayed any conspicuous gift for tactics. An incident that took place after the war reveals, I think, all we need to know about Washington the tactician. As president he made a tour of the South in the spring of 1791, during which he inspected the field of Guilford Courthouse in North Carolina, where Nathanael Greene and Lord Cornwallis had waged their big, bloody battle ten years before. In that battle Greene borrowed from Daniel Morgan's tactics at the Battle of Cowpens and put the militia in the first two lines. Their mission was to soften up the advancing British and Hessians before they reached Greene's main line of defense, which was manned by Continentals. The militia more or less did their job before fleeing, and a vicious fight developed at the third line between British and American regulars. Technically Cornwallis won because Greene withdrew ten miles and left His Lordship in possession of the field, but the battle so decimated Cornwallis's army that he had to withdraw 175 miles, to Wilmington on the coast. Greene was disappointed in not winning, but he had done his job well in completing the ruin of Cornwallis's army.

Yet Washington, upon studying the field and contemplating Greene's deployment, criticized a man who otherwise stood high in his regard. Two years later, in a conversation with Thomas Jefferson, then secretary of state, Washington "said that he and Gen'l. Greene had always differed in opinion about the manner of using militia. Greene always placed them in his front; himself was of the opinion they should always be used as a reserve to improve any advantage, for which purpose they were the *finest fellows* in the world." Since at Guilford Courthouse the

British and German regiments had to pass over a large, open field before reaching Greene's first line, which was deployed behind a fence, Washington believed that "they must have been torn all to peices if troops had been posted there who would have stood their ground." He also thought that in the event of a withdrawal the tangled woods behind the first line would have made a retreat "perfectly secure." Yet in the battle British infantry proved themselves perfectly adept at woods fighting by slugging their way through those woods against two Virginia militia regiments, one of which put up significant resistance.[4]

Nor did Washington take into account the regular troops available to Greene. Only 1st Maryland and two small companies of the Delaware Line were hardened veterans. The two Virginia regiments, raised to replace those lost at Charleston the previous year, had seen little if any action, while recruits composed most of 2nd Maryland. In the fighting at the main line of defense, 2nd Maryland had taken one look at the shining bayonets of British 2nd Guards advancing on them and fled as fast as the North Carolina militia before them. We can safely speculate that they would have done the same had they been in the first line. Greene knew that he could not, he must not, lose the army. Thus his deployment, thus his decision to break off the fighting and conduct an orderly withdrawal, to be able to fight another day. Had Washington forgotten by 1791 this cardinal rule of the Revolutionary War, that the army, which had become the Revolution, must be preserved? Had the Continental regiments been placed in the first line and failed to halt the numerically superior British and Hessians, it would have been a disaster. At the first sight of the American regulars breaking, the militia behind them would have run fast, run far, without putting up any resistance. Not only would the battle have been lost, but almost certainly Greene's army as well.

Washington learned how to use militia as partisans, or irregular fighters, sniping, raiding, squashing Tory resistance, hanging on the flanks and rear of British columns, ambushing patrols and supply trains, and making a general nuisance of themselves. But had he known how to do it he also could have used militia for formal battles, since he rarely had enough Continentals. Yet he never learned the tactical lesson that Daniel Morgan taught at Cowpens. Washington said that because Greene posted the militia in the front line, and because they fired and fell back, "the whole benefit of their position was lost." Daniel Morgan taught just the opposite. Put the militia in the first line or two, he said, but don't depend upon them to stand fast against advancing regulars. Their mission was to deliver one or two volleys, with special aim taken at officers and sergeants, before retiring, hopefully in an orderly manner, while the regulars at the main line of defense waited to deliver their own volleys at a weakened enemy and use their bayonets if it came to that. That deployment worked in near-textbook manner at Cowpens and not without effectiveness at Guilford Courthouse.

But Washington failed to appreciate what Morgan had accomplished beyond winning the Battle of Cowpens, and what Greene had tried to do and in effect did by severely punishing Cornwallis's army before withdrawing. Washington, Jefferson wrote, "thinks that the regulars with their field pieces would have hardly let a single man get through that field." All of this leads us to an inescapable judgment on Washington as tactician—how fortunate that Greene, not Washington, commanded at Guilford Courthouse, that Morgan, not Washington, led the troops at Cowpens.

How did Washington fare in operations—that is, maneuvering troops to put them in a position to either fight, or to withdraw from a perilous position? Here the record is mixed. His penchant for complex night marches with half-trained troops risked disaster, but when he did it—the escape across the East River from Brooklyn to Manhattan, the attack on Trenton, the withdrawal from Trenton, the attack on Germantown—luck was with him because his overconfident enemies allowed themselves to be surprised. The march on Trenton by his own command was almost perfectly executed, but his reliance on two other columns to cross the Delaware at different points, at night and in a fierce storm, and arrive at their assigned places on time was asking for more than could be delivered. The escape from Brooklyn and the withdrawal before Cornwallis's force at Trenton were masterly. But the approach march to Germantown was far too complicated, even had his troops been fully trained and disciplined.

At times indecision plagued him, the two most notable being his failure to overrule Nathanael Greene and evacuate Fort Washington, and the discussion with Henry Knox before the Chew mansion at Germantown, when he finally sided with Knox and failed to bypass the British stronghold.

If Washington lacked the gifts of a tactician, and was prone to overly complicated operations, how does he rate as a strategist? He cannot be faulted for trying to defend either New York City or Philadelphia, as it was politics, not military reality, that dictated that some sort of effort be made, even though neither city was of critical importance to the Rebels from a military point of view. That the British captured each got them no further in their search for a way to end the rebellion. They could only hope to do that by destroying Washington's army. He came early to that realization, and even though he put the army at risk a few times, on the whole he zealously protected it by what has been described as an aggressive defense.

His Fabian strategy during the winter and spring of 1777 was correct and effective. He was rightly praised for it at the time and should be praised for it today. But he was not a Fabian at heart. He was a fighter, and whenever he thought he could do the British damage he struck.

He was obsessed with retaking New York City, and I think that was because of the humiliating way in which he was driven from it in 1776. He was a proud man, even vain, and on Long Island and Manhattan he had been made to look quite amateurish. As it turned out, the Franco-American move in 1781 against Cornwallis in Virginia was a master-piece of timing and cooperation—augmented by the ever-necessary ingredient of luck—between Washington and French army and naval commanders. But Yorktown was not Washington's first choice. Five years after the war he wrote to Noah Webster that for an entire year before the Yorktown campaign he had pretended that New York was the target "for the important purpose of inducing the eastern and middle States to make greater exertions in furnishing specific supplies than they otherwise would have done, as well as for the interesting purpose of rendering the enemy less prepared elsewhere." He would only have attacked New York, he claimed, if its garrison had been sufficiently weak-ened by sending reinforcements to the South. That passage should be taken with a large grain of salt, as should his diary entry of 1 August 1781, in which he wrote that since "there was much reason to believe that part (at least) of the Troops in Virginia were recalled to reinforce New York and therefore I turned my views more seriously (than I had before done) to an operation to the Southward." A leading historian of the war, John Shy, has questioned whether diary entries for 1781 were written on the dates given or later.[5]

The decision to march south with the combined French and Ameri-can armies was made for Washington by the French. Washington learned of it on 14 August, and if we accept Timothy Pickering's testimony, as related by his son, the news produced one of Washington's rare eruptions of wrath. On that day Colonel Pickering, with Robert Morris, went to Washington's headquarters to confer with him and found the great man "striding to and fro in such a state of uncontrolled excitement that he did not seem to notice their presence. They immediately withdrew." Half an hour later they were summoned and "found him clothed with his usual serene dignity of countenance and mien. The terrific storm had wholly passed, and was succeeded by a perfect calm." Once they had concluded their business, Washington apologized for the outburst they had witnessed and explained "how bitterly and utterly he had been disappointed" that morning to receive a letter from the French admiral, de Grasse, stating that instead of proceeding to New York he was going to the Chesapeake. As angry as he was, however, Washington the realist took over and immediately began planning for the march to Yorktown.[6]

Given Washington's strategic shortcomings, mixed operational record, and serious tactical deficiencies, what positive things can we say about him as a field commander? First, there is no doubt that he was an inspired battle captain, or as we say today, combat commander. Once the shooting started, character and instinct took over. He knew where he belonged, rode to the guns, and there acted as an inspiration to his officers and men.

Second, he was a gifted administrator whose attention to the duties of his office was awesome. The potential existed for total confusion, but Washington's sure command of the reins of administration prevented chaos, and he demanded of subordinates strict attention to their duties as well.

Third, and most importantly, we must always keep in mind that Washington commanded a revolutionary army, and that is how he must be judged. He was a revolutionary leader of the first rank, a skillful politician, and a charismatic figure throughout the land. He was a nationalist in a nation where political allegiances were all too often tied to localities and states. His nationalism was one of his greatest gifts to his fellow Americans, for he became a symbol throughout the nation of America, not Virginia or Pennsylvania or Massachusetts, as one's country.

Fourth, a revolutionary army does not necessarily have to win many battles, only the key battles, and this Washington did in the Trenton/ Princeton campaign. All of those other battles and campaigns won by the British were for naught. The main responsibilities of a revolutionary army are to survive as a fighting force, allow the enemy the cities if you must, but deny him the permanent occupation of the countryside, and all the while whittle away at his will to continue the struggle. In these Washington was a smashing success. But those goals conflicted with his fighting instinct. He understood early on, after the disasters on Long Island and at Kips Bay, that the army could not stand against the British in formal battle. This began to change with the army of 1777 that marched out of Morristown, but it was not until von Steuben's lessons at Valley Forge that the Continental Army came to resemble British regulars in the open field. Even then, however, the army could not be risked in a winner-take-all slugfest. For the army had become the Revolution, and without it the Cause was doomed. To Washington the fighting general, however, this was a bitter pill, and at Brandywine and Germantown he placed the army at risk and got away with it because of the fighting abilities of the common soldier and the nature of his enemy.

What of Washington as commander in chief? Here we are on solid ground. Through eight long years of war he kept the army in the field in the face of crushing adversities. In doing this, he saved the Revolution. He was able to do it not only because he was a great leader of men but also because he was a very good politician, and I use the word *politician* in the very best sense, of one who can get things done while on the whole maintaining one's principles. And with regard to the necessity in war and peace of keen political leadership, I should add that the modern reader who holds our contemporary extreme distaste for politicians should be aware that our great presidents also were canny politicians; otherwise they would not have been great presidents. Washington had to be in almost daily contact with Congress, either by correspondence, or face-to-face when congressmen visited headquarters. He was acutely aware that Congress was his boss, and he was devoted to the principle of civil supremacy. He also had to deal often with state governors and legislators. Here is where his many years of experience as a legislator himself paid off, first in the Virginia House of Burgesses, which he entered in 1759, then in both the First and Second Continental Congresses. A democratic legislature is not an efficient body, and never can be if it does its job of bringing about compromise among conflicting needs, desires, concerns, and interests, of stroking egos, stoking passions, and quelling revolts among members, who will range from minds brilliant to mediocre to, shall we say, of limited comprehension. It was imperative that commander in chief and Congress work effectively together. And so firmly, patiently, but always with the utmost courtesy, often bitterly frustrated yet never giving up, Washington dealt successfully with this critical aspect of his job. It is impossible to imagine the arrogant Conway, the eccentric Lee, or the wily Gates, who once got into a shouting match with delegates on the floor of Congress, coping with this all-important part of the job of commander in chief.

Character was the overriding gift that Washington brought to the Cause. During the protracted discussions and communications with the French commanders over the target for a joint operation, at the end Washington revealed a character trait that was of immeasurable value to himself and the nation. Can we imagine Horatio Gates or Charles Lee handling the French fait accompli as smoothly as Washington did? Colonel Pickering's son related his father's description of Washington when he first learned of Admiral de Grasse's decision and shortly thereafter:

> In relating the details of this occasion, and describing the furious outburst of Washington's wrath at the first interview, and its entire dissapearance at the second, with so short an interval of time, Colonel Pickering used to say that such a complete triumph of a great mind, over adversity and over itself, he had never witnessed. The common impression, perhaps, is that Washington was a man of cold temperament. The truth is that he naturally had the strongest passions, and deepest sensibility of; and affords one of the most remarkable instances in human history of habitual and almost constant self-control.[7]

Washington was a great coalition commander, and that is precisely what was needed. Add to that his strength of character and his leadership abilities and we find, in James Thomas Flexner's words, the "Indispensable Man." His ability to lead a coalition army went beyond the touchy task of operating smoothly with his French allies once a French army and fleet arrived. We have caught glimpses of the sectionalism that existed in America then, of the hard feelings between northern and southern troops and politicians, feelings that would one day erupt into the maelstrom of civil war. Washington was above such feelings and strove throughout the war to build a national army and weld the country into one, efforts that lasted beyond the war and into his presidency. In that regard Washington the nationalist stood head and shoulders above another general from Virginia, Robert E. Lee, who more than eighty years later chose his state over his country.

John Adams often harshly criticized Washington during the war and loathed his deification. But "I loved and revered the man." He explained Washington's greatness in terms of the control the Virginian had over his passions. Adams wrote that Washington "possessed the gift of silence. This I esteem as one of the precious talents. He had great self-command. It cost him a great exertion sometimes, and a constant constraint; but to preserve so much equanimity required a great capacity." Thomas Jefferson supported Adams's judgment. "His temper was naturally high toned; but reflection and resolution had obtained a firm and habitual ascendency over it." To drive home his point, Jefferson added, "If ever, however, it broke its bonds, he was most tremendous in his wrath." When we consider the inhuman pressures that Washington underwent during eight years of war, the assessments of Adams and Jefferson take on added meaning. That august figure, tall and commanding, silently listening and observing, coming to his decisions slowly but firmly, struck awe into his contemporaries. His was the starring role, and he knew it, and he played it to the hilt.[8]

Writing in 1814, drawing "on an acquaintance of thirty years," briefly and in simple language, Jefferson gave us the essence of the man:

> He was, indeed, in every sense of the words, a wise, a good, and a great man.[9]

Notes

Abbreviations

Anderson, *Recollections*   *Personal Recollections of Captain Enoch Anderson* (1896; repr., New York, 1971).

André, *Journal*   John André, *Major André's Journal . . . June 1777 to November 1778* (Tarrytown, N.Y., 1930).

AR   Henry Clinton, *American Rebellion: Sir Henry Clinton's Narrative of His Campaigns, 1775–1782*, ed. William B. Willcox (New Haven, 1954).

Baurmeister   Carl Leopold Baurmeister, *Revolution in America: Confidential Letters and Journals 1776–1784 of Adjutant General Baurmeister of the Hessian Forces*, trans. and ed. Bernhard J. Uhlendorf (New Brunswick, N.J., 1957).

Bostwick, *Memoirs*   "A Connecticut Soldier under Washington: Elisha Bostwick's Memoirs of the First Year of the Revolution," ed. William S. Powell, *William and Mary Quarterly*, 3rd ser., 6, no. 1 (1949): 94–107.

Commager and Morris   Henry Steele Commager and Richard B. Morris, *The Spirit of 'Seventy-six: The Story of the American Revolution as Told by Participants*, 2 vols. (Indianapolis, 1958).

"Contemporary British Account"   "A Contemporary British Account of General Sir William Howe's Operations in 1777," *Proceedings of the American Antiquarian Society*, ed. Robert Francis Seybolt, new ser., 40, no. 1 (1930): 69–92.

Davies, *Documents*   *Documents of the American Revolution, 1770–1783: Colonial Office Series*, 21 vols., ed. K. G. Davies (Shannon, Ire., 1972–1981).

Ewald, *Diary*   Johann Ewald, *Diary of the American War: A Hessian Journal*, trans. and ed. Joseph P. Tustin (New Haven, 1979).

Force, *American Archives*   Peter Force, ed., *American Archives*, 9 vols. (Washington, D.C., 1837–1853).

Graydon, *Memoirs*   Alexander Graydon, *Memoirs of his Own Time, with Reminiscences of the Men and Events of the Revolution* (Philadelphia, 1846).

Gruber, *Howe Brothers*   Ira D. Gruber, *The Howe Brothers and the American Revolution* (Chapel Hill, N.C., 1972).

Hamond Naval Papers   Hamond Naval Papers, 1766–1825, Special Collections, University of Virginia Library.

Heath, *Memoirs*   *Memoirs of Major-General Heath* (Boston, 1798).

Howe, Narrative   "The Narrative of Lieut. Gen Sir William Howe," in Bellamy Partridge, *Sir Billy Howe* (London, 1932).

JCC   *Journals of the Continental Congress.*

Johnston, *Campaigns of 1776*   Henry Phelps Johnston, *The Campaigns of 1776 Around New York and Brooklyn* (1878; repr., New York, 1971).

Lee Papers   Charles Lee, *The Lee Papers,* Collections of the New-York Historical Society for the Year 1871–[1874], 4 vols. (New York, 1872–1875).

Letters of Delegates   *Letters of Delegates to Congress, 1774–1789,* 26 vols., ed. Paul H. Smith (Washington, D.C., 1976–2000).

Ludlum *Weather*   David M. Ludlum, "The Weather of American Independence," *Weatherwise* 26–30:33.

McCarty, *Journal*   "The Revolutionary War Journal of Sergeant Thomas McCarty, ed. Jared C. Lobdell, *Proceedings of the New Jersey Historical Society* 82, no. 1 (1964): 29–46.

Mackenzie, *Diary*   Frederick Mackenzie, *Diary of Frederick Mackenzie, Giving a Daily Narrative of His Military Service as an Officer of the Regiment of Royal Welch Fusiliers during the Years 1775–1781 in Massachusetts, Rhode Island and New York* (Cambridge, Mass., 1930).

McMichael, *Diary*   "Diary of Lieutenant James McMichael of the Pennsylvania Line, 1776–1778," PMHB 16, no. 2 (1892): 129–159.

Martin, *Private Yankee Doodle*   Joseph Plumb Martin, *Private Yankee Doodle: Being a Narrative of the Adventures, Dangers and Sufferings of a Revolutionary Soldier,* ed. George E. Scheer (1962; repr., n.p.: Eastern National, n.d.).

New Letters   Abigail Adams, *New Letters of Abigail Adams, 1788–1801,* ed. Stewart Mitchell (Boston, 1947).

New Records   *New Records of the American Revolution: The Letters, Manuscripts and Documents sent by Lieut.-General Sir Charles Stuart to his Father, the Earl of Bute, 1775–79* (London, 1927).

Peckham, *Toll*   Howard Peckham, *The Toll of Independence: Engagements and Battle Casualties of the American Revolution* (Chicago, 1974).

Peebles, *Diary*   *John Peebles' American War: The Diary of a Scottish Grenadier, 1776–1782,* ed. Ira D. Gruber (Mechanicsburg, Pa.: Stackpole Books, 1998).

PGW: Col. Ser.   George Washington, *The Papers of George Washington: Colonial Series,* 10 vols., ed. W. W. Abbot et al. (Charlottesville, Va., 1983–1988).

PGW: Rev. War   George Washington, *The Papers of George Washington: Revolutionary War Series,* 13 vols. to date, ed. W. W. Abbot et al. (Charlottesville, Va., 1985–   ).

PMHB   *Pennsylvania Magazine of History and Biography.*

PNG   *The Papers of General Nathanael Greene,*   vols. 1 and 2, ed. Richard K. Showman et al. (Chapel Hill, N.C., 1976, 1980).

Rhodehamel, *AR Writings*   John Rhodehamel, *The American Revolution: Writings from the War of Independence* (New York: Library of America, 2001).

Robertson, *Diaries*   Archibald Robertson, *Archibald Robertson: His Diaries and Sketches in America, 1762–1780* (New York, 1971).

Rodney, *Diary*   *Diary of Captain Thomas Rodney, 1776–1777* (1888; repr., New York: Da Capo Press, 1974).

Scheer and Rankin   George F. Scheer and Hugh Rankin, *Rebels and Redcoats: The American Revolution through the Eyes of Those Who Fought and Lived It* (1957; repr., New York, 1987).

Serle, *Journal*   Ambrose Serle, *The American Journal of Ambrose Serle, Secretary to Lord Howe, 1776–1778* (San Marino, Calif., 1940).

Tallmadge, *Memoir*   Benjamin Tallmadge, *Memoir of Benjamin Tallmadge*, ed. Henry Phelps Johnston (New York, 1904).

Tilghman, *Memoir*   Tench Tilghman, *Memoir of Lieut. Col. Tench Tilghman* (1876; repr., New York, 1971).

Von Münchhausen, *Diary*   *At General Howe's Side, 1776–1778: The Diary . . . of Captain Friedrich von Münchhausen* (Monmouth Beach, N.J.: Philip Frenau Press, 1974).

Preface

1. Winston S. Churchill, *Marlborough: His Life and Times*, 6 vols. (New York: Charles Scribner's Sons, 1933–1938), vol. 1, p. 3.

2. Edmund Burke, "Speech on Moving Resolutions for Conciliation with the Colonies," 3/22/1775, in *Edmund Burke: Selected Writings and Speeches on America*, ed. Thomas H. D. Mahoney (Indianapolis, 1964), pp. 131–132.

1. Invasion! 1776

1. The previous and following quotations are from Robertson, *Diaries*, 86; Charles Stuart to his father, 7/9/1776, in *New Records*, p. 9, for the width of the Narrows; on navigating the approaches to New York Harbor see John A. Tilley, *The British Navy and the American Revolution* (Columbia: University of South Carolina Press, 1987), p. 84.

2. For the first quote, Ira D. Gruber in *American National Biography*; Joseph Townsend, *Some Account of the British Army under the Command of General Howe . . . Which Came to the Knowledge and Understanding of Joseph Townsend* (Philadelphia: T. Ward, 1846), p. 25.

3. Quoted in John Alden, *A History of the American Revolution* (New York: Alfred A. Knopf, 1969), p. 304.

4. H. W. Wilkin, *Some British Soldiers in America* (London: Hugh Rees, 1914), pp. 1, 23; Robert Wright, *The Life of Major General James Wolfe* (London: Chapman, 1864), p. 468.

5. Stuart to his father, 7/9/1776, *New Records*, 9; General Robertson quoted in William B. Willcox, *Portrait of a General: Sir Henry Clinton in the War of Independence* (New York: Alfred A. Knopf, 1964), p. 99 n. 2.

6. Manning's Report, 7/3/1776, *PGW: Rev. War*, vol. 5, pp. 194–195.

7. Robertson, *Diaries*, p. 87; Sidney Ohrenstein, "Geology of the Revolutionary War in Metropolitan New York," lecture 3/8/2001 at the American Museum of Natural History.

8. Abigail Adams to her sister, 8/9/1789, *New Letters*, p. 19; Rush to Thomas Ruston, 10/29/1775, Benjamin Rush, *Letters of Benjamin Rush*, 2 vols., ed. Lyman H. Butterfield (Princeton, N.J.: Princeton University Press, 1951), vol. 1, p. 92;

Mercer to a Friend, 1760, *PGW: Col. Ser*, vol. 6, p. 192; Jefferson to Walter Jones, 1/2/1814, *Thomas Jefferson: Writings*, ed. Merrill D. Peterson (New York: Library of America, 1984), p. 1319.

9. For the story see Max Farrand, *The Records of the Federal Convention of 1787*, 4 vols. (New Haven: Yale University Press, 1911), vol. 3, pp. 85, 86n.

10. Frank E. Grizzard Jr., *George Washington: A Biographical Companion* (Santa Barbara, Calif.: ABC:CLIO, 2002), 151–154, contains several examples of GW's humorous side; GW to John Augustine Washington, 7/18/1755, *PGW: Col. Ser.*, vol. 1, p. 343; Abigail Adams to her sister, 7/12/1789, *New Letters*, 15.

11. Martha Bland to Francis Randolph, 5/12/1777, in Scheer & Rankin, p. 224.

12. Address to the Continental Congress, 6/16/1775, GW to Burwell Bassett, 6/19/1775, *PGW: Rev. War*, vol. 1, pp. 1, 12; JCC, vol. 2, p. 91.

13. *The Journal of Major George Washington*, fcs. ed. (1754; repr., Williamsburg, Va.: Colonial Williamsburg Foundation, 1959), for Washington's account.

14. "Journal of the Proceedings of Conrad Weiser in His Way to and At Auchwick . . in the year 1754," entry of 3 September, printed in Paul A. W. Wallace, *Conrad Weiser, 1696–1760, Friend of Colonist and Mohawk* (Philadelphia, 1954), p. 367; for excellent, detailed accounts of Washington's two expeditions to the Ohio country see Fred Anderson, *Crucible of War: The Seven Years' War and the Fate of Empire in British North America, 1754–1766* (New York: Vintage Books, 2001), pp. 5–7, 42–65.

15. GW to Mary Ball Washington, 7/18/1755, *PGW: Col. Ser.*, vol. 1, p. 336.

16. This paragraph is based on Don Higginbotham, "Washington and the Colonial American Tradition," in Don Higginbotham, ed., *George Washington Reconsidered* (Charlottesville: University Press of Virginia, 2001), pp. 38–66, with the Forbes quote on p. 54.

17. GW to John Hancock, 6/17/1776, *PGW: Rev. War*, vol. 5, p. 21.

18. Robertson, *Diaries*, for the date of Howe's departure from Halifax.

19. For the British invasion of the Carolinas see John Buchanan, *The Road to Guilford Courthouse: The American Revolution in the Carolinas* (New York: John Wiley & Sons, 1997).

20. GW to Charles Lee, 1/8/1776, Adams to GW, 1/6/1776, GW to Lord Stirling, 3/14/1776, *PGW: Rev. War*, vol. 3, pp. 37, 53, 407.

21. Lee to GW, 1/5/1776, 2/19/1776, ibid., pp. 30, 340; for more assessments and activities by Lee in New York City see his letters to GW of 2/14/1776 and 2/29/1776 in this source, pp. 310–312, 389–392.

22. JCC, vol. 4, pp. 180–181; John Hancock to Lee, 3/1/1776, *Letters of Delegates*, vol. 3, p. 317.

23. Ohrenstein, "Geology of the Revolutionary War in . . . New York," lecture of 3/15/2001, and field trip in New York Harbor, 6/12/2001.

24. Serle, *Journal*, p. 28.

25. There is no decent biography of Lord Howe. The quotation and those that follow are from the *Dictionary of National Biography*.

26. Dartmouth to Gage, 4/9/1774, *The Correspondence of General Thomas Gage with the Secretaries of State, and with the War Office and the Treasury, 1763–1775*, vol. 2, ed. Clarence Edwin Carter (New Haven, Conn.: Yale University Press, 1933), p. 160.

27. "Declaration and Resolves of the First Continental Congress, 10/17/1774," in *Documents of American History*, 7th ed., ed. Henry Steele Commager (New York: Appleton-Century-Crofts, 1963), p. 83.

28. George III to Lord North, 12/15/1774, 11/18/1774, 2/15/1775, *The Correspondence of King George III*, 6 vols, ed. Sir John Fortescue (1927–1928; repr., London: Frank Cass & Co., 1967), vol. 3, pp. 154, 156, 175; *The Journal of Nicholas Cresswell, 1774–1777* (New York: Dial Press, 1924), p. 259.

29. For the debate in London see Gruber, *Howe Brothers*, chap. 1; see also Gruber's important article "George III Chooses a Commander in Chief" in Ronald Hoffman and Peter. J. Albright, eds., *Arms and Independence: The Military Character of the American Revolution* (Charlottesville: University Press of Virginia, 1984), pp. 177–181.

30. Unless otherwise indicated, the following discussion, to the end of the chapter, is based on Gruber, *Howe Brothers*, chap. 2, and passim.

31. Howe to Germain, 4/25/1776, 7/7/1776, both quoted in Ira D. Gruber, "America's First Battle: Long Island, 27 August 1776," in Charles E. Heller and William A. Stofft, *America's First Battles, 1776–1965* (Lawrence: University Press of Kansas, 1986), 14–15.

32. Anna M. D. W. P. Stirling, *The Hothams: Being the Chronicles of the Hothams of Scarborough and South Dalton from their hitherto Unpublished Family Papers* (London: H. Jenkins, 1918), pp. 130–131.

33. Gruber, *Howe Brothers*, p. 57.

2. "I scarcely know which way to turn"

1. For more details of the ensuing action see Richard J. Koke, "The Struggle for the Hudson: The British Naval Expedition under Captain Hyde Parker and Captain James Wallace," *The New-York Historical Society Quarterly Bulletin*, vol. 40, no. 2 (1956), pp. 114–175, from which I have benefited; the quotations are on pp. 118–119.

2. Howe to Germain, 8/6/1776, Davies, *Documents*, vol. 12, p. 178.

3. Lee to GW, 2/14/1776, *PGW: Rev. War*, vol. 3, p. 310; Franklin to Anthony Todd, 3/29/1776, *Letters of Delegates*, vol. 3, p. 463.

4. GW to John Hancock, 7/12/1776, *PGW: Rev. War*, vol. 5, p. 284.

5. Diary of Rev. Mr. Shewkirk, Pastor of the Moravian Church, New York, 7/12/1776, in Johnston, *Campaigns of 1776*, part II, p. 110.

6. GW to the New York convention, 8/17/1776, GW's General Orders, 7/13/1776, *PGW: Rev. War*, vol. 6, p. 54; vol. 5, p. 290.

7. Scheer & Rankin, 156; Serle, *Journal*, p. 28.

8. AR, p. 40.

9. GW to Orange County Committee of Safety, 7/14/1776, Ann Hawkes Hayes to George Clinton, 7/14/1776, Clinton to GW, 7/15/1776, *PGW: Rev. War*, vol. 5, pp. 314–315, 319–320, 321n. 4.

10. GW to Orange County Committee of Safety, 7/14/1776, ibid.

11. GW to Benson and Clinton, 7/13/1776, draft, Clinton to GW, 7/23/1776, ibid., pp. 291–292, 436n. 4.

12. Koke, "Struggle for the Hudson," pp. 130–169, for details on the actions at Tappan Zee and the Hudson Highlands.

13. Koke, ibid., pp. 170–171, for Shuldham's quotes.

14. GW to Hancock, 7/14/1776, *PGW: Rev. War,* vol. 5, p. 305; Knox to Lucy Knox, 7/15/1776, in Commager and Morris, vol. 1, 426–427; Serle, *Journal,* pp. 32–33, for a British account.

15. GW to Hancock, 7/14/1776, *PGW: Rev. War,* vol. 5, pp. 306, 308n. 7.

16. Lord Howe to GW, 7/13/1776, ibid., pp. 295–296.

17. Serle, *Journal,* p. 32.

18. See Gruber, *Howe Brothers,* pp. 93–100, for a good discussion of these matters.

19. *Correspondence and Diaries of Samuel Blachley Webb,* 3 vols, ed. Worthington Chauncey Ford (New York, 1893–94), vol. 1, p. 156.

20. Commager and Morris, vol. 1, p. 427.

21. Paterson's account, 7/20/1776, *PGW: Rev. War,* vol. 5, p. 402, ed. note.

22. Memorandum of an Interview with Lieutenant Colonel James Paterson, 7/20/1776, ibid., pp. 400–401.

23. Ibid.; Paterson's account (see n. 21); *Correspondence and Diaries of Samuel Blachley Webb,* vol. 1, p. 156.

24. Howe to Germain, 8/6/1776, Davies, *Documents,* vol. 10, p. 348.

25. Serle, *Journal,* 35; André, *Journal,* p. 54 and passim.

26. GW to Lund Washington, 8/19/1776, *PGW: Rev. War,* vol. 6, pp. 82–83.

27. Gruber, *Howe Brothers,* 27–29; for the documents, Benjamin Franklin Stevens, *Facsimiles of Manuscripts in European Archives Relating to America, 1773–1783,* 26 vols. (London: 1889–1895), vol. 5, nos. 454, 459.

28. GW to Lund Washington, 8/19/1776, *PGW: Rev. War,* vol. 6, pp. 82–83, for the quotation. For a more detailed description of eighteenth-century battlefield tactics and the standard smoothbore musket see John Buchanan, *The Road to Guilford Courthouse: The American Revolution in the Carolinas* (New York: John Wiley & Sons, 1997), pp. 158–161.

29. Livingston to GW, 7/4/1776, GW to Livingston, 7/5/1776, *PGW: Rev. War,* vol. 5, pp. 205, 214; Pickering quoted in Higginbotham, *George Washington and the American Military Tradition* (Athens, Ga.: University of Georgia Press, 1985), 22, p. 154n.; For GW's aides-de-camp, see Arthur Lefkowitz, *George Washington's Indispensable Men: The 33 Aides-de-Camp Who Helped Win American Independence* (Mechanicsburg, Pa.: Stackpole, 2003).

30. GW to Schuyler, 7/16/1776, *PGW: Rev. War,* vol. 5, p. 7.

31. GW to Hancock, 7/3/1776, ibid., p. 193.

32. Orders and instructions to Major General Horatio Gates, 6/24/1776, ibid., pp. 84–86.

33. Schuyler to GW, 7/12/1776, ibid., pp. 286, 289n. 3.

34. General Orders, 8/1/1776, ibid., pp. 534–535.

35. GW to Hancock, 8/14/1776, ibid., vol. 6, p. 23 and n. 4.

36. General Orders, 7/2/1776, 8/6/1776, ibid., vol. 5, pp. 179, 575–576.

37. General Orders, 7/11/1776, ibid., p. 263.

38. In order of quotations, GW to Hancock, 7/11/1776, GW to Gold Selleck Silliman, 7/6/1776, Webb to Jonathan Trumbull, 7/18/1776, Field Officers of the

Connecticut Light Horse to GW, 7/16/1776, and GW's reply, 7/17/1776, ibid., pp. 225, 265–266, 337, ed. notes, pp. 335, 336.

39. GW to Hancock, 12/11/1776, ibid., vol. 7, p. 297.

40. Ward to GW, 7/22/1776, GW to Ward, 7/29/1776, Ward to GW, 8/4/1776, GW to Ward, 8/13/1776, ibid., vol. 5, pp. 427, 505, 562, vol. 6, p. 14.

41. GW to McKean, 7/13/1776, ibid., vol. 6, p. 6.

42. Mercer to GW, 8/19/1776, ibid., p. 78 and n. 2.

43. Livingston to GW, 8/2/1776, GW to Heath, 8/21/1776, ibid., pp. 98–99.

3. "It was hard work to Die"

1. Serle, *Journal*, p. 71; GW to Hancock, 8/22/1776, *PGW: Rev. War*, vol. 6, p. 102; letter from New York, 8/22/1776, Force, *American Archives*, 5th ser., vol. 1, pp. 1111–1112.

2. Greene to GW, 7/25/1776, 8/15/1776, PNG, vol. 1, pp. 262, 287–288; Chambers to Kitty Chambers, 9/3/1776, in Dennis P. Ryan, ed., *A Salute to Courage: The American Revolution as Seen through the Wartime Writings of Officers of the Continental Army and Navy* (New York: Columbia University Press, 1979), pp. 37–38; Baurmeister, p. 35.

3. Serle, *Journal*, pp. 71–72, 74.

4. For my discussion of topography I have relied on maps; my own inspections in Brooklyn; the Ohrenstein lectures; the reports of participants, especially Baurmeister, p. 36, and Samuel Holden Parsons to John Adams, 10/8/1776, in Johnston, *Campaign of 1776*, part II, p. 35, and part I: 142–143, and passim.

5. Greene to GW, 8/15/1776, Greene to Jacob Greene, PNG, vol. 1, pp. 288, 291–292, and n. 2; General Orders, 8/20/1776, *PGW: Rev. War*, vol. 67, p. 89.

6. AR, p. 41n. 3; William B. Willcox, *Portrait of a General: Sir Henry Clinton in the War of Independence* (New York: Alfred A. Knopf, 1964), p. 105; Charles Stuart, "Memorandum of 1776," *New Records*, pp. 15–16.

7. Willcox, *Portrait of a General*, p. 105.

8. Ibid.

9. AR, pp. 41, 42n. 4.

10. GW to Putnam, 8/25/1776, and editorial note, *PGW: Rev. War*, vol. 6, pp. 126–128; Reed to his wife, 8/24/1776, in William Bradford Reed, *Letters and Correspondence of Joseph Reed*, vol. 1 (Philadelphia, 1847), p. 220.

11. General Greene's Orders, 6/1/1776, PNG, vol. 1, pp. 221–222 and n. 2; Baurmeister to Baron von Jungkenn, 9/2/1776, Baurmeister, p. 39; Johnston, *Campaign of 1776*, part 1, pp. 65–87 (Montresor quotation on p. 67n. 1), is the best and most detailed description of the defensive works.

12. GW to Putnam, 8/24/1776, *PGW: Rev. War*, vol. 6, pp. 126–128; NG Papers, p. 293n. 3, for reasonable speculation by the editors with regard to Greene's intentions.

13. Eric Schmitt, "U.S. Review of Deadly Afghanistan Battle Finds Lapses," *New York Times*, 5/2/5/2002, p. A3.

14. AR, p. 42; Charles Stuart Manuscript, *New Records of the American Revolution*, p. 18.

15. Letter of a Pennsylvania Officer, 8/27/1776, in Thomas W. Field, *The Battle of Long Island*, Memoirs of the Long Island Historical Society, vol. 2 (Brooklyn, 1869), p. 485; Samuel Holden Parsons to John Adams, 10/8/1776, Edward Burd to Jasper Yeates, 9/3/1776, in Johnston, *Campaign of 1776*, part 2, pp. 35, 48.

16. "Extract from the Journal of Col. Atlee," *Pennsylvania Archives*, 2nd ser., ed. John B. Linn and William H. Egle (Harrisburg, Pa., 1874), vol. 1, p. 515; Parsons to John Adams, 10/8/1776, in Johnston, *Campaign of 1776*, part 2, p. 35.

17. *AR*, p. 42; William Glanville Evelyn, *Memoir and Letters of Captain W. Glanville Evelyn: of the 4th Regiment ("Kings Own") from North America, 1774–1776, edited and annotated by G. D. Scull* (Oxford: J. Parker, 1879), p. 90n.

18. *AR*, p. 42.

19. "Journal of Col. Samuel Miles, Concerning the Battle of Long Island, 1776," *Pennsylvania Archives*, 2nd ser., vol. 1, pp. 520–522, for this paragraph and to the end of the section.

20. Baurmeister, p. 37.

21. Ibid., pp. 36–37; Brodhead to the Convention of the State of Pennsylvania, 9/5/1776, in Johnston, *Campaign of 1776*, part 2, pp. 64–65.

22. Tallmadge, *Memoir*, p. 11.

23. Stirling to GW, 8/29/1777, *PGW: Rev. War*, vol. 6, pp. 159–161.

24. John C. Dann, ed., *Revolution Remembered: Eyewitness Accounts of the War for Independence* (Chicago: University of Chicago Press, 1980), p. 50.

25. Jabez Fitch, *The New York Diary of Lieutenant Jabez Fitch of the 17th (Connecticut) Regiment from August 22, 1776 to December 15, 1777* (New York: Colburn and Tegg, 1954), pp. 31, 33–35, to the end of the chapter.

4. The Night of the Fox

1. Howe to Germain, 9/3/1776, Davies, *Documents*, vol. 12, p. 216.

2. "The Narrative of Lieutenant General Sir William Howe," in Bellamy Partridge, *Sir Billy Howe* (London: Longmans, Green), p. 264.

3. Stuart, "Retrospect of Events in America, for the operation in New York and New Jersey, 1776," *New Records*, p. 16; Gruber, *Howe Brothers*, pp. 113–114 and no. 67 discusses the reactions of British officers.

4. Robertson, *Diaries*, p. 94, and for readers interested in siege warfare as practiced in the eighteenth century, see John Buchanan, *Road to Guilford Courthouse: The American Revolution in the Carolinas* (New York: John Wiley & Sons, 1997), pp. 53–57 and p. 406n. 12 for citations to detailed studies; Robert Hanson Harrison to John Hancock, 8/27/1776, *PGW: Rev. War*, vol. 6, p. 142; Graydon, *Memoirs*, pp. 164–166; Serle, *Journal*, p. 80.

5. General Orders, 8/29/1776, *PGW: Rev. War*, vol. 6, p. 152; William B. Reed, *Life and Correspondence of Joseph Reed*, vol. 1 (Philadelphia: Lindsay & Blakiston, 1847), pp. 226–227n; *The Diary of Lieutenant von Bardeleben and other von Donop Regiment Documents*, tr. Bruce E. Burgoyne (Bowie, Md.: Heritage Books, 1998), p. 60; Robertson quoted in Piers Mackesy, *The War for America, 1775–1783* (Cambridge, Mass.: Harvard University Press, 1964), p. 88; Tallmadge, *Memoir*, p. 11; Graydon, *Memoirs*, p. 166.

6. Shewkirk Diary in Johnston, *Campaign of 1776*, part 2, pp. 114–115, for the "prodigious" rain that day; Fithian quoted in Ludlum, *Weather* 28, no. 3 (1975): 121; Scott to John Jay, 9/6/1776, *The Correspondence and Public Papers of John Jay*, ed. Henry Phelps Johnston, 4 vols. (New York: G. P. Putnam's Sons, 1890–1893), vol. 1, p. 79.

7. Council of War, *PGW: Rev. War*, vol. 6, pp. 153–154; an excellent discussion of the weather, based on primary sources, is Ludlum, *Weather* 28, no. 3 (1975): 118–121, 147.

8. Martin, *Private Yankee Doodle*, pp. 28–29.

9. Chambers to Kitty Chambers, 9/3/1776, Dennis P. Ryan, ed., *A Salute to Courage: The American Revolution as Seen through the Wartime Writings of Officers of the Continental Army and Navy* (New York: Columbia University Press, 1978), p. 39.

10. Samuel Eliot Morison, *The Maritime History of Massachusetts, 1783–1860* (Boston: Houghton Mifflin, 1921), p. 24; Graydon, *Memoirs*, p. 148; George Athan Billias, *General John Glover and His Marblehead Mariners* (New York: Henry Holt, 1960), pp. 97–104, for details of the crossing well told, and for leading me to the Morison quotation.

11. Tallmadge, *Memoir*, pp. 308–309.

12. "Account of General Edward Hand," *Pennsylvania Archives*, 2nd ser., vol. 10, pp. 308–309.

13. Tallmadge, *Memoir*, pp. 12–13.

14. Ibid., p. 13.

15. Shewkirk Diary in Johnston, *Campaign of 1776*, part 2, p. 115.

16. Serle, *Journal*, p. 88; Louis L. Tucker, ed., "'To my inexpressible astonishment': Admiral Sir George Collier's Observations on the Battle of Long Island," *The New-York Historical Society Quarterly Bulletin*, vol. 48, no. 4 (1964), p. 304.

17. GW to Hancock, 9/2/1776, *PGW: Rev. War*, vol. 6, p. 199.

18. Collier, "'To my inexpressible astonishment,'" p. 305.

19. Lord Howe to Germain, 9/20/1776, Davies, *Documents*, vol. 12, p. 225; Gruber, *Howe Brothers*, pp. 116–117, on which much of this paragraph is based.

20. GW to Hancock, 8/31/1776, *PGW: Rev. War*, vol. 6, p. 178; JCC, vol. 5, pp. 737–738; Lewis Morris to John Jay, 9/8/1776, Bartlett to William Whipple, 9/3/1776, *Letters of Delegates*, vol. 5, pp. 84–95, 126.

21. Franklin to Lord Howe, 7/20/1776, Commager and Morris, vol. 1, p. 449.

22. John Adams, *Diary*, ed. L. H. Butterfield, vol. 3, pp. 417–420.

23. Unless otherwise indicated, the quotations in this paragraph and those following are from "Henry Strachey's Notes on Lord Howe's Meeting with a Committee of Congress," in *Letters of Delegates*, vol. 5, pp. 137–142. Accounts by two of the American representatives, conveniently found in the same source, are Rutledge to GW, 9/11/1776 (p. 137), Adams to Abigail Adams, 9/14/1776 (pp. 158–159), and Adams to Samuel Adams, 9/14/1776 (pp. 159–161); see also Committee's Report to Congress, JCC, vol. 5, pp. 765–766; *Diary of John Adams*, vol. 3, pp. 419–423; and Lord Howe to Germain, 9/20/1776, Davies, *Documents*, vol. 12, pp. 225–227.

24. Serle, *Journal*, pp. 100–101.

5. Manhattan Transfer

1. GW to Hancock, 8/31/1776, *PGW: Rev. War*, vol. 6, p. 177.

2. GW to Hancock, 9/2/1776, 9/8/1776, ibid., pp. 199–200, 252.

3. Haslet to Rodney, 9/4/1776, *Letters to and from Caesar Rodney, 1756–1784*, ed. George Herbert Ryden (Philadelphia: University of Pennsylvania Press, 1933), p. 112.

4. John Alsop to Alexander McDougall, 2/12/1776, and Hancock to New Jersey Provincial Convention, 2/12/1776, *Letters of Delegates*, vol. 3, pp. 99, 234–235.

5. GW to Hancock, 9/8/1776, *PGW: Rev. War*, vol. 6, pp. 248–252; AR, pp. 44–45.

6. GW to Hancock, 9/8/1776, *PGW: Rev. War*, vol. 6, pp. 249–250.

7. Ibid., p. 251.

8. JCC, vol. 5, p. 749; From Certain General Officers to GW, 9/11/1776, *PGW: Rev. War*, vol. 6, p. 279; Greene to GW, 9/5/1776, PNG, vol. 1, p. 295.

9. GW to Hancock, 9/14/1776, *PGW: Rev. War*, vol. 6, p. 308.

10. GW to Hancock, 9/16/1776, ibid., p. 313.

11. AR, pp. 44–45.

12. Martin, *Private Yankee Doodle*, pp. 32–33.

13. Mackenzie, *Diary*, p. 45.

14. Ibid., p. 46.

15. Ibid.; Martin, *Private Yankee Doodle*, p. 33.

16. Martin, *Private Yankee Doodle*, p. 34; *Journal of Rear-Admiral Bartholomew James, 1752–1828*, vol. 6, ed. John Knox Laughton et al., Publications of the Navy Records Society (London, 1896), p. 31.

17. Rodney Atwood, *The Hessians: Mercenaries from Hesse-Kassel in the American Revolution* (Cambridge, Eng.: Cambridge University Press, 1980), p. 71.

18. Mackenzie, *Diary*, p. 47; James, *Journal*, vol. 6, p. 31; Martin, *Private Yankee Doodle*, p. 35.

19. "Letters Written during the Revolutionary War by Colonel William Douglas to his Wife Covering the Period July 19, 1775, to December 5, 1776," *The New-York Historical Society Quarterly Bulletin*, vol. 13, no. 3 (1929), p. 122.

20. Martin, *Private Yankee Doodle*, pp. 36–38.

21. GW to Hancock, 9/16/1776, *PGW: Rev. War*, vol. 6, pp. 313–314.

22. See Douglas Southall Freeman, *George Washington*, 7 vols. (New York, 1948–1957), vol. 4, p. 194n. 118 for judicious commentary on these secondhand accounts.

23. James, *Journal*, vol. 6, p. 31.

24. Howe to Germain, 9/21/1776, *Davies, Documents*, vol. 12, p. 228; AR, pp. 46–47; Robertson, *Diaries*, pp. 98–99; Mackenzie, *Diary*, p. 50.

25. Mackenzie, *Diary*, pp. 49–50.

26. Commager and Morris, vol. 1, p. 467.

27. GW to Nicholas Cooke, 9/17/1776, GW to Hancock, 9/16/1776, *PGW: Rev. War*, vol. 6, pp. 314, 324.

28. GW to Hancock, 9/18/1776, ibid., p. 331; Reed to his wife, 9/17/1776, quoted in Henry Phelps Johnston, *The Battle of Harlem Heights, September 16, 1776* (New York: Columbia University Press, 1897), pp. 134–136.

29. Reed to his wife, 9/17/1776, quoted in Johnston, *Battle of Harlem Heights,* pp. 134–137; GW to Hancock, 9/18/1776, *PGW: Rev. War,* vol. 6, p. 331.

30. GW to Hancock, 9/18/1776, *PGW: Rev. War,* vol. 6, p. 333; Tilghman to James Tilghman Sr., 9/19/1776, Tilghman, *Memoir,* pp. 138–139.

31. GW to Nicholas Cooke, 9/17/1776, GW to Hancock, 9/18/1776, *PGW: Rev. War,* vol. 6, pp. 325, 333; Reed to his wife, 9/17/1776, quoted in Johnston, *Battle of Harlem Heights,* pp. 136–137.

6. "This is a most unfortunate affair"

1. Robertson, *Diaries,* pp. 99–101; Mackenzie, *Diary,* p. 64.

2. GW to Samuel Washington, 7/20/1775; GW to John Hancock, 7/21/1775; Address from the Massachusetts Provincial Congress, 7/3/1775, *PGW: Rev. War,* vol. 1, pp. 134, 138, 52.

3. Schuyler to GW, 7/15/1775, ibid., p. 120.

4. GW to Schuyler, 7/28/1775, ibid., p. 188.

5. Address from Massachusetts Provincial Congress to GW, 7/3/1775, ibid., p. 53.

6. GW to Yates, 8/30/1776, ibid., vol. 6, p. 170.

7. New York Committee of Safety to GW, 8/31/1776, ibid., p. 185.

8. *The Revolutionary War Sketches of William Richardson Davie,* ed. Blackwell P. Robinson (Raleigh: North Carolina Department of Cultural Resources, Division of Archives and History, 1976), p. 13.

9. Greene to Jacob Greene, 9/28/1776, *PNG,* vol. 1, p. 103.

10. Jay to Alexander McDougall, 3/13/1776, *Letters of Delegates,* vol. 3, p. 374.

11. Greene to Jacob Greene, 9/28/1776, *PNG,* vol. 1, p. 303; GW to Hancock, 9/2/1776, *PGW: Rev. War,* vol. 6, pp. 199–200.

12. *JCC,* vol. 5, pp. 762–763; see also Hancock to GW, 9/24/1776, *PGW: Rev. War,* vol. 6, pp. 388–390.

13. Andrew Snape Hamond to Hans Stanley, 9/24/1776, Hamond Naval Papers.

14. Howe to Germain, 11/30/1776, Davies, *Documents,* vol. 12, pp. 258–264; *AR,* pp. 48–49.

15. Robertson, *Diaries,* p. 102; *AR,* ibid.

16. GW to Hancock, 10/11–13/1776, *PGW: Rev. War,* vol. 6, pp. 534–535 and n. 3.

17. GW to John Augustine Washington, 3/31/1776, ibid., vol. 3, p. 570.

18. For the Battle of Sullivan's Island and Lee's role see John Buchanan, *The Road to Guilford Courthouse: The American Revolution in the Carolinas* (New York: John Wiley & Sons, 1997), chap. 1; *Familiar Letters of John and His Wife Abigail Adams during the Revolution,* ed. Charles Francis Adams (1875; repr., Freeport, N.Y.: Books for Libraries Press, 1970), p. 79; John C. Dann, *The Revolution Remembered:*

Eyewitness Accounts of the War for Independence (Chicago: University of Chicago Press, 1980), p. 105.

19. Lee to Gates, *Lee Papers*, vol. 2, pp. 261–262.

20. For Lee's life before the Revolution see John Richard Alden, *General Charles Lee: Traitor or Patriot?* (Baton Rouge: Louisiana State University Press, 1951), chaps. 1–4.

21. Hamilton to Hancock, 10/14–17/1776, Council of War, 10/16/1776, *PGW: Rev. War*, vol. 6, pp. 564–565, 576–577; Alden, *Charles Lee: Traitor or Patriot?*, p. 144; Tilghman to William Duer, Force, *American Archives*, 5th ser., vol. 2, p. 1077.

22. GW to Joseph Trumbull, 10/21/1776, *PGW: Rev. War*, vol. 7, p. 12; Douglas to his wife, 10/25/1776, "Revolutionary War Letters of Colonel William Douglas," *The New-York Historical Society Quarterly Bulletin*, vol. 13, no. 4 (1930), p. 161; Martin, *Private Yankee Doodle*, p. 51.

23. Robertson, *Diaries*, p. 103; unless otherwise indicated, my account in this and the following paragraphs of the action is based on Glover's letter of 10/22/1776, in Force, *American Archives*, 5th ser., vol. 2, p. 1188; Loammi Baldwin to Mary Baldwin, 10/20/1776, quoted in Billias, below, p. 115; and the excellent article by George A. Billias, "Pelham Bay: A Forgotten Battle," *Narratives of the American Revolution: A Collection of Articles from The New-York Historical Society Quarterly Bulletin* (New York: New-York Historical Society, 1975), pp. 105–119.

24. William Glanville Evelyn, *Memoir and Letters of Captain W. Glanville Evelyn: of the 4th regiment ("King's Own") from North America, 1774–1776*, ed. G. D. Scull (Oxford, Eng., 1879), p. 11.

25. *AR*, p. 51.

26. The argument for the importance of Glover's action is in the Billias article cited above, n. 23; Robert Hanson Harrison to Hancock, 10/20/1776, *PGW: Rev. War*, vol. 6, pp. 592–593; Robertson, *Diaries*, pp. 103–104; Peebles, *Diary*, p. 58.

27. Ewald, *Diary*, p. 7; Serle, *Journal*, p. 127.

28. General Orders, 10/23/1776, *PGW: Rev. War*, vol. 7, p. 16.

29. Heath, *Memoirs*, p. 78; Christopher Ward, *The War of the Revolution*, vol. 1 (New York: Macmillan, 1952), p. 262.

30. Ewald, *Diary*, pp. 12–13.

31. Tilghman to his father, 10/31/1776, Tilghman, *Memoirs*, p. 145; Haslet to Rodney, 11/12/1776, *Letters to and from Caesar Rodney, 1756–1784*, ed. George Herbert Ryden (Philadelphia: University of Pennsylvania Press, 1933), p. 142; Bostwick, *Memoirs*, pp. 94–107.

32. Howe, *Narrative*, 265–266; see Gruber, *Howe Brothers*, pp. 132–133, for speculation by Sir William's closest student.

33. Council of War, 11/6/1776, GW to Hancock, 11/6/1776, GW to Nathanael Greene, 11/8/1776, Instructions to Ezekiel Cheever, 11/10/1776, Instructions to Colonel Henry Knox, 11/10/1776, *PGW: Rev. War*, vol. 7, pp. 92, 96, 116, 130–131, 133.

34. Instructions to Major General Charles Lee, 11/10/1776, ibid., vol. 7, pp. 133–135.

35. Instructions to Major General William Heath, 11/12/1776, ibid., vol. 7, p. 147; Heath, *Memoirs*, p. 95.

36. GW to Greene, 11/8/1776, GW to an anonymous officer, 10/21/1776, ibid., vol. 7, pp. 3, 116; *JCC*, vol. 6, p. 866.

37. GW to Greene, 11/8/1776, *PGW: Rev. War*, vol. 7, pp. 115–116.

38. Greene to GW, 11/9/1776, *PNG*, vol. 1, p. 120.

39. GW to Hancock, 11/14/1776, Greene to GW, 11/15/1776, *PGW: Rev. War*, vol. 7, pp. 154, 162.

40. Magaw to Greene, 11/15/1776, *PNG*, vol. 1, pp. 350–351; see also Mackenzie, *Diary*, p. 108, for corroboration of the terms delivered by Paterson.

41. GW to Hancock, 11/16/1776, *PGW: Rev. War*, vol. 7, p. 163; Greene to Knox, 11/17/1776, *PNG Papers*, vol. 1, p. 352.

42. Mackenzie, *Diary*, p. 108.

43. Bruce E. Burgoyne, ed., *The Trenton Commanders* (Bowie, Md.: Heritage Books, 1997), p. 6; Mackenzie, *Diary*, p. 6; Rodney Atwood, *The Hessians: Mercenaries from Hesse-Kassel in the American Revolution* (Cambridge, Eng.: Cambridge University Press, 1980), p. 79.

44. Mackenzie, *Diary*, pp. 109–111.

45. Ibid., pp. 111–112.

46. Graydon, *Memoirs*, pp. 206–207.

47. Ibid., p. 222.

48. Greene to Knox, 11/17/1776, *PNG*, vol. 1, p. 352.

49. GW to John Augustine Washington, 11/6–19/1776, *PGW: Rev. War*, vol. 7, p. 103; GW to Reed 8/22/1779, George Washington, *The Writings of George Washington, from the Original Manuscript Sources, 1745–1799*, 39 vols, ed. John C. Fitzpatrick (Washington, D.C.: U.S. Government Printing Office, 1931–1944), vol. 16, pp. 151–152; Lee to Benjamin Rush, *Lee Papers*, vol. 2, p. 288.

50. Mackenzie, *Diary*, pp. 112–113.

7. "Constant perplexities and mortifications"

1. Arthur K. Lefkowitz, *The Long Retreat: The Calamitous American Defense of New Jersey, 1776* (New Brunswick, N.J.: Rutgers University Press, 1998), p. 42, n. 2, 3; Ewald, *Diary*, p. 17; Howe to Germain, 11/30/1776, Davies, *Documents*, vol. 12, p. 263.

2. Lefkowitz, *Long Retreat*, p. 45n. 1, for an excellent analysis of the British landing place; Adrian C. Leiby, *The Revolutionary War in the Hackensack Valley: The Jersey Dutch and the Neutral Ground, 1775–1783* (New Brunswick, N.J.: Rutgers University Press, 1962), p. 66n. 1, for Wayne's assessment; Howe to Germain, 11/30/1776, Davies, *Documents*, vol. 12, p. 263.

3. *Thomas Paine, Collected Writings*, ed. Eric Foner (New York: Literary Classics of the United States, 1995), vol. 1, p. 93; Ewald, *Diary*, p. 18; Johann Hinrichs, "Extracts from the Letter-Book of Captain Johann Hinrichs of the Hessian Jager Corps, 1778–1780," *PMHB* 22, no. 2 (1898): 139.

4. Ewald, *Diary*, p. 18.

5. Greene to GW, 10/29/1776, 11/18/1776, Greene to Nicholas Cooke, 12/4/1776, *PNG*, vol. 1, pp. 327, 359–362; Robert Hanson Harrison to Philip

Schuyler, 11/20/1776, Force, *American Archives*, 5th ser., vol. 3, p. 781, for the news reaching Washington.

6. Green to Cooke, *PNG*, vol. 1, p. 362; "Journal of a Pennsylvania Soldier, July–December 1776," *Bulletin of the New York Public Library* 8, no. 11 (1904): 549.

7. Lord Rawdon (?) to Robert Auchmuty, 11/25/1776, Commager and Morris, vol. 1, p. 497; description of Greene's troops quoted in Leiby, *The Revolutionary War in the Hackensack Valley*, p. 72; Greene to GW, 10/29/1776, *PNG*, vol. 1, pp. 326–327.

8. Ewald, *Diary*, p. 18; Greene to Catherine Greene, 12/4/1776, *PNG*, vol. 1, p. 365.

9. GW to John Augustine Washington, 11/6–19/1776, *PGW: Rev. War*, vol. 7, pp. 104–105.

10. Lord Rawdon (?) to Robert Auchmuty, 11/25/1776, Commager & Morris, vol. 1, p. 497.

11. Greene to Nicholas Cooke, 12/4/1776, *PNG*, vol. 1, p. 362; Harrison to Lee, 12/20/1776, Force, *American Archives*, 5th ser., vol. 3, p. 780; GW to Lee, 12/21/1776, *PGW: Rev. War*, vol. 7, p. 194.

12. Lee to Bowdoin, 11/21/1776, *Lee Papers*, vol. 2, pp. 291–292.

13. Unless otherwise indicated, the details of the Lee-Heath dispute and the quotations to the end of the section are from Heath, *Memoirs*, pp. 88–96.

14. Heath to GW, 11/24/1776, GW to Lee, 11/24/1776, *PGW: Rev. War*, vol. 7, pp. 205–208; Lee to Reed, 11/21/1777, *Lee Papers*, vol. 2, p. 301.

15. GW to Lee, 12/27/1776, Lee to GW, 11/30/1776, *PGW: Rev. War*, vol. 7, pp. 224, 235.

16. Quoted in ibid., p. 218n. 1.

17. Heath, *Memoirs*, p. 7, for his description of himself.

18. Hancock to GW, 11/24/1776 and n. 6, GW to Hancock, 11/27/1776, *PGW: Rev. War*, vol. 7, pp. 204–205, 223–224.

19. GW to William Livingston, 11/21/1776, *PGW: Rev. War*, vol. 7, p. 195; *AR*, pp. 55–56n. 34; Mackenzie, *Diary*, pp. 116–118; George O. Trevalyan, *The American Revolution*, part 2, 6 vols. (London, 1909–1914), vol. 2, p. 20.

20. Webb to Trumbull, *Correspondence and Journals of Samuel Blachley Webb*, 3 vols., ed. Worthington Chauncey Ford (New York, 1893), vol. 1, pp. 172–173.

21. GW to Hancock, 11/23/1776, GW to Livingston, 11/23/1776, GW to Forman, 11/24/1776, *PGW: Rev. War*, vol. 7, pp. 196, 198, 203.

22. Ewald, *Diary*, p. 22. Ewald's use of the word *plantation* should not be confused with the big cotton and rice plantations worked by slaves in the antebellum South. The word then meant simply land cultivated, especially in what Ewald would have considered a new land, even though many of the farms, which is what they were, would have existed for well over a century.

23. Reed to Lee, 11/21/1776, *Lee Papers*, vol. 2, pp. 293–294.

24. Lee to Reed, 11/24/1776, ibid., pp. 305–307.

25. GW to Reed, 11/30/1776, *PGW: Rev. War*, vol. 7, p. 237.

26. McMichael, *Diary*, p. 139 (McMichael was a sergeant when he began his diary; he was promoted to lieutenant in March 1777); Greene to Nicholas Cooke,

12/4/1776, *PNG*, vol. 1, p. 362; GW to Hancock, 12/1/1776, *PGW: Rev. War*, vol. 7, p. 244.

27. GW to Lee, 12/1/1776, *PGW: Rev. War*, vol. 7, p. 249.

28. Greene to Cooke, 12/4/1776, *PNG*, vol. 1, p. 362; GW to Hancock, 12/3/1776, *PGW: Rev. War*, vol. 7, p. 255.

29. Anderson, *Recollections*, p. 27.

30. Ibid., pp. 28–29.

31. GW to Hancock, 12/3/1776, GW to Lee, 12/3/1776, *PGW: Rev. War*, vol. 7, pp. 255–257; *JCC*, vol. 6, p. 1000.

32. Lee to GW, 12/4/1776, *PGW: Rev. War*, vol. 7, pp. 259–260.

33. John Richard Alden, *Charles Lee: Traitor or Patriot?* (Baton Rouge: Louisiana State University Press, 1951), p. 154.

34. GW to Hancock, 12/5/1776, GW to Humpton, 12/5/1776, *PGW: Rev. War*, vol. 7, pp. 262–263, 265.

35. Force, *American Archives*, 5th ser., vol. 3, pp. 927–928, for the proclamation; Serle, *Journal*, p. 151; Ewald, *Diary*, p. 125.

36. GW to Hancock, 12/8/1776, *PGW: Rev. War*, vol. 7, p. 273; McMichael, *Diary*, p. 139; Ewald, *Diary*, p. 25.

37. Von Münchhausen, *Diary*, p. 6.

38. GW to Hancock, 12/8/1776, Greene to GW, 12/7/1776, Lee to GW, 12/8/1776 (two letters), *PGW: Rev. War*, vol. 7, pp. 269, 273, 276–277.

39. Von Münchhausen, *Diary*, pp. 6–7.

40. Lee to GW, 12/11/1776, GW to Lee, 12/14/1776, *PGW: Rev. War*, vol. 7, pp. 301, 335.

41. I have based this paragraph on Alden, *Charles Lee: Traitor or Patriot?*, pp. 155–158, as well as "New War Letters of Banastre Tarleton," *Narratives of the Revolution in New York: A Collection of Articles from The New-York Historical Society Quarterly Bulletin*, ed. Richard M. Ketchum (New York: New-York Historical Society, 1975), pp. 126–129, and also on the sources cited below.

42. Lee to Gates, 12/13/1776, *Lee Papers*, vol. 2, p. 348.

43. Force, *American Archives*, 5th ser., vol. 3, p. 1247; Sullivan to GW, 12/13/1776, GW to Hancock, 12/15/1776, *PGW: Rev. War*, vol. 7, pp. 328, 344.

44. Frank Moore, *Diary of the American Revolution*, vol. 1 (New York: Charles T. Evans, 1863), p. 361; Edward W. Harcourt, ed. *Harcourt Papers*, 14 vols. (Oxford, Eng.: 1880–1905?), vol. 11: 180–181.

45. Rodney, *Diary*, pp. 18–19.

8. "I conclude the troops will be in perfect security"

1. GW to Lund Washington, 12/10–17/1776, *PGW: Rev. War*, vol. 7, pp. 289–292 and no. 4 for this and the preceding paragraph.

2. Douglas to his wife, 12/5/1776, "Letters Written during the Revolutionary War by Colonel William Douglas to His Wife Covering the Period July 19, 1775, to December 5, 1776," *The New-York Historical Society Quarterly Bulletin*, vol. 14, no. 1 (1931), p. 42.

3. Douglas to his wife, 10/15/1776, ibid., 13, no. 4 (1930): 180.

4. Howe to Germain, 12/20/1776, Davies, *Documents*, vol. 12, p. 266; von Münchhausen, *Diary*, pp. 6, 56n. 13.

5. General Orders, 12/12/1776, Orders to Colonel John Cadwalader, 12/12/1776, *PGW: Rev. War*, vol. 7, pp. 303–305.

6. Orders to Brigadier General James Ewing, 12/12/1776, Orders to Brigadier General Philemon Dickinson, 12/12/1776, ibid., pp. 305–307.

7. GW to Hancock, 12/12/1776, ibid., pp. 309–310, and p. 320n. 1 for the resolution ordering Philadelphia defended; *JCC*, vol. 6, pp. 1024–1027.

8. GW to Hancock, 12/12/1776, *PGW: Rev. War*, vol. 7, p. 309.

9. Howe's order quoted in Christopher Ward, *The War of the Revolution*, vol. 1, ed. John Alden (New York: Macmillan, 1952), p. 291; Howe to Germain, 12/20/1776, Davies, *Documents*, vol. 12, p. 267.

10. Thomas Jones, *History of New York during the Revolutionary War*, vol. 1, ed. Edward F. DeLancey (New York, 1879), p. 351.

11. GW to Brigadier Generals James Ewing, Hugh Mercer, Adam Stephen, and Lord Stirling, 12/14/1776, *PGW: Rev. War*, vol. 7, p. 332.

12. GW to Gates, 12/14/1776, ibid., p. 333.

13. Joseph Reed to GW, 12/22/1776, ibid., pp. 415–416.

14. GW to the Pennsylvania Council of Safety, 12/15/1776, ibid., p. 348.

15. GW to Gates, GW to Heath, GW to Trumbull, 12/14/1776 (all), ibid., pp. 333–334, 340.

16. GW to Hancock, 12/20/1776, Knox's Plan for Artillery, 12/18/1776, ibid., pp. 321n. 1 (for Congress's grant of power to Washington), 381, 387n. 4.

17. GW to Hancock, 12/21/1776, ibid., p. 382.

18. Greene to Hancock, 12/21/1776, *PNG*, vol. 1, pp. 370–374; Gerard to Comte de Vergennes, 3/8/1779, in *George Washington as the French Knew Him*, ed. and trans. Gilbert Chinard (New York, 1969), pp. 73–74.

19. *PGW: Rev. War*, vol. 7, pp. 462–463n. 1.

20. GW to Gates, 12/23/1776, ibid., p. 418; Paul David Nelson, *General Horatio Gates: A Biography* (Baton Rouge: Louisiana State University Press, 1976), p. 75. Concerning my assertion that Gates had never led troops into battle, he did command 4th Independent Company of Foot at Braddock's defeat on the Monongahela in 1755, where he was badly wounded. But since it was his first troop command, and to that date he had not experienced combat, he was accompanied by Captain Robert Cholmley, whose assignment was to make all combat decisions. When the shooting started, it was Cholmley who led the company. At Saratoga, Gates stayed in his headquarters tent while Arnold, Morgan, Dearborn, Poor, and others led the troops into battle. In 1780 at Camden Gates was so far behind his main line of defense he had no idea what was going on during the British attack, and when the militia broke and ran he went with them, leaving the Continentals and his deputy, the gallant Major General de Kalb, to fight on alone. For Gates's inept and disgraceful performance at Camden see John Buchanan, *The Road to Guilford Courthouse: The American Revolution in the Carolinas* (New York: John Wiley & Sons, 1997), chap. 12.

21. Orders to Carpenter Wheaton, 12/20/1776, 12/21/1776, *PGW: Rev. War*, vol. 7, pp. 391, 408.

22. GW to Joseph Reed, 12/23/1776, ibid., p. 423.

23. *The Autobiography of Benjamin Rush*, ed. George W. Corner (1948; repr., Westport, Conn.: Greenwood Press, 1970), p. 124.

24. GW to Cadwalader, 12/24/1776, ibid., p. 425; Charles H. Lesser, *Sinews of Independence: Monthly Strength Reports of the Continental Army* (Chicago: University of Chicago Press, 1976), p. 43.

25. Dickinson to GW, 12/14/1776, *PGW: Rev. War*, vol. 7, pp. 427–428.

26. For this and the following three paragraphs, including the quotations, see General Orders, 12/25/1776, ibid., pp. 435–438, the variant in editorial note, and notes 1–4.

27. Ibid., p. 261n. 1 for La Rochefermoy's background and subsequent history.

9. "Success of an Enterprize"

1. The Piel quote is in Bruce E. Burgoyne, ed., *The Trenton Commanders* (Bowie, Md.: Heritage Press, 1997), p. 9; the Wiederhold quote is in "Colonel Rall at Trenton," *PMHB* 22, no. 4 (1898): 462; the rest of the paragraph is based on Rodney Atwood, *The Hessian Mercenaries from Hesse-Kassel in the American Revolution* (Cambridge, Eng.: Cambridge University Press, 1980), pp. 84–96.

2. Quoted in Atwood, *The Hessians*, p. 84.

3. Ibid.

4. Grant to von Donop, 12/17, 21/1776, quoted in Atwood, *The Hessians*, pp. 91–92; the paragraph is based on Atwood.

5. GW to Hancock, 12/27/1776, *PGW: Rev. War*, vol. 7, p. 454; George W. Corner, ed., *Autobiography of Benjamin Rush* (Westport, Conn.: Greenwood Press, 1970), p. 125.

6. My description of the weather is based on Ludlum, *Weather* 29, no. 2 (1976): 74–76.

7. Knox to Lucy Knox, 12/28/1776, Rodney to Caesar Rodney, 12/30/1776, in Commager and Morris, vol. 1: 513–514; Ludlum, *Weather* 29, no. 2 (1976): 76–78.

8. Washington to Humpton, 12/1/1776, *PGW: Rev. War*, vol. 7, p. 248; Alfred Hoyt Bill, *The Campaign of Princeton, 1776–1777* (Princeton, N.J.: Princeton University Press, 1948), pp. 28–29.

9. GW to Hancock, 12/27/1776, *PGW: Rev. War*, vol. 7, p. 454.

10. Ibid; Henry Knox to Lucy Knox, 12/28/1776, Commager and Morris, vol. 1, p. 513; McCarty, *Journal*; Bostwick, *Memoirs*, p. 102.

11. "Colonel Rall at Trenton," p. 465.

12. Hull to Andrew Adams, 1/1/1777, Johnston to Leven Powell, 12/29/1776, *PGW: Rev. War*, vol. 7, p. 457n. 6; Tilghman to his father, 12/27/1776, Tilghman, *Memoir*, p. 149.

13. McMichael, *Diary*, p. 140; "Colonel Rall at Trenton," p. 466; GW to Hancock, 12/27/1776, *PGW: Rev. War*, vol. 7, p. 454.

14. "Colonel Rall at Trenton," p. 466.

15. Tilghman to his father, 12/27/1776, Tilghman, *Memoir*; GW to Hancock, 12/27/1776, *PGW: Rev. War*, vol. 7, p. 454; "Colonel Rall at Trenton," pp. 466–467; Scheffer quoted in Atwood, *The Hessians*, p. 93.

16. Wiederhold quoted in Atwood, *The Hessians*, p. 95.

17. McCarty, *Journal*, p. 45; GW to Hancock, 12/27/1776, *PGW: Rev. War*, vol. 7, p. 454; *Annual Register*, 20 (1777), p. 17; for casualties see editorial notes in *PGW: Rev. War*, vol. 7, pp. 459–461, Tilghman to his father, 12/27/1776, Tilghman, *Memoir*, p. 149, who gives American casualties, but cf. Peckham, *Toll*, p. 27, who agrees with the *Annual Register*.

18. Von Münchhausen, *Diary*, entry of 12/27–31/1776, p. 9.

19. Don Higginbotham, *The War of American Independence: Military Attitudes, Policies, and Practice, 1763–1789* (New York: Macmillan, 1971), p. 166.

20. Rodney to Caesar Rodney, 12/30/1776, Commager and Morris, vol. 1, p. 514.

21. Ludlum, *Weather*, 29, no. 2 (1776): 78, for ice conditions on the Delaware; Christopher Ward, *The War of the Revolution*, vol. 1, ed. John Alden (New York: Macmillan, 1952), p. 304; GW to Hancock, GW to Morris, 12/27/1776 (both), *PGW: Rev. War*, vol. 7, pp. 456, 463; "General Joseph Reed's Narrative of the Movements of the American Army in the Neighborhood of Trenton in the winter of 1776–77," *PMHB*, vol. 8, p. 391.

22. Bostwick, *Memoirs*, pp. 102–103.

23. "General Joseph Reed's Narrative," p. 397; John Cadwalader to GW, Executive Committee to GW, GW to William Heath, GW to Alexander McDougall, 12/28/1776 (all), General Orders, GW to Hancock, 12/29/1776 (both), *PGW: Rev. War*, vol. 7, pp. 464–472, 476–478; Sergeant R———, "The Battle of Princeton," *PMHB*, vol. 20 (1896), p. 515; McMichael, *Diary*, p. 140.

24. *The Journal of Nicholas Cresswell* (New York: Dial Press, 1924), pp. 179–181.

25. General Orders, 12/30/1776, *PGW: Rev. War*, vol. 7, p. 484; Sergeant R———, "The Battle of Princeton," pp. 515–516.

26. Bostwick, *Memoir*, p. 103; "Sergeant John Smith's Diary of 1776," ed. Louise Rau, *Mississippi Valley Historical Review*, vol. 20, no. 2 (1933), pp. 269–270.

27. "Sergeant John Smith's Diary," p. 27n. 51.

28. Ludlum, *Weather*, p. 80; Robertson, *Diary*, p. 118; Ewald, *Diary*, p. 48.

29. Ewald, *Diary*, p. 49; Knox to Lucy Knox, 1/7/1777, in Scheer and Rankin, p. 217; Sergeant White quoted in Richard M. Ketchum, *The Winter Soldiers: The Battles for Trenton and Princeton* (1973; repr., New York: Henry Holt, 1999), p. 290.

30. Jefferson to Walter Jones, 1/2/1814, *Thomas Jefferson: Writings* (New York: Library of America, 1984), p. 1318; James Wilkinson, *Memoirs of My Own Time*, vol. 1 (Philadelphia, 1816), p. 140; John Lardner to Captain Smith, 7/13/1824, GW to Hancock, 1/5/1777 *PGW: Rev. War*, vol. 7, p. 527n. 5, pp. 519–521.

31. Ludlum, *Weather*, 29, no. 2 (1976): 82; Rodney, *Diary*, p. 32; *PGW: Rev. War*, vol. 7, p. 527n. 5.

32. GW to Hancock, 1/5/1777, *PGW: Rev. War*, vol. 7, pp, 521–523; Greene to Nicholas Cooke, 1/10/1777, *PNG*, vol. 2, p. 4; Rodney, *Diary*, p. 32.

33. Wilkinson, *Memoirs*, vol. 1, p. 141.

34. Rodney, *Diary*, pp. 33–34.

35. McMichael, *Diary*, p. 14.

36. Cadwalader quoted in *PGW: Rev. War*, vol. 7, p. 528n. 8; Sergeant R̀———, "The Battle of Princeton," p. 517; Horace Wells Sellers, ed., "Charles Willson Peale,

Artist-Soldier," *PMHB* 38, no. 3 (1914): 280; Greene to Nicholas Cooke, 1/10/1777, *PNG*, vol. 2, p. 5.

37. Sergeant R____ , "The Battle of Princeton," pp. 517–518.

38. Peckham, *Toll*, p. 29; Varnum Lansing Collins, ed., *A Brief Narrative of the Ravages of the British and Hessians at Princeton in 1776–1777* (1906; repr., New York: Arno Press, 1968), pp. 36–37.

39. Rush to Lee, 1/7/1777, *Letters of Benjamin Rush*, vol. 1, ed. L. H. Butterfield (Princeton, N.J.: Princeton University Press, 1951), pp. 125–127.

40. Ewald, *Diary*, pp. 49–50; Robertson, *Diary*, p. 120.

41. GW to Hancock, 1/5/1777, *PGW: Rev. War*, vol. 7, p. 523; Rodney, *Diary*, p. 38; "Charles Willson Peale, Artist-Soldier," p. 283.

42. McMichael, *Diary*, p. 141; Sergeant R———, "The Battle of Princeton," 518–519.

43. Robertson, *Diary*, pp. 120–121.

10. "Harrass their troops to death"

1. Ewald, *Diary*, p. 50; Harcourt to Lord Harcourt, 3/17/1777, in Commager and Morris, vol. 1, p. 524.

2. Howe to Germain, 1/20/1777, quoted in Gruber, *Howe Brothers*, pp. 156–157; this paragraph also draws partly on Gruber, pp. 156–157.

3. GW to Putnam, 1/5/1777, GW to Hancock, 1/7/1777, *PGW: Rev. War*, vol. 7, p. 535, vol. 8, pp. 9–10; McMichael, *Diary*, p. 141.

4. GW to Heath, GW to Putnam, 1/5/1777 (both), GW to Joseph Reed, 1/14/1777, *PGW: Rev. War*, vol. 7, pp. 531, 535, vol. 8, p. 68.

5. Von Münchhausen, *Diary*, p. 9.

6. Ibid.

7. Christopher Ward, *The War of the Revolution*, vol. 1, ed. John Alden (New York: Macmillan, 1952), p. 322; Adams to John Sullivan, 2/22/1777, quoted in Douglas Southall Freeman, *George Washington*, 7 vols. (New York, 1948–1957), vol. 4, p. 382n. 10; GW to Heath, 2/3/1777, GW to Reed, 1/14/1777, GW to Hancock, 1/7/1777, *PGW: Rev. War*, vol. 8, pp. 68–69, 230.

8. Ewald, *Diary*, p. 51.

9. Ibid., p. 52.

10. Ibid.

11. Robertson, *Diary*, p. 122; GW to Hancock, 1/22/1777, *PGW: Rev. War*, vol. 8, pp. 125–126, 128n. 1.

12. Robertson, *Diary*, p. 122.

13. Ibid., pp. 123–124.

14. Ewald, *Diary*, pp. 53–55.

15. Ibid., p. 55.

16. Peebles, *Diary*, pp. 95–97.

17. Ibid., pp. 97–98.

18. Ewald, *Diary*, p. 55.

19. Frederick the Great quoted in Dave R. Palmer, *The Way of the Fox: American Strategy in the War for America, 1775–1783* (Westport, Conn: Greenwood Press,

1975), p. 20; Peter Green, *Alexander of Macedon, 356–323* B.C.: *A Historical Biography* (1974; repr., Berkeley: University of California Press, 1991), p. 394; for amusing examples of two field officers, Nathanael Greene and William Richardson Davie, trying to avoid the jobs of quartermaster general and commissary general, respectively, see John Buchanan, *The Road to Guilford Courthouse: The American Revolution in the Carolinas* (New York: John Wiley & Sons, 1997), pp. 271–275, 293–294.

20. GW to Duer, 1/14/1777, New York Committee of Safety to Washington, 1/22/1776, *PGW: Rev. War*, vol. 8, pp. 63–64, 129–131.

21. Hamilton to Putnam, 6/9/1777, in Harold C. Syrett, ed., *The Papers of Alexander Hamilton, vol. 1, 1776–1778* (New York: Columbia University Press, 1961); Putnam to GW, 6/8/1777, GW to Putnam, 6/10/1777, GW to Mease, 6/13/1777, Mease to GW, 6/13/1777, 7/22/1777, *PGW: Rev. War*, vol. 9, pp. 649, 667, vol. 10, pp. 30, 37–38, 357–359.

22. GW to Jeremiah Wadsworth, 2/3/1777, ibid., p. 238.

23. This paragraph draws heavily on E. Wayne Carp's seminal work *To Starve the Army at Pleasure: Continental Army Administration and American Political Culture, 1775–1783* (Chapel Hill: University of North Carolina Press, 1984), pp. 219–222, and passim for examples (the quotation is on p. 219). For a thorough look at American political culture throughout the Revolutionary era see the excellent book by John Ferling, *A Leap in the Dark: The Struggle to Create the American Republic* (New York: Oxford University Press, 2003).

24. Sergeant R——, "The Battle of Princeton," *PMHB*, vol. 20 (1896), p. 519.

25. This paragraph and the following are based on Elizabeth Fenn's fine book *Pox Americana: The Great Smallpox Epidemic of 1775–1782* (New York: Hill & Wang, 2001), pp. 4–9, 31–43, and passim; throughout this section I have benefited from her scholarship and insights; although it appeared after my manuscript had gone into production, readers interested in this topic should also read Ann M. Becker, "Smallpox in Washington's Army: Strategic Implications of the Disease during the American Revolutionary War," *Journal of Military History*, vol. 68, no. 2 (April 2004), pp. 381–430.

26. Adams to Abigail Smith, 4/13/1764, *The Book of Abigail and John: Selected Letters of the Adams Family, 1762–1784*, ed. L. H. Butterfield et al. (Cambridge, Mass.: Harvard University Press, 1975), p. 30.

27. Adams to Abigail Smith, 4/26/1764, Adams to Abigail Adams, 6/26/1776, ibid., pp. 39–40, 138.

28. This paragraph is based on Fenn, *Pox Americana*, pp. 36–39; see also Abigail Adams to John Adams, 7/21/1776, 8/5/1776, *Book of Abigail and John*, pp. 148–151.

29. Fenn, *Pox Americana*, p. 49; GW to Hancock, 7/21/1775, General Orders, 4/14/1776, *PGW: Rev. War*, vol. 1, p. 140, vol. 4, pp. 58–59.

30. GW to Jonathan Trumbull Sr., 2/10/1777, GW to Hancock, 2/5/1777, GW to William Shippen Jr. 2/8/1777, *PGW: Rev. War*, vol. 8, pp. 251, 264, 304.

31. GW to Shippen, 2/6/1777, GW to Cooke, 2/10/1777, GW to Parsons, 2/10/1777, GW to Baylor, 3/28/1777, ibid., vol. 8, pp. 264, 296–297, 300, vol. 9, p. 1.

32. Martin, *Private Yankee Doodle*, pp. 65–67.

33. Quoted in Scheer and Rankin, p. 224.

34. Citizens of Hanover, Pennsylvania, to GW, 2/12/1777, *PGW: Rev. War,* vol. 8, p. 317.

35. Unless otherwise indicated, this paragraph and those to the end of the chapter are based on Gruber, *Howe Brothers,* pp. 179–188 and passim; "Letters of Charles O'Hara to the Duke of Grafton," *South Carolina Historical Magazine* 65, no. 3 (1964): 177.

36. Gruber, *Howe Brothers,* p. 188.

11. "The American Fabius"?

1. Spencer to GW, 3/2/177, GW to Spencer, 3/11/1777, *PGW: Rev. War,* vol. 8, pp. 489–491, 554–555.

2. GW to Hancock, 1/19/1777, ibid., pp. 102–103.

3. GW to Jonathan Trumbull Sr., 3/6/1777, GW to Hancock, 3/14/1777, return of American forces in New Jersey, 3/15/1777, ibid., pp. 531, 572, 576.

4. For the attitude of the general public, see James Kirby Martin and Mark Edward Lender, *A Respectable Army: The Military Origins of the Republic, 1763–1789* (Wheeling, Il.: Harlan Davidson, 1982), pp. 89–97.

5. GW to Harrison, 1/12/1777, ibid., p. 47, quoted in editorial note.

6. Peebles, *Diary,* p. 108; Hamond Naval Papers; this paragraph is drawn from Gruber, *Howe Brothers,* pp. 224–227 (quotation on p. 227).

7. For Weedon's letter see *PGW: Rev. War,* vol. 9, p. 552n. 1.

8. GW to Sullivan, 5/29/1777, ibid., pp. 558–559.

9. Greene to GW, 5/25/1777, Greene to Trumbull, 5/28/1777, *PNG,* vol. 2, pp. 92–93, 101.

10. GW to Lee, 5/17/1777, *PGW: Rev. War,* vol. 9, pp. 453–454.

11. In addition to the letter quoted, the problem of foreign officers at this time can be traced in GW to Lee, 6/1/1777, Knox to GW, 6/5/1777, GW to Hancock, 6/6/1777, ibid., pp. 580–581, 610–611, 618–620; and Nathanael Greene to Hancock, 7/1/1777, John Adams to Greene, 7/7/1777, *PNG,* vol. 2, pp. 109–114.

12. GW to Hancock, 5/31/1777, *PGW: Rev. War,* vol. 9, pp. 570–572 and n. 1 and 2.

13. General Orders, 6/8/1777; Robertson, *Diaries,* p. 135; "Contemporary British Account," p. 73.

14. Robertson, *Diaries,* p. 136; von Münchhausen, *Diary,* pp. 10, 14, 16.

15. GW to Morgan, 6/13/1777, GW to Richard Peters, 6/20/1777, *PGW: Rev. War,* vol. 10, pp. 31, 88; von Münchhausen, *Diary,* p. 16.

16. General Orders, Order of March, *PGW: Rev. War,* vol. 10, pp. 33–36.

17. Von Münchhausen, *Diary,* p. 16; GW to Sullivan, 7/14/1777 (two), 7/15/1777, ibid., pp. 40–41, 45–46.

18. Robertson, *Diaries,* p. 137; Ewald, *Diary,* pp. 64–65; von Münchhausen, *Diary,* p. 18.

19. Von Münchhausen, *Diary,* p. 18; Ewald, *Diary,* p. 65; GW to Hancock, 6/11/1777, *PGW: Rev. War,* vol. 10, pp. 104–105; Cresswell, *Journal,* p. 252.

20. GW to Hancock, 6/22/1777, 6/25/1777, Matthias Williamson Jr. to GW, 6/24/1777, *PGW: Rev,. War*, vol. 10, pp. 105, 119–124.

21. GW to Hancock, 6/25/1777, ibid., p. 124.

22. Peebles, *Diary;* p. 117; Ewald, *Diary*, p. 69; *The Selected Papers of Charles Willson Peale and His Family*, vol. 1, ed. Lillian B. Miller (New Haven, Conn.: Yale University Press, 1983), p. 236.

23. Ewald, *Diary*, p. 69; Peebles, *Diary*, p. 118; Serle to Lord Dartmouth, 8/30/1777, quoted in Gruber, *Howe Brothers*, p. 230.

24. Freeman, *George Washington*, vol. 4, pp. 362–363n. 16, citing *Dodsley's Annual Register* for 1777, p. 20.

25. John Adams to Abigail Adams, 6/18/1777, *Letters of Delegates*, vol. 7, p. 207; sonnet from Domenico Bertini of Florence, c. 11/12/1777, *PGW: Rev. War*, vol. 12, pp. 220–221.

26. Sam Adams to Greene, 5/12/1777, *PNG Papers*, vol. 2, pp. 77–78; Sam Adams to Warren, 6/18/1777, *Letters of Delegates*, vol. 7, p. 208; Arthur Lee to GW, 7/15/1777, *PGW: Rev. War*, vol. 10, p. 44; Hamilton to Robert R. Livingston, 6/28/1777, *The Papers of Alexander Hamilton, Volume 1: 1768–1778*, ed. Harold C. Syrett (New York: Columbia University Press, 1961), pp. 274–277.

27. Philip Schuyler to GW, 6/28/1777, GW to George Clinton, 7/1/1777, GW to Israel Putnam, 7/1/1777, GW to Hancock, 7/2/1777, *PGW: Rev. War*, vol. 10, pp. 140–143, 163, 165–166, 168–170.

28. This paragraph is drawn from Gruber, *Howe Brothers*, chap. 2, which treats the subject in detail (quotation on p. 187).

29. Hamilton to New York Committee of Correspondence, 4/5/1777, *The Papers of Alexander Hamilton, Volume 1: 1768–1778*, ed. Harold C. Syrett (New York: Columbia University Press, 1961), pp. 220–221; see also the excellent discussion in Don Higginbotham, *The War of American Independence* (New York: Macmillan, 1971), pp. 176–178.

30. The departure of the fleet from New York is based on the following contemporary accounts: Ewald, *Diary*, pp. 71–72; Peebles, *Diary*, p. 121; Serle, *Journal*, pp. 239–240; von Münchhausen, *Diary*, p. 22; Robertson, *Diaries*, p. 140.

31. Matthais Williamson Jr. to GW, 7/18/1777, GW to William Livingston, 7/12/1777, Moylan to GW, 7/23/1777, GW to Benjamin Lincoln, 7/24/1777, *PGW: Rev. War*, vol. 10, pp. 256, 330, 378, 385.

32. Hamond Naval Papers, Diaries.

33. Hamond Naval Papers, Diaries; Serle, *Journal*, p. 241; Howe to Clinton, 7/30/1777, quoted in Howe, "Narrative," p. 279.

34. GW to Gates, 7/30/1777, GW to Hancock, 7/30/1777, *PGW: Rev. War*, vol. 10, pp. 459–460.

35. This paragraph is drawn from correspondence in ibid., pp. 464–496.

36. General Orders, 8/4/1777, ibid., p. 406.

37. GW to John Langdon, 8/4/1777, GW to John Augustine Washington, 8/5–9/1777, ibid., pp. 501, 514–515.

38. Council of War, 8/21/1777, Hancock to GW, 8/21/1777, GW to Hancock, 8/21/1777, Hancock to GW, 8/22/1777, ibid., vol. 11, pp. 19–20, 25–26, 41.

12. "Come boys, we shall do better another time"

1. General Orders, 8/23/1777, GW to Hancock, 8/23/1777, *PGW: Rev. War*, vol. 11, pp. 49–52; John Adams to Abigail Adams, 8/24/1777; *The Book of Abigail and John: Selected Letters of the Adams Family, 1762–1784*, ed. L. H. Butterfield et al. (Cambridge, Mass.: Harvard University Press, 1975), p. 191; Henry Marchant to Nicholas Cooke, 8/24/1777, Lee to Jefferson, 8/25/1777, *Letters of Delegates*, vol. 7, pp. 540–542, 550–552.

2. Adams to Abigail, 8/24/1777, *Book of Abigail and John*, p. 192.

3. General Orders, 8/24/1777, *PGW: Rev. War*, vol. 11, p. 55; McMichael, *Diary*, pp. 147–148.

4. Philip Schuyler to GW, 8/19/1777, Burgoyne to Baum, 8/9/1777, Hancock to GW, 8/24/1777, *PGW: Rev. War*, vol. 11, pp. 7–8, 16–17, 56n. 1; Peckham, *Toll*, p. 38; Philip Lord Jr., *War over Wallomscoick: Land Use and Settlement Pattern on the Bennington Battlefield—1777*, New York State Museum Bulletin no. 473 (Albany, N.Y.: University of the State of New York, 1989), p. 70.

5. Sullivan to GW, 8/24/1777, GW to Sullivan, 8/27/1777, Hancock to GW, 9/3/1777, General Orders, 10/16/1777, *PGW: Rev. War*, vol. 11, pp. 57–60, 80, 134–135, 523; *AR*, p. 68n. 20.

6. Ewald, *Diary*, pp. 73–75; Robertson, *Diary*, pp. 142–143; Peebles, *Diary*, pp. 127–128; von Münchhausen, *Diary*, p. 26; Baurmeister, p. 95; "Contemporary British Account," p. 75. Robertson, p. 143, is the only eyewitness who says the admiral's flag was on HMS *Roebuck*.

7. GW to Hancock, 8/25/1777, 8/27/1777; GW to Landon Carter, 10/27/1777, *PGW: Rev. War*, vol. 11, pp. 69 and 78n. 1, vol. 12, pp. 25–26; von Münchhausen, *Diary*, p. 26.

8. Von Münchhausen, *Diary*, p. 26.

9. Arnold to Gates, 8/24/1777; Gates to GW, 8/28/1777, GW to Gates, 9/1/1777, *PGW: Rev. War*, vol. 11, pp. 84 and no. 1, 107.

10. GW to Cadwalader, 8/28/1777, *PGW: Rev. War*, vol. 11, p. 83; Ewald, *Diary*, p. 76; André, *Journal*, pp. 41–42; von Münchhausen, *Diary*, p. 26; Peebles, *Diary*, p. 129.

11. GW to Bland, 8/30/1777, General Orders, 8/28/1777, 8/30/1777, GW to Hancock, 8/30/1777, GW to Maxwell, 8/30/1777, 9/1/1777 (two), 9/2/1777 (two), 9/3/1777, *PGW: Rev. War*, vol. 11, pp. 82, 91, 93, 95, 114–115, 127–128, 139–140.

12. Ewald, *Diary*, p. 78; von Münchhausen, *Diary*, p. 28; André, *Journal*, in Rhodehamel, *Writings*, p. 335.

13. Ewald, *Diary*, p. 78; von Münchhausen, *Diary*, p. 28; GW to Hancock, 9/5/1777, *PGW: Rev. War*, vol. 11, p. 150, Howe to Germain, 10/10/1777, Davies, *Documents*, vol. 14, pp. 202–209.

14. General Orders, 9/5/1777, *PGW: Rev. War*, vol. 11, p. 148.

15. General Orders, 9/6/1777, *PGW: Rev. War*, vol. 11, p. 158; McMichael, *Diary*, p. 149; von Münchhausen, *Diary*, p. 30; Ewald, *Diary*, pp. 79–80.

16. General Orders, 9/9/1777, GW to Hancock, 9/9/1777, *PGW: Rev. War*, vol. 11, pp. 174–175; McMichael, *Diary*, p. 149; Ewald, *Diary*, p. 81; "Contemporary British Account," p. 78.

17. Joseph Townsend, *Some Account of the British Army, Under the Command of General Howe, and of the Battle of Brandywine, on the Memorable September 11th, 1777, and the Adventures of That Day, Which Came to the Knowledge and Understanding of Joseph Townsend* (Philadelphia: T. Ward, 1846), p. 8.

18. Greene to Catherine Greene, 9/10/1777, *NG Papers*, vol. 2, pp. 154–156; General Orders, 9/4/1777, *PGW: Rev. War*, vol. 11, p. 142.

19. Greene to Catherine Greene, 9/19/1777, *NG Papers*, vol. 2, pp. 154–156.

20. Ewald, *Diary*, p. 81; Ludlum, *Weather* 30, no. 3 (1977): 116. For readers interested in a discussion of Ferguson's rifle see John Buchanan, *The Road to Guilford Courthouse: The American Revolution in the Carolinas* (New York: John Wiley & Sons, 1997), pp. 196–198.

21. Unless otherwise indicated, I have based my discussion of the Battle of Brandywine in this and all following paragraphs on the sources in this note. The sources of the quotations are identified in the text. The excellent editorial note, and its own citations in *PGW: Rev. War*, vol. 11, pp. 187–195, and in the same source, Robert Hanson Harrison to John Hancock (two), James Ross to GW, GW to Theodoric Bland, John Sullivan to GW (two), Theodoric Bland to GW, GW to John Hancock, all on 9/11/1777, pp. 195–201, and Sullivan to GW, 10/24/1777, GW to Sullivan, 10/24/1777, pp. 600–602; General Greene's Orders, 9/13/1777, with the long editorial note describing the battle, Greene to Henry Marchant, 7/25/1777, *PNG*, vol. 2, pp. 156–162, 470–472; Ewald, *Diary*, pp. 81–88, is an excellent, detailed account; Townsend, *Some Account of the British Army*, pp. 19–29; Baurmeister, pp. 106–112; von Münchhausen, *Diary*, pp. 31–32; Robertson, *Diary*, pp. 146–147; Anderson, *Recollections*, pp. 36–38; André, *Journal*, in Rhodehamel, *AR Writings*, pp. 337–338; McMichael, *Diary*, p. 150; Commager and Morris: vol. 1, pp. 613–616.

22. James Ferguson, *Two Scottish Soldiers, A Soldier of 1688 and Blenheim, A Soldier of the American Revolution, and a Jacobite Laird and His Forbearers* (Aberdeen: D. Wyllie & Sons, 1888), p. 68.

23. Graydon, *Memoirs*, pp. 455–456.

24. Cooper to Editor, 1/28/1831, *New-York Mirror*, 8:31, p. 327.

25. John Ferling, *A Leap in the Dark: The Struggle to Create the American Republic* (New York: Oxford University Press, 2003), p. 48.

26. Peckham, *Toll*, p. 40, for American losses; *PGW: Rev. War*, vol. 11, p. 193, for British losses.

13. "Perplexing Maneuvres"

1. Joseph Townsend, *Some Account of the British Army, Under the Command of General Howe, and of the Battle of Brandywine, on the Memorable September 11th, 1777, and the Adventures of the Day, Which Came to the Knowledge and Understanding of Joseph Townsend* (Philadelphia: T. Ward, 1846), pp. 26 and 29, for both paragraphs.

2. General Orders, 9/12/1777, GW to Charles Stewart, 9/13/1776, *PGW: Rev. War,* vol. 11, pp. 204–205, 221.

3. Wharton to GW, 9/12/1777, GW to Hancock, 9/13/1777, GW to Wharton, 9/13/1777, ibid., pp. 210–211, 213–214, 222.

4. GW to Smallwood, 9/12/1777, ibid., 209–210.

5. General Orders, 9/13/1777, ibid., pp. 211–212.

6. Hancock to GW, 9/14/1777, GW to Hancock, 9/15/1777, Hancock to GW, 9/16/1777, ibid., pp. 226–227, 236–237, 248–249.

7. Von Münchhausen, *Diary,* p. 32.

8. Council of War, 9/23/1777, *PGW: Rev. War,* vol. 11, p. 295; "A British Officer's Revolutionary War Journal, 1776–1778," ed. S. Sydney Bradford, *Maryland Historical Magazine* 56 no. 2 (1961): 171; Colonel Timothy Pickering, quoted in Thomas J. McGuire, *Battle of Paoli* (Mechanicsburg, Pa.: Stackpole Books, 2000), p. 33; Ewald, *Diary,* pp. 88–89.

9. Ewald, *Diary,* p. 89; Baurmeister, p. 114; Pickering and Upham, *Life of Pickering,* vol. 1, pp. 159–161; McMichael, *Diary,* p. 151, Joseph Reed to GW, 9/30/1777, GW to Hancock, 9/17/1777, *PGW: Rev. War,* vol. 11, pp. 251, 253; Shaw to his father, 9/30/1777, in Josiah Quincy, ed., *The Journals of Major Samuel Shaw* (Boston: Wm. Crosby & H. P. Nichols, 1847), p. 37; John C. Dann, *The Nagle Journal* (London: Weidenfeld & Nicholson, 1989), p. 8.

10. GW to Maxwell, 9/17/1777, GW to Hancock, 9/18/1777, 9/19/1777, *PGW: Rev. War,* vol. 11, pp. 258, 262, 268; McMichael, *Diary,* p. 151; *The Journals of Henry Melchior Muhlenberg, 1711–1787,* vol. 3, ed. and trans. Theodore G. Tappert and John W. Doberstein (Philadelphia, 1958), p. 78.

11. Muhlenberg, *Journals,* pp. 76–78.

12. GW to Wayne, 9/18/1777 (two), *PGW: Rev. War,* vol. 11, pp. 265–266.

13. Wayne to GW, 9/19/1777 (two), 9/19/1777, ibid., p. 273.

14. Von Münchhausen, *Diary,* p. 34.

15. André, *Journal,* in Rhodehamel, *AR Writings,* p. 340. For the Paoli incident I have drawn on an excellent work by Thomas J. McGuire, *The Battle of Paoli* (Mechanicsburg, Pa.: Stackpole Books, 2000), chaps. 12–19 and passim, which covers far more than the title indicates, describing, for example, the maneuvers of the two armies between the Battle of Brandywine and the British occupation of Philadelphia. In this regard see also John F. Reed, *Campaign to Valley Forge, July 1, 1777–December 19, 1777* (Philadelphia: University of Pennsylvania Press, 1965), pp. 141–167.

16. Both quotations in McGuire, *Battle of Paoli,* pp. 84–87.

17. Unless otherwise indicated, beginning with this paragraph my description of the Battle of Paoli is based on Captain André's *Journal* in Rhodehamel, *AR Writings,* pp. 340–341, and McGuire, *The Battle of Paoli,* pp. 95–131; the quotations of eyewitnesses other than André are taken from McGuire, within the pages cited.

18. The standard source is Peckham, *Toll;* the closest student of the action is McGuire, *The Battle of Paoli.*

19. James Murray, *An Impartial History of the War in America Etc.* (Newcastle upon Tyne: T. Robeson, 1783), vol. 2, pp. 271–272.

20. Laurens to John Lewis Gervais, 10/6/1777, *Letters of Delegates*, vol. 8, pp. 69–70.

21. Council of War, 9/23/1777, GW to McDougall, 9/22/1777, *PGW: Rev. War*, vol. 11, pp. 292–293, 295; McMichael, *Diary*, p. 152.

22. Von Münchhausen, *Diary*, p. 35; Robertson, *Diary*, p. 150; Council of War, 9/23/1777, GW to Hancock, 9/23/1777, *PGW: Rev. War*, vol. 11, pp. 294–296, 301–302.

23. McGuire, *The Battle of Paoli*, pp. 1–2; "Contemporary British Account," p. 83; "The Diary of Robert Morton," *PMHB*, 1, no. 1 (1877): 7–8.

24. Adams, *Diary*, 9/21/1777.

14. "Our army is in higher spirits than ever"

1. GW to Colonel Arendt, 9/23/1777, *PGW: Rev. War*, vol. 11, p. 298; John W. Jackson, *The Delaware Bay and River Defenses of Philadelphia, 1775–1777* (Philadelphia: Philadelphia Maritime Museum, 1977), pp. 5–7, and the entire text of this brief but authoritative study of the events that finally led to the fall of Forts Mifflin and Mercer.

2. GW to Arendt, GW to Hazelwood, GW to Smith, all 9/23/1777, Smith to GW, 9/26/1777, *PGW: Rev. War*, vol. 11, pp. 298, 303–304, 308, 328.

3. GW to Putnam, 9/23/1777, GW to Gates, 9/24/1777, ibid., pp. 305–306, 310–311.

4. GW to Caesar Rodney, 9/24/1777, *PGW: Rev. War*, vol. 11, p. 315; Pickering to John Pickering, 9/25/1777, Pickering and Upham, *Life of Pickering*, vol. 1, pp. 162–165.

5. GW to Thomas Nelson Jr., 9/27/1777, Hancock to GW, 9/30/1777, council of war, 9/28/1777, *PGW: Rev. War*, vol. 11, pp. 333, 338–339, 349–350.

6. GW to Jonathan Trumbull Sr., 10/1/1777, ibid., p. 365.

7. General Orders, 10/1/1777, *PGW: Rev. War*, vol. 11, p. 356; *The Journals of Henry Melchior Muhlenberg, 1711–1787*, vol. 3, ed. and trans. Theodore G. Tappert and John W. Doberstein (Philadelphia, 1958), p. 82.

8. GW to Hancock, 10/5/1777, *PGW: Rev. War*, vol. 11, p. 395.

9. General Orders for Attacking Germantown, 10/3/1777, *PGW: Rev. War*, vol. 11, pp. 375–376; McMichael, *Diary*, p. 152.

10. I have drawn on many sources, both primary and secondary, for the Battle of Germantown. Primary accounts are General Orders for Attacking Germantown, 10/3/1777, Wayne to GW, 10/4/1777, GW to Hancock, 10/5/1777, GW to Benjamin Harrison, 10/5/1777, Adam Stephen to GW, 10/9/1777, and all relevant editorial notes, *PGW: Rev. War*, vol. 11, pp. 375–382, 389–390, 393–402, 468–470; General Greene's Orders, 10/7/1777, Report of a Court of Enquiry, 11/1/1777, and all editorial notes, *PNG*, vol. 2, pp. 171–177, 188–189; McMichael, *Diary*, pp. 152–153; "Orderly Book of General Peter Gabriel Muhlenberg, March 26–December 20, 1777, *PMHB* 35 (1911): 63; Loftus Cliffe to Jack Cliffe, 10/24/1777, Loftus Cliffe Papers, William L. Clements Library, University of Michigan; Pickering and Upham, *Life of Pickering*, vol. 1, pp. 166–168; "Pickering's Letter," 8/23/1826, *North American Review* 26 (1826): 425–430; Sullivan to Meshech Weare, 10/25/1777, *Sul-*

livan Papers, vol. 1, pp. 542–547; John Armstrong to Thomas Wharton Jr., 10/5/1777, *Pennsylvania Archives*, 1st ser., vol. 5, pp. 645–646; Henry Miller to his family, 10/10/1777, in Henry Miller Watts, "A Memoir of General Henry Miller, by His Grandson, Henry Miller Watts," *PMHB* 12 (1888): 426–427; T. Will Heth to John Lamb, 10/12/1777, Commager and Morris, vol. 1, pp. 629–630; Elias Dayton, "Notes on the Battle of Germantown," in Dayton, "Papers of General Elias Dayton," *Proceedings of the New Jersey Historical Society* 9 (1857): 183–185; "Revolutionary Services of Captain John Markland," *PMHB* 9 (1885): 107–108; "Memoirs of Brigadier–General John Lacey, of Pennsylvania," *PMHB* 26 (1902): 105–106; Tallmadge, *Memoirs*, pp. 22–25; Charles Cotesworth Pinckney to Harold Johnson, 11/14/1820, *Historical Magazine* 10 (1886), pp. 202–204; John Eager Howard to Timothy Pickering, 1/29/1827, *Maryland Historical Magazine* 4 (1909), pp. 314–320; William Howe to Lord Germain, 10/10/1777, Davies, *Documents*, vol. 14, pp. 202–209; André, *Journal*, pp. 55–57; von Münchhausen, *Diary*, pp. 38–39; Robertson, *Diaries*, pp. 151–152; Baurmeister: 119–122; Ewald, *Diary*, pp. 92–96; Morton, *Diary*, pp. 14– 15; Martin, *Private Yankee Doodle*, pp. 72–74; recommended secondary accounts are Alfred C. Lambdin, "Battle of Germantown," *PMHB* vol. 1 (1877): 368–403, not to be ignored because of its age; Thomas J. McGuire, *The Surprise of Germantown, or, the Battle of Cliveden* (Gettysburg, Pa.: Cliveden and Thomas Publications, 1994); Christopher Ward, *The War of the Revolution*, vol. 1, ed. John Alden (New York: Macmillan, 1952), pp. 362–371; Freeman, *George Washington*, vol. 4, pp. 490–519; John F. Reed, *Campaign to Valley Forge, July 1, 1777–December 19, 1777* (Philadelphia: University of Pennsylvania Press, 1965), pp. 214–239; Mark M. Boatner III, *Encyclopedia of the American Revolution* (Mechanicsburg, Pa.: Stackpole Books, 1994), pp. 426–430.

11. Marquis de Chastellux, *Travels in North America, in the Years 1780, 1781, 1782*, vol. 1 (1787; repr., New York: Arno Press, 1968), p. 215.

12. Ibid., p. 216; Henry Lee, *Memoirs of the War in the Southern Department of the United States*, ed. Robert E. Lee, new ed. (1869; repr., New York: Arno Press, 1969), p. 96.

13. Chastellux, pp. 214–215.

14. Weedon quoted in Freeman, *George Washington*, vol. 4, p. 517; Wayne quoted in Michael J. McGuire, *The Battle of Paoli* (Mechanicsburg, Pa.: Stackpole Books, 2000), p. 174; Martin, *Private Yankee Doodle*, pp. 73–74; Heth to John Lamb, 10/12/1777, Commager and Morris, vol. 1, pp. 629–630.

15. Henry Miller Watts, "A Memoir of General Henry Miller," *PMHB* 12 (1887), pp. 426–427.

15. "We . . . took post near the Valley Forge"

1. John Joseph Stoudt, *Ordeal at Valley Forge: A Day-by-Day Chronicle from December 17, 1777 to June 18, 1778 Compiled from the Sources* (Philadelphia: University of Pennsylvania Press, 1963), p. 25; McMichael, *Diary*, p. 157; Varnum to Alexander McDougall, 2/7/1778, "*A Degree of Patience which will ever astonish the better part of Mankind*": *Writings from the Valley Forge Encampment of the Continental*

Army, December 19, 1777–June 19, 1778, ed. Joseph Lee Boyle (Bowie, Md.: Heritage Press, 2000), p. 45.

2. Robert Graves, *Count Belisarius* (1938; repr., New York: Farrar, Straus, & Giroux, 1982), p. 81.

3. For a good description of the agricultural riches of southeastern Pennsylvania see Wayne Bodle, *The Valley Forge Winter: Civilians and Soldiers in War* (University Park, Pa.: Pennsylvania State University Press, 2002), pp. 5–10; for the breakdown of the logistical system and Congress's culpability see E. Wayne Sharp, *To Starve the Army at Pleasure: Continental Army Administration and American Political Culture, 1775–1783* (Chapel Hill: University of North Carolina Press, 1984), pp. 43–45, passim; Greene to GW, 9/3/1779, *PNG*, vol. 3, p. 427.

4. Committee to Inspect Beef to GW, 12/20/1777, *PGW: Rev. War*, vol. 12, pp. 648, 671n. 2.

5. GW to Laurens, 12/22/1777, ibid., pp. 667–668.

6. Commager and Morris, vol. 1, pp. 641–642.

7. Clark to GW, 12/19/1777, Jameson to GW, 12/31/1777, *PGW: Rev. War*, vol. 12, p. 635, vol. 13: 81–82.

8. GW to Greene, 2/12/1778, ibid., vol. 13, pp. 514–515.

9. Greene to Clement Biddle, 2/14/1778, *PNG*, vol. 2, p. 283.

10. Greene to GW, 2/15/1778, *PGW: Rev. War*, vol. 13, p. 546.

11. John Brooks to ? , 1/5/1778, Massachusetts Historical Society; Poor to Meschech Weare, 1/21/1778, Peter Force Papers, 7E, item 97.4, New Hampshire Council Correspondence, Library of Congress; Lewis to Jesse Partridge, 2/1/1778, Governor and Council Letters, Massachusetts State Archives.

12. Butler to Thomas Wharton Jr., 2/12/1778, André de Coppet Collection, Box 4, Fldr. 71, Princeton University Library; Van Cortlandt to George Clinton, 2/13/1778, *Public Papers of George Clinton, First Governor of New York, 1777–1795, 1801–1804*, 10 vols. (New York: Wynkoop Hollenbeck Crawford, 1900), vol. 2, pp. 843–844; James Paterson to Thomas Marshall, 2/23/1778, Ely Collection MG 14, New Jersey Historical Society.

13. Gibbs to his brother, 3/5/1778, Valley Forge; Cropper to Margaret Cropper, 3/13/1778, Boyle, *Writings*, p. 80; Charles Royster, *A Revolutionary People at War: The Continental Army and American Character, 1775–1783* (1979; repr., New York: W. W. Norton, 1981), p. 195.

14. Sergeant to Lovell, 11/20/1777, *Letters of Delegates*, vol. 8, p. 296.

15. James Lovell to Joseph Whipple, 11/21/1777, ibid., pp. 302–303. The best brief summary of the Conway Cabal is Don Higginbotham, *The War of American Independence: Military Attitudes, Policies, and Practice, 1763–1789* (New York: Macmillan, 1971), pp. 216–222; other good discussions are in Royster, *A Revolutionary People at War*, pp. 179–189; John E. Ferling, *The First of Men: A Life of George Washington* (Knoxville, Tenn.: University of Tennessee Press, 1988), pp. 225–230; and Stephen R. Taaffe, *The Philadelphia Campaign, 1777–1778* (Lawrence, Kans: University Press of Kansas, 2003), pp. 157–168, which has copious citations. The first book-length revisionist study of the Conway Cobal and other matters, including an undeserved apologia for Horatio Gates, is Bernhard Knollenberg, *Washington and the Revolution, a Reappraisal: Gates, Conway, and the Continental Congress* (New York: Macmillan, 1940); another important study is Jonathan Gregory Rossie, *The Politics*

of Command in the American Revolution (Syracuse, N.Y.: Syracuse University Press, 1975), esp. chap. 13.

16. Lovell to Joseph Whipple, 11/21/1777, *Letters of Delegates,* vol. 8, p. 302.

17. Gerry to Adams, 12/3/1777, 12/8/1777, ibid., pp. 373–374, 388.

18. Rush to Adams, 10/13/1777, 10/21/1777, ibid., pp. 158–160.

19. Quoted in Rossie, *Politics of Command,* pp. 191–192, along with the original French.

20. Hinrichs, *Diary,* in *The Siege of Charleston, with an Account of the Province of South Carolina: Diaries and Letters of Hessian Officers from the von Jungkenn Papers in the William L. Clements Library,* trans. and ed. Bernhard A. Uhlendorf (Ann Arbor: University of Michigan Press, 1938), p. 213.

21. Henry Laurens to John Laurens, 10/16/1777, *Letters of Delegates,* vol. 8, p. 125.

22. GW to Lee, 10/16/1777, *PGW: Rev. War,* vol. 11, p. 529.

23. Stirling to GW, 11/3/1777, GW to Conway, 11/5/1777, ibid., vol. 12, pp. 111, 129n. 4.

24. Conway to GW, 11/5/1777, ibid., p. 130.

25. John Fitzgerald to GW, 2/16/1778, ibid., vol. 13, pp. 555–556 and n. 3.

26. Gates to GW, 12/8/1777, GW to Gates, 1/4/1778, ibid., vol. 12, p. 577, vol. 13, p. 138.

27. Craik to GW, 1/6/1778, ibid., vol. 13, pp. 160–161.

28. Rush to Henry, 1/12/1778, *Letters of Benjamin Rush,* vol. 1, ed. L. H. Butterfield (Princeton, N.J.: Princeton University Press, 1951), p. 183.

29. Laurens to Lafayette, 1/12/1778, *Letters of Delegates,* vol. 8, p. 571.

30. Laurens to GW, 1/27/1778, *PGW: Rev. War,* vol. 13, pp. 364–366, with Robert Hanson Harrison copy of the anonymous letter in n. 1.

31. Gerry to Knox, 2/7/1778, Dyer to Jeremiah Wadsworth, 3/10/1778, *Letters of Delegates,* vol. 9, pp. 45–47, 257.

32. Henry to GW, 2/20/1778, GW to Lee, 8/26/1794, *PGW: Rev. War,* vol. 13, pp. 608, 611n. 1.

33. Franklin and Silas Deane to GW, 9/4/1777, ibid., vol. 12, p. 568n. 1.

34. Philander D. Chase, in his essay on von Steuben in *American National Biography.*

35. GW to Laurens, 2/27/1778, *PGW: Rev. War,* vol. 13, p. 687.

36. Quoted in Stoudt, *Ordeal at Valley Forge,* pp. 157–158.

37. Ibid., p. 193.

38. Von Steuben to Baron von der Goltz, n.d., quoted in Scheer and Rankin, p. 307; John Laurens to Henry Laurens, 2/28/1778, quoted in Philander D. Chase's essay on von Steuben in *American National Biography.*

39. Wayne Bodle laid out his case in *The Valley Forge Winter: Civilians and Soldiers in War* (University Park, Pa.: Pennsylvania State University Press, 2002), pp. 245–249.

40. First Hamilton quotation in Christopher Ward, *The War of the Revolution,* vol. 2, ed. John Alden (New York: Macmillan, 1952), p. 582; second Hamilton quotation in Hamilton to Elias Boudinot, 7/5/1778, *The Papers of Alexander Hamilton, Volume 1, 1768–1778,* ed. Harold C. Syrett (New York: Columbia University Press, 1961), p. 513; Bodle, *Valley Forge Winter,* p. 248; Greene to Jacob Greene, 7/2/1778, *PNG,* vol. 2, p. 450.

41. Bodle, *Valley Forge Winter*, pp. 13, 250.

42. "A Narrative of the Campaign of 1780, by Colonel Otho Holland Williams," in William Johnson, *Sketches of the Life and Correspondence of General Nathanael Greene*, vol. 1 (Charleston, 1822), p. 496; for the Battle of Camden see John Buchanan, *The Road to Guilford Courthouse: The American Revolution in the Carolinas* (New York: John Wiley & Sons, 1997), chap. 12.

43. Howard in Henry Lee, *The Campaign of 1781 in the Carolinas* (Philadelphia, 1824), p. 97n., and Howard to [Bayard?], n.d., Bayard Papers, Ms. 109, Maryland Historical Society; for the Battle of Cowpens, see Buchanan, *The Road to Guilford Courthouse*, chap. 21, and for book-length treatment, Lawrence E. Babits, *A Devil of a Whipping: The Battle of Cowpens* (Chapel Hill: University of North Carolina Press, 1998), esp. pp. 116–117.

44. For details of Guilford Courthouse see Buchanan, *The Road to Guilford Courthouse*, chap. 24.

45. McMichael, *Diary*

Epilogue

1. Information on Lord Howe's postwar career is drawn from the *Dictionary of National Biography*.

2. My comments on Sir William's resignation are a combination of my own thoughts and my readings in Gruber, *Howe Brothers*; the quotations in the paragraphs describing the fete are from either Baurmeister, pp. 77–78, or von Münchhausen, *Diary*, p. 52, with the narrators identified in the text.

3. John R. Alden, *A History of the American Revolution* (New York: Alfred A. Knopf, 1969), p. 308.

4. The views and quotations in this paragraph and following on Washington's opinion on the Battle of Guilford Courthouse are from Jefferson's notes on conversations with John Beckley and George Washington, 7 June 1793, *The Papers of Thomas Jefferson*, ed. John Catanzariti et al. (Princeton, N.J.: Princeton University Press, 1950–), vol. 26, pp. 219–220.

5. GW to Noah Webster, 1788, cited in Harold A. Larrabee, *Decision at the Chesapeake* (New York: Clarkson N. Potter, 1964), p. 246; *Diaries of George Washington*, ed. Donald Jackson et al., 6 vols. (Charlottesville: University of Virginia Press, 1976–1979), vol. 3, pp. 404–405; for comment on Washington's diary of 1781 see John Shy, "General Washington Reconsidered," *The John H. Biggs Cincinnati Lectures in Military Leadership and Command, 1986*, ed. Henry S. Bauman (Lexington, Va.: The VMI Foundation, 1986), p. 46n. 11.

6. Octavius Pickering, *The Life of Timothy Pickering, by His Son*, vol. 2 (Boston: Little, Brown, 1867–1873), pp. 54–57.

7. Ibid., p. 56.

8. Adams quoted in Page Smith, *John Adams*, 2 vols (Garden City, N.Y.: Doubleday & Co., 1962), vol. 1, p. 1084; Jefferson to Walter Jones, 1/2/1814, *Thomas Jefferson: Writings*, ed. Merrill D. Peterson (New York: Library of America, 1984), p. 1319.

9. Jefferson to Jones, 1/2/1814, *Writings*, p. 1319.

Suggestions for
Further Reading

The notes contain citations for those interested in orignal sources and periodical literature. For this essay I have restricted myself largely to secondary works easily available in either bookstores or libraries. For those books that are out of print, readers should keep in mind our wonderful system of interlibrary loans. Almost all of the books mentioned have bibliographies that can lead the enthusiast as far as he cares to go.

If I were limited to one book on the military phase of the Revolution in all of its aspects, my choice would be that splendid study by Don Higginbotham, *The War of American Independence: Military Attitudes, Policies, and Practice, 1763–1789* (New York: Macmillan, 1971).

An excellent work by another master historian is John Richard Alden, *A History of the American Revolution* (New York: Alfred A. Knopf, 1969). John Ferling, *A Leap in the Dark: The Struggle to Create the American Republic* (New York: Oxford University Press, 2003), is an insightful and highly readable analytical political history covering the period from 1754 to Jefferson's inauguration in 1801 that provides the framework for readings on the Revolutionary War. For readers beguiled by the so-called "new history" and its emphasis on common folk, Ray Raphael, *A People's History of the American Revolution: How Common Folk Shaped the Fight for Independence* (2001; repr., New York: Perennial, 2002) is first-rate, as long as one remains aware that dead, white, upper-class males had a little something to do with it, too. A good narrative history is Robert Middlekauff, *The Glorious Cause: The American Revolution, 1763–1789* (New York: Oxford University Press, 1982). Well worth reading is John Shy, *A People Numerous and Armed: Reflections on the Military Struggle for American Independence* (New York: Oxford University Press, 1976). A slim volume by one of the most perceptive students of the Revolution is Gordon S. Wood, *The American Revolution: A History* (New York: Modern Library, 2002). An earlier work by Professor Wood, *The Radicalism of the American Revolution* (New York: Alfred A. Knopf, 1992), is one of the best books ever written on the rebellion.

Readers who would rather stick strictly to the fighting will find that Christopher Ward, *The War of the Revolution*, 2 vols., ed. John Alden (New York: Macmillan, 1952), is indispensable and has not been superseded. Briefer but very good is Willard M. Wallace, *Appeal to Arms: A Military History of the Revolution* (New York: Harper & Brothers, 1951). These two books can be supplemented by George Athan Billias, ed., *George Washington's Generals and Opponents: Their Exploits and Leadership* (New York: Da Capo Press, 1994), originally published as two volumes but now conveniently brought together in one.

The excitement of reading the words of participants is splendidly provided in two works: Henry Steele Commager and Richard B. Morris, eds., *The Spirit of 'Seventy-six: The Story of the American Revolution as Told by Participants*, 2 vols. (Indianapolis, Ind.: Bobbs-Merrill, 1958), and George F. Scheer and Hugh F. Rankin, *Rebels and Redcoats: The American Revolution through the Eyes of Those Who Fought and Lived It* (1957; repr., New York: Da Capo Press, 1987). Pension applications by veterans are a mine of information, and a selection is presented in John C. Dann, *The Revolution Remembered: Eyewitness Accounts of the War for Independence* (Chicago: University of Chicago Press, 1980). Delightful is the right description for Joseph Plumb Martin, *Private Yankee Doodle: Being a Narrative of Some of the Adventures, Dangers, and Sufferings of a Revolutionary Soldier*, ed. George F. Scheer (Boston: Little, Brown, 1962). Another good book for those who like their history firsthand is *The American Revolution: Writings from the War of Independence*, ed. John C. Rhodehamel (New York: Library of America, 2001).

The literature on George Washington is voluminous. Here are my choices. For the serious student the monumental biography is Douglas Southall Freeman, *George Washington*, 7 vols. (New York: Charles Scribner's Sons, 1948–1957). Note that volume 7 is by John A. Carroll and Mary W. Ashworth. Better in some respects and with literary flair is James Thomas Flexner, *George Washington*, 4 vols. (Boston: Little, Brown 1965–1972). But for readers who lack the time or inclination for multi-volume works, Flexner's distillation of the four volumes in one is recommended: *Washington: The Indispensable Man* (Boston: Little, Brown, 1974). Other solid one-volume works are John R. Alden, *George Washington: A Biography* (Baton Rouge: Louisiana State University Press, 1984); John E. Ferling, *The First of Men: A Life of George Washington* (Knoxville: University of Tennessee Press, 1988); Paul K. Longmore, *The Invention of George Washington* (Charlottesville: University Press of Virginia, 1999); Marcus Cunliffe, *George Washington: Man and Monument* (Boston: Little, Brown, 1958); and Richard Brookhiser, *Founding Father: Rediscovering George Washington* (New York: Free Press, 1996).

Don Higginbotham has been studying Washington for many years. In addition to his general work described earlier in this essay, I heartily recommend the following, the first two written by Professor Higginbotham, the third one edited by him: *George Washington and the American Military Tradition* (Athens: University of Georgia Press, 1985); *George Washington: Uniting a Nation* (Lanham, Md.: Rowman & Littlefield, 2002); and *George Washington Reconsidered* (Charlottesville: University Press of Virginia, 2001).

There are three good books on the Continental Army: E. Wayne Carp, *To Starve the Army with Pleasure: Continental Army Administration and American Political Culture, 1775–1783* (Chapel Hill: University of North Carolina Press, 1984); James Kirby Martin and Mark Edward Lender, *A Respectable Army: The Military Origins of the Republic, 1763–1789* (Wheeling, Ill.: Harlan Davidson, 1982); and especially good and well written is Charles Royster, *A Revolutionary People at War: The Continental Army and American Character, 1775–1783* (1979; repr., New York: W. W. Norton, 1981).

Three works overlap with specific periods covered in my book: Richard M. Ketchum, *Winter Soldiers: The Battles for Trenton and Princeton* (1973; repr., New York: Henry Holt, 1999); John F. Reed, *Campaign to Valley Forge: July 1, 1777–December 19, 1777* (Philadelphia: University of Pennsylvania Press, 1965); and Stephen R. Taaffe, *The Philadelphia Campaign, 1777–1778* (Lawrence: University Press of Kansas, 2003).

Supplementing the work by Ray Raphael described above are three works about people who have only recently received their due. The world of eighteenth-century camp followers has disappeared (replaced by the military-industrial complex), but Holly A. Mayer describes in fine fashion those indispensable support troops in *Belonging to the Army: Camp Followers and Community during the American Revolution* (Columbia: University of South Carolina Press, 1996). Then there are Mary Beth Norton, *Liberty's Daughters: The Revolutionary Experience of American Women, 1750–1800* (Boston: Little, Brown, 1980) and Benjamin Quarles, *The Negro in the American Revolution* (1961; repr., Chapel Hill: University of North Carolina Press, 1996).

In a category by itself is a fascinating and important work by Elizabeth A. Fenn, *Pox Americana: The Great Smallpox Epidemic of 1775–1782* (New York: Hill & Wang, 2001).

Finally, let us not forget the foe. Of great help in writing this book was Ira D. Gruber, *The Howe Brothers and the American Revolution* (Chapel Hill: University of North Carolina Press, 1972), a very scholarly book written for specialists that demands careful reading but is immensely rewarding. Another work, which is among the best ever written on the war and a model of scholarship and the biographer's art, is William B. Willcox, *Portrait of a General: Sir Henry Clinton in the War of Independence* (New York: Alfred A. Knopf, 1964). Almost the entire war is covered, since Sir Henry was present for most of it, from Bunker Hill through Yorktown. The only caveat I have with regard to Willcox's book is the final chapter, which is a psychological study of Clinton. Although it neither descends to psychobabble nor detracts from the rest of the book, it should not be taken seriously— if one bothers to read it. Piers Mackesey, *The War for America, 1775–1783* (1964; repr., Lincoln: University of Nebraska Press, 1993), is by a British historian who is often criticized for being too easy on Lord Germain and other ministers but offers a strong corrective to the sometimes parochial American view that nothing else was going on in the world, for the War of the Revolution became a world war, especially for Britain; this had a significant effect on the war in America, and Mackesey shows the way. Another excellent work by a British historian is Jeremy Black, *War for America: The Fight for Independence, 1775–1783* (New York: St. Martin's Press, 1991). The best observer of the war close up is Captain Johann Ewald, *Diary of the American War: A Hessian Journal*, ed. Joseph P. Tustin (New Haven, Conn.: Yale University Press, 1979), who wrote with verve, humor, insight, and feeling.

Index

Page numbers in *italics* indicate illustrations.